SEARCHING

for

YOUR

SOUL

Writers of Many Faiths Share
Their Personal Stories of
Spiritual Discovery

EDITED AND WITH AN INTRODUCTION BY

KATHERINE KURS

SCHOCKEN BOOKS / NEW YORK

All rights reserved under International and Pan-American
Copyright Conventions. Published in the United States by
Schocken Books Inc., New York, and simultaneously in Canada
by Random House of Canada Limited, Toronto. Distributed by
Pantheon Books, a division of Random House, Inc., New York.

SCHOCKEN and colophon are trademarks of Random House, Inc.

Permissions Acknowledgments are on pages 471 through 475.

Library of Congress Cataloging-in-Publication Data

Searching for your soul : writers of many faiths share their personal stories
of spiritual discovery / edited and with an introduction by
Katherine Kurs.
p.   cm.
ISBN 0-8052-1111-X
1. Spiritual biography.   2. Christian biography.   I. Kurs,
Katherine, 1956–
BL72.S38 1999
291.4—dc21   99-21266

Random House Web Address: www.randomhouse.com

Book design by JoAnne Metsch

Printed in the United States of America

First Edition

2 4 6 8 9 7 5 3 1

For my beloved teachers,

Marshall Meyer (z"l),
who taught me—and teaches me still—
how to live in this world;

and

Jonathan Omer-Man,
who teaches me how to live in the
midst of all worlds.

Contents

Acknowledgments

I COULD NOT have begun or completed this book without the encouragement and vision of a number of significant individuals to whom I would like to express my thanks.

I am very grateful for the interest and responsiveness that I received from Arthur Samuelson, Editorial Director of Schocken Books. Cecelia Cancellaro offered wise and sensitive editing and was wholehearted in her enthusiasm for this project from the outset. Editorial assistant Jennifer Turvey gave thoughtful feedback and was helpful and welcoming at all times.

Virginia Baron, former co-editor of *Parabola* magazine, first encouraged me to do a book on this subject, and, on a hot summer day in 1997, she sent me to the computer at last. Amir Shaviv provided numerous Indian lunches and support throughout. Early on, Emmanuel Kaftal offered insight from his own work in the area of psychoanalysis and "the mystery of Otherness."

In the academic community, I am thankful to Professor Alan Mandell of Empire State College, S.U.N.Y., not only for his friendship but for making a place for spiritual autobiography; and to Dean Nancy Bunch who, along with my colleagues, has continued to support these studies. Thanks as well to Dr. Sarah Winter, Dr. Bea Banu, and Dr. Toni Oliviero who brought spiritual autobiography to undergraduates at Eugene Lang College of the New School for Social Research. For those who have been willing to share their spiritual lives with me in a pastoral counseling context, and for all my students, my deepest gratitude, that we may continue to learn and grow together. My appreciation also to those who, in years past, taught me with such generosity of mind and spirit: Margaret Miles, David Eckel, Robert Cathcart, Parke Burgess, Gary Gumpert, and Robert Carey.

Even in its most solitary moments, the spiritual life is, in my experience, a life lived seeking after relationship and encounter. Like many of the autobiographies found in this book, my own journey has been very complex, riven with both joy and pain. Hence, my thanks and love to those beloved friends who have understood and helped in so many ways: Pamela Oline, Stephen Day, Alan Spain, Page Spain, Mark Horn, Sherry Kohn, Deb Meyers, Cecily Broderick y Guerra, Al Raboteau, Bill Monaghan, Christopher McIntosh, David Eckel and Sarah Vance, Laura LaRosa, Jonah Friedmen, Kusumita Pedersen, Paula Fredriksen, Ira Wohl, Shifra Sharlin, Mary Boys, Deborah Bly, Jack McMullen, Lyle Poncher, Evelyn Baran, my dear "sister" Merryl Weber, and the blessed memory of Georgianna Berry, James Gabriel Thompson, and Bruce Kenyon.

I am grateful to those clergy friends, colleagues, and communities of faith from a variety of religious traditions who, over a period of many years, made a home for me and encouraged my vocation; above all, the Rev. Donald Reeves, former rector of St. James's, Piccadilly in London, along with that community, for all they taught me. Also Emmanuel Church, Boston; The Cathedral Church of St. John the Divine; St. Mark's Church in-the-Bowery; the Psalms Gospel Choir, especially Maurice Colridge and Vivian Bonaparte; and especially the Rev. Robert Brashear and West Park Presbyterian Church. Also, my thanks to the Rev. Dr. Daniel Hardy; the Rev. William Boatwright; the Rev. Barbara Crafton; the Very Rev. Petero Sabune; the Rev. Canon Mary Simpson; the Rev. Canon Jonathan King; the Very Rev. James Parks Morton, the Rev. Diana Phillips, Sister Kathy DeVico and Mother Myriam of the Monastery of the Redwoods; the Rev. Constance Hammond; Rabbi Mark Sameth; the Rev. Lark d'Helen, and especially the Rev. Canon Cecily Broderick y Guerra. Rabbis Rolando Matalon and Marcelo Bronstein provide the most extraordinary love and understanding for which I am forever grateful. Rabbi Marshall Meyer (of blessed memory) and Rabbi Jonathan Omer-Man remain for me, each in their very different ways, the ideal of spiritual commitment.

My appreciation to the many friends at Congregation B'nai Jeshurun in New York who have taught me so much through their countless deeds of loving kindness: Jane Baum, Robert Baum, Ted Berger,

Jonathan Berger, Asya Berger, Ellen Perecman, Jack David Marcus, Robert Pollack, Amy Pollack, Judith Berman, Estare Weiser, Lenny Picker, Hella Moritz, Paula Dubrow, Bob Owens, soul bro' Todd Chanko, Susan Bodnar, Gary Schatsky, Ellen Zimmerli, Phyllis Schatsky, Sam Schatsky, David Schatsky, Jacob Bender, Helen Radin, Johanna Skilling, Pamela Cohn-Allen, Aviva Hay, Carol Zwick, Rachel Cowan, Seth Kasten, Mim Warden, Eric Levine, Amala Levine, Alice Fisher, Linda Thal, Helen Stark, Robert Stark, Brielle Stark, Cindy Ginsburg, Andrea Schwartz, Lois Sharzer, Len Sharzer, Susan Horowitz, Saul Rosenberg, and the blessed memory of Masha Tumarkin and Suzanne Tumarkin.

Finally, my deepest thanksgiving for those special relationships which hold so much love: my cherished M. E. Armstrong, who scanned the horizon and called me home; and my wonderful partner, John Hudson, whose unparalleled understanding, sensitivity, and loving support makes every good thing possible.

K.K.
Autumn, 1999
New York City

Introduction

KATHERINE KURS

EVER SINCE I can remember, I have known two worlds. The concrete, day-to-day physical world—deadlines, desks, dinner— the world of manifestation; and another world, the spiritual world of mystery, the world of God.

When I search now through the earliest recesses of my spiritual memories, I can see a little me, begging my mother to let me watch *The Nun's Story* for the umpteenth time on the *Late, Late, Late Show.* When Audrey Hepburn and the other, less beautiful nuns make full prostration in their long, stark habits, I do the same in a secret place inside myself.

I was seven when *The Sound of Music* was released. I went with my second-grade class and rooted for Maria, the flibbertigibbet postulant, to forget about Captain von Trapp and all those children and go right back into the serene, God-infused world of the convent perched on top of a snowy Salzburg mountain.

I must have been nine or so when I fixed my heart on a doll called Lonely Lisa from a B. Altman's catalogue. With her golden blonde hair and large brown eyes, Lisa was toddler size and probably about my age in doll years. She was the perfect companion for an only child and I was thrilled when my mother agreed that I could have her for Christmas. When she arrived, after admiring her for a brief period as she was, I took off her calico dress and carefully laid it aside. I found some material in my mother's sewing basket and worked for several days with an inner determination. Soon my project was finished. I dressed Lisa in a new outfit I had made specially for her—a nun's habit, including black "rosary beads" at her waist.

Lisa got to keep her black slippers (they matched her new, true identity), but her blonde hair was hidden behind her wimple. Her spiritual transformation was now complete.

For a little Catholic girl, perhaps there would be nothing very remarkable about these yearnings, but it was different for me. I was born a Jew.

My father was a hard-headed realist who came of age during the Depression on the Lower East Side of New York, the first-generation son of Russian immigrants. Taking over his father's paper-box business, he had no time for anything other than utter self-reliance. Work hard, rise early, and mind your business. Believe in only what you can bank on—and he meant it, literally. The Almighty Dollar, he used to call it, and on Yom Kippur this Jew would get up and go to work.

The only respite was on certain Sunday mornings in winter. While my mother slept late, I would dress myself, and my father and I would drive to the edge of Brooklyn to buy "appetizing"—smoked sable carp, lox, and pickled herring—Jewish food. As the car windows slowly defrosted, I settled in next to him for the drive, breathing in the reassuring smell of his worn-in tan windbreaker. The parkways merged into highways, Queens blurring into Brooklyn, while I listened sleepily to the stories of the Bal Shem Tov that he tuned in on the car radio. This was all I knew of Judaism.

My mother was no better equipped to show me the religious tradition of my birth. She came from a poor but arty Jewish family, her father a temperamental tailor who thought he was sewing couture and preferred finishing a seam to studying the *parashah*.* Her mother—dark, flamboyant, and part Mongolian—gave her only son, my mother's brother, a pat on the head and violin lessons instead of a bar mitzvah.

My mother's rite of initiation was to join the Ringling Brothers circus. She became the lady on the flying trapeze, defying gravity, trusting the inner rhythm of the body as she was swinging into outer space with nothing to hold her here below.

In every way, her sense of the physical went beyond this world. For my mother, the universe teemed with souls and spirits, disincarnate entities, all somehow governed by the valence and pull of heavenly

---

*One of the fifty-four consecutive portions of the Torah read during synagogue services on Saturday morning, and studied weekly.

bodies. When I was growing up, people routinely phoned to let her know about their most recent trip to Mars or Jupiter, to which she responded as enthusiastically as if they had just returned from Europe or a posh Caribbean cruise. Others pleaded with her to read their cards or to accept an invitation to an upcoming seance.

I'd wake in the middle of the night, as children often do, for a visit to the bathroom or to get some juice, and I'd see her in the den, lighting candles, reading little books on spell casting or astrology, throwing the I Ching or laying out the tarot deck in a new pattern. Her present was bleak; perhaps the future would be better.

"You have a good head on your shoulders," my father told me on one of those rare occasions when he felt like complimenting me, but it was really to remind me that I belonged to his side of the family. I was practical, quick, and organized, and I positively reeked with a sober maturity.

But I also had *no* head on my shoulders at all. I could touch and see things that were not there, at least not there in a normal, everyday sense. Traveling ecstatically in inner space, I would sit in meditation for hours, watching my breath drop to nothing and feeling my body fade far away as I left my constantly arguing parents and this confusing world behind to draw closer and closer to God.

As a child, the stillness of empty churches called to me. When I reached the age when I was able to venture out on my own, I would retrace my steps toward my elementary school, passing through the arch that separated the outside, predominantly Jewish, area of Forest Hills where I lived, from the high-WASP precincts of turreted mansions, hidden closes, and cul-de-sacs. There, streets were quiet, voices were hushed, and Protestant churches abounded: silent, stately, and serene.

Episcopal, Congregational, Presbyterian, they were indistinguishable to me. At that age, I knew nothing of denominations. What I sought was the cool silence of these spaces where, on a weekday afternoon, I could kneel alone in front of a cross and pray to Jesus Christ. Was he human or divine? I did not know, but the sibilant sound of his name rang holy inside me. I felt his power, the power of another world merging with this one, moving through me as I uttered his name like a secret prayer. I stayed there for hours, transfixed, with Christ riding on my breath.

But then there was the weekend warmth of listening to elderly rebbes from the old country, real Jews, telling stories on the radio layered with meaning and sad irony. And my craving for the weight of my father's bread and potatoes that my mother, who traveled through the ethers, derided as "peasant food."

The world of the mind. The world of the spirit. The world of the rational. The world of the intuitive. The world of the Christian. The world of the Jew.

In which world, then, would I live?

Standing in the fading lavender light of an April afternoon the day before Easter, now nearing my mid-twenties, I bend over the baptismal font at the cavernous Cathedral Church of St. John the Divine. Everything feels cool here. The stone floor. The gaze of the priest. Especially the air, like having climbed to a high altitude where the atmosphere is thin and rarefied. I can hardly breathe. A cross, given me by a friend moments before, grazes my skin and I shiver. After years of waiting, I am about to belong to Him.

As the Cathedral grows dark, the rose window at the end of the nave hovers seemingly in mid-air. In a white silk blouse and a long, beige Brooks Brothers skirt, I kneel in front of the majestic, patrician bishop as he seals me in baptism with water and the holy chrism. Tracing the sign of the cross on my forehead with the oil he has blessed, he nearly boxes my ears as he holds my head in his enormous hands and marks me as "Christ's own forever."

I thought of my adult baptism into the One Holy Catholic and Apostolic Episcopal Church of the Anglican Communion as my spiritual homecoming, the culmination of all those years of living like a Marrano in reverse—the Jew who knew Christ in secret.

Over the years, I had gradually trained myself to move away from the contemplative, solitary meditation and prayer of my youth to participation in the life of the Church. I altered my inner, spiritual rhythms of yearning and longing, praying and dreaming, to suit the rhythm of the *ecclesia:* Now you stand; now you kneel. When you pass the altar, always genuflect. Cross yourself at the Benedictus. At the name of Jesus, bow your head. Guide the chalice to your lips and then remember to say "Amen."

There was much to learn and I craved every detail, studied every nuance, as though encountering up close for the very first time the revelation of the true nature of my Beloved, and I wanted my responses to be almost instinctive. Every movement, every act in the Church, was charged with meaning and mystery, and every gesture I mirrored took me past another boundary. I wanted to absorb—and become—everything that would allow me to know Christ more intimately, and, at the same time, enable me to pass undetected as an insider, as though I had been born to love Him this way.

One wintry Sunday, after the conclusion of the liturgy, I sat far back near the crossing in the frigid cathedral where no one might see me. Balancing *The Book of Common Prayer* on my lap, my fingers cramping from the icy air and the clandestine urgency of my task, I hurriedly copied out the Nicene Creed into a little notebook so that I could memorize it at home, not knowing that one could buy an inexpensive edition of the prayer book just steps away in the swanky cathedral gift shop. I was convinced that all this ecclesiastical knowledge and etiquette were the privilege and the birthright of "cradle Episcopalians"—I found out early on what "the natives" were called—and intuited that I would have to learn it all in secret, and learn it well.

And so I did. But each time the liturgy began and I heard the far-off approach of the incense-bearer preparing the way of the Lord, rhythmically swinging the thurible on its chain down that impossibly long cathedral nave, I was transported by a spiritual ecstasy that was no learned response. The clouds of frankincense and myrrh that hung heavy in its wake, the scent of anointing the body for love or death, simultaneously veiled and unveiled God before my eyes.

Even then, I did not wish for myself the nun's habit I swooned over as a child. The mystery of the Eucharist called me closer to the altar than that. I searched and listened, waiting to learn the name of what I was made to be.

One very still morning in church, while I was kneeling in the pew and watching the consecration of bread and wine during the Mass, another reality became visible to me, beyond what was apparent at the altar. As a child, I had often experienced two different, but always separate, realities—the world of the material and the world of the spiritual. However, in this moment, when the bread and wine were transformed into the Body and Blood of Christ through the words and hands of the priest, in my spiritual "sight" these two worlds commingled. Each was somehow made holy by the other, and Christ's presence, so real to me then, suffused them both.

In some mysterious way, the separation of "worlds" within me began to come together as Christ's presence passed through me as well. I realized that all my youthful hours of meditation and prayer had laid the spiritual groundwork for what I had just witnessed in the

Mass. It was then that I knew instinctively that Christ had been preparing me all these years so that I might now serve him as a priest at his altar.

Such was the urgency with which I experienced this calling to priesthood that it never occurred to me not to respond, or even to say no. Wanting to begin preparing for the ordained ministry at the first possible opportunity, I had applied to divinity school months before my formal initiation into the Church took place. The party at my favorite Indian restaurant on the night of my baptism also celebrated the acceptance letter I'd received the week before from Harvard, welcoming me to its hallowed halls of *veritas* that coming fall. Newly Episcopalian, immersing myself in the nuances of the Bible and Church history, sipping sherry at the Dean's tea in wood-paneled drawing rooms with leaded glass windows and roaring fires, at Harvard Divinity School I would receive not only first-rate preparation for the ministry but would at last possess that genteel Ivy League "finishing school" education that had, thus far, eluded me.

My call, once named—though at the beginning, whispered just within the confines of my own heart—was so strong, and I felt so full of God's desire, that I believed my path from the baptismal font to the altar would be as clear as the straight highway in the desert that Isaiah saw laid out, unbroken, through the wilderness of this world. But the long road I traveled from the moment of baptism when I lifted my face streaming with sanctified water, to a moment fifteen years later when I would stand in synagogue in front of the Ark of the Covenant, feeling the weight of the Torah on Yom Kippur, the Day of Atonement, was a journey that I never could have imagined.

One divinity degree. One Ph.D. Three years spent in England, the Anglican homeland, where I had been part of the clergy team at a prominent, progressive London parish. I prepared for ordination in every way I knew how: through prayer and practice, study and service; through endless hours pastoring and preaching, teaching and leading church services. The call to priesthood grew ever stronger in my soul as I took on more and more parish responsibilities and congregation members affirmed my ministry. Sunday after Sunday, assisting the priest at the altar, utterly immersed in the life of the Church, I imagined myself soon being able to celebrate the Eucharist, standing in that place where God's worlds "came together."

But shortly after I returned to New York from England and began the Episcopal Church's process for Holy Orders, I was turned down for ordination. In a single moment, I experienced the shattering of my reason for being in the world. I thought I had known something about how to listen to the still voice of God, how to give expression to this fire, this passion, that I felt within. All these years, I thought I had done everything that God had asked of me. What could God possibly be asking of me now?

As I reeled from the shock of learning that I would not be ordained a priest in the Episcopal Church, I struggled to be supportive of my then-husband, a Prince Charles look-alike who disdained the Anglican Christianity of his upper-crust, English birthright and hoped one day to embrace Judaism. One Saturday, I reluctantly agreed to accompany him to a synagogue he had discovered near our Upper West Side apartment. I figured that some religious commitment was better for him than none, since he had always been unwilling to attend church. But I was in no way prepared for my own response.

I, who had only known rapture in those high Gothic spaces reaching toward heaven, was astonished with what I found in this particular synagogue—my first significant encounter with Judaism. Instead of the "three point," twenty-minute sermons I was used to in church, here were rabbis who were eloquent and learned on the subjects of meaning and being, spontaneously questioning each other in a lengthy dialogue in which the congregation joined in! I alternated between staring outright and averting my eyes in embarrassment as I watched them praying to God with unabashed love and passion, the kind of holy adoration and abandon that I, too, had once known before I became so well-trained in the restrained, highly choreographed movements of Anglican liturgy.

In church, I always wanted to wrestle with the Bible passages, bridling when I was instructed to tone down my intellectual streak. But here in this synagogue, the rabbis revered the text yet still challenged it—and God—and to do so, they said, was, in Judaism, a sacred act. No longer was I out of place with my love of learning and voracious reading habits, my desire to talk late into the night with all my friends over food and more food, uncovering layer after layer of meaning—in ideas, in books, in life. Suddenly, so many of the things that had made me stick out as "too intense" in church all had a context.

Alongside of the Anglican I had become, I found I was also a Jew.

It is years later now. The early autumn light is dimming; the Yom Kippur fast has begun. I surround myself in my *tallit*, white Ethiopian homespun riven with silver and black, drawing this prayer shawl over my head. I reach for the Torah without hesitation, the force of my body ready to receive it. I accept its weight, its curved bulk, against me, as I take it in my arms at last.

Just beyond where I stand in front of the Ark, the cantor begins to chant the *Kol Nidrei**—solemn and dark. My eyes closed, I rock from side to side, shutting out the enormous congregation, the rising heat of this unusually warm fall day, and the sight of my beloved rabbis nearby dressed in Yom Kippur white.

I am utterly focused within this embrace. I touch the scroll gently through its velvet covering, questioning, stroking, as though I could penetrate its layers and somewhere, among all its words in a language I barely understand, I would find—and grasp—my lineage at last.

For years, I remained caught in the gravitational pull between the two spheres that transited through me, Christian and Jew, these two ways through which I knew God. Holding the Torah so close to me now in front of the eyes of the assembly, seven years after my first encounter with Judaism, I have passed through the gate. Having embraced this covenant, now there is no turning back.

Moments later, at my seat in the crowded synagogue, we all joyously sing the *Shehechyanu—Praised are you, Adonai our God, for granting us life, for sustaining us, and for helping us to reach this day*. The solemnity of the *Kol Nidrei* lifts, and the sudden contrast jars me to attention and I wonder: Had I somehow been led deliberately on this painful and perplexing path that had once seemed so singular and clear? Had it all, somehow, been inevitable? Looking back over these years, can I discern the hand of God at work?

As I moved back and forth from church to synagogue, searching for my spiritual identity and my sense of place in the world, I began to intentionally, deliberately, seek out and read spiritual autobiography. In short, I needed to find another kind of spiritual "company." Had anyone else ever searched the way I did? Made wrong turns?

---

*The opening words of the declaration chanted three times at the beginning of the evening service of Yom Kippur, the Day of Atonement. Its mournful melody ushers in the most solemn day of the year for Jews.

Tried to realize a deep calling? And, even more confusing and embarrassing perhaps, had not succeeded and needed then to re-create and reevaluate his or her life?

I began to comb the religion section of my local bookstores, but I also explored the literature, memoir, biography, history, poetry, anthropology, and psychology shelves looking for the life stories of others who had tried to respond to a spiritual imperative. I needed to learn what had catalyzed as well as impeded them, and how they made spiritual sense out of outwardly random yet deeply connected events and occurrences. In the face of disappointment, I craved to know how they continued to serve and pray, watch and listen. I wanted to hear what had happened to their faith, to their families and communities, to their engagement with the world around them, to their sense of self, their experience of God, and to their response to the holy. What did they do with their pain and despair?

During this process, I revisited the writings of Thomas Merton and Mohandas Gandhi that I'd read years earlier as a teenager, trying to make sense of my spiritual inclinations. I also discovered a whole range of new autobiographical writings on spirituality and religion that spoke to me with urgency. I pondered the many Christian, Jewish, Hindu, and Muslim mystics who offered profound testimonies of living lives in a state of deep longing for God. And I looked again at the early Church apologists and martyrs whom I had read in my divinity school classes, then only on the lookout for their theological constructions.

As I read through these diverse stories, I began to notice familiar markers on the spiritual landscape. There were, indeed, patterns in the spiritual life that began to emerge as these writers, each in their own way, explored their lives.

In 1994, I began to teach religious studies at the college level and, unsurprisingly, one of the first courses I put together was "Readings in Spiritual Autobiography." It seemed to me that my students, many of whom were returning to school at an older age, had more than just an academic interest in the topic. It soon became clear that their spiritual and existential questions sat right alongside of the more scholarly concerns that they hoped to pursue.

But once again, just as when I began to read these accounts with my own circumstances in mind, there was no book, no compendium, of spiritual autobiographies which I could hand to them to read. It was then that the idea for this book was born.

The spiritual autobiographies that follow offer reflections upon some of the most meaningful and most difficult questions many of us ask of ourselves: Who or what is God, or the holy, for me? What are the sources of my spirituality? Who are my spiritual "ancestors"? When did I begin to lose my sense of "connection" to the holy and to the world around me and how do I regain it? How do I "come home," spiritually speaking? What is my life for? What am I meant to express or do or be in this world? Is my life part of a greater plan? Who am I, truly, in God's sight?

When I face a crisis, what inner resources will I have within me to help me through? What will endure from my life? What is my relationship to mainstream religious observance? If I don't pray or believe in God, can I still have something called a "spiritual life"?

The majority of writings in this anthology are by contemporary Western writers from a range of beliefs and backgrounds. But historical voices are also included; concern with the state of one's soul and one's relationship to God is not just a preoccupation of the late twentieth century.

I have cast the net of spiritual autobiography widely. While some writers refer to God in highly theistic terms and experience God as a central figure in their lives, for others, God is barely hinted at or even mentioned by any name at all. Some of these writers may have embraced a non-theistic spiritual path, such as Buddhism. Others may be more comfortable focusing on their ethnic or cultural heritage and their storehouse of family customs and memories. All describe a profound search and process of self-transformation that is, in my view, spiritual in nature.

Written by women and men from a wide range of backgrounds, these autobiographies illustrate lives filled with questioning and quest. Some are raw and disturbing; others are transporting in their lyrical, poetic power. Markers of identity such as race, gender, ethnicity, sexual orientation, physical ability, location in time, and a sense of place often play a significant role in their narratives, helping to frame and give context to their experiences. Yet despite the diversity and differences in the backgrounds of these writers, a number of common themes emerge, and these themes have inspired the five sections that organize this book.

What is central to all the autobiographies found in the first section, "Secrets and Revelation," is the quest for, or the discovery of, concealed information about ourselves and others that has the ability to affect our spiritual identity and sense of self.

There are three "kinds" of secrets found in this section. In the excerpts from books by Julius Lester, Mary Gordon, and Louise Kehoe, we read about the secrets that others, sometimes our families, keep from us about who they really are in terms of religious background or heritage, and the spiritual "detective work" that finally reveals what we have inherited.

And then there are those secrets about ourselves which we know, consciously or unconsciously, but do not fully reveal—to others or to ourselves. For Jan Morris, Antonio Feliz, and Lauren Slater, secrets about self-identity and spirituality are interwoven.

Finally, as we read in Nancy Mairs's essay, there are those devastating secrets that others reveal to us, catching us totally unaware and unsuspecting. Once disclosed, we are forced to use all our spiritual resources to cope and respond.

The second section, "Ancestors and Tradition," focuses on our spiritual and religious lineage and background; those connections and customs, rites, and rituals that we have inherited from our families and the religion into which we were born. Looking back, how do we locate our spiritual selves in relation to where we came from? What have we held on to and what have we left behind?

Sometimes our spiritual and religious lineage is centered on a specific place or time. Beverly Coyle, bell hooks, James McBride, Mary McCarthy, and Rita Dove all bring us back to their early years, offering moving recollections of their childhood faith and worshipping communities. Charles Fenyvesi, Kathleen Norris, and Albert Raboteau travel to ancestral homelands in search of the sources of their spirituality.

Our connections to the religious traditions of our birth can often be touched with sadness and estrangement. The selections by Randall Balmer and Carl Jung relate the often painful process of disenchantment—moving away from the religious traditions in which they were each raised. Yet the late Paul Cowan describes the joyous reconnection with the religious roots and spiritual "home" he had never really, fully, known. And Margot Adler, who grew up with multiple traditions and influences, shows us that we can be powerfully linked to another kind of spiritual lineage, perhaps not of birth, but of soul or temperament.

The stories in "Flesh and Spirit," the third section, describe the complex and often uneasy relationship between the physical longings of the body and the spiritual longings of the soul. Many of the writers explore the tension between their desire for sensual, sexual, embodied love and companionship with another person, and their desire to renounce those yearnings and commit themselves wholly to God.

Mohandas Gandhi, so filled with shame because of his lust, finally takes a vow of celibacy so that he might focus all his energy on the struggle for India's freedom and on his own quest for God. Though separated by centuries, Thomas Merton and St. Augustine, as well as the married medieval mystic Margery Kempe, are all united in their holy callings, leaving behind the pleasures of physical relationships. Social activist Dorothy Day painfully recounts the relationship that she sacrificed when she decided to be baptized. Kim Barnes struggles with the prohibitions of her strict Christian family and church community while her adolescent desire for the boy in the next pew blossomed. Barbara Grizzuti Harrison recalls the stirrings that filled her with the fear of sin and the judgment of God as a teenage Jehovah's Witness.

For some, such as Don Belton, Jyl Lynn Felman, and bell hooks, the themes of flesh and spirit are interwoven with their spirituality rather than in opposition to it. The powerful, same-sex longings of Belton and of Felman are tied to their families' respective religious and cultural expectations of what makes a real—that is, a heterosexual—man or woman. bell hooks, however, offers a sensual, poetic description of her preparation for baptism in which flesh and spirit, body and soul, at last come together.

Finally, the excerpt from Richard Gilman's memoir treats this theme in yet another way—focusing on the flesh and spirit of Jesus Christ, embodied and united in the sacraments of bread and wine, body and blood, and consumed to assuage both physical and spiritual hunger.

"Suffering and Mortality" groups the essays in the fourth section, which includes a range of human experiences involving physical and emotional pain, loss, and crisis.

Bradford Morrow recollects, moment by moment, thought by thought, the illness that delivered him close to death while the long-forgotten verses of the 23rd Psalm streamed through his mind. Jarvis Jay Masters, on San Quentin's Death Row, relies on the Buddhist practice of meditation and compassion to get him peacefully through whatever is left of his life. Dan Wakefield faced despair, depression, and addiction prior to his own spiritual transformation. Martin Luther King, Jr., who so often preached about the sufferings of a people, writes of his own faith in light of personal difficulties and danger.

Jeanne DuPrau turns to the non-theistic teachings of Zen Buddhism to help her face the loss of Sylvia, her beloved life partner. Kathryn Harrison, a convert to Catholicism, creates a complex "Trinitarian" narrative that unites "Mother, Death, and God." When Terry Tempest Williams's mother dies of cancer, her faith and tradition provide her with comfort and strength; but when Letty Cottin Pogrebin's mother dies all-too-suddenly from cancer, the boundaries of her religion, policed by her father, deny her from truly mourning this profound loss.

In the final section, "Exploration and Encounter," we see what can happen when we venture forth from the "safe harbor" of the religion in which we were raised, to encounter another tradition and a different set of beliefs.

Some of the writers in this section—Lawrence Shainberg, Sue Bender—are spiritual seekers, intentionally exploring religious traditions or practices other than the ones in which they were raised. Perhaps they are responding to feelings of spiritual dissatisfaction or restlessness. Or perhaps unexpected circumstances bring them into contact with new religious experiences, such as when journalist Dennis Covington goes to rural Appalachia to cover a murder trial and finds himself worshiping in a snake handling Holiness church.

James Oakley, the youngest writer in this collection, recalls his search for God in the midst of perilous encounters with Christian fundamentalism followed by years of drugs and then rehabilitation.

Encountering a different religious tradition can often force us to look more closely and more deliberately at who we are and what we believe. Roman Catholic George Dardess's encounter with Islam, and Methodist Christian Diana Eck's and James Karpen's encounters with Hinduism and Judaism, respectively, bring them right up to the edge of their own beliefs. Ari Goldman, an Orthodox Jew who goes to Harvard to study religion, faces the spiritual challenge of "the Other" with trepidation and wariness. Mohja Kahf, a Syrian Muslim who grew up isolated in the Midwest, experiences years of racial and religious slurs aimed at her "otherness"; yet when she and her family relocate to a more diverse city, she finds herself ill-prepared and reluctant to reach out beyond her Muslim community.

Karen McCarthy Brown, a professor of anthropology, pushes past the boundaries imposed by her scholarly work and is initiated into the Haitian vodou culture that she has studied for so long. In an excerpt from his autobiography, Malcolm X remembers the difficulty he faced within himself as he prepared to accept Islam.

Finally, unlike the other writers in this section, Bernadette Roberts, a former nun, engages in spiritual exploration not through embracing different practices as Shainberg does with Zen Buddhism; or through travels to other lands and cultures like Bender's visit to the Amish or Eck's sojourn in Banaras, but inwardly, through contemplation. There, Roberts encounters a vast Otherness, equal to any outward journey or spiritual challenge described here.

It is probably clear by now that a number of these essays, slotted into one particular category might easily fit into another. In fact, the themes that divide this anthology also unite a great many of these essays. Therefore, I invite you to read some of these pieces through the "lens" of a different category and see what emerges through a second, or even a third, reading.

Yet even on the printed page, we are, ultimately, "works in progress," and what I believe these stories demonstrate is that the spiritual life is much more nuanced, and much more riddled with trepidation and ambiguity, than we might have ever imagined or foreseen. Spiritual autobiographies often resound with what we might call "outsiderness." Many of the people whose work we read here experience themselves to be significantly different in some way, not "fitting in," or even alienated from the world around them—a state that sometimes seems to be caused or exacerbated by their quest. Frequently, they maintain an uneasy relationship to organized religion, and their seeking takes place "on the margins."

While a few authors describe a strong sense of "having arrived" at a place of spiritual stasis, many more suggest that the spiritual life is dynamic, always in flux. We read of transcendence and enlightenment that lasts for a millisecond and ecstasy that is fleeting at best and very hard to sustain. The depression and feelings of immense loss that sometimes follow spiritual "highs" become, for many, intertwined with a relentless longing that, in turn, continues to fuel the search.

Attempting to live a spiritual life can indeed be a confusing and painful experience beset with obstacles and detours, rather than filled with the bliss we might have expected. The autobiographies collected in this anthology offer companionship, helping us to understand our own frequently perplexing journeys. They recall moments of profound meaning and insight that are part of the process of human transformation, how we all get from "here to there"—even if we are only talking about the movement that takes place within our souls.

These testimonies can inspire us when our own connection to anything spiritual seems just a vague memory. They can provide reassurance when we feel isolated and misunderstood in our quest. When we are about to stumble, they can be the "lookout" just ahead. When we get "uppity" or spiritually complacent or lazy, they challenge us to begin again. And in those moments of union when we are indeed filled with a sense of the holy, they echo our joy.

I

SECRETS

and

REVELATION

HERE: GRACE

Nancy Mairs

From her proper New England Protestant upbringing, to her adult conversion to the "oxymoron" of Roman Catholic feminist, author Nancy Mairs writes with startling candor about God's daily presence in her life in the midst of extreme circumstances. Mairs uses the often difficult "text" of her life—her husband's cancer, their mutual infidelities, her own multiple sclerosis and depression—as the spiritual context within which to find God, again and again, even in the midst of betrayal, as illustrated in this essay from Ordinary Time: Cycles in Marriage, Faith, and Renewal.

"**You will** love me?" my husband asks, and at something in his tone my consciousness rouses like a startled cat, ears pricked, pupils round and onyx-black.

Never voluble, he has been unusually subdued this evening. Thinking him depressed about the mysterious symptoms that have plagued him for months and that we know in our heart of hearts signal a recurrence of cancer, although the tests won't confirm it for several more days, I pressed up against him on the couch and whispered against his neck, "This may be the most troublesome time of our lives, but I'm so happy." This awareness of joy, though it's been growing for several years now, has recently expanded in response to my own failing health. A few weeks ago, pondering the possibility that I might die at any time, I posed myself a new question: *If I died at this very moment, would I die happy?* And the answer burst out without hesitation: *Yes!* Since then, in spite of my fears, I've felt a new contentment. What more could I ever ask than to give an unequivocal response to such a question?

His silence persisted. "Scared?" I asked him after a few moments, thinking of the doctor's appointment that morning, the CAT scan scheduled for later in the week. Head resting on the back of the couch, eyes closed, he nodded. More silence. Finally I said, "George, you know how I love words. I need words!"

And now, words: "You will love me?" Behind his glasses, his eyes have the startled look I associate, incongruously, with the moment of orgasm.

"Yes," I tell him, alert, icy all over. "I can safely promise you that. I will always love you."

"You asked the other day whether my illness could be AIDS," he says unevenly. "I'm pretty sure it isn't, because I had the test for HIV some time ago, after I had an affair for a couple of years with another woman."

The sensation is absolutely nonverbal, but everybody knows it even without words: the stunned breathlessness that follows a jab to the solar plexus. What will astonish me in the days to come is that this sensation can sustain itself long after one would expect to be dead of asphyxiation. I have often wished myself dead. If it were possible to die of grief, I would die at this moment. But it's not, and I don't.

A couple of years. *A couple of years.* This was not fit of passion, no passing fancy, but a sustained commitment. He loved her, loves her still: Their relationship, until he broke it off—for reasons having little to do with me—was a kind of marriage, he says. Time after time after time he went to her, deliberately, telling whatever lies he needed to free himself from me and the children, and later from his mother when she came for a protracted visit after his father's death, throughout at least a couple of years.

More. He'd fallen in love with her six years earlier, I could sense at that time, and they'd had a prolonged flirtation. She was a bitter, brittle woman, and something about her rage inflamed him. Their paths had parted, however, and I had no way of knowing of their later chance encounter, courtship, years-long "marriage." And after that ended—here, in this room, which will ever hereafter be haunted by her tears—four years of silence: too late to tell me, he says, and then too later, and then too later still. Twelve of our twenty-seven years of marriage suddenly called, one way or another, into question. I recall my brother's description of his framing shop after the San Francisco earthquake, how miraculously nothing in it was broken, not even the sheets of glass for covering pictures, but it looked as though some giant gremlin had come in and slid everything a few feet to one side. My past feels similarly shoved out of whack, not shattered but strangely reconfigured, and out of its shadows steps a man I have never seen before: Sandra's lover.

If I were that proverbial virtuous woman, the one whose price is far above rubies, perhaps I would have the right to order George out of my sight, out of my house, out of my life. But I'm not that woman. I'm the other one, the one whose accusers dropped their stones and skulked away. I've desired other men, slept with them, even loved them, although I've never felt married to one. I guess I took my girlhood vow literally: I have always thought of marriage as something one did once and forever. All the same, in brief passionate bursts I've transgressed the sexual taboos that give definition to Christian marriage.

I'm not a virtuous woman, but I am a candid one. Many years ago, George and I pledged that we would not again lie to anyone about anything. I haven't been strictly faithful to the spirit of this promise, either, because I've deliberately withheld information on occasion (although not, according to my mother, often enough, having an unfortunate propensity for spilling the family beans in print); but I have not, when directly challenged, lied. This commitment can have maddening consequences: One night I listened for half an hour or longer to the outpourings of a total stranger in response to an essay in one of my books because I couldn't tell her that I had a pot on the stove about to boil over when I actually didn't. Had Daddy and I meant that vow for *everybody*, my daughter asked after I hung up the telephone, not just for each other? Not even, I can see now, for each other: especially not for each other.

"How can you ever believe me again after this?" George asks, and I shrug: "I've believed you all this time. I'm in the habit of it. Why should I stop now?" And so I go on believing him, but a subtle difference will emerge over time: belief becomes a matter of faith, no longer logically connected to the "truth" of its object, which remains unknowable except insofar as it chooses to reveal itself. I suppose I could hire a private detective to corroborate George's tales, but I'm not going to because George's whereabouts are no less his own business now than they ever were. I can envision some practical difficulties in my being unable to locate him at any given time, but no moral ones, whereas I perceive a serious problem in seeking information that would curb his freedom to lie, a freedom without which he can't freely tell me the truth. I don't want to come by my belief through extortion. Once, I believed George because it never occurred to me not to believe him; now I believe him because I prefer belief, which affirms his goodness, to doubt, which sneers and sniggers at it. No longer an habitual response, belief becomes an act of love.

It does not thereby absolve George of responsibility for the choices he has freely made, however. The years while he was slipping away to sleep with Sandra were among the most wretched of my not conspicuously cheerful life; and by lying to me, he permitted—no, really encouraged—me to believe that my unhappiness was, as always, my own fault, even though, thanks to the wonders of psychopharmacology, I was at least no longer clinically depressed. I remember lying awake, night after night, while he stayed up late grading papers and then dropped into bed, and instantly into sleep, without a word or a touch; as he twitched and snored, I'd prowl through the dark house, sip milk or wine, smoke cigarettes, write in my journal until, shuddering with cold and loneliness, I'd be forced to creep back into bed. Past forty, he must have been conserving his sexual energies, I realize now, but when I expressed concern and sadness, he blamed our chilling relationship on me. I was distracted, too bitchy, not affectionate enough. . . . Ah, he knew my self-doubts thoroughly.

Breakdowns in our relationship, especially sexual ones, had habitually been ascribed to me. "I'm very tired," I wrote in my journal early in this period of misery, twenty years into our marriage, "of his putting me down all the time—telling me that I'm too involved with Anne, that I don't handle Matthew well, that I'm not affectionate (the only signs of affection he recognizes are physical, which I suppose makes sense, since he doesn't communicate verbally). In short, that I'm a bad mother and wife. I just don't know how to feel much affection for someone I feel sorry for, for being married to me." Tired of disparagement I may already have been, but I took over two years more to recognize myself as a collaborator in it: "He survives—thrives—on my culpability. Without it, where would he be today? We've *both* built our lives on it, and if I remove it, our relationship will no longer have any foundation."

This awareness of complicity precipitated out of a homely crisis (the form of most of my crises), in the winter of 1985, involving the proper setting of the thermostat, which George persistently left at sixty degrees even though I couldn't bear the temperature below sixty-five (and, as came out in the course of the dispute, neither could he). When I told him that the coldness of the house represented my growing feelings of neglect and abandonment, he countered that he had to go elsewhere (leaving the thermostat set at sixty) in order to get the touching and affection he needed. It was, I noted, "the same old ploy, trying to trigger my guilt for not being a physically affectionate wife. Only this time I could feel myself not quite biting. Because he wants the physical part to continue regardless of the pain I'm in, even if he causes the pain, and he blames me if I won't put out, come across, what have you. And I'm sick unto death of bearing the blame." He could, I suddenly understood, turn up the heat himself. He chose not to.

Or rather, he chose to turn it up in some other woman's house. In spite of the sexual stress underlying this controversy, he gave no hint that his longing for "warmth and light" was taking him from the crumbling converted Chinese grocery where the children and I lived to a spacious, immaculate, perfectly appointed home in a tranquil neighborhood miles away; and I didn't guess. Just as he knew how to exploit my self-doubts, he knew how to escape me. Teaching in two programs, he was out of the house from at least eight-thirty in the morning until eight-thirty at night; he devoted his spare time to good works like cooking at Casa María soup kitchen, observing the federal trial of the people who had arranged sanctuary for refugees from El Salvador, and editing *¡Presente!,* the local Catholics for Peace and Justice newsletter. With such a schedule, of course he'd have little enough energy left for sex, or even a leisurely family dinner. Another woman (his lover, for instance) might have judged his devotion to illiterate, poor, and oppressed people sanctimonious, even morbid, but I found it natural and necessary.

As a result, he put me in a conscientious bind: I felt abandoned, and I believed that George was neglecting our troubled teenaged son dangerously, but I couldn't make our needs weigh heavily enough against those of five hundred empty bellies at the kitchen door or a Salvadoran woman who'd fled her village in terror when the last of her sons disappeared. Still, I wondered uneasily why the spiritual growth he said he was seeking necessitated his setting out on what appeared to be "a quest—Galahad and the Holy Grail—noble and high-minded and above all out there, beyond the muck and mire of daily living in a decaying house with a crippled wife and a rebellious adolescent son." Forced to let him go, I did so with a bitter blessing: "Feed the poor, my dear. Shelter the refugees. Forget the impoverishment you leave in your wake. It's only Nancy and Matthew and Anne, after all—nothing spiritual there, nothing uplifting, no real needs, just niggling demands that drag at you, cling to you, slow your lofty ascent into the light and life of Christ."

Our approaches to ministry were hopelessly at odds: "I think that the life of Christ is only this life, which one must enter further and further. And I hate the entering. I'd give anything to escape. . . . There's no glamor here, no glory. Only the endless grading of papers. The being present for two difficult children. The making of another meal. The dragging around of an increasingly crippled body, forcing it to one end of the house and back again, out the door, into the classroom, home again, up from the bed, up from the toilet, up from the couch. The extent of my lofty ascent. I want only to do what I must with as much grace as I can." That George, finding these conditions squalid and limiting, sought to minister elsewhere embittered but hardly surprised me. And so, whenever he wanted Sandra, he had only to murmur "Soup. Sanctuary. *¡Presente!*" in order to be as free of them as he liked.

I have been, it appears, a bit of a fool. "Where did I think you'd gone?" I ask George. "What lies did I believe?" He claims not to remember. He will always claim not to remember such details, which is his prerogative, but the writer in me obsessively scribbles in all the blanks he leaves. I imagine the two of them sitting half-naked beside her pool, sipping cold Coronas and laughing at my naïveté, and then I have to laugh myself: I would have been the last thing on their minds. This sense of my own extinction will prove the most tenacious and terrifying of my responses, the one that keeps me flat on my back in the night, staring into the dark, gasping for breath, as though I've been buried alive. For almost thirty years, except during a couple of severe disintegrative episodes, my presence to George has kept me present to myself. Now, at just the moment when cancer threatens to remove that reassurance of my own reality from my future, it's yanked from my past as well. Throughout his sweet stolen hours with Sandra, George lived where I was not.

"Are you all right?" my daughter asks on the day following George's revelation when she stumbles upon me huddled in my studio, rocking and shivering. I shake my head. "Shall I cut class and stay here with you?"

"No, go to class," I say. "Then come back. We'll talk."

"You're not going to do anything rash while I'm gone?" It's the question of a child seasoned in suicide, and I wish she didn't have to ask it.

"I promise. Scoot."

I hadn't planned to tell Anne, at least not yet; but George is getting sicker by the day, his mother is about to arrive for several weeks, Christmas is coming, and I don't think I can deal with this new complication alone. I have George's permission to tell whomever I wish. "I want you to write about this," he says. "I want you to write about us." For himself, he has never revealed it to anyone except once, early on, the psychotherapist with whom we've worked, together and apart, over the years. But he believes in the value of what I try to do in my work: in reclaiming human experience, insofar as I can find it embodied in my own experience, from the morass of secrecy and shame into which Christian and pre-Christian social taboos have plunged it, to rescue and restore God's good creation. (And if at times the work proves as smelly as pumping a septic tank, well, shit is God's creation, too.) George supports it, but the work itself is mine. If any bad tidings are to be borne, I am the one to bear them.

"But Mom," Anne says when I've finished my tale of woe, "men *do* these things." Transcribed, these words might look like a twenty-five-year-old's cynicism, but in fact her tone rings purely, and characteristically, pragmatic. It's just the tone I need to jerk my attention back from private misery to the human condition. She's right, of course. In the Judaic roots of our culture, as Uta Ranke-Heinemann points out in *Eunuchs for the Kingdom of Heaven*, "a man could never violate his own marriage. The wife belonged to her husband, but the husband did not belong to his wife," and a couple of thousand years of Church teaching on the subject of marital fidelity—not all of it a model of clarity and consistency—has never entirely balanced the expectations placed on the two partners. *People* do these things, Anne means (I know: I have done them myself); but ordinary men, men possessed of healthy sexual appetites, have been tacitly *entitled* to do them. They're just *like* that.

Except for my man. One reviewer of my first book of essays, *Plaintext,* wrote: "The reader will also wish to see more closely some of the people who simply drift through these essays, especially Mairs' husband, who comes across as a saint, staying through extreme mood swings, suicide attempts, severe illness, and a number of love affairs." That's *my* man: a saint. Through my essays I've publicly canonized him. Any man who could stay with a crazy, crippled, unfaithful bitch like me had to be more than humanly patient and loving and long-suffering and self-abnegating and . . . oh, just more than human.

Admittedly, I had help in forming this view, especially from other women; a man whose bearing is as gentle and courtly as George's can seem a true miracle, one my inconstancy plainly didn't merit. "But hasn't he ever slept with another woman?" more than one person has asked, and I've said proudly, gratefully, "No. I've asked him, and he tells me he never has." I often told myself that he "ought to go, get out now, while he's still fairly young, find a healthy woman free from black spells, have some fun. No one could blame him." And occasionally, trying to account for his physical and emotional unavailability, I'd conjecture: "Perhaps another woman—he's so attractive and romantic that that thought always crosses my mind." My guess was dead on, it turns out, formed at the height of his affair with just the sort of healthy woman I'd had in mind, but I took him at his word and felt humbled—humiliated—that he had responded to my infidelities with such steadfastness.

A saint's wife readily falls prey to self-loathing, I discovered, since comparisons are both common and invidious, and recuperation, if it occurs at all, is a protracted and lonely process. One evening a couple of years ago, when I'd been invited to discuss *Plaintext* with a local women's reading group and the conversation turned, as such conversations always seem to, to my infidelity and George's forbearance, I blurted: "Wait a minute! Did it ever occur to you that there might be some advantage to being married to the woman who wrote *Plaintext?*" At last I'd reached the point where I could ask that question. But as I sipped coffee and nibbled a chocolate cookie in the company of these polite and pleasant but plainly distressed strangers, my chances of getting an affirmative answer seemed remote as ever. In this tale, I was decidedly not the Princess but the Dragon.

George has conspired in his own sanctification. Why wouldn't he? The veneration of others must be seductive. And if, in order to perpetuate it, he had to affirm—to me, and through me to others familiar with my writings—his faithfulness even as he shuttled between Sandra and me, well, what harm was he doing? For her own reasons, Sandra was just as eager as he to keep the affair clandestine. They seldom went out and never got together with friends; he never even encountered her child, who was always, magically, "not there"; she'd even meet him in a parking lot and drive him to her house so that the neighbors wouldn't see his car. He could maintain this oddly hermetic relationship without risk to the sympathy and admiration of friends, family, and book reviewers alike. No one need ever know.

Until, ultimately, me. That is, I don't need to know, not at all, I've done very well indeed without knowing, but he has come to need to tell me. At first, he thought merely breaking with Sandra would calm the dread his father's death and the discovery of melanoma in a lymph node stirred in him, but now he needs a stronger remedy. "I feel this awful blackness inside. I just want to die," he says after confessing, and I shudder, because an awful blackness is precisely what he has inside— a six-centimeter melanoma attached to his small bowel—and I don't want him to die, he can tell me anything, I'll accept whatever he confesses, any number of awful blacknesses, if only please he won't die. He hasn't any control over that, alas, but at least now he has cleared his conscience thoroughly. I think he's after another clarity as well, one that involves putting off sainthood and standing naked—bones jutting under wasted flesh, scars puckering arm and belly, penis too limp now for love—as a man. He wants to be loved as he is, not as we—his mother, my mother, my sisters, our daughter, his students, our friends, maybe even Sandra herself—have dreamed him. I most of all. I look anew at the reviewer's words: "The reader will wish to *see more closely* some of the people who *simply drift* through these essays. . . ."

George is accustomed to holding himself slightly aloof. The only child of adoring parents, he grew up believing himself entitled to act on his own desires without regard for the needs of others: There weren't any others. If he wanted the last cookie, it was his. (In fact, even if he didn't want it, his mother probably made him take it.) No noisy wrangles, no division of the coveted cookie followed by wails that "he got the bigger half," no snitching a bite while the other's head was turned or spitting on the other's half to spoil it for both, just complacent munching down to the last sweet crumb. But, by the same token; no whispers and giggles under the covers after Mother has put out the light *for absolutely the last time*. No shared cookies. No shared secrets, either. No entanglements, true. But no intimacy.

Having grown up in an extensive family linked by complicated affections, with a slightly younger sister who still sometimes seems hooked into my flesh, I don't think I ever quite comprehended George's implacable self-sufficiency. Maybe for that reason I allowed, even encouraged, his remoteness. And I did. The reviewer is talking, after all, not about George's nature but about my essays. If the reader wants to "see" George "more closely," then I have not seem him closely enough. George "drifts" through my essays because I permitted him to drift through my life. "I couldn't imagine," he tells me now, "that what I was doing, as long as I kept it in a separate little box, had any effect on the rest of you." Like his indulgent mother, I let him persist in such manly detachment. I'd have served him better as a scrappy sister.

What I might have thought of, in good aging-hippy fashion, as "giving him space," letting him "do his own thing," strikes me now as a failure of love. Respecting another's freedom does not require cutting him loose and letting him drift; the lines of love connecting us one to another are stays, not shackles. I do not want to fail again. After the children and I have each spoken with him separately about the affair, I say to him: "You may have hoped, in confessing to us, that we'd punish you by sending you away, but now you see that we won't do that. If you want to leave, you'll have to go on your own initiative. As far as we're concerned, you're not an only child, you're one of us. We love you. We intend, if you will let us, to keep you."

"You will love me?" George asked at the beginning of this terrible test, and I find, to my relief, that I can keep my promise. "But can you forgive him?" asks our friend Father Ricardo when we seek his counsel, and I reply, without hesitation, "I already have."

I *have*? How can this be? I have never felt more hurt than I do now. I am angry. I am bitter. I try to weep but my eyes feel blasted, although occasionally I shudder and gasp in some stone's version of crying its heart out. I dread going out into the city for fear I'll encounter Sandra. I torment myself with images of George pressing his lips to hers, stroking her hair, slowly unbuttoning her blouse, calling her "sweetheart," too. *She got the sex,* I reflect sardonically as I keep my vigil through surgery and its horrific aftermath, then through chemotherapy, *and I get the death*. I despise her for her willingness to risk my marriage without a thought; and yet in a queer way I pity her because, as it has turned out, she has to live without George and, for the moment, I do not.

Worst of all, ghastly congratulatory cheers ring in my head: *Good-o, George! You've finally given the bitch her comeuppance: tit for tat, an eye for an eye, and not a whit more than she deserves.* "What do you care what people think?" he shrugs when I tell him of this fantastic taunting, but the truth is that, with new comprehension of the suffering my adultery must have caused him, I'm tempted to join the chorus. Still, although our affairs may be connected chronologically (mine all took place before his) and causally (bitterness about mine offered him permission for his), morally they stand separate. I don't merit the pain I'm now in, any more than George ever deserved to be hurt, but we have unquestionably wounded each other horribly and we each bear full moral responsibility for the other's pain. George is right to dismiss my demonic chorus: What matters is not mockery and blame, whether our own or others', but mutual contrition. Over and over when he clings to me and weeps as I cannot and says, "I'm sorry, I'm sorry," I hold him, stroking his back and murmuring reassurances: that I love him, that I'll be all right, that he hasn't "spoiled" us, that through this pain we can grow. Forgiveness is not even in question. It is simply, mysteriously, already accomplished.

Week after week he has stood beside me telling me what I have not wanted to know: *I confess to Almighty God, and to you, my brothers and sisters, that I have sinned, through my own fault, in my thoughts and in my words, in what I have done and in what I have failed to do.* Now that he's divulged the specific contents of his conscience to me, I'm curious what this little ritual of general confession meant during the time he so plainly wasn't sorry for what he was doing. "Did you ever think about Sandra as you said those words?" I ask. "Did you think what you were doing might be wrong?"

"Well, yes, I knew it was. But I also knew I didn't intend to stop. So I just had to hope that God had a sense of humor." Fortunately for George, God has a much better sense of humor than I do. But I've been working on it. Meanwhile, week after week his voice has spoken aloud at my side: *And I ask Blessed Mary ever virgin, all the angels and saints, and you, my brothers and sisters, to pray for me to the Lord our God.* As bidden, I have prayed for him, as for myself and for all the disembodied voices floating up behind me, that God might have mercy on us, forgive us our sins, and lead each one of us to everlasting life. Believing myself forgiven by God, I must believe George equally forgiven. And if forgiven by God, surely no less by me.

One of the elements that drew me into the Catholic Church was the concept of grace, although I've never been able to make more than clumsy sense of it. I am moved by the idea that God always already loves us first, before we love God, wholly and without condition, that God forgives us even before we have done anything to require forgiveness, as we will inevitably do, and that this outpouring of love and forgiveness fortifies us for repentance and reform. I am moved—but not persuaded. I am simply incapable of grasping an abstraction unless I can root it experientially, and nothing in my experience has revealed quite how grace works. Until now. The uncontingent love and forgiveness I feel for George, themselves a gift of grace, unwilled and irresistible, intimate that grace whose nature has eluded me.

For the most theologically unsophisticated of reasons, involving a dead father who went, I was told, to heaven up in the sky, together with continual reiterations, from about the same age on, of "Our Father, who art in heaven . . . ," I always expect spiritual insights to shower like coins of light from on high. When instead they bubble up from the mire like will-o'-the-wisps, I am invariably started. Grace *here,* among these lies and shattered vows, sleepless nights, remorse, recriminations? Yes, precisely, here: Grace.

But forgiveness does not, whatever the aphorism says, entail forgetfulness. Never mind the sheer impossibility of forgetting that your husband has just told you he's had an affair, a strenuous version of that childhood game in which you try, on a dare, *not* to think about a three-legged green cat licking persimmon marmalade from the tip of its tail. Never mind memory's malarial tenacity, the way that, weeks and months and even years after you think the shock has worn off, as you recall a trip you made to Washington to receive a writing award, it occurs to you that in your absence they may have made love for the first time and all your words, the ones you'd written before and the ones you've written since, shrivel and scatter like ashes. Never mind.

Mind what matters: his presence here, for now. Love is not love, forgiveness is not forgiveness, that effaces the beloved's lineaments by letting him drift, indistinct, through the lives of those who claim him. That way lies lethargy, which is the death of love. I am not married to Saint George, after all. I am married to a man who is, among many other things neither more nor less remarkable, an adulterer. I must remember him: whole.

from *IN THIS DARK HOUSE*

L O U I S E   K E H O E

Growing up in a remote English farmhouse called "World's End," Louise Kehoe knows that there is something unutterably different about her family, especially her mysterious, despotic Russian father. A journalist who now lives in Massachusetts, Kehoe writes in her memoir, In This Dark House, *of her struggle to decipher the clues to her own identity in the midst of self-shattering isolation and a profound sense of "otherness."*

In the southwest of England, where the river Severn ambles gently through the undulating Cotswold countryside, the scenery is timeless and unmistakably agricultural. The landscape is latticed with natural hedgerows—prickly and impenetrable thickets of sweetbrier and hazel, hawthorn and elder—which divide field from field and farm from farm along ancient boundaries. The narrow, winding roads are used by livestock more than by cars, and the few drivers who do negotiate those twists and turns do so at snail's pace, knowing that they may at any moment come upon a flock of sheep or a herd of cattle plodding sedately toward their barn at milking time.

The village of Upper Killington does not appear on any map. Indeed, despite its rather grandiose name, it can hardly be described as a village at all, nor even a hamlet. There are just three houses there; three seventeenth-century stone-built farmhouses nestling comfortably in the shelter of a little valley.

My parents discovered Upper Killington entirely by accident. It was 1939, just before the outbreak of the Second World War, and they had not long been married. They lived in London then, where my father's architectural practice was based, and were driving back to London after spending a weekend with friends in the west country when a particularly beautiful sunset made them want to stop for a while and just look. Leaving their car beside a ramshackle hay barn, they wandered down an anonymous-looking dirt road and suddenly found themselves in the little valley, its patient old houses suffused with the sunset's triumphant light. One of these houses stood empty and abandoned, is garden waist-high in grass and weeds, its rough-hewn front door obscured by a heavy curtain of wisteria whose inquisitive tendrils had wormed their way through the keyhole and around the doorjamb, and could be seen advancing greedily across the flagstoned floor within.

To my parents, the pull of this beautiful backwater must have seemed irresistible. The country was on the brink of war; uncertainty permeated every aspect of daily life. Bomb shelters were hurriedly being constructed in towns and cities all over England, and propaganda posters had begun appearing everywhere. "Careless Talk Costs Lives," the posters proclaimed apocalyptically, warning people not to talk unguardedly to anyone: you never knew who might be listening, who might be a spy or a Nazi sympathizer. In this atmosphere of mounting dread and queasy instability Upper Killington, isolated and untouched by the troubles of the twentieth century, offered an oasis of immutable calm and reassuring predictability.

They returned to London but could not settle. Before the end of that year they had bought the empty house at Upper Killington and the hundred acres of farmland that went with it. Because of its blissful remoteness—but also, I suspect, because of the catastrophe which was about to engulf Europe—they called the house World's End.

· · ·

Quite why my parents had chosen to withdraw from the world in this way it never occurred to me to ask; it was simply a fact of life. The hermetic isolation of Upper Killington was the only thing I had ever known—I was born there, after all—and besides, I had no memory of my parents as the gregarious people they had reputedly been when they first met. As far as I was concerned, they had always been militantly antisocial. When people did visit, they were not encouraged to stay for long—I cannot recall there ever being an overnight guest at World's End—and after they had gone my parents would express enormous relief at the lifting of what they saw as a painful intrusion. There would follow a lengthy and detailed postmortem, during which they would subject their erstwhile visitors to minute and scathing criticism, dissecting their conversation, their opinions and even their table manners without pity, something I found enormously disconcerting in view of the apparent cordiality with which the fleeting guests had been received.

A child raised in an atmosphere of such resolute misanthropy cannot fail to be affected by it, and even before I reached school age I had begun to entertain the uneasy suspicion that my family was somehow different from other families, and that, for reasons I could neither understand nor articulate, I was destined to be an outsider.

School did little to dispel my misgivings. For a start, sheer distance put a well-nigh insurmountable barrier between me and my peers. The bus that took me to school and back—an hour's ride in each direction—left from the village of Hawkesworth, itself a half-hour ride by car from Upper Killington. My parents found the trip to Hawkesworth and back twice daily tiresome enough, and were unyielding in their opposition to my taking part in any after-school activities, for this would of necessity involve them in extra fetching and carrying. It was therefore rare indeed for me to go to the home of a classmate or to experience a taste of life outside the quarantined existence at World's End—and when I did, it only served to confirm my belief that the Lubetkin family was like no other, and that I was a misfit through and through.

But more than simply mileage stood between me and comfortable assimilation at school. Far from being separate, church and state in England were deeply and inextricably enmeshed with each other: all the schools were to a greater or lesser extent parochial, and prayer and religious education were an integral part of the curriculum. My parents, both avowed atheists, objected vehemently to my participation in any religious activity, and demanded that I pursue purely academic study during the periods when the rest of the school attended to devotional matters. This set me apart at once from every other child in the school, branding me indelibly in the eyes of pupils and staff alike. I dread to think what would have happened if I had been rash enough to reveal to my parents that the academic study arranged by the school for me as an alternative to religious education consisted of my sitting in an empty classroom, rote-learning the Psalms in numerical order and reciting from memory in front of the entire class at the end of the study period. It is an irony which I am sure would not have been lost on my teachers that I can, to this day, summon up whole chunks of the lyrical hymns of King David, while remembering little or nothing about my other studies.

There was no escape, either, from the consequences of my parents' passionate political convictions. Contemptuously dismissing the mounting evidence of Stalin's monstrous crimes as nothing more than vicious anti-Soviet propaganda, Dad clung doggedly to his communist faith, while Mama echoed his pronouncements as though they had come down from the mountain carved on tablets of stone. Like a loyal commissar Dad stood guard over me, jealously policing my contact with the outside world and taking it upon himself to protect me from influences which he considered undesirable. Every day, as he drove me along the narrow, winding road to Hawkesworth to catch the school bus, he would take advantage of the time we had together to catechize me on current affairs, the car accelerating sharply with every forceful point he made, and meandering alarmingly while its driver's attention was wholly occupied elsewhere. As we neared Hawkesworth, he would sum up the lesson of the vertiginous journey with this homily, identical every day: *Now we are approaching the last and most dangerous corner, and the time at my disposal is strictly speaking limited. Nevertheless, before I release you to the school there is still time for me to express the fervent hope that when I return to fetch you this evening you will have become a worthier citizen than you are now.*

Many was the time I landed myself in hot water at school by regurgitating some wildly irreverent remark or transparently doctrinaire statement of Dad's. I was summoned by the headmistress of my junior school and made to apologize publicly, before the entire school, for blaspheming, after I made the mistake of referring to the Holy Ghost the way Dad did, as the Holy Goat. And I have never forgotten the explosive silence that descended on the classroom—a classroom packed with the children of dairy farmers—when I, eight years old and terrifyingly truthful, answered a teacher's question about the dietary value of milk by solemnly denouncing that paragon of health and natural purity, declaring it carcinogenic on account of the dangerously high strontium 90 levels which were present in it as a direct result of fallout from the testing of nuclear weapons in the atmosphere.

I was on no less perilous ground at home. After picking me up from the school bus at Hawkesworth in the evening, Dad would put me through what amounted to a full debriefing on the way home, demanding to know what I had learned that day—particularly in history classes—and would savagely dismember the information I dutifully relayed to him, condemning it as bourgeois revisionism and drumming his own—Marxist—interpretation mercilessly into me. The dilemma induced by these conflicting forces was agonizing: if I defended the version supplied by my teachers I would incur Dad's most withering scorn and anger, whereas if I expounded on Dad's ideas to my teachers they responded with crushing rebukes and punitive grading. Homework to which Dad had given the seal of doctrinal approval would regularly come back to me run through with an angry cat-scratch of red ink, the page puckered by the vehemence of the pen stroke. "I'm not interested in your pet theories; I asked for the FACTS!" wrote my furious history teacher on one memorable occasion. But to Dad these were the words of an idiot. He never tired of telling me, then and later on in my life, that the very notion of fact was itself a fantasy, particularly where history was concerned. "Facts," he said, "do not exist. The data one chooses to select and record depend solely upon the theory one is trying to prove. Facts are purely a matter of opinion."

Little did I realize, as I wrestled, exasperated, with the seemingly insoluble problem of how to do my history homework to the satisfaction of both my judges, that Dad's disdain for facts was not the product of some lofty philosophical purism, nor even of simple sophistry, but came instead from the desperate desire he felt to escape from the awful realities of his own sad past.

．　．　．

It did not pay to argue with Dad. He had an explosive temper, and nothing triggered it more inexorably than being defied by one of his children. It made no difference if he was clearly in the wrong, or if the issue was entirely trivial: he simply could not tolerate dissent. You knew it was too late the second you opened your mouth. "IDIOT!" he would roar at you, in his thick Russian accent, whipping his glasses off and glaring at you with bulging eyes, contempt and fury combining to harden his features into something resembling a samurai war mask. There was no stopping him then: although he lost his composure with frightening ease, it often took him days to regain it, and during that time you were a pariah. He would neither speak to you nor look at you, and if you should happen to touch him he would flinch, pulling sharply, disgustedly away from you as though you were leprous.

He punished all transgressions, no matter how minor, by turning cold in this way, and the restoration of peace required of the offender a painfully long drawn-out process of self-abasement and ever more abject apologizing, until finally Dad would signal a thaw by delivering a solemn monologue about the fragility of love—parental love included—and the dangers of putting it to the test. "Love is like a wall," he would say, drawing a splendidly bathetic architectural analogy, "and each time there is a quarrel a new crack appears, a chunk of mortar crumbles. In time, the wall becomes so weak that it simply collapses, and once it has fallen it can never be rebuilt the way it used to be." Naturally he saw himself as the one whose love was being tested to the limit; it never occurred to him, I am sure, that his children might identify with the wall in his analogy, casting him as the cracker of stones and the crumbler of mortar. He was nothing if not vain.

Nor was he willing to let bygones be bygones once a quarrel had finally came to an end. He often nursed grievances for long periods, returning to them again and again as if to whet the pain which might otherwise long since have dulled and died away. Hidden behind the books on the top shelf in his study he kept a series of notebooks—dubbed by us the Book of Grievances—in which he chronicled our wrongdoings, omissions, and shortcomings. Writing sometimes in Russian, sometimes in English, and sometimes in a mixture of the two, he recorded incidents of such banality that it is difficult to imagine how they could have precipitated the seismic and seemingly unquenchable anger that they did.

Three apples on kitchen table at breakfast; only two left at lunchtime. I questioned Steven, who repeatedly denied taking apple, but was obviously lying because he blushed.

Louise's bed unmade despite two reminders.

Sasha stole piece of fudge from kitchen.

He viewed these misdemeanors, inconsequential as they truly were, not as random childish peccadillos but as sinister portents, symptoms of an underlying malaise; and he saw himself as the benign, concerned physician, carefully watching his afflicted patients and collecting clinical evidence, the better to assess their pathology and devise effective treatments.

Often the precise nature of the original transgression would become overshadowed by its supposed significance as a marker for something deeper and more ominous, and one would find oneself being asked to apologize not for the taking of an apple without permission but for the essential mediocrity of one's character. It was not uncommon, either, to be accused of something one had not done, and yet to incur Dad's wrath nonetheless, simply on account of the spiritedness of one's denial—vehemence being a quality which the good doctor, although himself a master of the art, could not abide in others. We were children of Stalinism, and we very early learned that one didn't necessarily need to have done anything; attitudes were even more important than actions, since attitudes were truer windows on one's ideological and intellectual development, and sensitive barometers of its orthodoxy.

It was in these situations above all that we would turn to Mama for support, begging her to intercede on our behalf. And this, with great selflessness and not a little raw courage, she would do, pleading with Dad to be gentler to his children, and not to draw such sweeping conclusions about their worth on the basis of such tenuous evidence. Inevitably, this would cause him to turn the full force of his wrath on her like a water cannon, for, as he saw it, she was willfully opposing him—an act that showed her to be as shallow and disloyal as the children themselves, and deserving of no lesser punishment. Their voices would be heard coming from the kitchen, Mama's measured appeals crowded out and shouted down by Dad's relentless harangue. And whichever one of us it was who had unleashed Dad's fury would listen at the kitchen door, or creep across the uneven floor of my bedroom, which was directly above the kitchen, praying for the creaky floorboards to stay silent, and would make use of the numerous cracks between the boards to observe the proceedings taking place below.

To watch oneself being tried by kangaroo court in this way was a terrible experience: the sense of utter powerlessness was overwhelming. But worse by far was to witness Dad's deliberate cruelty to Mama, the way he berated her and called her an idiot, the way he reduced her to tears and made her sob so heartrendingly, all to punish her for taking her child's part instead of his. That was truly unbearable. Despite the murderous hatred we felt for him at these times, all that really mattered to us was to alleviate Mama's suffering, and if that meant apologizing profusely—even for something we hadn't done— and subjecting ourselves to remorseless self-criticism, so be it: for her sake we would acknowledge the trumped-up charges, sign the confession, admit to being enemies of the people.

But Dad was an autocrat in the true Russian tradition: an extraordinary union of heartlessness and humanity; Cossack cruelty coexisting with grand sentimentality; the knout in one hand, the balalaika in the other; and the man who could arouse both abject fear and incandescent resentment in his children could also inspire them with an insatiable hunger for his affection. The father who denigrated his children without mercy and harbored festering grievances against them was also the father who could disarm them with a sudden kindness, embrace them with his ready laughter, beguile them by blowing smoke rings and wiggling his ears, and play the piano for them like Paderewski, throwing open the windows of the old farmhouse and filling the entire valley with the cascading, kaleidoscopic music of Chopin.

Mama was as bewitched by him as we were, and it was she who fed and fueled the natural longing we had to be loved by him, and who shielded the flame and kept it alive when his volatile temper and blistering anger threatened to extinguish it entirely. She it was, too, who insisted against all the evidence that he did indeed love us, and that if only we knew him better—*really* knew him, as she did—then we would understand what made him the monster he could sometimes be, and would forgive him for it. "One day," she said, "he'll explain everything to you. Then you'll understand."

One thing is certain: the people who thought they knew Dad didn't know him at all, and that was as true for his children as it was for the few friends he and Mama still kept. Only Mama really knew him, really understood him, but her understanding of him owed more to faith than to insight: she simply accepted him unquestioningly, recognizing his faults but giving them no weight. And although she knew him inside out she kept that knowledge doggedly to herself, meeting my every plea for an explanation with a curious reticence, and quietly insisting that Dad must be the one to tell his story, and no one else.

This meant, of course, that the story never got told, and that was exactly the way Dad wanted it, for he was clearly not inclined to explain himself to anyone, least of all to his children. Indeed, on the few occasions when I plucked up courage and made timid overtures in that direction, he jumped at the chance to tell me that he considered me too stupid to understand anything more challenging than Mickey Mouse—a taunt which Mama, in her usual placatory way, dismissed as merely Dad's clumsy attempt at humor, but which stung and bruised me nonetheless, causing me to shy away from asking any question which might invite a similar rebuff.

Being the youngest, I had had ample opportunity to watch my brother and sister battling their way through childhood ahead of me, and I harbored few illusions as to what lay in store for me. I was therefore a great deal more interested in avoiding conflict with Dad than I was in plumbing his psychology. And even if there was, as Mama had so often told me, some mitigating explanation for his fulminant temper and tyrannical behavior, it was largely academic as far as I was concerned. After all, this was by no means the only mystery surrounding Dad: almost nothing about him was straightforward or simple. Even his personal history was shrouded in obscurity. Whereas Mama was forever recounting stories of her childhood, her schooling, her aunts and uncles, cousins and grandparents, Dad never spoke about his family at all, and would not be drawn on the subject. And while Mama kept a photograph album full of pictures of her family, from the straitlaced, scowling Victorian worthies of her grandparents' generation all the way through her own childhood and right up to the time she met Dad, there was no corresponding album for Dad's side. Indeed, I never saw a single photograph of Dad's family, nor any of him as a child. It was almost as though his life had begun only upon his arrival in England in 1930. Before that there was no trace, no record, and to all intents and purposes, no memory.

The little I knew about Dad's past I gleaned from Mama, who, with the evasiveness and palpable discomfort which characterized our conversations about Dad (she clearly felt that she was somehow being disloyal to him), told me only that he had been born in 1901 in czarist Russia, that he had been the child of a wealthy family with homes in St. Petersburg and Moscow, and that the family had been wiped out by the Bolsheviks in the Russian Revolution of 1917. Dad was the only survivor.

I forget how old I was when Mama first imparted this information to me—six, maybe, or seven—but I do remember that it troubled me enormously, evoking a deep compassion for Dad which ran entirely counter to the cringing submissiveness he typically inspired, and serving to worsen the miserable ambivalence I felt toward him. As I grew older, of course, and began to fight more and more fiercely with him, that compassion withered, and in its place there arose a great bitterness toward him for remaining a communist in spite of the fact that his family had been butchered on the altar of Marxism, and a silent, angry cynicism toward the ideology he so obstinately espoused.

Just about the only aspect of Dad's past about which there was no doubt, and of which he made no secret, was that Berthold Lubetkin was not his real name. This he freely admitted, although, even so, neither he nor Mama would ever reveal what his real name was. He had acquired the name, he told me, in order that he could enter the University of Warsaw to study architecture. It was at a time shortly after the Russian Revolution, when a tide of nationalistic fervor was sweeping through Poland, a country which lay open and vulnerable on the western doorstep of the emerging Soviet Union. In an attempt to shore up its independence and guard against being engulfed by the civil war that was still raging unabated inside Russia, the Polish authorities decreed that Soviet citizens would not be allowed to reside in Poland, nor attend Polish universities; these privileges would be reserved exclusively for Poles. Since Dad was then still a Soviet citizen, it became imperative for him to acquire Polish nationality at once, and he did so by clandestinely purchasing the name and forged identity papers of a long-dead Polish citizen, one Berthold Lubetkin, native of Warsaw. Newly minted citizenship in hand, he entered and duly graduated from the University of Warsaw, leaving his real name behind forever.

While I understood almost instinctively that the secrecy surrounding Dad's real name sprang from his need to put the painful memory of the fate of his family firmly behind him, I was nevertheless fascinated by the whole idea of his assumed identity. There was something intriguing and glamorous about it, and I used to daydream endlessly about what our real family name might be, who we really were, and why it had to be kept such a profound secret. In my mind's eye, depending on how well or badly Dad and I happened to be getting along, I would imagine him as the last of the Romanovs, hiding his royal ancestry behind a commoner's name; or he would be a heartless criminal, like Raskolnikov in Dostoyevsky's *Crime and Punishment,* hoping to escape the consequences of his own villainous past.

And so Dad remained a complete enigma to me, a man entirely made up of contradictions and inconsistencies, a man who had no qualms about preaching one thing with passionate conviction whilst practicing quite the opposite; a man who systematically isolated himself behind a wall of secrecy, emerging only to punish, criticize, or pass judgment on his children. The wonder of it is not that I lived in fear of him, but that I so desperately wanted him to love me, and would go to the most extraordinary lengths to please him. But his praise was always fleeting. He dispensed affection as though it were a cash payment to an odd-jobber: no promises, no long-term commitment; you did it right this time, but that doesn't mean I consider you reliable.

Knowing that I could only earn his love on piecework, I constantly sought ways to prove myself useful to him. Quietly and unbidden I would empty his ashtray, polish his shoes, bring him cups of coffee, being called a creep by my brother and sister, and incurring their jealousy for the small gratuity of affection Dad would occasionally pay me for my attentiveness. I was fiercely proud of the nickname he gave me—*kurrinny eyes* ("chicken eyes" in Russian)—for my sharp-sightedness and my useful ability to find even tiny objects which had been misplaced. To me it seemed such a milestone: I had earned myself a permanent place in his life at last.

How ironic it is that my most treasured gift from him is one he never intended that I should have, and which I therefore never dared mention to him, still less thank him for. I was only eight or nine at the time, but the memory of that strange incident has stayed with me ever since, luminous and powerful. Late one night I stirred from a deep sleep to find Dad sitting beside my bed, gently stroking my hair. He thought I was still fast asleep, of course, but I wasn't. There was a full moon that night, and in its light I could clearly see the tears which filled his eyes and trickled down his cheeks. "You look so much like my mother," he whispered. Then he kissed my forehead and quietly slipped out of the room.

After he'd gone I lay awake for a long time listening to the slow, sad sound of a Chopin nocturne coming softly from the piano downstairs.

• • •

With school being such a lifeline for my beleaguered psyche, the long summer vacation presented a uniquely gloomy and purgatorial prospect. So when, in the summer of my seventeenth year, I received an invitation from my German pen-friend to spend the entire month of August at her home in Bavaria, I closed my eyes and begged every conceivable deity to soften Dad's heart and make him consent to let me go. Amazingly, he did agree. Who knows why? Maybe he, too, was worn out by the endless conflict between us and relished the chance to spend a month alone with Mama at World's End, just him and her, the way things had been in those wonderful, childless early days. Whatever his reasons, I was at last being set free, and I can clearly remember the exhilaration I felt as I boarded the train at the start of that long journey, kissing my parents a joyful good-bye and promising, in my gratitude, to visit every Baroque palace within striking distance of my friend Sabine's home.

Sabine lived in the town of Prien, on the shore of Lake Chiemsee, not far from Munich. She and her family spent a lot of time sailing on the lake, which was certainly a complete change for a lifelong landlubber like me; but very soon I tired of sailing, and, giddy with my newfound sense of independence, I longed to go off on my own and explore. One afternoon, while Sabine and her family were out sailing on the lake as usual, I opted instead to borrow her bicycle and go for a ride into town by myself. I didn't tell Sabine this, of course, but I had never ridden a bicycle before, and moreover, coming as I did from one of the most sparsely populated areas of rural England, I was entirely unused to traffic, especially traffic which drove on the right. Meandering wildly, I provoked yells of annoyance and remonstration from passing motorists. I tried to keep as far to the right as I could to enable cars to pass me uneventfully, but soon found myself wobbling dangerously, and before I knew what had happened, I had plowed into a parked car, plunging my hand clean through the side-view mirror.

Passersby began gathering around me at once, clucking over my badly mangled hand, which was now bleeding enthusiastically; but my immediate worries were more for Sabine's crumpled bicycle and the scratched and dented car I'd hit than for the injury I'd inflicted on myself. Who would pay for the damage I'd done? How would I explain what had happened to the owner of the car, or to Sabine's parents? I was in trouble, no doubt about it; and as I sat there fretting on the sidewalk, a dozen anxious citizens of Prien fussing over the young *Engländerin* with the badly bleeding hand, I was struck by the irony of the fact that here I was, really on my own for the first time in my life, yet what I wanted most in all the world was for Mama and Dad to be there to help me.

A taxi took me to a local hospital, a grim place, as they all are. The hospital was staffed by an order of Carmelite nuns in full traditional habits, including starched headdresses so elaborately folded and so white that there was not room for two to pass each other in the dismal, paneled hallway. I was bleeding impressively by now, and without further ado I was ushered into a small operatory where a doctor was waiting for me.

He was in his middle to late fifties, a gray-haired, bespectacled man with a stiff and unsmiling demeanor. He wore a long green rubber apron which reminded me vividly of the one the veterinarian wore when attending to the obstetrical needs of the World's End cattle. The nuns must have told him that I was English, for he spoke to me with the slow, exaggerated elocution that people use when addressing idiots and foreigners. He seemed particularly interested in my name. "Lubetkin," he said. "Lubetkin. What sort of a name is that?" "Russian," I replied. "My father came from Russia." "Oh?" he returned. "But Lubetkin is a Jewish name. Are you Jewish?" "No," I replied, wondering whether I should even try to embark upon the convoluted saga of Dad and his assumed name. I wasn't at all sure my very basic German could be stretched to cover such a long and involved story, and besides, I was beginning to feel distinctly faint with shock and fear. If this was the doctor's attempt at polite conversation, if he was trying to put me at my ease, he had failed miserably. There was something profoundly disturbing about him, and I was immensely thankful for the presence of the nun-nurse in her starched butterfly headdress.

And then the doctor set to work. Stretching my hand out on a stainless steel table, he took a hard-bristled nailbrush and began scrubbing the ragged wounds with an unnatural zeal—and since he had not seen fit to bother with niceties such as local anesthesia, the pain was excruciating. There was no anesthesia, either, for the eighteen stitches it took to close all the wounds. I lay there, face averted, biting my lip so hard that it bled, conjuring up images of my beloved Mama, who set such store by bravery and dignity, and I fought will all my might to do her justice by not crying.

The doctor stood up and, after dismissing the nun from the room, told me he would now give me antitetanus shots. In England nearly all shots are given in the upper arm, so I pushed back the sleeve of my T-shirt as best I could for him. He stopped me. "No," he said. "Take off your clothes." I did as he said. With his face wearing the expressionless mask of clinical detachment, and with his hand unshaken by shame or compassion, he administered a tetanus shot with studious precision into the nipple of both my breasts. Then without a word, he turned on his heel and left the room. A short while later, the nun returned and told me I could go.

I went home to England a couple of days later, my month of freedom abruptly at an end. The incident had laid me so low that my hosts became worried and called Mama and Dad to tell them that they were putting me on a plane for London.

I wasn't really sure how Mama and Dad would react. I was prepared for outrage and indignation toward that doctor, whose vile agenda had been so clearly visible in the questions he had asked about my name, and the cruel, perverted way he had treated me, I was even prepared for anger: after all, I should never have taken such a risk, especially not all alone, in a foreign country, unused as I was to traffic. What I wasn't prepared for was indifference—and that was exactly what I got.

Neither Mama or Dad showed the slighted surprise or resentment toward the doctor. On the contrary, they dismissed the questions he had asked me as being perfectly innocent—simply a natural curiosity on his part, they said, concerning a patient with an unusual name. They told me I was being hysterical and melodramatic when I suggested that he might be a former Nazi bent on humiliating me because he thought I was Jewish. And as for the injections in my breasts, well, they did things differently on the Continent. Sometimes they gave shots in one's behind, Mama said, and sometimes in other parts; just different customs, that's all. Nothing to worry about. He must have had good reason to choose that particular technique.

I was devastated by their reaction. I had been through something savage and unspeakable, and there they were telling me I was making a mountain out of a molehill, that nothing untoward had happened, and that I was the one with the problem. I could not accept it. Surely I was worth more than that? I felt abandoned—and worse, violated all over again, this time by my own parents—and I told them exactly that.

The result was predictable. Whipping his glasses off, Dad leaped to his feet and glared at me, his face suddenly suffused with rage. "You will take that remark back and apologize for it immediately!" he roared. "No, I won't," I replied, strangely calm, and full of an unfamiliar sensation of self-assurance. "I meant every word."

The force of the blow Dad struck me sent me reeling to the floor. I got up slowly, my head spinning and my ears humming. Mama was sitting at the kitchen table, her head in her hands, sobbing. "Get out!" Dad shouted at me. "Okay," I said. And that night, taking only the clothes I stood up in, and the little money I had in my purse, I left World's End forever.

from *CONUNDRUM*

JAN MORRIS

To all outward appearances, James Humphrey Morris was a solitary yet well-adjusted boy who grew up in the 1930s in a cultured home, not far from the mountains of Wales. Yet since his earliest years, he possessed a secret: that he "had been born into the wrong body, and should really be a girl." These excerpts from Conundrum, *writer and journalist Jan Morris's classic autobiography on transexuality, eloquently chronicle the gradual revelation of this self-knowledge as Morris embarks on a spiritual quest for unity: to align inner essence with the physical body.*

I WAS THREE or perhaps four years old when I realized that I had been born into the wrong body, and should really be a girl. I remember the moment well, and it is the earliest memory of my life.

I was sitting beneath my mother's piano, and her music was falling around me like cataracts, enclosing me as in a cave. The round stumpy legs of the piano were like three black stalagmites, and the sound-box was a high dark vault above my head. My mother was probably playing Sibelius, for she was enjoying a Finnish period then, and Sibelius from *underneath* a piano can be a very noisy composer; but I always liked it down there, sometimes drawing pictures on the piles of music stacked around me, or clutching my unfortunate cat for company.

What triggered so bizarre a thought I have long forgotten, but the conviction was unfaltering from the start. On the face of things it was pure nonsense. I seemed to most people a very straightforward child, enjoying a happy childhood. I was loved and I was loving, brought up kindly and sensibly, spoiled to a comfortable degree, weaned at an early age on Huck Finn and *Alice in Wonderland,* taught to cherish my animals, say grace, think well of myself, and wash my hands before tea. I was always sure of an audience. My security was absolute. Looking back at my infancy, as one might look back through a windswept avenue of trees, I see there only a cheerful glimpse of sunshine—for of course the weather was much better in those days, summers were really summers, and I seldom seem to remember it actually raining at all.

More to the point, by every standard of logic I was patently a boy. I was James Humphry Morris, male child. I had a boy's body. I wore a boy's clothes. It is true that my mother had wished me to be a daughter, but I was never treated as one. It is true that gushing visitors sometimes assembled me into their fox furs and lavender sachets to murmur that, with curly hair like mine, I should have been born a girl. As the youngest of three brothers, in a family very soon to be fatherless, I was doubtless indulged. I was not, however, generally thought effeminate. At kindergarten I was not derided. In the street I was not stared at. If I had announced my self-discovery beneath the piano, my family might not have been shocked (Virginia Woolf's androgynous *Orlando* was already in the house) but would certainly have been astonished.

Not that I dreamed of revealing it. I cherished it as a secret, shared for twenty years with not a single soul. At first I did not regard it as an especially significant secret. I was as vague as the next child about the meaning of sex, and I assumed it to be simply another aspect of differentness. For different in some way I recognized myself to be. Nobody ever urged me to be like other children: conformity was not a quality coveted in our home. We sprang, we all knew, from a line of odd forebears and unusual unions, Welsh, Norman, Quaker, and I never supposed myself to be much like anyone else.

I was a solitary child in consequence, and I realize now that inner conflicts, only half-formulated, made me more solitary still. When my brothers were away at school I wandered lonely as a cloud over the hills, among the rocks, sloshing through the mudbanks or prodding in the rockpools of the Bristol Channel, sometimes fishing for eels in the bleak dikes of the inland moors, or watching the ships sail up to Newport or Avonmouth through my telescope. If I looked to the east

I could see the line of the Mendip Hills, in whose lee my mother's people, modest country squires, flourished in life and were brass-commemorated in death. If I looked to the west I could see the blue mass of the Welsh mountains, far more exciting to me, beneath whose flanks my father's people had always lived—"decent proud people," as a cousin once defined them for me, some of whom still spoke Welsh within living memory, and all of whom were bound together, generation after generation, by a common love of music.

Both prospects, I used to feel, were mine, and this double possession sometimes gave me a heady sense of universality, as though wherever I looked I could see some aspect of myself—an unhealthy delusion, I have since discovered, for it later made me feel that no country or city was worth visiting unless I either owned a house there, or wrote a book about it. Like all Napoleonic fantasies, it was a lonely sensation too. If it all belonged to me, then I belonged to no particular part of it. The people I could see from my hilltop, farming their farms, tending their shops, flirting their way through seaside holidays, inhabited a different world from mine. They were all together, I was all alone. They were members, I was a stranger. They talked to each other in words they all understood about matters that interested them all. I spoke a tongue that was only mine, and thought things that would bore them.

·   ·   ·

I was intensely self-conscious, and often stood back, so to speak, to watch my own figure stumbling over the hills, or sprawled on the springy turf in the sunshine. The background was, at least in my memory, brilliant and sharp-edged, like a Pre-Raphaelite painting. The sky may not always have been as blue as I recall it, but it was certainly clear as crystal, the only smoke the smudge from a collier laboring up-Channel, or the blurred miasma of grime that hung always over the Swansea valleys. Hawks and skylarks abounded, rabbits were everywhere, weasels haunted the bracken, and sometimes there came trundling over the hill, heavily buzzing, the daily de Havilland biplane on its way to Cardiff.

My emotions, though, were far less distinct or definable. My conviction of mistaken sex was still no more than a blur, tucked away at the back of my mind, but if I was not unhappy, I was habitually puzzled. Even then that silent fresh childhood above the sea seemed to me strangely incomplete. I felt a yearning for I knew not what, as though there were a piece missing from my pattern, or some element in me that should be hard and permanent, but was instead soluble and diffuse. Everything seemed more determinate for those people down the hill. *Their* lives looked preordained, as though like the old de Havilland they simply stuck dogged and content to their daily routes, comfortably throbbing. Mine was more like a glider's movements, airy and delightful perhaps, but lacking direction.

This was a bewilderment that would never leave me, and I see it now as the developing core of my life's dilemma. If my landscapes were Millais or Holman Hunt, my introspections were pure Turner, as though my inner uncertainty could be represented in swirls and clouds of color, a haze inside me. I did not know exactly where it was—in my head, in my heart, in my loins, in my dreams. Nor did I know whether to be ashamed of it, proud of it, grateful for it, resentful of it. Sometimes I thought I would be happier without it, sometimes I felt it must be essential to my being. Perhaps one day, when I grew up, I would be as solid as other people appeared to be; but perhaps I was meant always to be a creature of wisp or spindrift, loitering in this inconsequential way almost as though I were intangible.

• • •

. . . I myself see the conundrum in another perspective, for I believe it to have some higher origin or meaning. I equate it with the idea of soul, or self, and I think of it not just as a sexual enigma, but as a quest for unity. For me every aspect of my life is relevant to that quest—not only the sexual impulses, but all the sights, sounds, and smells of memory, the influences of buildings, landscapes, comradeships, the power of love and of sorrow, the satisfactions of the senses as of the body. In my mind it is a subject far wider than sex: I recognize no pruriency to it, and I see it above all as a dilemma neither of the body nor of the brain, but of the spirit.

• • •

I have never been a true Christian, and even now wish the great churches of Europe were devoted to some less preposterous exercise than worship. I except, though, from my iconoclasm your true-blue English cathedrals, if there are any left, where the Book of Common Prayer survives untampered, where the Bible is still King James's version, where fiery brides keep their fingers crossed as they promise to obey, where the smell is of must and candles, where the hassocks have been embroidered by the Diocesan Mothers' Guild, where the clergymen's vowels are as pure as their musical intonation is shaky, where gold plate gleams beneath rose windows, where organists lean genially from their organ-lofts during the sermon, where Stanford in C, *The Wilderness* or *Zadoc the Priest* thunder through the arches on feast days, and where at the end of evensong the words of the Benediction come frail, half inaudible but wonderfully moving from the distant coped figure raising his hand in blessing before the high altar. All these conditions were satisfied to perfection during my childhood attendance at the cathedral of Christ Church, Oxford, and beneath the orison of their mysteries I brooded and wondered, day after day, about the mystery of myself.

Investigators into transsexuality often comment upon the mystic trappings in which it is likely to be clothed. The ancients frequently saw something holy in a being that transcended the sexes, and sympathetic friends have detected, in the heart of my own quandary, some sort of inspiration. I first felt it myself, profane or ludicrous though it may appear to skeptics, during my years in that cathedral. Every day for five years, holidays apart, I went to service there, and its combination of architecture, music, pageantry, literature, suggestion, association, and sanctity powerfully affected my introspections. I knew that building almost as I knew my own home; or rather I knew *part* of it, for out of sight beyond the choir stalls were chantries and chancels we seldom had cause to penetrate, alcoves which sprang into life only on particular days of ceremony, and were usually obscured in shadow, dimly hung with the gossamer ensigns of disbanded regiments, and sometimes shuffled into, as into anonymity, by lonely bowed figures in search of solitude. But the bright-lit circle around the choir stalls became as it were my own, and it was there more than anywhere that I molded my conundrum into an intent.

An ancient holy building is conducive to secrets, and my secret became so intermingled with the shapes, sounds, and patterns of the cathedral that to this day, when I go back there to evensong, I feel an air of complicity. I found a passing fulfillment in the building, in a kind of dedication. Over at the choir school I increasingly felt myself an imposter among my friends, and winced, silently but in pain, when people in their ignorant kindness expected me to be as the others. . . . I wondered sometimes if it were all a punishment. Could I perhaps have done something fearful in a previous incarnation, to be condemned in this way? Or would I be compensated in an existence to come, by rebirth as Sonja Henie or Deanna Durbin? At other times I thought it might all be resolved by suffering, and when I sat in the dentist's chair, or lay miserable in the sickroom, or was being urged to be first off the diving-board into the cold pool, I called into play arcane formulae of my own: often I was told how brave I was, and this told me something about the meaning of courage, for I was really ticking off each moment of unhappiness as a contribution toward my release—truly storing up treasures in heaven.

But during our daily hours at the cathedral, I could be myself. There I achieved some childish nirvana. Pink, white, and scarlet in my vestments, genuinely inspired by the music, the words, and the setting, I was not exactly a boy anyway, but had undergone some apotheosis of innocence to which I aspire even now—an enchantment less direct than my abandonment beneath the chestnuts, but more complete in its liberation. Perhaps it is how nuns feel. Certainly I felt sure that the spirits of the place approved of it, and perfectly understood my desires. How could they do otherwise? The noblest aspects of the liturgy aspired to what I conceived as the female principle. Our very vestments seemed intended to deny our manhood, and the most beautiful of all the characters of the Christian story, I thought, far more perfect and mysterious than Christ himself, was the Virgin Mary, whose presence drifted so strangely and elegantly through the Gospels, an enigma herself.

Elevated in this guileless if soppy way, I began to dream of ways in which I might throw off the hide of my body and reveal myself pristine within—forever emancipated into that state of simplicity. I prayed for it every evening. A moment of silence followed each day the words of the Grace—"The grace of Our Lord Jesus Christ, and the love of God, and the fellowship of the Holy Ghost, be with us all evermore." Into that hiatus, while my betters I suppose were asking for forgiveness or enlightenment, I inserted silently every night, year after year throughout my boyhood, an appeal less graceful but no less heartfelt: "*And please, God, let me be a girl. Amen.*"

How He could achieve it, I had no idea, and I was doubtless as vague as ever myself about the details of my desire. I still hardly knew the difference between the sexes anyway, having seldom if ever seen a female body in the nude, and I prayed without reason, purely out of instinct. But the compulsion was absolute, and irrepressible, and those cathedral days seemed to give it a sacred encouragement. I felt that there were Powers waiting to help me, someday. I did not despair, and being by temperament a cheerful child, and by circumstance a lucky one, I conditioned myself to cherish my secret more as a promise than a burden. . . . I do not wish to imply that I imagined some godly purpose working itself out in me: it is merely that those influences of my childhood, those English tolerances, those attitudes and sensations of Oxford, those consolations of Christian form, wove their own spell around my perplexities, softening them and giving them grace.

from *THE SHADOW MAN*

Mary Gordon

Best-selling novelist Mary Gordon's adored, enigmatic father died when she was seven, shattering her world, leaving a trail of clues to his life of lies. Gordon's painful search for his true identity, detailed in her memoir, The Shadow Man, *reveals a Jew converted to Catholicism, a virulent anti-Semite, and a pornographer. In these excerpts, a very young Mary, enshrining her idealized dead father in her memory, is alternately comforted and frightened by morbid Church piety: the thorns, the tears, and the open wounds.*

THERE IS a sound of disaster, and a quiet after it, when the universe becomes still from shock, the wind stops, the light is colorless, and humans have no words because no words fit the enormity. Then a hum enters the air, and normal activity begins again, but slowly, as if everyone were underwater. People move, pick things up in their hands, walk from place to place, but the hum supports each action. You can mark the time when the disaster is complete and something else—the rest of life—begins. You know this because the hum no longer supports each act. I have never been in an earthquake, or the aftermath of battle, but I know their sound: the shocked sound of proximity to death. I heard it when my mother hung up the phone and said, "Your father's had a heart attack."

For thirty days, my mother drove to the hospital each evening to see my father. I wasn't allowed to go. I stayed with my grandmother. I slept in her dark room with the frightening pictures: the brown replica of the Shroud of Turin, a picture of Christ with long, smooth, girlish hair, pointing to his Sacred Heart, the size and shape of a pimento or a tongue. Most mysterious: a picture made of slats. You turned your head one way: it was the Scourging at the Pillar. Another turn of the head produced Jesus Crowned with Thorns. If you looked absolutely straight ahead, you saw the Agony in the Garden. I was kept awake by these pictures and by the room's bitter smells: lavender, ammonia, hair oil, liniment. Pine Sol always at the bottom of the commode: a green pool reminding you inevitably of the corruption that you, as a human, had no right pretending you could rise above.

One Monday night, I woke for nothing. It was nearly midnight. I went into the living room. My mother let me sit on the couch beside her and watch television. We watched Jack Paar. Ten minutes later, the phone rang. It was the hospital. My father had just died.

It was then that my life split in two, into the part when my father was alive and the part when he was not. Since the first part lasted only seven years, my life has always felt unbalanced. The part of my life after his death kept growing; there was no way to stop it, except by my own death. There was no way to lengthen the other, to have more time with my father as a living man.

I understood what had come to an end. My mother and I moved out of our apartment into my grandmother's house. I never saw the apartment again, and I never saw most of the things I'd had there.

I don't know what happened to it all. The furniture, the lamps, the cheerful dishes. And my toys: my windup Cinderella, my tin dollhouse, the Alice in Wonderland rug. They were banished. Were they burned, sold, put upstairs in the attic? I was afraid to ask. My aunt who lived with my grandmother, with whom I would now live, said I had to remember there was very little room in the house. I understood. But nobody said anything to me about what had happened to my things. Everything was simply gone, no longer on earth. It had disappeared, as my father's body, for no better reason, had disappeared.

My mother bought twin beds and flowered cardboard dressers. We moved into an empty room in my grandmother's house. My mother impressed upon me that my aunt and grandmother were doing us a big favor in letting us live with them, that we mustn't seem to be in the way. I saw that she was happy. She had come back home. She wouldn't have to work so hard; she wouldn't have to come home from the office and cook the supper and do the washing and the ironing.

But she seemed to have forgotten what we'd had. She didn't miss our apartment, which was clearly much more like the movies than my grandmother's house. She didn't miss the Pyrex dishes in Technicolor shades, her wedding china with its playful patterning of unnaturally colored fruits. She didn't miss our trips to the movies, or listening to the radio (we'd had no television; my father wouldn't allow it). She didn't miss the songs we sang from musicals, our imitations of Irish priests and Italian barbers. She didn't miss going out to eat. She seemed to prefer my grandmother's dark living room, the lamps with golden handles and maroon bases and pictures of men and women with flowing hair and hats with feathers. The bust of Christ crowned with thorns, the tears flowing down his cheeks, which I enjoyed touching, feeling I'd stolen grace. And beside the head of Christ, a thin black stork riding on a turtle's back. It was said to be bronze, but no one believed that. Next to the stork there was a clump of peat, wedge-shaped and porous, that my grandmother had brought from Ireland. She wasn't frightened, as I was, of the bathroom upstairs with its blue-black linoleum and its pitcher full of overripe philodendron, whose stems I could imagine rotting in the yellowish water in which they stood.

She didn't seem to miss my father. There was no trace of him in my grandmother's house, and he was talked about only if I brought him up. I understood that if he was to be remembered, it would be up to me.

For a while, I thought he would come back. At night, I'd climb the dark stairs, certain that when I lit the light in the bedroom, he'd be there waiting.

Sometimes I wasn't sure whether or not I too had died. Often when I was near the edge of sleep, or ill, or cold, or when I became hypnotized by a repetitive physical event—the water going down the bathtub drain, a record spinning on the turntable—I would be caught up in a frightening spiral of language. I would hear a voice, my own, but speaking from so far away that it was barely recognizable. The voice was saying, "What does it mean to be alive?" And the words had no meaning. Particularly the two important ones: "mean" and "alive." I was looking down at myself like a spirit peering at a corpse. And yet neither the spirit nor the corpse had any connection with each other or with me, the thing once comprehensibly known as "I" but now something else, something I couldn't name.

I had to allow for the possibility that I might be only an idea—but in the mind of whom? Or what? Not God, certainly. I knew it wasn't God; at that moment God was only one more instance of failed language. I longed for someone to rescue me, but I didn't know what would be rescued or what rescue would entail. The past was blotted out and memory obliterated. I inhabited a sickening present without words. Without, therefore, a future. If I was dead, I must always have been, and I would always be. The region I inhabited wasn't one where I would be reunited with my father. What was my father? Only another word I didn't understand. A figure in a mist, stirring no impulse of recognition or recall.

After a few minutes, a few hours, a few days (time had become unmeasurable), I would return to a place where I could use words without terror, that is to say, use them without questioning their meaning as I spoke. I could understand, be understood. I still felt unrooted, but at least I knew what I was about. I had a task. I was looking for the place where my father and I once were and where we could be once again. I peered through fog for a glimpse of a man who could not be touched or joined. I knew I wouldn't see my father's face again, or feel his breath, or hear his voice, but if I was journeying back in memory to places we had been together, I was engaged in a quest that was not only admirable but, most important, meaningful.

But this search wasn't my only job. I had another one, only partially connected with my father: I was trying to obey the law. A law that was not monochrome and flat but complex, full of color and gradation and interlocking design. Law like a peacock's tail that spread and spread and could repay endless attention. At the center of the fan, in the densest, most vivid place, were the Ten Commandments; then lighter, less crucial, the Six Commandments of the Church, related to the rules of worship. There were the Seven Deadly Sins; and then, farther out, more remote, and opposite them, their reverse, the Virtues, Theological, Cardinal, Moral; and the Works of Mercy, Corporal and Spiritual. But the law I continually broke was one of the most basic. My specialized knowledge did me no good. Every few days found me in a state of mortal sin. Impurity was its name.

My experience of mortal sin wasn't like the ones I've read about in semicomic memoirs. I wasn't afraid of going to hell. Knowing the law so well, I knew that even if I were hit by a car, there would be one moment of consciousness that would allow me to say the word "sorry," even the syllable "sor," and that would be enough. Perhaps I would have years and years of Purgatory, but Purgatory was, in its way, desirable. Yes, the agonies would be real, but all the fine people, the interesting sinners, would be there, undergoing a process of chastening or burnishing that in its communal aspects seemed noble. So it wasn't eternal damnation that I feared; it wasn't even fear that moved me. It was shame, a sense of my defilement in relation to the infinite purity of God's love. A filthiness that seemed as if it should be public, made worse because in the public eye, in fact, I was perceived to be exceptionally good. The nuns in school who chose me as class monitor, the slow or unruly children who were made to sit next to me and look up to me as an example of probity and industry—what would they think if they knew the degradation that was the truth of my inner life? I went to confession every three or four days, always confessing the same sin in the same words: "I was impure with myself." The worst moments occurred before I spoke, when I could see the priest's shadow on the screen that separated us, and imagine his chastisement, which mostly never came. The priests wanted me out quickly; they were probably more embarrassed than I. But the words of self-accusation, once spoken, were the gate that led to my exaltation. Only by saying them could I earn absolution and the most perfect sentence I have ever yet heard spoken: "Go in peace."

Since I came to life, or a kind of incorporeal life, in these moments of exaltation, it was natural that I should try to do my job—remembering my father—by enclosing my understanding of his life and death in one of the shining vessels that the Church provided. Ecclesiastical language is full of names for vessels: chalice, ciborium, monstrance, pyx; there must be containers to enclose, keep safe, keep intact, keep protected from the world's contamination the sacred matter—the Body and Blood of Christ—in the form of the natural and the ordinary—bread and wine. This transformation of the ordinary into the sacred is called transubstantiation, and that was what I needed for my father's history.

I needed to think of it as only appearing to be ordinary—like the host and the wine—so I could bring myself to life, or back to life, so I could save myself or resurrect myself. His history was my lifeblood, as the Eucharist was the lifeblood of the Church. And so I contained my father's life and death in one of the forms the Church provided, as it provided the containers of precious metals for the Host, the wine. The mysteries of the faith were held in sacred stories. And I wrote my father's history as one of the Lives of the Saints.

By doing this, I could see my father's death not as something that could have happened to anybody, an expected consequence of living, and therefore without meaning. Loss, absence, the half-life of my life, weren't ordinary or purposeless. My father's life and death became part of something grand, enormous. And so mine did, too.

But what I am saying is an understanding come to in 1992 by a woman in her forties, whose father had been dead thirty-five years. When he died, I was a child of seven. I didn't know what I was doing. What I was doing was telling myself stories. They were richer, more colorful, and more enjoyable than the texture of my daily life, which was marked by wrongness and loss. Everything about me was wrong, and I had lost the part of my life that, like a false, colorful beam illuminating some minor theatrical tableau, had transformed it from pathetic to heroic.

It is very easy for me to call back the atmosphere of that earlier time, even the quality of the light in which I lived. When I think of it, I think of the light in the Holland Tunnel. It was a yellowish, acidic light, like the breath of a lethal chemical. Even with my father, I'd always been afraid in the Holland Tunnel. It wasn't being underground that disturbed me. When we took the Lincoln Tunnel I was quite relaxed; it seemed well-tended, clean, its light was violet-blue, the color of the neon letters of familiar signs: PHARMACY, FLORIST, BAR AND GRILL.

When we drove through the Holland Tunnel, saturated in that yellow light, I knew we were driving into and through death. And I knew I couldn't say anything about it, even to my father. I had only one consolation. I saw that in our danger we weren't quite alone. There was a policeman in the tunnel, walking its length on a narrow ledge six feet or so above the cars, tapping his nightstick on the palm of his free hand. He looked down at the travelers, the workers, the puzzled foreigners, the families on their way to pleasant destinations. I trusted him, and I worried for him, breathing the bad air and kept all day from sunlight. I was immensely proud of him for enduring those conditions for our sakes. I thought of him often, even if I hadn't gone into the tunnel for months.

After my father's death, I became the policeman. On patrol, vigilant and apart, in the yellow light of the dead. I was alert, looking out, in case my father would appear; maybe he was not really dead but was missing or banished, a political exile, and I, by the right word or signal, would be able to recall him.

• • •

The details of my life with my father require a language for which there is often no place in what has become my present life.

The next summer, of 1960, when I was ten, I asked Father D. if he thought it was possible that my father was the prophet Elijah. I'd been thinking about it a lot because I'd learned that Elijah had to come back to earth to die a human death, since he hadn't died, merely been carried up in a fiery chariot. I said that it made sense, because my father had been born Jewish. Father D. said that anything was possible with God.

My father's Jewishness presented no problem for the form of the saint's life; conversion was a staple of the genre. But my Jewishness was a problem for me.

Because of my father, I was a Jew. But he'd placed me in an Irish Catholic world, where I was visibly an outsider, a stranger. I looked like him, not like the people we lived among. I often cried because I wasn't pretty. He said I was beautiful, but I knew better than to believe him. He wasn't one of them; he wasn't right either. How could he know their standards or their rules? One night when I cried because I didn't have blue eyes, he said, "But you have eyes like mine, you have my eyes." I told him those were not the eyes I wanted. "They're the color of steak," I told him. "Light brown. Like when you cut into a steak." My mother, like many of the Irish, served our meat well-done.

I walked the streets of the neighborhood marked by my dark hair, my large nose, my full lips. During any lull, at any quiet point in a game, when the neighborhood children were bored or lustful for a cruelty, the words they always had a right to say came readily to them. "We know your father's a Jew. So you must be one too."

What did that mean to me? Except for my father, the only Jews I thought of had been exterminated by the millions only a few years before I was born. I thought of them, as I thought of the devastation of the war, as part of myself, something that would catch up with me one day, but in a way I couldn't see. The starving children, the separated children, the skeletal children, would take their place in my life sometime, but not yet, not yet. I knew I wasn't one of them, although my father blessed me every night in Hebrew. But my father seemed to think we were connected with them in some way. He said to me once, "If Hitler is still alive somewhere, in South America, and the Nazis come back into power, you and I will have to go to a concentration camp, but Mommy won't." I remember knowing he was right, and I knew that when the moment came, I would go with him happily, and that our departure would have the grandeur of all inevirable acts.

But how could I know what it was to be a Jew? I had Jewish blood, but no knowledge of those whose blood I shared. We had one picture of my father's mother—not a beauty, with an almost grotesquely wide nose in the middle of a wide, benign face, and eyes that could charitably be called quizzical, though it might have been a cast. There was no picture of his father.

My father kept the details of his Jewish childhood a darkness to me. But he did tell me the family had sat shiva for him when he converted. He didn't use the word "shiva"; he said that he'd been declared dead.

They had buried a living man, a son. They had sat in a circle and mourned his passing from this life. Yet not far from them, in Cleveland, in Chicago, in Los Angeles, and then in New York, someone with the name they mourned was living a life. I wasn't yet born, so in consigning him to nonaliveness, they were consigning me, prematurely, to nonbeing. Somewhere in his body, dry, encoded, was the story of my future life, which they insisted could not be told. Yet when my father and I spoke about this, neither of us was angry. We both understood that in his passing from Judaism to Catholicism, one man had, indeed, to die. We felt the justice of the Old World's acknowledgment of this, the rightness all around.

And so it seemed right that my father's family didn't inquire about me. And how could I think about them? I had no picture of what a Jewish family might be. In fact, most of the references to Jews I heard were a product of the anti-Semitism of some members of my mother's family. Jewish dialects. Jewish jokes. A song they made up, communally, one Christmas, called "Finkle Bells," sung to the tune of "Jingle Bells." I remember three lines: "We don't believe, you know/ But still we take their dough/ Oh, what fun to sit and watch the lovely sheckels grow." I remember feeling sick and frightened, knowing I ought to speak, but fearing their scorn.

Mostly, they referred to Jews as "Hebes," but they also had a family code. They referred to Jews as "the Persians," a habit that puzzled not only me but also my uncle's wife, whose father had been born in Iran. The explanation was that a character in the musical *Oklahoma!*, a peddler, clearly Jewish, tries to pass himself off as "Persian." They also spoke the sentence that was most horrible to me, one I would hear from time to time, the tone of which gave me the only clue I have ever needed to the timbre of real hate. "That's the *Jew* in you," they would say whenever I did something they didn't like. Even now the memory of their emphasis on the word "Jew" frightens me like the reports of the noise of Kristallnacht.

I would have had to be braver and more imaginative than I was to want to identify myself with, to think of belonging to, the Jews, my father's people. I couldn't really think of them as my father's people, since he didn't want to be a Jew, and if he didn't want it for himself, had worked so hard to separate himself, surely he wouldn't have wanted Jewishness for me.

Also, my only moments of certainty emanated from the Church. My identity was too unsure for me to risk those moments for a setting I would have had to invent. And like most people in a weak position, I needed to feel that I was allied with the party of the winners. Catholics did seem to be winning in those years: John XXIII was in the Vatican and JFK was in the White House. Why wouldn't I want to be part of that triumph?

.   .   .

My father died in winter. I remember how I always felt on the day of his anniversary. My mother and I went to early Mass. It was dark when I woke up, but for once I didn't mind waking up early because it was a day of honor. February 13. The deep end of winter. A somber time. Lent to look forward to. Sometimes Ash Wednesday followed soon after. And Valentine's Day, which the day of his death always overshadowed. Clearly mourning took precedence over ordinary romance.

I would often cry on the day of his anniversary, or stoically hold back tears. It was a secret only my father knew: the depth and constancy of my sorrow. But I was trying to be a saint, and the saints kept their sorrow to themselves. After the Mass, in the car, our Rambler, with my mother, I drank hot cocoa from a thermos and ate an egg sandwich: This was my rushed breakfast (we had to fast between midnight and Communion) between Mass and school. I was proud of it all: my early-morning hunger and alertness, my furtive breakfast, my position as a public mourner, and the unknowable depths of my real mourning.

On his anniversary day, I knew exactly who I was, as I know exactly who I am when I read his letters. I am the daughter that he loved. Not witness, not critic.

This is an impossible position for me, reading everything else he wrote.

Because, reading what he wrote, I have to understand that he did other things in his life than love me.

. . .

When I knew him, we were a father and a daughter, and the world was nothing to us. Then he died, leaving me a hunger for a living man. I looked for this man in what he left me. But what harm would there have been if all the words he left me had been made to disappear? Wiped out by a benevolent, obliterating wing. The angel of erasure. The angel of forgetfulness. What harm would there have been if I had been able to make everything up, to rely only on memory, or on objects, with their malleable testimony, their cut-out tongues?

If only he hadn't been a writer, leaving a trail. If only I had no other words from him than his letters from the hospital.

If he hadn't been a writer, would I have been one? It was because of him that I never doubted, as many women do, that I had a right to be a writer; it was because of him that it never occurred to me to be anything else. I am a writer because he was one, although reading what he published sometimes embarrasses me, sometimes tears my heart.

If only neither of us was a writer. If only we were both saints.

If only I could think of him as the writer of one sentence: "I wish I could see your face just one minute."

I am trying to make a resting place for him in words, a place that won't be torn apart by the words he insisted upon using: words that make me feel I have no right to love him. That I must bear witness against him. But then I want to run into his arms, headlong, like the child who was the only one to know him as a father. I want to say, my tearful face resting against the place on his chest that was to me the place of safety: "Let those for whom you wrote those other words, those published words, let them condemn you. Only the words in your letters are mine. Only they are my text. To be commented on, illumined, and interpreted."

But what I am to say of those crumbling magazines that fall apart when I touch them, those pages that turn to flakes that I could put upon my tongue and melt like the Communion Host. They, too, fit into the gear of the machine that produces the image of my father. I know also from the sound of those words who he is. The sound of the words, the worlds they created, are a way I came to know him after he was dead, even if I abandoned them, misplaced them, was unable to persevere and finish them, refused to hear them, radically misremembered them, forgot the first thing they said. They were a way I knew my father and a way I knew myself.

I am a writer because he was one. And not only that: I write the way I do because of the way he wrote. Some dream of purity, or style. Some way of naming and distinguishing. Some taste for exclusion and embellishment. And a desire for a point of silence, emptiness, and rest.

But he does not allow me, the reading daughter, the writing daughter, a place of rest. I hear him speak in tones of ecstasy and madness, of foolishness, vulgarity, love, hatred, humility, devotion, destruction, desperation, joy. The waters of his contradictions rise around my head and I am drowning in the seas that surround me. The sea of the impossible love of a child for her father, the sea of oblivion, the sea of a daughter's shame.

This is the story of my father I must simultaneously read and write. This is what it is to be his daughter.

THREE SPHERES

LAUREN SLATER

In this chapter from Welcome to My Country, *her first book, Boston psychologist Lauren Slater reminds us that she has been well trained to maintain her professional distance and not identify too closely with her patients. But when she is assigned the case of a woman close to her own age, diagnosed with borderline personality disorder, Slater's secret of her own emotionally fragmented early years resurfaces, blurring the boundary between doctor and patient. Remembering the sense of spiritual connection she felt when her mother would recite the Sh'ma, Judaism's proclamation of God's Oneness, Slater uses her own memories of pain and healing to reach out to her troubled patient.*

LINDA COGSWELL: INITIAL INTAKE NOTES

Ms. Cogswell is a thirty-seven-year-old SWF who has had over thirty hospitalizations, all for suicide attempts or self-mutilation. She scratches her arms lightly when upset. Was extensively sexually abused as a child. Is now requesting outpatient therapy for bulimia. Ms. Cogswell says she's vomiting multiple times during the day. Teeth are yellowed and rotting, probably due to stomach acids present during purges.

Client has been in outpatient therapy with over seventy (!) social workers, psy-

chologists, and psychiatrists. She has "fired" them all because she cannot tolerate their limit-setting. She has threatened to sue "at least eight, maybe more," because "they never gave me what I needed. They were a menace to the profession." Please note: Client has never carried through with any of her threats to sue. She does, however, demand complete access to her health-care providers. Has a history of calling her therapists in the middle of the night, screaming that she needs to see them right away, and self-mutilating when her requests are refused.

During her intake and evaluation appointment, client presented as teary and soft-spoken. She wore large hoop earrings and much makeup. She said she believes she has gout and asked to be prescribed medication for it. Became belligerent when refused. Possibly this client is delusional, although she was fully oriented to all three spheres—person, place, and time—knowing who and where she was, and demonstrating capacity to locate historical figures in their appropriate periods. Proverb interpretation: somewhat concrete. Serial sevens: intact. Recommendation: *psychological testing; 1x weekly behavioral therapy to address eating disorder; possible admission as an inpatient if she cannot get bulimia under control.*

"So who wants to take the case?" asks Dr. Siley, the director of both the inpatient and outpatient facilities where I work. He folds the initial intake evaluation from which he's been reading back into its green file.

None of the other clinicians offer. A woman as outrageously demanding and consistently suicidal as this one is would add a lot of pressure to anyone's job. Ellen looks away. Veronica busies herself with the pleats on her skirt. The staff room stays quiet.

"What about you?" Dr. Siley says, looking in my direction. He knows my numbers are down. My job description states I'm responsible for seeing at least twenty in his outpatient clinic, in addition to the chronic schizophrenics in his residential program.

"Well," I say, "she sounds like a lot of work."

"Who isn't?" Veronica says.

"Why don't you take her, then?" I say.

"I'm full," Veronica says.

"And you aren't," Dr. Siley adds, pushing the file across the table toward me.

The phone rings six, maybe seven times, and then I hear a tiny voice on the other end—"Hello," it whispers, and I announce myself, the new therapist, let's make an appointment, look forward to meeting you, here's where the clinic is, in case you forgot—

"Can't," the voice weeps. "Can't, can't." I hear the sound of choking, the rustle of plastic. "Ten times a day," the voice says. "Into thirty-three gallon bags. I've spent"—and sobbing breaks out over the line—"I've spent every last penny on frozen pizzas. There's blood coming up now."

"You need to be in a hospital, then," I say.

"Oh, please," the voice cries. "Put me in a hospital before I kill myself. I'm afraid I'm going to kill myself."

I tell her to sit tight, hang on, and then I replace the receiver. I know the routine by heart. I call 911, give the ambulance company her name and address, tell them there's no need to commit her because she said she'd go willingly. Next they'll take her to an emergency room, and after that she'll be placed on an inpatient unit somewhere in the state. She can't come into our own program's inpatient unit because she's neither schizophrenic nor male, the two criteria for admission. She'll stay wherever she is put anywhere from three days to four weeks, enough time, probably, for her to forget I ever called, to forget she ever wandered into the clinic where I work. At the hospital they'll likely set her up with an aftercare psychologist affiliated with their own institution, and he or she will have to deal with what sounds like her enormous neediness. And I, lucky I, will be off the case. Or so I think.

Two days later a call comes through to my office. "Ms. Linda Cogswell tells us you're her outpatient therapist. Could you come in for a team meeting next Monday afternoon?"

"Well, I don't even know her, actually. I was assigned the case, but before I could meet her she had to be hospitalized. Where is she?"

"Mount Vernon, I'm her attending psychologist here. Would you be willing to meet with us regarding her aftercare plans?"

Mount Vernon, Mount Vernon. And suddenly, even though it's been years, I see the place perfectly all over again, the brick buildings, the green ivy swarming the windows. The nurses who floated down the halls like flocks of seagulls, carrying needles in their beaks. My heart quickens; a screw tightens in my throat.

"Mount Vernon?" I say. Of all the hundreds of hospitals in Massachusetts, why did it have to be *this* one? And another part of me thinks

I should have been prepared, for eventually past meets present; ghosts slither through all sealed spaces.

"Look, I don't know the woman at all," I repeat, and I hear something desperate in my voice. I try to tamp it down, assume a professional pose. "I mean, the patient, although technically assigned to me, has not begun a formal course of psychotherapy under my care."

A pause on the line. "But *technically*," the voice retorts, "she is under your care, yes? You have some sort of record on her? Your clinic agreed to take the case?"

"Yes," I say. "Well . . . yes."

"Next Monday, then, one o'clock, North—"

"Two," I interrupt bitterly. "North Two."

"Good," she says. "We'll see you then."

What else can I do? Technically, I *have* been assigned the case. But this isn't any longer about the case; my hesitations now don't have to do with Linda Cogswell and her stained teeth, but with ivy on the brick, the shadow of a nurse, a needle, the way night looked as it fell beyond the bars and the stars were sliced into even segments. I remember looking out the windows on North Two; I remember Rosemary swallowing her hidden pills, how she danced the Demerol onto her tongue and later sank into a sleep so deep only the slamming cuffs of a cardiac machine could rouse her. Liquid crimson medicines were served in plastic cups. The rooms had no mirrors.

But the reflections came clear to me then, come still in quiet moments when past meets present so smoothly the seams disappear and time itself turns fluid. Sometimes I wish time stayed solid, in separable chunks as distinct as the sound of the ticking clock on my mantel. In truth, though, we break all boundaries, hurling forward through hope and backward on the trail made by memory.

But what else can we do except reach, except remember? What else can I do, having been assigned this case? I will go in, go down. Go back.

American culture abounds with marketplace confessions. I know this. And I know the criticisms levied against this trend, how such open testifying trivializes suffering and contributes to the narcissism polluting our country's character. I agree with some of what the critics of the confessional claim. I'm well aware of Wendy Kaminer's deep and, in part, justified scorn for the open admissions of Kitty Dukakis, who parades her alcoholism for all to observe, or for Oprah, who extracts admissions from the soul like a dentist pulls teeth, gleefully waving the bloodied root and probing the hole in the abscessed gum while all look, without shame, into the mouth of pain made ridiculously public. Would it not be more prudent to say little or nothing, to hold myself back like any good doctor, at most admitting some kind of empathic twinge? For what purpose will I show myself? Does it satisfy some narcissistic need in me—at last I can have some of the spotlight? Perhaps a bit, yes? But I think I set aspects of my own life down not so much to revel in their gothic qualities, but to tell you this: that with many of my patients I feel intimacy, I feel love. To say I believe time is fluid, and so are the boundaries between human beings, the border separating helper from the one who hurts always blurry. Wounds, I think, are never confined to a single skin but reach out to rasp us all. When you die, there's that much less breath to the world, and across continents someone supposedly separate gasps for air. When, Marie, Joseph, Peter, Moxi, Oscar, when I weep for you, don't forget I weep as well for me.

I have to drive out of the city to get there, down forty miles of roads I've avoided for the past eight years. Where there was once farmland, horses spitting sand as they galloped, wide willow trees I sat under when the nurses let me out on passes, there are now squat, square houses dotting the hills. But the building's bubbled dome rises unmistakably over a crest as I round the corner, floating there in the distance like a glittering spaceship, looking exactly the same as it did almost a decade ago. Walking back from passes, I would see that domed bubble, that silver blister bursting against a spring sky, and I would count, *One . . . two . . . three . . .* getting closer, my heart hammering half with fear, half with relief. Safe again. Trapped again. Safe again. Trapped aga—

And I have the same heart in the same socket of chest, and it hammers the way it used to, and I find myself thinking the same words, *Safe again, trapped again.* My palms sweat on the steering wheel. I remind myself: I am *not* that girl. I am *not* that girl. I've changed. I've grown. It's a long time ago. I am now a psychologist, who over the years has learned to give up her Indian-print sundresses and bulky smocks for tailored skirts, who carries a black Coach leather briefcase. How often, though, I've marveled at the discrepancy between this current image of me and the tangled past it sprang from. Sometimes I've imagined shouting out in staff meeting, in front of all my colleagues, who know me as a spunky confident doctor, how often I've wanted to say, *Once I, too—*

And what I would tell them goes something like this. On five separate occasions, spanning the ages from fourteen to twenty-four, I spent considerable portions of my life inside the very hospital whose graveled drive I am now turning into. Until what could be called my "recovery" at twenty-five or so, I was admitted to this institution on the average of every other year for up to several months. And even today, at thirty-one years old, with all of that supposedly behind me, with chunks of time in which to construct and explain the problems that led me to lockup, I find myself at a loss for words. Images come, and perhaps in the images I can illuminate some of my story. I am ten years old, sitting under the piano, as my mother, her face a mask of pain, pummels the keys. Beneath the bench I press the golden pedals, hold them all down at the same time so our house swells with raw and echoing sounds, with crashing crescendos and wails that shiver up inside my skin, lodging there a fear of a world I know is impossible to negotiate, teetering on a cruel and warbling axis. And later, while I am lying in my bed, she murmurs a Hebrew prayer and I imagine her hands exploring me, and a darkness sprouts inside my stomach. A pain grows like a plant, and when I was twelve, thirteen, I decided to find the plant, grasping for its roots with a razor blade. Stocked solid with the romance of the teenage years, with the words of the wounded Hamlet and the drowned Virginia Woolf, whom I adored, I pranced on the lawn of my school, showing off the fresh gashes— Cordelia, a dwarf, a clown, Miss Havisham. I loved it all. I wept for the things inserted into me, the things plucked out of me. And I knew, with the conviction of adolescence, that pain confers a crown. I was removed to the hospital, then a foster home, then the hospital, again and again. Later on, in my late teens and early twenties, I starved myself, took pills to calm myself down, wanted a way out. And finally I found one, or one, perhaps, found me.

I am not that girl any longer. I tell that to myself as I ride up the hospital's elevator. I found some sort of way into recovery. But I know, have always known, that I could go back. Mysterious neurons collide and break. The brain bruises. Memories you thought were buried rise up.

I rise up in the elevator and the doors part with a whisper. Stepping off, I find myself face-to-face with yet another door, this one bolted and on it a sign that says ENTER WITH CAUTION. SPLIT RISK.

And now I am standing on the other side of that door—the wrong, I mean the right, side of the door, and I ring the buzzer. I look through the thick glass window and see a nurse hustle down the hall, clipboard in hand. I recognize her. Oh, my God, I recognize her! I hunch, dart back. Impossible, I tell myself. It's been over eight years. Staff turnover in these places is unbelievably high. But it could be her, couldn't it? And what happens if she recognizes me? My mouth dries and something shrivels in my throat.

"Dr. Slater?" she asks, opening the door. I nod, peer into her eyes. They're the blue of sadness, thickly fringed. Her lips are painted the palest sheen of pink. "Welcome," she says, and she steps back to let me pass. I was wrong—I've never seen this woman in my life. I don't know those eyes, their liquid color, nor the voice, in whose tone I hear, to my surprise, a ring of deference. Doctor—she actually calls me doctor. She bends a bit at the waist, in greeting, acknowledging the hierarchies that exist in these places—nurses below psychologists, psychologists below psychiatrists, patients at the bottom of the ladder.

With a sudden surge of confidence, I step through. The reversal is remarkable, and for a second it makes me giddy. I'm aware of the incredible elasticity of life, how the buckled can become straight, the broken mended. Watch what is on the ground; watch what you step on, for it could contain hidden powers and, in a rage, fly up all emerald and scarlet to sting your face.

And here I am, for the briefest moment, all emerald, all scarlet. "Get me a glass of water," I imagine barking to her. "Take your pills or I'll put you in the quiet room."

Then the particular kind of dense quiet that sits over the ward comes to me. Emerald goes. Scarlet dies down. I am me again, here again. I grip my briefcase and look down the shadowy hall, and it's the same shadowy hall, loaded with the exact same scents, as it was so many years ago. The paint is that precise golden green. The odor is still undefinable, sweet and wretched. Another woman comes up, shakes my hand. "I'm Nancy," she says, "charge nurse on the unit."

"Good to meet you," I say. And then I think I see her squint at me. I've the urge to toss my hair in front of my face, to mention a child-hood in California or Europe, how I've only been in this state for a year.

"We're meeting in the conference room," Nancy says. Clutching my briefcase, I follow her down the corridor. We pass open doors, and I hold my breath as we come to the one numbered 6, because that was my bedroom for many of the months I stayed here. I slow down, try to peer in. Just as they used to, heavy curtains hang over a large, thickly meshed window. *There are the stars,* I want to say, for in my mind it's night again, and someone is rocking in a corner. Now, in the present time, a blond woman lies in what used to be my bed. On that mattress swim my cells, the ones we slough off, the pieces of ourselves we leave behind, forever setting our signatures into the skin of the world. As she sleeps, my name etches itself on her smooth flesh, and my old pain pours into her head.

And just as we are passing her by, the woman leaps out of bed and gallops to the door. "Oh, Nancy," she keens. "I'm not safe, not safe. Get my doctor. I want my doctor."

"Dr. Ness will be up to see you at four," Nancy says.

Suddenly the woman snarls, "Four. Dr. Ness is always late. Always keeps me waiting. I want a new doctor, someone who'll really care. A new doctor, a new—"

Her voice rises and she sucks on her fist. "Stop it, Kayla," Nancy says. "Take your fist out of your mouth. You're twenty-nine years old. And if you want a new doctor, you'll have to bring it up in community meeting."

Kayla stamps her foot, tosses her head like a regal pony. "Screw you," she mutters now. "Screw this whole fucking place," and then she stomps back into her bed.

When we're a few feet beyond the scene, Nancy turns to me, smiles conspiratorially. I feel my mouth stretched into a similar smirk, and it relieves yet bothers me, this expression toward a patient. "Borderline," Nancy says matter-of-factly, giving a crisp nod of her head.

I sigh and nod back. "They're exhausting patients, the ones with borderline personalities." I pause. "But I prefer them to antisocials," I add, and as I say these words I feel safe again, hidden behind my professional mask. I am back on balance, tossing jargon with the confidence of a Brahman in a village of untouchables. There is betrayal here, in what I do, but in betrayal I am finally camouflaged.

Of all the psychiatric illnesses, borderline personality disorder may be the one professionals most dislike to encounter. It's less serious than, say, schizophrenia, for the borderline isn't usually psychotic, but such patients are known for their flamboyant, attention-getting, over-demanding ways of relating to others. Linda, according to her intake description, is surely a borderline. Patients like her are described with such adjectives as "manipulative" and "needy," and their behaviors are usually terribly destructive and include anorexia, substance abuse, self-mutilation, suicide attempts. Borderlines are thought to be pretty hopeless, supposedly never maturing from their "lifelong" condition. I myself was diagnosed with, among other things, borderline personality disorder. In fact, when I left the hospital for what I somehow knew would be the very last time, at twenty-four years old, I asked for a copy of my chart, which is every patient's right. The initial intake evaluation looked quite similar to Linda's, and the write-ups were full of all kinds of hopeless projections. "This young woman displays a long history marked by instability in her interpersonal and intrapsychic functioning," my record read. "She clearly has had a long career as a mental patient and we will likely encounter her as an admission again in the future."

I recall these words now, as we enter the conference room, where several other nurses and doctors sit around a table with a one-way mirror on the far wall. I scan their faces quickly, praying I look as unfamiliar to them as they do to me. I don't recognize any of the people in here, and I'm hoping against hope they don't recognize me. Still, even if we've never met, I feel I know them somehow, known them in a deep and private part of me. "Ta da," I have the angry urge to shout out, bowing to the bearded psychiatrist at the oval's head, standing arms akimbo, twirling so my skirt swells out. "Here I am," I'd like to yell. "Yes, sireee, encountered again. Guess who you're looking at; guess who this is. The Borderline! And sure enough, folks, I *did* mature out, at least a little . . ."

Of course I won't say such a thing, wouldn't dare, for I would lose my credibility. But the funny thing is, I'm supposedly in a profession that values honesty and self-revelation. Freud himself claimed you couldn't do good analytic work until you'd "come clean" with yourself in the presence of another, until you'd spoken in the bright daylight your repressed secrets and memories. Freud told us not to be so ashamed, to set loose and let waltz our mothers and fathers, our wetness and skins. Training programs for psychologists like me, and the clinics we later work in, have as a credo the admission and discussion of countertransference, which by necessity claims elements of private conflict.

But at the same time, another, more subtle yet powerful message gets transmitted to practitioners in the field. This message says, *Admit your pain, but only to a point. Admit it but keep it clean. Go into therapy, but don't call yourself one of us if you're anything more than nicely neurotic.* The field transmits this message by perpetuating so strongly an us-versus-them mindset, by consistently placing a rift between practitioners and patients, a rift it intends to keep deep. This rift is reflected in the language only practitioners are privy to, in words like *glossolalia* and *echolalia* instead of just saying *the music of madness,* and then again in phrases like *homicidal ideation* and *oriented to all three spheres* instead of *he's so mad he wants to kill her* or *he's thinking clearly today, knows who, what, and where he is.* Along these same lines, practitioners are allowed to admit their *countertransference* but not the *pain pain pain the patient brings me back to, memories of when I was five, your arms, my arms, and the wound is one.* No. To speak in such a way would make the rift disappear, and practitioners might sink into something overwhelming. We—I—hang on to the jargon that at once describes suffering and hoists us above it. Suddenly, however, here I am, back in an old home, lowered.

I recognize the conference room as the place where, when I was fourteen, I met with my mother and the social worker for the last time. My father had gone away to Egypt. My mother, abandoned by him, somehow always abandoned and lonely, even as she surrounded herself with people, was wearing a scarf around her neck and a gold Star of David wedged between the hills of her breasts. Years later, seeing the mountains of Jerusalem, cupping the scathing sand of the desert, hearing the primitive wails of the Hasids who mourned the Temple's destruction, I would think of my mother's burning body, a pain I could never comprehend.

This is the conference room where she, unstable, rageful, maybe delusional at times, shot through with a perpetual anxiety that made her hands shake, told me she was giving me up, giving me over to become a foster child. "I can't handle you anymore," she'd said to me, spit at me. "I no longer want you in my house."

I bow my head in deference to something I cannot name, and enter the room. Things are screaming inside me and my eyes feel hot. Nancy introduces me all around, and I take a seat, pull out a notebook, try to act as calm and composed as possible. "The patient Ms. Cogswell," the bearded psychiatrist begins, "is not able to make good use of the hospital. She's an extreme borderline, wreaking havoc on the unit. We suspect her of some factitious posturing as well." He pauses, looks at me, clears his throat. I smile back at him but my mouth feels uncoordinated, tightness at its corners. I won't cry, won't cry, even though in the one-way mirror, in the criss-crossing of the creamy branches beyond the ward's windows, I see my mother again, her face coming to me clearly, her eyes haunted with loneliness and rage. I feel her fingers at my breasts and flinch.

"We think," a social worker named Miss Norton continues, "that we'll be discharging her in a matter of days, as soon as we get her stabilized on some meds. We take it you'll be picking up her case on an outpatient basis. Any ideas of how you'll work with her?"

I nod, pretend to make some notes on the pad. As my voice rises through my throat, I'm surprised at how smooth it sounds, a sleek bolt of silk. "Lots of limits," I say. "We know borderlines do well with lots of limits. This is the only context in which a workable transference can begin."

The bearded doctor nods. In the tree, my mother tongues her teeth and wind lifts her lovely skirt, embroidered with fragile flowers. And then she is not my mother anymore, but a little girl whose legs are white, a single ruby scar on scrubbed knee. And while part of me sits in the conference room, part of me flies out to meet this girl, to touch the sore spot, fondling it with my fingers.

For I have learned how to soothe the hot spots, how to salve the soreness on my skin. I can do it so no one notices, can do it while I teach a class if I need to, or lead a seminar on psychodiagnosis. I can do it while I talk to you in the evenest of tones. "Shhhh," I whisper to the hurting part, hidden here. You can call her borderline—call me borderline—or multiple, or heaped with posttraumatic stress—but strip away the language and you find something simple. You find me, part healthy as a horse and part still suffering, as are we all. What sets me apart from Kayla or Linda or my other patients like Oscar, Marie, Moxi—what sets me apart from these "sick" ones—is simply a learned ability to manage the blades of deep pain with a little bit of dexterity. Mental health doesn't mean making the pains go away. I don't believe they ever go away. I do believe that nearly every person sitting at this oval table now has the same warped impulses, the same scarlet id, as the wobbliest of borderlines, the most florid of psychotics. Only the muscles to hold things in check—to channel and funnel—are stronger. I have not healed so much as learned to sit still and wait while pain does its dancing work, trying not to panic or twist in ways that make the blades tear deeper, finally infecting the wounds.

Still, I wonder. Why—how—have I managed to learn these things while others have not? Why have I managed somehow to leave behind at least for now what looks like wreckage, and shape something solid from my life? My prognosis, after all, was very poor. In idle moments, I still slide my fingers under the sleeves of my shirt and trace the raised white nubs of scars that track my arms from years and years of cutting. How did I learn to stop cutting and collapsing, and can I somehow transmit this ability to others? I don't know. It's a core question for me in my work. I believe my strength has something to do with memory, with that concept of fluid time. For while I recall with clarity the terror of abuse, I also recall the green and lovely dream of childhood, the moist membrane of a leaf against my nose, the toads that peed a golden pool in the palm of my hand. Pleasures, pleasures, the recollections of which have injected me with a firm and unshakable faith. I believe Dostoevski when he wrote, "If one has only good memory left in one's heart, even that may be the means of saving us." I have gone by memory.

And other things too. E. J. Anthony wrote in his landmark study, *The Invulnerable Child,* that some children manage to avoid or grow out of traumatic pasts when there is the presence in their lives of at least one stable adult—an aunt, a neighbor, a teacher. I had the extreme good fortune to be placed in a foster home where I stayed for four years, until I turned eighteen, where I was lovingly cared about and believed in. Even when my behavior was so bad I cut myself in their kitchen with the steak knife, or when, out of rage, I swallowed all the Excedrin in their medicine cabinet and had to go back to the unit, my foster parents continued to believe in my abilities to grow, and showed this belief by accepting me after each hospital discharge as their foster child still. That steady acceptance must have had an impact, teaching me slowly over the years how to see something salvageable in myself. Bless those people, for they are a part of my faith's firmness. Bless the stories my foster mother read to me, the stories of mine she later listened to, her thin blond hair hanging down in a single sheet. The house, old and shingled, with niches and culverts I loved to crawl in, where the rain pinged on a leaky roof and out in the puddled yard a beautiful German shepherd, who licked my face and offered me his paw, barked and played in the water. Bless the night there, the hallway light they left on for me, burning a soft yellow wedge that I turned into a wing, a woman, an entire army of angels who, I learned to imagine, knew just how to sing me to sleep.

• • •

At a break in the conference, a nurse offers me a cup of coffee. "Sure," I say, "but first the ladies' room." And then I'm off, striding down the hallway I know so well, its twists and turns etched in subterranean memory. I go left, then right, swing open the old wooden ladies' room door, and sit in a stall.

When I come back, the nurse is ready with a steaming plastic cup. She looks at me, puzzled, as she hands me my hot coffee. "You've been here before?" she asks.

My face must show some surprise, for she adds, "I mean, the bathrooms. You know where they are."

"Oh," I say quickly. "Right. I've visited some of my patients on this ward before, yes."

"You don't have to use the patient bathroom," she says, smiling oddly, looking at me with what I think may be suspicion. "We don't recommend it," she adds. "Please use the staff bathroom, through the nurse's station."

"OK," I say. I bend my face into the coffee's steam, hoping she'll think the redness is from the rising heat. Of course. How stupid of me. What's she thinking? Can she guess? But in a way I *am* one of the patients, and she could be too. I'm not ready to say it yet, though. Weak one. Wise one. This time, memory has led me astray.

The conference resumes. I pay little attention. I'm thinking about the faux pas with the bathroom, and then I'm watching the wind in the tree outside the window. I am thinking about how we all share a similar, if not single pain, and the rifts between stalls and selves is its own form of delusion. And then I hear, through a thin ceiling, wails twining down, a sharp scream, the clattering of footsteps. I sit up straight.

"Delivery room," the social worker says, pointing up. "We're one floor under the maternity ward."

I smile. That's right. North Two is just one floor of what is an old large public hospital. The psychiatric unit we're on has always been wedged between labor rooms upstairs and a nursery downstairs. When I was a patient, I could often hear, during group therapy or as

I drifted into a drugged sleep, the cries of pushing women as their muscles contracted and in great pain their pink skins ripped, a head coming to crown.

"Why don't you meet with Linda now," the psychiatrist says, checking his watch and gathering his papers. Everyone stands, signaling the end of the conference.

"You can take one of the interview rooms," Nancy, the charge nurse, adds. "They're nice places for doing therapy, comfortable."

I nod. I've almost forgotten about Linda and how she is the reason for my return here today. Now I walk with the rest out of the conference room and Nancy points down the long hall. "There," she says, her finger aiming toward a door on the left. "The third room. We'll bring Linda to you." And then, to my surprise, Nancy fishes deep into her pocket and pulls out a large steel ring of keys, placing them in my hand. They're the same keys, I know, from all those years ago, keys I was not allowed to touch but that I watched avidly whenever I could, the cold green gleam and mysterious squared prongs opening doors to worlds I didn't know how to get to. Keys, keys, they are what every mental patient must dream of, the heart-shaped holes keys fit into, the smart click as they twist the secret tumblers and unlatch boxes, velvet-lined and studded with sea jewels. Keys are symbols of freedom and power and finally separateness. For in a mental hospital, only one side has the keys; the others go to meals with plastic forks in their fists.

Slowly, I make my way down the hall to the interview room, stand outside the locked door holding the key ring. It feels cool, and I press it to my cheek. A hand there once, feeling me for a fever, stroking away my fear. Bless those who have helped.

A woman who looks far older than her thirty-seven years is now making her way down the hall. Stooped, she is, with tired red ringlets of hair. As she gets closer I see the dark ditches under her eyes, where years of fatigue and fear have gathered. I would like to put my finger there, sweep away the microscopic detritus of suffering.

"Linda," I say, and as she comes close to me, I extend my hand. "Hello," I say, and I can hear a gentleness in my voice, a warm wind in me, for I am greeting not only her, but myself.

We stand in front of the locked interview room and I fumble for the correct key. I start to insert it in the lock, but then, halfway done, I stop. "You," I say to my new patient, Linda. "You take the key. You turn the lock."

She arches one eyebrow, stares up at me. Her face seems to say, *Who are you, anyway?* I want to cry. The hours here have been too long and hard. "You," I say again, and then I feel my eyes actually begin to tear. She steps forward, peers closely, her expression confused. Surely she's never seen one of her doctors cry. "It's OK," I say. "I know what I'm doing." And for a reason I cannot quite articulate at the moment, I make no effort to hide the wetness. I look straight at her. At the same time, for the first time today, my voice feels genuinely confident. "Take the keys, Linda," I say, "and open the door."

She reaches out a bony hand, takes the keys from me, and swings open the door. The interview room is shining with sun, one wall all windows. I've been in this room too, probably hundreds of times over the years, meeting with the psychiatrists who tried to treat me. I shiver with the memory. Ultimately it was not their treatments or their theories that helped me get better, but the kindness lodged in a difficult world. And from the floor above comes the cry of a protesting baby, a woman ripped raw in birth. She is us. We are her. As my mother used to say, rocking over the Shabbat candles, chanting Jewish prayers late, late into the night, "Hear, O Israel. The Lord our God, the Lord is one, and so are we as a people."

She would pause then, her hands held cupped over the candlesticks. "We are one," she would repeat to me after a few moments, her strained face peering at me through shadows. "As a people we are always one."

Sometimes I miss her.

My patient and I sit down, look at each other. I see myself in her. I trust she sees herself in me.

This is where we begin.

PERSONAL DICHOTOMIES

ANTONIO FELIZ

In his memoir, Out of the Bishop's Closet, *Antonio Feliz describes his rapid rise through the priestly ranks of leadership in the Mormon Church. This excerpt recounts a day in the early 1970s in Los Angeles when, as Branch President of a Spanish-speaking congregation, he is called to preside at the excommunication of a young man accused of being homosexual. Though Feliz draws strength from the profound love of his wife, of his family, and of God, he fears that one day, he, too, will be faced with the very same charge.*

"HOLINESS TO the Lord." The familiar words greeted me as I prepared to enter the temple in Los Angeles, California. It was the autumn of 1973 and the temple was solemn and majestic against the blue California sky. This holy edifice truly was for me a place where heaven and earth met, a window through which I personally could step into heaven. A young couple would kneel before me today at one of the altars in this place that was so sacred to me, and with the power that had been given to me through a Prophet of God, I would seal them to each other for the rest of their eternal lives.

I had the power spoken of in the scriptures. According to the belief of my Church, I had been given that power to bind on earth in such a way that those I sealed to each other could be together not only in this place and time but in all places and times: Marriage for Eternity, unique to our belief in some respects, but so common a desire throughout the human family. I was the agent. As always, the weight of it was heavy on me. But today, somehow that weight was even heavier than usual.

What presumption is it in us that lets us think we can act for God? Who was I to exercise such a power as this? To speak for God? To act in God's place? I knew I had the power. It wasn't that. I had stood often enough in that place and had my mind opened to know exactly what it was a particular man and woman needed to hear, needed to know and remember as they began their life together. I knew how close heaven and earth really were. But today, I felt strangely unworthy to use that power. I sought assurance. I needed to feel again, as I'd felt before, that I really was worthy to do what I was going into the House of The Lord to do.

I changed to my white clothing. It was some time before the ceremony was to begin. The carpeted hallways softened my steps as the noise of the world began to recede. These walls protected me. The distractions, the rush were left behind. I checked the necessary paper work. Everything was in order. I needed to be alone. I climbed the massive circular staircase to the upper chambers of the temple. It encircled the huge chandelier around which this spiral took my steps. At the top, I stopped and looked down at the brightness of the thousands of lights in the chandelier. Beauty filled the hollow shaft which I'd just climbed. I went on.

Where could I go to be alone? The serenity of this place was around me as I passed the Terrestrial Room, a wonderful place of light and growing things where a large group of people was gathered. I entered the Celestial Room of the temple. Here was our effort to create a place that was as much like heaven as we mortals could imagine. A place where God could come. The large room was empty. I walked slowly around it. The adjoining hallways and sealing rooms were likewise unoccupied. I chose a chair and sat down, trying to focus my troubled thoughts. In this beautiful and sacred place of peace my mind was not at rest. The more I tried to clear my mind, the worse it was. I couldn't.

Today especially, I needed to feel that God heard me. In my mind, I addressed him as one would speak to another person: "God, Father, let me know you hear me." I still felt very much alone. I took a deep breath and clasped my hands in my lap, and I tried to let go of my connection to earth.

I had tried all my life to do what God wanted me to do. I'd conse-crated my time and talents and all I'd been blessed with to the build-ing up of the Kingdom of God on earth. I'd been a missionary in South America, preaching for two years at my own expense, because I wanted others, everyone, in fact, to know what I knew and feel what I felt. I'd been a Bishopric Counselor and High Councilor. I'd blessed many people through those callings. Somehow I felt the need to remind God of that now. Why should I be feeling what I was feeling today when I had tried so hard to do what I felt God wanted me to do. I'd tried to be the man God wanted me to be.

The room was quiet. The peace of the place began to filter into me. I felt a gentle reminder that, as the Branch President of the Spanish-speaking branch in Los Angeles, I had the right to seek guidance con-cerning the needs of those saints. But it was I who needed guidance today.

Three days before, I had been required to hold a Church court for a young man in my congregation who had been accused of living in a homosexual relationship with his roommate. "No unclean thing can enter into the Kingdom of God," we'd been taught. It was my respon-sibility to determine if Sergio would be allowed to remain a part of the Church, or be cast out. The memory of the "trial," as ominous and weighty as any physical burden, would not leave me . . .

"Sergio," I'd asked gently in Spanish, "do you understand the seri-ousness of the charge against you?"

He shrugged his bent shoulders, but didn't look up at me.

I tried again. "We want to hear your side, Sergio. Tell us what hap-pened."

He raised his gaze hesitantly to meet mine and I saw how his dark eyes were full of the tears he was struggling to hold back. I waited for him to speak.

"Yes," he said at last. "It's true what you say of me. I do love another man. And I know you say it's wrong for me to love him in this way." He paused. "I want to do what's right, President." He said it as if he were afraid we wouldn't believe him. I believed him.

"But it doesn't feel wrong to me! Aren't you supposed to be able to feel it when things are wrong? Can't we tell?"

"Then tell us how it did make you feel," I prompted.

"Sometimes I'm afraid," he said. "Sometimes I feel so alone. Some-times I think no one will ever love me. Then he puts his arms around me. He holds my body close to his. He makes me part of him." We waited until he was ready to go on. "Then, then it's all right. He loves me. He holds me. We love each other. How can it be wrong to love someone?" He was pleading with us to see it his way. I wanted to. I didn't want to condemn him. I felt the same need to be loved, to be held, to be made whole. He had faced us with courage. A courage I lacked. He'd shared his deepest feelings. Mine remained unspoken.

I had to ask the next question. The part of me that loved my Church and my God wanted to ask it sincerely, but the words did not come easily. "You've taken the first step, Sergio, in coming to us and confessing your sins. Are you now willing to forsake them and make your life right with the Lord?"

He looked at me steadily without answering, and though there was no condemnation in his look, I felt he somehow knew more about me than almost anyone else. That he knew exactly what I'd been feeling as he described his lover's touch and the warmth of his friend's body close to his. Finally, his eyes still locked to mine, he shook his head slowly. "No," he said. "No, I guess I'm not willing to do that."

We invited him to leave the room for a few minutes and I asked my two counselors for their impressions. "He's not sorry," one said. "He's not the least bit repentant. For his own good, we have no option but excommunication." I knew they were right, but I didn't want them to be right. Why should people be condemned because they were honest? I was the one who had sat there in silence. I felt torn.

Sergio rejoined us. I pronounced the verdict. At the word "excommunication," a kind of stubborn defiance replaced the hesitancy with which he'd spoken before. With his hands outstretched, as if he would grab me and shake the truth into me if he had to, he said, almost spitting out the words in his anger and frustration, "President Feliz, aren't you ever going to learn that there are other ways of looking at things? I tell you, the Church is wrong on this one! Why can't you see that?"

I had no answer.

What would it be like to be touched intimately by a man? In the quiet of the temple, my turbulent thoughts would not be still. To be hugged sensually, even kissed tenderly by another man, and to return those intimate sensual approaches?

I forced the thought away. No! It was wrong to feel that way. It was wrong to want that. It was a sin even to think about it. I knew that. I tried to pray again.

"Heavenly Father," I began silently. "I'm married to a beautiful and sweet woman who loves me and loves you . . ." Laura's face came into my mind. So serious, so sincere, so concerned whenever she sensed a strain between us. How I'd prayed and fasted and prayed again before I'd proposed to her, begging the Lord to bless me with the ability to love a woman so that I could marry and have children and learn to fill the measure of my creation. And what wonder it had been when I'd finally felt it. And I did love her. Didn't I? I'd been sealed to her. We'd knelt across from each other at the altar, our hands clasped, and had been promised that if we were true and faithful, we would be companions in Eternity. But then why, why couldn't I feel for her what I'd felt for . . other faces blurred with hers . . .

Terry. When I was near him in the early morning seminary class we'd shared as teenagers, the strength of my incomprehensible desire to touch him and be close to him had simply bewildered me. I remembered the morning after class when Terry looked at me with that same desire, how he'd touched me and how that had called out yearnings for him deep within me. I remembered how much I'd wanted his look, his touch.

Then Ken. He'd pulled me innocently into his sleeping bag one freezing night so we could keep each other warm as we tried to fall asleep in the back of his pickup on our way to Salt Lake City for Conference. He'd been so warm next to me. I'd felt so guilty enjoying the closeness of his warm body.

Other faces came to my memory, faces of other guys to whom I'd felt attracted in my teen years. Were they all infatuations, a stage, a part of youth?

I tried to repeat the prayer I'd prayed then. The prayer I sometimes felt I'd been praying ever since: "Please, God, take these feelings away from me. I want to love my wife. Keep me strong. Don't let me do anything I shouldn't. Please."

But I felt totally alone. Abandoned even. Pulled and stretched in too many directions. Laura. Terry. Ken. Sergio and others. Unanswered questions hammered at me, relentless and demanding. "Please, God. Please." I realized I was crying. I reached for my handkerchief to dry my face.

Just like Sergio, I wanted to do what was right. I wanted desperately to do what was right. I knew that the men who led the Church were inspired. And if they said that what I was feeling was wrong, then it must be. I wanted to follow them.

I had decided when I was 16 that I needed to know for myself if David O. McKay, then President of the Church, really was a Prophet of God. Somehow I knew that if I went to Salt Lake City for a General Conference of the Church, I'd find some way to meet this man and, when I did, I'd know if he really did speak for God.

The memory of that experience has never left me; it probably never will . . .

Temple Square glowed in the spring sunshine. Ken's parents were saving our seats in the Tabernacle balcony as he and I went out to get a newspaper before the Conference session started. In the warmth of the sunlit April morning, it was hard to believe that only two days before Ken and I had been caught in a snowstorm in central Utah and had spent the night huddled together in one sleeping bag in the back of his truck trying to keep warm. We hadn't done anything but hold each other to keep warm, but the guilt surrounded me like a dark cloud, blocking out the glory of the morning.

As Ken and I walked around the Tabernacle, a large, gray limousine drove past us and parked near the west doors of the Tabernacle. For some reason, I froze at the sight of it, but Ken ran right up to the rear door of the car. We both knew it could only be one person—the President of the Church.

Part of me wanted to do just what Ken was doing—to get as close to the car as I could and shake the Prophet's hand and look into his eyes. But the memory of what I'd felt in the back of that pickup was still too vivid. I couldn't move. I stood by the west gate to Temple Square. Ken waved for me to come over and join him, but I stayed where I was.

Through the open doors of the Tabernacle I could hear the choir rehearsing their songs for the next session of Conference. I could hear the excited voices of the crowd that had gathered around the limousine. On the other side of the wall around Temple Square, a police siren blared. But louder than any of the other sounds was the voice in my head: "If you go over there, and if he really is a true Prophet of God, he'll look right through you and he'll know you're queer!" What would his reaction be if he could tell? I didn't want to be queer but I knew that somehow, I was.

The limousine door opened. There he was. From my earliest memory I'd been taught he was a Prophet. Was he? Did he communicate with God in the same way that Moses and Jeremiah and Isaiah had? I wanted to know, but at the same time I was afraid to find out. The spring breeze fluttered his white hair. His smile looked just like the pictures of him I'd seen in Sunday School. He seemed taller than I'd imagined he'd be. Ken stepped forward from the crowd to talk to him. They both looked toward me. I wished I could simply disappear, fade invisibly into the wall. Ken pointed at me. President McKay looked in my direction and gave me the warmest look I'd ever received from anyone in my whole life. But I couldn't feel any joy in it. I was terrified. He beckoned me to come over to them, and I found myself walking slowly over to where they stood.

The man I had come so far to meet grabbed my right hand in both of his and looked right into my eyes. "It's beautiful weather for Conference, isn't it?" he asked me. I just nodded, still unable to speak.

Ken introduced me and told President McKay how we'd driven from California to be at General Conference for the first time in our lives. As the Prophet listened, his clear eyes were framed by what seemed to be a steady and irrepressible glow. I rubbed my eyes to soften the sudden brightness. It must have been the sunlight, I thought to myself.

Back inside the Tabernacle again, Ken told his parents about what had happened. Was he really a Prophet? It had felt good to shake his hand. Could he see through me? Did he know what I really was? What if he weren't a true Prophet?

The Tabernacle was crowded. We'd come early in order to get seats, and we were standing and talking in the balcony so we wouldn't be tired of sitting by the time the meeting was finally ready to start. A few of the General Authorities of the Church were already in their seats. To Mormons, these men were holy men, what Popes and Archbishops are to Roman Catholics. Others were shaking hands with one another and greeting the members seated near the front of the hall. The organ played a soft prelude.

Suddenly, I knew he was in the room. Nothing appeared to be any different than it had been just a minute before, but a powerful feeling of warmth and peace surrounded me and filled me. I turned to Ken. "The Prophet is in the Tabernacle," I told him.

He looked at me strangely, then glanced toward the stand where the First Presidency and Apostles sat. "No, he isn't. Look, his chair is empty."

I couldn't see him, but still I knew he was in the room. Ken looked all around, and finally leaned over the balcony railing so he could see the doors beneath us. He turned to me in surprise. "You're right! He just came in through the doorway right below us. How did you know?"

My eyes filled with tears. I watched my Prophet make his way slowly toward the front of the Tabernacle. His whole body seemed to radiate light. He was filled with light. I could not stop looking at him. It seemed almost too much to believe. I realized that the glow from his face I'd seen as we stood shaking hands outside the Tabernacle must not have been the sunlight, after all. I couldn't hold back the tears of joy and Ken's mother hugged me as I stood there. Then, I felt a voice declare, "Behold, your Prophet." For the first time in my life, God had shown me a sign. I'd asked, and God had given me an answer.

I wouldn't speak of this experience until years later in an address at a BYU student devotional assembly.

As I sat in the temple reminiscing about that experience, I knew God knew how I felt about His Prophets. He knew that after that experience in the Tabernacle in Salt Lake, I'd tried to read every word President McKay spoke or wrote. He knew I'd committed myself, seriously and solemnly, to obey the teachings of this Prophet and of every other Prophet that would follow him in the leadership of the Church.

God had shown me personally that I should follow this man and I had done my best to do that. For me, he was no different than Moses or Elijah or any of the other men of the Bible who walked and talked with God. I became known as a defender of the Prophets. People had told me, after hearing me speak, that the strength of my conviction was enough to make them want to believe.

God knew that. He knew my heart. He knew how much I wanted to do what was right. But I just didn't know any more what that was. The Prophets said it was wrong for me to want to be close to another man in the way that I had always inwardly and irrepressibly desired to be. Their sermons left no room for any discussion whatsoever on the subject. I'd heard them many times. Homosexuality was a sin, a despicable, degrading, awful sin, one of the "unholy and impure practices" spoken of in the temple.

Because I supported the Prophets in all they'd taught since the time that I'd received my personal witness of David O. McKay's call, I had sustained the Prophets in all they taught, including their teachings on homosexuality. I could not control what I felt, but I could control what I did. I'd vowed to myself that, no matter how strong my desires were for another man, I would never act on those impulses.

And God knew I'd been true to that commitment. But if I was doing what I was supposed to be doing, if I was doing what the Prophets taught, then why did I feel so . . . so unhappy? So frustrated. Why did I feel that what we'd done to Sergio was very wrong? My tears seemed to increase.

No comfort came. God who, in this place above all others, should have been close to me, had left me totally alone. He wouldn't hear me. Why? So many times before this, I'd received answer to my prayers in the temple. What was wrong this time? Was it Sergio?

I remembered pondering homosexuality as a missionary in Peru many years earlier . . .

Elder Hatch, my missionary companion, knocked half-heartedly on the next door in the small apartment complex where we'd been "tracting" most of the afternoon without much success. Tracting was our method of going door to door in an effort to meet prospective converts for our Church. We were both very tired.

"Let's go after this one," he suggested. I agreed. A door opened across the way and a young woman called out to us to come over and talk to her.

"What are you doing here?" she asked as we approached her front step.

"We're missionaries," I answered. "And we have a very important message for you." As she listened, I recited the carefully memorized story of Joseph Smith, the founder of Mormonism, who as a young boy had wanted to know the truth about God and religion. "He read in the Bible," I told her. "'If any of you lack wisdom, let him ask of God,' and then he decided that that's just what he would do."

"¿Y . . . qué pasó?" She asked. "What happened?"

I told the familiar story. "Joseph went to a grove of trees near his home. He knelt down and began to pray to God, to ask which of all the many churches he should join. As he prayed, he felt overcome by an overpowering darkness; it pushed him to the ground. When he came to himself, he saw two heavenly beings standing above him in the air. One spoke to Joseph and said, pointing to the other, 'This is my beloved son. Hear him.'"

She wanted us to come in and tell her more. We asked if her husband was home. "No, but he'll be here later. Come back and eat with us tonight."

She was pleased when we called her "Hermana Griego." She said she'd like to be our sister. We assured her we'd be back in the evening.

When we returned, Mr. Griego wasn't home, but another man was there. He had an interest in our message. This man was Sister Griego's brother, and he introduced himself to us as Pepe Gomez. He indicated to us that his wife was in the back of the house.

"Why doesn't she come out and join us too?" Elder Hatch asked.

"No," her husband answered, shrugging his shoulders uncomfortably. "You see, she's not able to speak and her noises would be too distracting."

We persisted and finally he went to the curtain separating the rooms and called, "Ven, Chica." A thin, pleasant woman ducked nervously into the room and sat down by her husband. Though she was unable to speak, she sat and listened as Elder Hatch and I taught her, her husband, and Sister Griego about the gospel.

Through the next two weeks, we continued to teach the two couples. They were eager to learn and listened earnestly as we taught of the apostasy that had followed Christ's crucifixion, and then of the promised restoration that had brought the full sealing blessings of the Holy Priesthood power back to the earth.

One afternoon, as I was speaking on the power the Priesthood has, I felt a gentle pull on the sleeve of my shirt. Chica had come silently up beside me. She put her hands out together in front of her and moved them in a small tentative circle, her eyes all the time watching mine to see if I understood. I shook my head to show my confusion, and she repeated the gesture, this time making a small, definite downward motion with her two hands as if she were laying hands on someone's head.

"She wants to be healed by your Priesthood, Elder Feliz," her husband told me. "She's already told me she knows she'll be healed."

I looked at Elder Hatch. He gave me a small scared half-smile that let me know he'd support me in whatever I decided. But I couldn't tell her no. I'd blessed others, of course, and I'd seen healings, but this was the first time I'd been asked to anoint and lay hands on someone who was totally unable to speak. Would she be healed?

Elder Hatch poured the holy oil on the crown of Chica's head. I then put my hands over his and, after sealing his holy anointing on her head as one from a servant of God, I waited for the Spirit to give me the words. Through me, God then commended her faith, and blessed her that if she had sufficient faith, her affliction would be lifted from her. She was also told that her healing was not for her alone, but in order that this might be a witness of the power of the Priesthood which we had brought with us to bless them.

After the blessing, she thanked me in the only way she could, grasping my hands in hers, and smiling her happiness as she made the small awkward noises that were her only form of communication.

We left to attend to our other appointments. By late afternoon, we'd finished all we'd planned for the day and were returning to our apartment for dinner. As we walked down the main commercial street of the downtown area, I heard someone calling me from the bottom of the hill.

"Elder Feliz! Elder Feliz!" I turned to see who it was. Chica and Pepe were running up the hill and she was shouting my name! They had been scouring the town all afternoon to find me and tell me that right after we'd left their home, her speech had come. We laughed and shouted, cavorting like fools in the street, sharing her joy in her wonderful, new-found power.

It did not take Chica long to learn that she had much to say to everyone. Sometimes it seemed she was trying to make up for a lifetime of not being able to speak. She talked and talked. And of course we let her.

A few days after the healing, however, as we sat around the Griego's dinner table, Chica broke into the conversation and said, "I need to clear something up."

"Oh, no, don't listen to her Elders," her sister-in-law warned. She turned to Chica. "You hush now. That's enough of that."

Elder Hatch glanced at me. We both stood at the same time. It seemed best for us to leave, and let the family resolve this problem, whatever it was. But she was not going to let us leave without saying what was on her mind. "El es maricón!" she shouted as we made our way toward the door.

Maricón? Homosexual? Who? She couldn't possibly be talking about me, could she?

Hermana Griego tried to smooth things over. "Don't believe it, Elder," she reassured us. "No es verdad."

Gradually we learned what the truth was. Hermano Gomez, our gentle Pepe, was not really Chica's husband at all. They were living together and Chica had just discovered that he was having an affair with a man he'd met at the casino where he worked.

I set up an appointment to meet with Brother Gomez privately. Elder Hatch and I left the house in turmoil. I knew we couldn't baptize him if he was a homosexual. As missionaries, we had been specifically instructed by our area leaders not to teach the gospel to anyone whom we knew to be homosexual. Homosexuals were not included in our call.

At our interview, Pepe begged me to hear his side of the story. He wanted to be baptized. "Sí, Elder Feliz," he admitted, "I am a homosexual. But I am also living with a woman and she has my child. Shouldn't I be baptized so I can raise my boy in the Church?" This man was my brother. I didn't want to be the one to have to make this kind of decision about his future. "I've known it for a long time," he went on. "I started to live with Chica so no one would know. Your Church has so much truth. I thought maybe you'd understand."

I didn't understand. It would be a long time before I'd understand.

from *LOVESONG: BECOMING A JEW*

JULIUS LESTER

"I have become who I am," writes Julius Lester in Lovesong, *his autobiographical journal of spiritual quest and self-revelation, intermingled with years of restlessness and uncertainty. As a black man never quite at home with the Christianity of his Methodist minister father or in the activism of the civil rights movement, Lester, now a noted author and professor at the University of Massachusetts at Amherst, explores his family's secrets and finds his spiritual home at last in the tradition of his great-grandfather, a Jew who married a former slave.*

I AM EIGHT or nine years old. I am playing Bach on the upright piano in the living room. Though it is a simplified arrangement of a Bach fugue, the lines of music move away from and back to each other, never merging or separating, like windblown ribbons on the tail of a kite. I forget that I am playing, and I slip through the lines to the other side of the music where I understand all that was, is, and will be. When the music ends, however, I return to this side and cannot remember what I understood.

I love Bach's music more than that of any composer, but my favorite composition is in a thick book Momma bought me. There is no composer's name and I do not know how to pronounce the title because it is in a foreign language. Every day after I finish practicing, I play it over and over. It is not lines or chords; neither does it move, but it does not stand still. It simply is. It is happy and sad at the same time. I play and beauty becomes pain and then beauty again and in a half-step is inverted into pain once more until beauty and pain wrap around each other like the braids of a girl's hair, and beauty and pain become a piercing that holds me pinioned and I feel old like "In the beginning," old as if I was never born and will never die. The music winds itself around me and wants to take me somewhere, but I am afraid and do not go. When I stop playing there is a painful yearning in my stomach, a wishing for something I have never had and thus do not know what it is, or a wishing for something which I had once and have forgotten what it was. The name of the composition is *"Kol Nidre."** It is a Hebrew melody.

I am eight or nine and sit on the floor in the living room before the big Philco console. The news announcer says that Sammy Davis, Jr., has converted to Judaism. "I'm going to do that someday," I say to myself.

·   ·   ·

[SPRING 1960]

. . . The sit-in movement has been victorious and the downtown merchants have agreed to desegregate all public eating places. There is a victory rally at a church near the Fisk campus, and I go.

I sit in a back pew, alone, listening to the joyous singing of freedom songs but not loosing my voice to join the others. I want to belong to the joy in the church, want to be a part of the camaraderie shared by those who have been arrested and jailed. I cannot. I must hold myself apart to know what God wants of me, or what I think He wants.

Is that arrogance, madness, or faith?

MAY 1961

On the front page of the *Nashville Tennessean* is a picture of Jim Zwerg, a white exchange student at Fisk last semester. He is slumped against

*See note on page xxii.

a wall, head bowed, blood streaming down his face like ribbons. Quickly I read the story to learn that students from Nashville were beaten in Montgomery, Alabama, protesting segregated seating on buses traveling between states.

I stare at the picture of Jim's bloody face. How can I justify myself? How can I say nothing matters but God, especially when I don't live as if God matters; I don't go to church; I don't study the Bible, pray daily or even once a year.

I want to go to Alabama and join the Freedom Riders, if only to rid myself of this guilt. I am weary of the aloneness, weary of uncertainty, the not knowing what it is God has called me to do. I want to be real to myself.

I leave Nashville and go to New York. It not a decision but a desperate fleeing to save myself from being impelled by guilt and isolation to do what I know in my soul I am not supposed to do. God has not called me to risk my life on a Freedom Ride.

SUMMER 1961

Working as a counselor at Camp Woodland in the Catskills near Phoenicia, New York, I have my first sustained contact with Jews. Within a week I am calling people *meshugge*,* referring to the camp food as *trayf*,† and muttering *oy gevalt*‡ under my breath. I fall in love with a fellow counselor, a large-eyed Jewish girl with long, dark hair, who tells me stories of her grandparents fleeing Russia, and invites me into her childhood through borscht, bagels, lox, sour cream and herring, and gefilte fish, and at the end of the camp season we unburden each other of virginity and think we are adults, at last.

Many nights I sit in the camp dining room with campers and I play my guitar and sing spirituals and songs from the civil rights movement, which is little more than a year old. They sing Jewish and Israeli songs. I don't know or understand the words, but the songs are familiar, and instinctively I know the odd intervals melodies will take. The simplest Israeli song—*"Shalom Chaverim,"* or "Every Man

---

*Yiddish, meaning "crazy, not right in the head."
†Referring to anything not kosher according to Jewish law.
‡A Yiddish exclamation, literally meaning "Oh, screams!" but used idiomatically to mean "Oh, my goodness!"

'Neath His Vine and Fig Tree"—brings tears to my eyes as spirituals never have.

Perhaps that is when I first see myself standing in a synagogue singing *"Kol Nidre."* The centuries of black suffering merge with the millennia of Jewish suffering as my voice weaves the two into a seamless oneness that is the suffering and at the same time the only appropriate and adequate response to it.

The following spring I sit in New York's Riverside Park every evening and watch bearded men walk by in black hats, black suits and white shirts without ties. They are Chasidim.* No one has told me, but I know that is who they are. I stare at the older ones and imagine I see the blue stenciled numbers on their forearms, only noticing later that I am rubbing my forearm as I stare. It is my suffering and theirs I want to avenge and give voice to—for them and for me.

I want to be a cantor. I sit in my tiny furnished room on West End Avenue in the fall of 1961 and yearn to sing Jewish music—as a Jew. When I pass synagogues, I hear melodies of pain and beauty rising toward heaven.

The following year I move to West Twenty-first Street, and between Sixth and Seventh avenues discover a tiny Sephardic cemetery amidst the factories. During the thirteen years I live in that neighborhood I go often to stand at the wrought-iron fence of the cemetery, looking at the tombstones, wishing I could be who they had been—Jews.

But, who has ever heard of a black Jew? Few seem to take Sammy Davis, Jr., seriously as a Jew.

AUTUMN 1975: AMHERST, MASSACHUSETTS

At seven each morning the alarm clock buzzes like killer bees, stunning me into consciousness. If that is what it is.

I'm not sure anymore.

For six months now I haven't given myself to the pictures rising from the grave of night, the nocturnal messages from unknown parts of my soul which the ancients knew as visitations from the gods.

Beside the bed I keep a notepad and pen to write down what God is

---

*Chasid (singular); Chasidism (plural). A member of any one of a number of ultra-Orthodox Jewish religious groups originating in Eastern Europe in the eighteenth century.

saying. I wish He would speak as directly to me as He did to Moses: "Hey, stupid! Go to Egypt and set My people free!" I would be content with Joseph's or Daniel's ability to interpret dreams. What am I to think of an elephant lumbering through one of my dreams with all the grace of a Himalayan avalanche? I doubt that Elijah dreamed about Kojak, Angie Dickinson, or Cher, and if he did, he was too ashamed to put those dreams on a scroll.

I'm ashamed, too, but I am not God's prophet. I am thirty-six years old, the divorced father of a nine-year-old daughter and seven-year-old son, and I am afraid my life is an unclean thing.

Is that what God wants me to know? If so, then why doesn't He tell me how to cleanse this life He has given me? I listen to Gregorian chants each morning; I pray; I read Merton and learn only that I am not the person I could be and I do not know what to do.

.   .   .

SPRING 1978

Every Sunday morning the university radio station plays Jewish music for two hours. I don't know why but I listen every week. I don't understand the words of the songs or what they are about, not even after the announcer explains. What is Purim? What is Pesach?

Yet there is something in Jewish music that makes me feel loved. I listen and that loneliness lying within me like a black hole threatening to suck the entire universe into its nothingness is destroyed and stars shine with a white heat and I become infinity.

Every week when I listen to the show "Zamir," I pretend that I am a Jew and the Hebrew words are my language and the melodies are my songs. But I am not a Jew and there is a pain in my soul so deep that it must have begun before I was born.

.   .   .

DECEMBER 18, 1981

I go to the office to turn in my final grades and get my mail.

"When does Chanukah begin?" the secretary, Jean, asks me.

"Sunday night," I respond without thinking.

"Well, you have a happy Chanukah."

"And a merry Christmas to you."

I am walking out of the building before I wonder why she wished me happy Chanukah. And why did I receive it? And how did I know when the first night of Chanukah is? I chuckle to myself as I think: She must think I'm Jewish.

Since I began teaching the "Blacks and Jews" course, I cancel classes if they come on Rosh HaShana, Yom Kippur or the first day of Passover. It's funny she thinks I would have to be Jewish to do that.

Night. I am lying in bed. My eyes are closed, but I am not asleep. Suddenly, I see myself dancing in the middle of a brick-laid street. A brown yarmulke is on my head and I am dancing around and around in a circle, my arms extended like the wings of an eagle. I am a Chasid and I am grinning and laughing, dancing, around and around and around.

The joy of the vision permeates my body and I smile. I want to laugh aloud, to get out of bed and dance. I want to shout: I am a Jew! I am a Jew! I am a Jew dancing the joy of God!

The next morning I awake and joy swirls around and within me like dandelion flowers dazzling the sun.

I am a Jew!

I want to run downstairs and tell my wife. But I am afraid. What will she say? What will she think? I am afraid of my joy. I will wait and say nothing. This joy may dissipate in tonight's sleep.

Two weeks pass. Joy is no longer an emotion I feel; it is who I am. I am so happy each day that I have to force myself not to burst out giggling for no reason.

When the children are in bed, I tell my wife. "I think I am going to convert to Judaism."

"I'm not surprised," she says.

Shocked, I ask, "What do you mean?"

"I don't know. I'm just not surprised."

Having said the words aloud, having heard her matter-of-fact response, I am afraid again. What am I talking about? Why do I want to be a Jew?

The answer is simple: I am tired of feeling guilty for not being in synagogue on Rosh HaShana and Yom Kippur. I am tired of feeling lost on the first night of Passover. I am tired of being jealous when I see Jews going to or coming from synagogue. I want my eyes to shine like sky as do those of my Jewish students when they return to class after having gone home for the first night of Passover.

I am a Jew. I wonder if I have been always and if playing *"Kol Nidre"* on the piano when I was seven was a tiny act of affirmation which I am able only now to embody. I will not be converting to Judaism. I am becoming, at long last, who I always have been. I am a Jew. I'm only sorry it has taken me forty-two years to accept that.

Two more weeks go by. I must be sure that this is what I want to do, what I need to do. But why do I doubt? The joy is there each morning when I awake. I not only see it smiling at me like a lover when I open my eyes, but it takes me in its arms and strokes my body.

I call Rabbi Lander.

.   .   .

AUTUMN 1982: ROSH HASHANA

The High Holy Days. I don't like the term. It makes me think of Anglican cathedrals with stone floors as cold as sin. The more traditional Jewish term for the ten days from Rosh HaShana to Yom Kippur is Days of Awe. I don't know what it means because I have not experienced any awe. Quite the contrary. I am depressed and discouraged. The more I read and the harder I study, the more difficult becoming Jewish is.

I sat in synagogue on this first day of Rosh HaShana and knew myself once again to be an Outsider. The service seemed to be without order or reason. The cantor sang and then he mumbled more rapidly in Hebrew than I can think in English, then exploded into song again, after which he mumbled some more. This is worship? I thought. This is chaotic primitivism!

I think every Jew in Amherst was there today. Even the balcony was filled. Then there was me. If people didn't know anyone else was there, they knew I was, with my black self. How can I become a part of the Jewish people when I don't look like other Jews? Three-quarters of the way through the service I left and came home.

I sit on the couch now, silent, angry, disappointed in myself, glad no one knows I am studying for conversion. I can't do it! I can't be a

Jew. What made me think I could? I wish I knew another convert, a black one, but I don't know Sammy Davis's phone number.

But if I do not become a Jew, who am I?

I cannot go back to who I was, and I do not know who I am becoming.

JANUARY 3, 1983

It is *erev** *Shabbat*. I wait for Rabbi Lander to begin services. Tonight I publicly proclaim that I have chosen to become part of the Jewish people.

Last week I appeared before my *bet din*.[†] Rather than be examined by Rabbi Lander and two other rabbis, I chose two members of the Jewish Community of Amherst whom I respect. This was unorthodox but allowable under Reform Judaism's rules of conversion.

One was Haim Gunner, who I respect for his knowledge of Judaism and Jewish history, and his love of the Jewish people and Israel. The other was Monroe Rabin. I don't know Monroe, but I love to listen to him lead services and chant from the Torah scroll. He does not have a melodic voice but there is such love for Torah in it. I listen to him and see myself standing in the market of some village in Israel two thousand years ago on a Monday or Thursday morning when the Torah was read.

Haim and Monroe are very serious about being Jews and I want to be taken seriously as a Jew. If my answers to their questions were not satisfactory, they would say I was not yet ready.

I expected to be examined on my knowledge. Their questions went deeper, however, to my motivations, my purpose in becoming a Jew, and what did I expect my life as a Jew to be, i.e., did I really understand what it was I was proposing to assume?

I wondered if Haim was remembering stories of converts in centuries past who betrayed the Jewish people in times of trouble. I wondered if either of them was battling doubts as to whether or not he could trust this black man, who, even though he had spoken out against black anti-Semitism, was nonetheless black.

---

*Evening; in this case, Friday night.
[†]The Jewish religious or civil court of law. As part of the process of conversion to Judaism, a person must be examined by a *bet din*.

I know there will be always be a gap between me and Jews rooted in *Yiddishkeit,** but *Yiddishkeit* does not represent all of Jewry. Neither is it the only way to express Jewishness.

When they finished questioning me I was asked to leave the room. I was shocked. Was there some doubt in their minds? Were they going to call me back into Rabbi Lander's office and tell me that I needed to study for another year? I paced the hallway for what seemed like hours before the office door opened and I was asked to return.

I looked at Haim because, whatever the verdict, I knew I would see it on his face. He was smiling. He offered me his hand, grinned and said, "Well, I hope you know what you're doing."

"I do," I replied seriously.

Rabbi Lander is disappointed that I decided not to be circumcised. He talked about it at length, affirming that in Reform Judaism circumcision was not necessary, but his own feelings were different. I knew that if he insisted on circumcision I would not continue with the conversion process. I have done as much as I can, and it has been more difficult and painful than I would have imagined. I will keep my foreskin.

Near the end of the service, Rabbi Lander calls me to the *bimah,*† and while four people hold over me a large *tallit,*‡ he recites the *kohanic*§ blessing:

May the Lord bless you and keep you.

May the Lord make his face shine upon you and be gracious unto you.

May the Lord lift up his face upon you and give you peace.

A chill goes through me and I think of my great-grandfather and great-grandmother and it is not in my imagination but in my body that I feel them joined once more. I feel also a deep peace, for at long last my great-grandfather is at peace.

So am I.

•   •   •

*The culture of Eastern European Jewry.
†The elevated platform in the synagogue at which the reading of the Torah takes place.
‡Prayer shawl.
§Priestly. The text of this benediction is taken from Numbers 6:24–26.

MAY 10, 1986

It is Shabbat, the first of Iyyar 5746, the 16th day of the Omer and the second day of Rosh Chodesh, the New Moon. My wife, David and I sit at the rear of the sanctuary of B'nai Israel.

A brown velvet *kippah** is on my head, my multi-colored *tallit* wrapped around me and flowing down to my hips. I am nervous, as I have been since the Saturday morning early in the spring when Rabbi Friedman said casually to me after services, "When are we going to get that bass voice of yours up on the *bimah*?"

I had not been aware that he could hear my voice. I know it is deep and loud, which is why I tried to sing quietly. But there had been Saturday mornings when joy banished timidity, especially during the repetition of *amidah†* when we sang *"Yismach Moshe"* and *"Sim Shalom."*

In a few moments the repetition of the *amidah* will be finished and Rabbi Friedman will say, "Julius Lester will lead us in the *Hallel*." I will rise, walk to the *bimah* and begin to sing Psalms 113 to 118, those special psalms of praise that are only sung on holidays and when Rosh Chodesh coincides with the Sabbath. At long last I will stand in a synagogue and sing Jewish liturgical music as a Jew. What if I fail? What if I forget the melodies?

I remember what we were told at the seminar last summer: "Sing sweetly. Sing sweetly." I will not be going to the *bimah* to perform but to lead the congregation in prayers to HaShem. That will be my only function.

"Julius Lester will lead us in *Hallel*. Please rise."

I squeeze my wife's hand, and taking her smile with me, walk slowly down the side aisle, ascend the steps to the *bimah* and stand behind the broad table on which the Torah scrolls are laid. I close my eyes and begin to chant the opening blessing: "*Baruch ata Adonai Elohenu melech ha olam asher kidshanu b'mitzotav v'tzivanu likro et ha hallel.*" ("Blessed are You, O Lord our God, Ruler of the Universe, who has sanctified us by Your precepts and enjoined upon us the reading of the *Hallel*.") The melody is my own and it is simultaneously joyous and mournful, because that is the essence of Chosenness.

As I hear the voices from the congregation rising to meet mine, there is no separateness between me and them. We have become

---

*Skullcap.
†Literally "standing"; refers to a central prayer in Jewish liturgy, recited standing.

music; we are embodied prayer. When I begin the up-tempo and very rhythmic melody for Psalm 115, I hear a soprano voice from the congregation doing an ascending obbligato at the end of each line and I smile, recognizing the voice of Janice Friedman, the rabbi's wife, and I think about the words we are singing: "*Ha shamayim shamayim l'adonai, v'haaretz natan livne adam*" ("The heavens are the heavens of the Lord, but the earth He has given to children of men"), and it is as if our voices are fusing the two into one so that heaven has now become earth and earth is heaven and the two are one as God is One.

I know now. At long last I know what my voice was meant to sing. All those years I sang folk songs, spirituals, blues, work songs, and always knew that something was absent, that as much as I loved spirituals, I was not wholly present when I sang them. Now I know why. It is this music my voice was meant to sing. It is this music of praise and love that releases my soul into my voice, and I have known that ever since I was seven years old and sat at the piano playing "*Kol Nidre*" over and over. I knew. It took only forty years for me to believe in what I knew.

All too soon it is over and I descend the *bimah* and begin walking up the aisle to return to my seat in the back of the synagogue. The oldest member of the synagogue offers me his hand and says "*Yasher koach.*" ("More strength to you.") There are tears in his eyes and I want to cry in my joy.

I know now who I am. I am a Jew and I am a lovesong to the God of Abraham, Isaac and Jacob, a praisesong to the God of Sarah, Rebecca, Rachel and Leah.

That is all the 613 *mitzvot** are, the *midrashim,*† the Talmud, the Torah, *kashrut,*‡ *tzdekah,*§ and everything else in Judaism. They are lovesongs to HaShem.‖

And so am I.

                                                                13 Elul 5746

---

*The 613 religious and moral precepts and obligations derived from the Torah.
†A method of study, investigation, and interpretation of Jewish biblical texts.
‡Literally, "fitness"; generally applies to things and persons meeting religious requirements, most often pertaining to Jewish dietary laws.
§Righteousness; generally used to refer to charity and acts of justice aiding the poor.
‖Literally, The Name. Used by observant Jews to refer to God.

II

ANCESTORS

and

TRADITION

from *BONE BLACK*

BELL HOOKS

Distinguished professor of English at City College in New York, bell hooks has written widely on feminist theory, art, culture, gender, and race. Here, in Bone Black, *she offers her own girlhood memories of Sundays spent in church, and of the powerful, wise elders with whom she found spiritual communion and companionship.*

EVERY SUNDAY Miss Emma sits on the third pew. No one ever sits in her place. Even if she is late it is there waiting—a space large enough for two people. She is short and plump like our Big Mama. She walks with a cane, wears funny hats. I do not want to grow up to be a woman who wears funny hats. I think we look silly in them, silly like clowns, silly like paper party hats, silly like Halloween. I do not want to come to church looking silly, knowing that children like myself are staring, wanting to laugh, holding their mouths with their hands, rolling their eyes at one another—anything to keep the laughing sounds from coming out. We noticed her not because of her funny hats, not even because of the way that she has a special place reserved for her but because she is old, because she has long been a member of this church. She is one of the church founders. She was there at the very beginning. From our seats in the children's choir we can tell that if she has been here from the beginning of the church 'til now—she is very old, older than we can imagine.

We notice her because during the sermon, just as the preacher is reaching the point at which what he says reaches into our hearts so that we feel it pressed against the passionate beating—she screams out in a loud and piercing voice, one long sentence. We understand the first part of it, the part where she says Thankgodthankyoujesus. We do not understand the second part. We hear her saying Thank god for hot paprika. This is forever puzzling, mysterious to us, until we grow older, until she is long dead and we come to know that what she has left piercing and ringing in our ears is a Thank god, thank you jesus for heartfelt religion. Although we know that in the home of the church god can be thanked for anything we are glad the mystery is solved—in our hearts we are glad.

Who can remember when this short plump woman wearing face powder that made it appear her skin was covered in ash first spoke to me. She is one who will tell you that she has been watching you from birth, that she has seen you grow. You stand rigid in her embrace, afraid of what it is she has seen, your young body pressed forever into her flesh as if she has died and you have been forgotten. She first spoke to me when I began reading the scripture for the morning offering, listening to my voice rising softly above the click of coins, the organ music, like smoke, drifting and settling. She waited for me after church, to hold me in those arms, to tell me that my reading (like the preacher's sermon) also found its way into the heart, also pressed itself against the beating. Because of this she wanted to give me something, some gesture of her confidence that the god voice that came out of me and touched her beating heart would go on speaking and name itself in this world. She tells me to tell my mama to send me to her house. I become a regular visitor. Never allowed to stay long— only as long as it takes to speak a little, to be handed the gift, the gesture of her regard, I return home soon.

Her house is clean and airy. It reminds me of bright new pennies. When I enter, the coolness touches me like feathers, like those bright bird feathers in the funny hats. I follow her through this house to the kitchen—where the gift awaits. It comes in a box, a little basket, a sack. I never open it until I am all the way home. It is a wonderful and mysterious love I must wait for the others to share.

.   .   .

To her child mind old men were the only men of feeling. They did not come at one smelling of alcohol and sweet cologne. They approached one like butterflies, moving light and beautiful, staying still for only a moment. She found it easy to be friends with them. They talked to her as if they understood one another, as if they were the same—nothing standing between them, not age, not sex. They were the brown-skinned men with serious faces who were the deacons of the church, the right-hand men of god. They were the men who wept when they felt his love, who wept when the preacher spoke of the good and faithful servant. They pulled wrinkled handkerchiefs out of their pockets and poured tears into them, as if they were pouring milk into a cup. She wanted to drink those tears that like milk would nourish her and help her grow.

One of those men walked with his body bent, crippled. The grown-ups frowned at her when she asked them why he didn't walk straight. Did he know how to walk straight? Had he ever learned? They never answered. Every Sunday he read the scripture for the main offering. His voice wrinkled like paper. Sometimes it sounded as if there were already tears in it waiting to spill over, waiting to wet the thirsty throats of parched souls. She could not understand the reading. Only one part was clear. It was as though his voice suddenly found a message that eased sorrow, a message brighter than any tear. It was the part that read, It is required and understood that a man be found faithful. He was one of the faithful.

She loved the sight of him. After church she would go and stand near him, knowing that he would give her his hand, covered old bones in wrinkled brown skin that reminded her of a well-worn leather glove. She would hold his hand tight, never wanting to give it back. In a wee pretend voice full of tears and longing he would ask for his hand back saying all the while that he would love for her to keep it but could not build his house without it. She loved to hear him talk about the house that he had been building for years, a dream house, way out in the country, with trees, wildflowers, and animals. She wanted to know if there were snakes. He assured her that if she came to visit the snakes would come out of their hiding places just for her, singing and playing their enchanted flutes.

It was a hot, hot day when she went to his house. She came all by herself slowly walking down the dirt road, slowly moving up the hill. He stood at the top waiting. The house was so funny she couldn't stop laughing, it was half-finished. She could not imagine how anyone could live in a half-finished house. He gave her his hand, strong and brown. She could see it sawing, nailing, putting together boards that contained the memories of all his unfulfilled dreams. She could see the loneliness in that hand. When she whispered to him that she always held that hand—the right one—because all the loneliness was stored there like dry fruit in a cool place, he understood immediately.

Sitting on the steps watching him work she could ask all the questions about being crippled that she had ever wanted to know. Was he alone because he was crippled. Was he not married because he was crippled. Was he without children because he was crippled. Her questions smoothed the wrinkles in his brow, took the tears from his voice, wet his dreams with the promise of a woman waiting faithfully with outstretched hands.

from *WHEN THE WORLD WAS WHOLE*

CHARLES FENYVESI

Washington, D.C.-based journalist Charles Fenyvesi was a small boy in eastern Hungary when the Nazis swept across Europe, and he came of age cherishing the stories of his ancestors who cultivated their land, enjoyed cordial relationships with Gentile neighbors, and harkened to the wise teaching of great rabbis. In these selections from his memoir, When the World Was Whole, *Fenyvesi revisits his ancestral village to search for the remnants of what survived, and to reconnect homeland with memory and dreams.*

EVER SINCE I remember remembering, I have heard stories about my ancestors, whose lives pulsed with the teachings of two rabbis who performed what people called miracles: the Baal Shem Tov, who wandered through the villages of the Carpathian mountains, and Isaac Taub, who shepherded a congregation of about a hundred souls in the little town of Kálló, on the northeastern edge of Hungary's Great Plain. These two eighteenth-century rabbis of blessed memory broke rank with their colleagues when they declared that misery and oppression are not inevitable, and that we can and must improve the world; that while suspicion and revenge unleash new cycles of hatred, it is always possible to start anew; that the vast Gentile world which surrounds the little Jewish world is not immutably and forever hostile, and that Gentiles are our partners in improving

93

the world. If there is one phrase that can sum up the advice of the two rabbis, it is this: Do not fear! Or, better yet: Keep the gates of your heart open!

I was seven when the Nazi noose tightened around us in Hungary, and every day I saw my mother wait anxiously for the mailman to bring postcards from her husband and her mother, her brothers and sisters and cousins, who were being taken to concentration camps or forced-labor battalions. For me, a bedtime story about a forefather overcoming his fear of bandits and other evil spirits and living an unusually long life was more reassuring than all the wishful rumors about the Americans and the British being on their way to liberate us.

Our family stories had a cast of characters who were wholesome and as rooted in the land of Hungary as an old walnut tree. They suggested to me that the thugs I saw on the streets of Budapest marching off men, women, and children to be shot on the banks of the Danube river were not real people, but ghouls as insubstantial as those in a nightmare. I thought that the high-pitched, high-speed, hysterical voice on the radio—and even a child couldn't mistake Adolf Hitler's voice—simply had to run out of words, breath, and life. One day he would choke on the poison that he spewed out, I thought, and his followers would be swallowed up by an angry earth.

In my heart I was certain that one day my grandfather or great-grandfather would come on a horse-drawn wagon and take us all to a safe and beautiful place, which to me always meant the countryside. Having heard bedtime stories about my ancestors, I believed that both these men were still on this earth, but somewhere far away where only those gained entrance who were just and kind and generous. I believed they were watching what was happening to us, and that if ever our lives were in real danger, they would surely leave their hiding place to rescue their family at the last minute.

My parents and I were fortunate in evading the Nazis, but the larger part of our family did not survive.

Though I soon outgrew bedtime stories, I still wanted to know more about my ancestors and I was annoyed that different relatives told different versions of the same story. Why couldn't my uncle Shumi and his cousin Shamu, both born in the last year of the nineteenth century, agree on how their grandfather Samuel acquired his wealth—or how and why their generation lost it? Just exactly when and where did a carriage axle break on a critical journey through the snowdrifts of the Carpathian mountains?

"But what is the truth?" I kept asking. My relatives were apologetic. "This is how I heard it," each of them said, and would add, as the ultimate excuse: "All that happened long, long ago."

•   •   •

In Belgrade's dingy railroad station, the time always seems to be half past midnight, and the trains are perpetually late. In the station's standing-room-only, cigarette-butt-littered tavern that never closes, an unshaven man in his mid-fifties sings one ditty after another in a throaty, hoarse baritone. His delivery suggests half entertainment, half prayer. Gripping a glass of wine, he addresses no one in particular. Most people pay no attention to him, but a few do listen, and one man even offers him money, which he declines with a wave of his bony hand.

One of his songs is about a Jewish virgin, the daughter of a rabbi who is arranging a marriage for her. Raven-haired and almond-eyed, she is as beautiful as he is wise, and no one from their hometown, a dusty overgrown village where two highways cross, is good enough for her, or for her father.

The song is in Serbo-Croatian, and the singer could be its author. Or, more likely, the song was passed down to him. Yugoslavia is in the Balkans, and the peninsula was Homer's wandering grounds, where the bardic tradition still lives.

It is possible that the singer has never knowingly met a rabbi's daughter, or a rabbi. It is also possible that he has never knowingly spoken with a Jew. Bards are keepers of memories that are seldom their own. They may add to the oral treasury—and ambitious bards do—but the norm is to draw on what others have contributed. As it is with plum brandy, the older the song, the more it is cherished.

In East-Central Europe, a region buffeted between the immensities of Mother Russia and the refinements of Western civilization, Jews stood out for centuries as a separate tribe whose members were both mysterious and familiar, enviably rich and pitifully poor, vulnerable and powerful. In these closing years of the twentieth century, the authentic, distinct, historical Jew is turning into a folk memory: a fabled people joining, in the consciousness of the surviving nations, with the Habsburg bureaucrat, the Ottoman pasha, the Hun horseman, and the Roman legionnaire.

Government statistics still list tens of thousand of Jews in the region, nearly all living in the capitals. The vast majority are assimilated, hard to tell apart from their fellow citizens. Rabbis still lead services in improbably splendid synagogues, built a century ago in a now faraway age that harnessed sudden new wealth generated by capitalist expansion to the classic piety handed down from the Middle Ages. Under the red star of communism, now breaking apart, there has been neither wealth nor piety, yet Jews still gather for purposes other than paying vestigial tribute to their ancestors once a year, on the Day of Atonement. The most idealistic among them collect, as do Gentile friends who are hard put to explain their motives, fragments of a Jewish world that was once whole.

These days in Central Europe it is quaint and intriguing to be part-Jewish, and a distant rabbinical forefather, discovered after decades of amnesia, gussies up a family tree the way the whisper of an archduke's dalliance once did. "I believe my grandmother must have been Jewish," an otherwise cynical Yugoslav journalist born in the early years of the People's Republic confesses to me wistfully. With the cheerless grin of a survivor, he cites the Nazis' law of racial purity which doomed an Aryan whose genealogical documents revealed a single Jewish grandparent. While walking through Belgrade's old inner city, now in the throes of a rehabilitation project, he points to a hole, the size of a bomb crater, where workmen recently stumbled upon thick stone walls that he is convinced one belonged to a synagogue. He concedes that thus far archeologists don't have much evidence to support his thesis beyond the fact that they have found neither a cross nor a crescent in what was probably a public building. "Jews have lived between the Adriatic sea and the Drava river forever," he cries out, "and at least as far back as the Roman empire. And Jews build their synagogues to endure. 'Endure'—isn't that the password, isn't that the secret of the Jews?"

I am reminded of a legend that says that after an eleventh century Russian general destroyed the capital of the Khazars, a tribe living between the Black Sea and the Caspian Sea that had converted to Judaism, the shadows of the houses held their outlines for many years even though all the walls had been razed. The shadows held in the wind, it is claimed, as did their reflections in the water. I am also reminded of my godfather, Yenö, who sent me seven sturdy pairs of shoes, in progressively larger sizes, shortly before he was taken by the Nazis in 1944. Owner of a pine forest and a sawmill in the Carpathian mountains, near the source of the river Tisza, Yenö was a close relative. He was my father's cousin, and his wife was my mother's cousin, and he was delighted to have an opportunity to observe a shared family tradition: a wealthy relative launches a poor one on "the highway of life" by providing his first pair of walking shoes.

We will never know if Yenö increased the number of shoes to seven pairs because he suspected that he would not live to buy any more presents, or because he believed that seven, a magic number, would multiply his godson's chances of survival. I was a teenager, soon to flee across the border of Austria and then off to the United States, and Yenö had long disappeared as a wisp of smoke over Auschwitz, when I grew out of the seventh pair of his shoes, which were a treasure in Hungary in the Stalinist poverty of the 1950s and fetched a good price after I was done with them. Every time I buy a pair of shoes I remember that out of Yenö's extended family of more than fifty people, only two survived the Nazis, and that no more than a handful of Jews are left in his town of Huszt, now part of the Soviet Union, and called Chust, where in his day more than twenty rabbis competed for the loyalties of five thousand Jews.

Nowhere along the Danube or its tributaries, the Drava and the Tisza, is there today a rabbi famous for his wisdom who attracts Jew and non-Jew looking to ease their troubled souls. The markets still smell of sausage and sheep cheese, apricots and dill and freshly baked bread, but there are no Jewish women shouting the praise of their wondrously fat geese, no Jewish bands playing at Jewish weddings, and no itinerant students of the Talmud eating at the table of a rich grain merchant or a poor but pious tailor. Jewish peddlers no longer wander from village to village, from county to county, selling ribbons and yarn and the latest cotton prints, and collecting from the peasants sacks of goosedown for filling comforters which are at the same time the warmest and the lightest, or pillows which prompt the sweetest of dreams; nor do the peddlers buy up the plum harvest to distill kosher slivovitz, the best in the world. There are no more Jewish innkeepers and no more Jewish landowners.

No more, no more, no more.

In the eastern Hungarian town of Debrecen, where I was born, I meet with a thoughtful county official, a patriot with a melliflu-ous voice and an aching heart. To define himself in 1988, he cites nineteenth-century Hungarian poetry: he is a sentinel on the frontier with Russia and Romania, and a caretaker of ruins left behind by four decades of the alien forces of communism. He hopes that by dint of hard work and under a new generation of leaders, his nation will recover its glory.

A descendant of Calvinist preachers, the county official represents the nationalist tradition of his community, the Protestant denomination which in the sixteenth and seventeenth centuries won over many Hungarians opposed to the Roman Catholic House of Habsburg. They constitute the majority in Debrecen, the city Hungarians call "the Calvinist Rome." It was in the austere Calvinist church that towers over Debrecen's main street and which is known simply as "the Big Temple" that the revolutionary parliament of 1849 voted to dethrone the Habsburgs, thus sealing Czar Nicholas I's decision to dispatch his armies to restore a fellow monarch overthrown by popular uprising.

The conversation goes on for hours and hours, and the county official's initial reserve, the armor of a Debrecen burgher, falls away layer by layer. Hungary has been a colony of the Russians, he says. While Russian jets land and take off from Debrecen's airport whenever they wish, a Hungarian plane needs a special permit. The Hungarian treasury has supplied Soviet occupation forces with food and was required to contribute to the upkeep of the Russian's far-flung empire in Cuba, Vietnam, Ethiopia, and Afghanistan. At the same time, the Kremlin did not allow itself a hint of sympathy for the plight of the two-million-strong Hungarian minority in Romania.

It is past midnight when he comes around to the subject of what he calls "the dear old Jews." He laments their passing the way Byron and Goethe lamented the vanishing of the ancient Greeks or of the scribes who had illuminated manuscripts. "What secrets they must have known," he says with a sigh, "we will never know. Those white-bearded old rabbis knew everything. I mean everything!"

Born after the Second World War, he has no firsthand knowledge of the twelve thousand Jews who once lived in his town. He is aware that Jews, including descendants of Hungarian Jews, survive and prosper in other lands. But to his way of thinking, Hungary is the fulcrum of the globe, and the virtual disappearance of Jews from Debrecen, the country's second-largest city with a population of two hundred thousand, constitutes a loss to Hungary, rather than to the Jewish people.

Hungary still boasts some hundred thousand Jews, 98 percent of them living in Budapest, a metropolis of more than two million. Nevertheless, the official in Debrecen asks, and his questions are not just rhetorical: "Where are the real Jews, the Jewish Jews? Aren't all our real Jews dead?"

.   .   .

I drive by the hospital where I was born, in 1937, during the night of Debrecen's first air-raid exercise in preparation for the Second World War. A local newspaper published a light-hearted report about all that happened in town during the first blackout and duly noted the birth of two children. The other child, a girl, also was Jewish. Her life ended in an Auschwitz gas chamber, but her mother, sent to work in a munitions factory, survived.

After the war my mother and I ran into her on a street in Budapest, I cannot forget the look in her eyes which asked me, wordlessly: Why are you alive and why is my daughter dead?

.   .   .

I walk over to the house where my grandmother Róza lived before she was deported to Auschwitz in 1944. The gate, loose on its hinges, is ajar. The one-story building seems about to collapse. The mortar is turning into powder and drifts out from in between the bricks, and the red roof tiles are splitting. Built in the nineteenth century, the house was once a fine structure. It had dignity, so important to my gentrified forebears, but now it looks as if it had been part of an abjectly poor medieval ghetto.

I walk around the courtyard, once planted thick with shrubs and flowers, the work of my mother Anna, a born gardener. The brick-covered pathway used to be swept every morning, to help start the day with a clean slate. Now there are only a few neglected, unhappy plants, and the pathway is only partially visible underneath layers of mud, bottle caps, and cigarette butts.

I search for the mezuzah—the finger-size talisman for protection that has a prayer encased in wood or metal—which Jews do not remove once they nail it to the doorpost and which Christians sometimes keep for good luck. But the doorframe is so riddled with nicks and nail holes that I can't even guess where the mezuzah might have been.

There is not a soul around, and I am thankful. For once I don't feel like having a conversation with locals, and I don't look for people who might have known my beloved, unforgettable grandmother. It is as if we had never lived in this town.

·   ·   ·

I drive a slick red Renault on the same roads where my ancestors once traveled on crude, horse-drawn wagons and elegant carriages. A flock of sheep the color of sand lumbers across the black asphalt, and I stop gladly. I watch them shove and bump one another, even after the shepherd leads them to a new pasture. The car behind me starts honking, and I reluctantly drive on. The pungent odor of the sheep stays with me.

A sign informs me that I have entered Szabolcs County, and soon I park the car next to a century-old walnut tree and get out to admire the sun, which is sinking into a plain as flat as a lake. There is a breeze, and the rustle of the leaves suggests the sound of evening prayers. I sense the presence of my ancestors the way I sense birds hidden in foliage.

I have been finding myself thinking my ancestors' thoughts and repeating phrases they used. When speaking of them, I add the words, "of blessed memory," after their names. When asked the length of my visit, I answer so, and add, "If God wills it," which is what they would have said.

I pick up a walnut from the ground. Its soft husk is half green, full of live tissue, and half black and dead, and I hear myself muttering the opening words of the Kaddish, the Hebrew prayer for the dead that does not once mention dying or death or the dead, but which helps the soul free itself from the body and rise to a higher sphere. In the Kaddish we "glorify, sanctify, bless, praise, exalt, extol, honor, adore, and laud God's name." The prayer is a wreath of synonyms of praise for the Lord, the God of our Fathers, and keeps us alive and give us peace. Suddenly it becomes clear to me that our prayer for the dead is our pledge of allegiance to life.

For the first time in my life I visit Derzs, a small village of less than thousand souls, and its slightly larger neighbor Gyulaj, which my widowed grandmother Róza and her seven children left tearfully in 1927, after their estate there went bankrupt.

Derzs is where my ancestors settled at least four, and possibly several more centuries ago. They might have lived there when Hungary was still ruled by the House of Árpád, whose kings descended from the legendary tribal chieftain who led his people out of the steppes on the banks of the Volga river and whose horsemen completed in the year 896 their conquest of the land that later became known as the Kingdom of Hungary. Then, as now, Derzs was at the end of a road, a cul-de-sac village. Even today it is half a day's bus ride from the nearest big town, Nyiregyháza.

While other Jews chose to live at busy crossroads to be in a better position to trade and to travel, and to move quickly when threatened by invading armies, murderous mobs, or plain bad times, my ancestors looked for a quiet haven where they could raise wheat and cattle and fruit, and later, sheep and potatoes. Theirs was a hideaway on a land so flat that the ruts left behind by wagon wheels are the lowest points into which rainwater drains.

My ancestors planted trees to anchor the faithless yellow sand that runs off with the wind that blows most of the time. From the early nineteenth century on, they relied on black locust trees. Some of the tallest trees in Derzs today were planted by them, while others sprouted from scattered seeds of the first plantings.

The sunlight filtered by the foliage and refracted by the sand offers a shifting mix of gold and green. The gold has the tint of late-afternoon sunshine that aficionados call old gold to distinguish it from the brassy nouveau riche glitter of newly minted gold. The green is the rampant elemental color of the rainforest, promising growth and vegetation everlasting. The gold tames and refines the green, and the green shows the gold to its best advantage. Together, the two colors stand for civilization, as it is defined in the poet's meshing of nature and artifice.

The landscape captures me instantly. I was not told how lovely and harmonious it is, and no story about my ancestors' ambition to create a rich dark soil prepared me for the sensation of scooping up a fistful and inhaling its fecundity.

The villagers and I find ourselves speaking the same language of land and time. One man who engages me in conversation is delighted to find out whose grandson I am. He points out perfect squares of plots surrounded by locust trees two to three stories high. He explains that the land once belonged to my grandfather, then the most prominent landowner in the village, who "thus defined what was his."

Now in his seventies, the farmer can identify every piece of real estate that my family owned or leased in the county. I tell him that he is too young to have been an eyewitness. He says that what he knows he heard from his father who worked for my grandfather and used to haul manure every winter, year after year, with two men on the wagon shoveling the stuff to cover the ground which was later plowed. "Your grandfather knew how to improve the land," the villager says, "and he knew how to deal with people. He know how to bring everything together. He was much liked here, and his name is remembered."

I ask him how and why my family lost its lands. "Your uncles Shumi and Mishi weren't good businessmen," he says, dismissing them as "just like other scions of the landed gentry: light-headed." He also finds fault with advice given by their cousins, whom he knows by name. He has some sharp words for the family lawyer as "the man who took advantage of your problems." But above and beyond every human factor, he blames "the war"—and he means the First World War—when "the world got smashed into pieces, and there was nothing anybody could do to stop that."

The farmer is a hardheaded realist and a Calvinist, which is the minority religion in the village. The majority are Greek Catholics, and their priest, in his fifties and in Derzs only for the past five years, reads Hungarian novels and poetry, and he struggles with books in German, French, and English. He refuses to have anything to do with Russian, even though his forebears and those of his parishioners were Slavs who migrated from the steppes east of the Carpathian mountain range more than a thousand years ago and who followed Byzantine Christianity when the invading Hungarian tribes were still pagans whose shamans sacrificed white horses. The son of a priest and born in a village some ten miles away, he is an amateur historian and archeologist, as well as a dreamer—a species for which Szabolcs County is well known. Dreamers can be unpredictable as the local birds who fill the air with loud, cheerful twitter one year and keep unaccountably quiet the next.

The priest talks about the forty years of communism as "a tragic era during which an entire generation dropped out of not just religion, but the possibility of a life lived by an ethical code." He tells me he has a plan to bring his flock back to religion, but a few minutes later he sees no hope because the world is breaking up into pieces faster than it can be repaired. Then he tells me that he teaches the history of my family as "an example of loyalty to a faith and a place."

.   .   .

He teaches the Hebrew alphabet to his parish children and shows me the primers he is using, which were printed for Jewish children in the 1930s. He acknowledges that his project is unrealistic—of what possible use can Hebrew be to Greek Catholic villagers? But he interrupts himself in midthought: "Must we always be so practical, so down to the mud and dust of the earth? Man must rise above and soar. . . . But Hebrew is tough." He sighs. "Oh God, our shared God, yours and mine, tell us why is the holy language so very, very tough?"

His eyes fill with tears when he mentioned my uncle Shumi, who died a year ago and who had sent him the primers. He cannot forgive himself for missing Shumi's funeral, he says, but the bishop summoned him on some silly business he now knows he should have ignored. . . . Shumi, he sighs, that dear man of the dear nineteenth century, used to visit with him and exchange letters with the children, and it is thanks to him that the children, who are almost adults now, are interested not only in the Schwarcz family but in the history of the village.

It is a sunny, languid, timeless village afternoon. The steady drone of honeybees from the priest's kitchen garden is in harmony with the clatter of hammers, trowels, and spades from the church reconstruction. When the workers stop for a snack, one of them crosses the street to offer to share with us their bread, bacon, and onions—all from his home, he assures us, not from any store.

The hours fly as the priest and I talk in the parsonage. Built some two hundred years ago, it is a spacious, pleasant, whitewashed house with nine-foot ceilings. The floor of unvarnished pine planks is worn down and the knots bulge like an old peasant's knuckles. Books, photographs, documents, and files are everywhere, in stacks on the floor and on chairs and in cupboards; letters are spiked on nails in the walls.

The priest and I talk about everything under the sun, as if we knew each other all our lives, and I make a donation for the church, just as my grandfather did before me. My forebears visited the parsonage countless times, just as the priest's predecessors visited my ancestral home, which my grandfather and his brothers rebuilt and turned into a synagogue in 1906. In 1945, two or three young village Jews who survived the Nazis returned home, dismantled the tin roof, dug up the Torah scroll their families had hidden, and sold whatever they could remove and sell quickly, and used the money to make their way to Palestine. The building, made of adobe and plaster, soon collapsed and was later rebuilt with bricks to serve as a kindergarten.

As we stand in front of the parsonage, saying an extended good-bye, villagers come by, and the priest introduces me. Once they hear my first name and whose grandson I am, they promptly call me Károly *bácsi*, the equivalent of Uncle Charles. Even those much older than I address me that way, rather than by my family name preceded by Mister, the appellation villagers normally use for a stranger and for a townsman. They know without asking that I am named after my grandfather. They all know of him, and the connection they make and the honor they extend to me are immediate and unmistakable. In Derzs, where my grandfather was born, and in Gyulaj where he set up his own estate, I am not just his descendant but his heir and proxy.

I recall what the Talmud says about time: that in the Torah—and by implication, in all matters truly important—there is no "before" and there is no "after," that the trials and triumphs of Abraham, Isaac, and Jacob were recorded not only before they were born but before Creation, and that every Jewish soul who has ever lived or will live was present in the wilderness of Sinai when Moses accepted the Torah on their behalf. Such notions would have been manna for Henry David Thoreau, who, living in wooded hills, thought of time as a stream to go a-fishing in. But what I see all around for miles and miles is sand—homogeneous, particulate, fathoms deep. It dents under the weight of each footstep. Its layers are endlessly shuffled by the wind, and each grain of sand is a fraction of time as measured by an hourglass. As I think of the skulls and the geraniums sharing space in the priest's grape arbor, it seems to me that what is illusory is history, and that it is for the census-taker's convenience that we limit ourselves to one lifetime, from birth to death. I hum to myself: linear time is reason's sweet dream.

The fields beckon. Spread out in what is called "the boundary," they are beyond the houses which cling to the two streets of the village. The road between the village and the fields suggests a stroll, and each bend offers an invitation to the next. My feet feel weightless. I look for a sliver of reedy marsh, known in Szabolcs County as *vadviz*, which translates as "wildwater." It is a twilight zone between land and water, and its contours shift from day to day. For a long time I wait for a shadow to fall suddenly across the water, as still as a tombstone, even though there is no one and nothing above to cast it. According to local tradition, that is how the presence of a spirit can be ascertained in broad daylight. The wind blows from the northeast, from the unseen mountains, and the cattails that sprouted from seeds which had found their way to the *vadviz*—not marked by any map—quiver, bend, and arch, their leaves fluttering like cavalry battle flags from another century. But I see no shadow that is unaccounted for.

I am hoping to catch a glimpse of an ancestor of mine on a deserted dirt road, as he sits on the edge by a drainage ditch, stretching his legs in the moist moonlight while he waits for a wayfarer who would wish him good evening, take him for a man still alive, and accept his invitation to halt and to listen to a story. That is what ghosts do, locals believe, and they fear the morose, silent spirit who crouches with knees drawn close to the chin, and the angry one who rattles a rusty chain while walking about, in search of revenge for having been cheated out of a plot of land or abandoned by a husband. But there are also gentle ghosts eager for a visit with the living. One may be troubled by some unfinished business—something of value he buried which he wants to point out to the proper person to dig up—while another is determined to remind the living of a story he treasures but which no one alive remembers anymore.

A ghost should not be interrupted, but he may be asked three questions before he begins to tell his story, which he completes by the time the first cock crows. He then vanishes in the dawn's mist, which is the color of apricots, shuttling back to his grave, passing through hedgerows of elderberry and the ground of the cemetery as if they too were made of mist.

How I wish I had met one of my ancestors and had a chance to ask my questions: when did we get to this part of the earth, what kept us here, and why are we still so attached to it?

The mists I saw swaddled the land, swirled toward the treetops, and then slipped beyond the horizon. But they appeared to be empty, hiding no one I could see.

Local lore also suspects that ghosts lurk in the adobe walls of the taverns where they once stopped off to sip plum brandy from squat, thick-bottomed shot glasses. It is said that some of them can't stay away from the Gypsy tunes they loved and that others eavesdrop to keep up with village gossip. There is no formula for coaxing them out of the walls, which can be more than a foot thick, but at least one necromancer, who is also Szabolcs County's greatest writer, Gyula Krudy, suggested at the beginning of this century that a descendant engaged in a project to the liking of his forebears and pleading for their help might get the ghost of one of them to step out of the wall and sit and talk. Should that ever happen to me, I don't think we would waste our time discussing the present century, with its fallen kings and corrupt bolsheviks, its devastation in the wake of the swastika and the current chaos as the red star finally fades. We would talk instead about what matters: the Torah of tending fruit trees and vineyards and wheat fields, and the art of keeping our children faithful to the covenant of forefather Abraham.

I keep eyeing the walls, whitewashed with quicklime and uneven like sand scoured by the winds. My ancestors, however, have visited me only in my dreams. They were kind and reassuring, and although their measured demeanor seemed to bear all sorts of secrets, they told me no story and answered no questions.

I walk the dirt road where relatives and villagers took turns in carrying my grandfather's coffin on a raw, blustery day in March 1920. I pass by the canal, straight as a ruler and paid for by my great-grandfather Samuel, which still drains swamps and protects against flooding. I admire the corn growing all around, smaller than in the United States but just as ornamental with its upright stalk and arching blades. No human is in evidence, and the silence is total, sundered from time to time by the piercing cry of a bird hidden in the fields.

The road is not only the shortest distance between my grandfather's house and the family cemetery—which is what the Jewish law prescribes for a funeral procession—it is also part of a network of dirt roads that crisscross the country, but which appear on no map. Sometimes a dirt road runs parallel to a paved road, sometimes perpendicular to it, and sometimes there is no visible connection. Faced by churches, taverns, and fine brick homes, the paved roads are the ancient main routes used by armies on the march and government officials collecting taxes. The dirt roads, now flanked by collapsing adobe huts and shacks housing old wine-presses, have served villagers who work in the fields, fugitives seeking a way to safety, as well as defeated armies and secret lovers.

The only Jews still in Derzs are those buried in our family cemetery, which is surrounded by locust trees and wedged in by cornfields. The graves are in precise rows. The headstones erected in the past one hundred years are made of marble and are upright, their Hebrew lettering clear even though the rains have washed out the gold paint. Headstones from the eighteenth century, made of grainy, coarse limestone quarried from nearby, lean to one side or another and crumble at the edges. Still earlier headstones have sunk into the soft sand long ago, and their presence is suggested by a dip in the flat surface. The oldest of them, next to the road, must be several feet in the earth.

A villager in his thirties walks over to find out who the visiting stranger is and what his purpose must be. He introduces himself as the next-door neighbor to the cemetery. As we shake hands, he looks into my eyes, examines my face, then he asks me, and his words float in the air like rose petals: "Aren't you one of our Jews?"

With a lump in my throat, I can only nod and keep nodding.

"Welcome home," he says.

GHOSTS: A HISTORY

KATHLEEN NORRIS

"Religion is in my blood and in my ghosts," acknowledges Kathleen Norris in this excerpt from her highly praised book, Dakota: A Spiritual Geography. *Norris, a writer and poet, left the frenetic Manhattan arts scene in 1974 to live on the Plains of South Dakota, inheriting both the physical and spiritual home of her fiercely Protestant ancestors.*

THE CHURCH was music to me when I was little, an enthusiastic member of the cherub choir in the large Methodist church in Arlington, Virginia, where my dad was choir director. We wore pale blue robes with voluminous sleeves, stiff white collars, and floppy black bow ties, which I thought made me look like one of the angels in my picture hymnal.

I sang from that book every day at home. One of my strongest memories of early childhood is of sitting on my mother's lap at our old, battered Steinway upright as she played the hymns and I sang. By the time I was three, long before I knew how to read, I'd turn the pages and on seeing the illustration would begin singing the right song in the right pitch.

But music was no longer enough once I discovered the rosary owned by a Catholic friend in first grade. I decided I should have one too, and when my parents said I couldn't, I took an old necklace my mom had given me and said my own grace with it at the table, after family prayers. I had to mumble, because I had no idea what I was supposed to be saying.

This was too much for my father's Methodist blood. His grandfather had been a circuit rider in West Virginia and a chaplain in the Confederate Army. His father, my grandfather, had been a stonemason, lumberjack, and jug band banjo picker who got saved one night at a tent revival, worked his way through West Virginia Wesleyan, and spent the rest of his life preaching the Word. My dad said, ominously, that I could become a Catholic if I wanted to, but he also told me they had a list of books and movies I'd be forbidden to see. For the first time in my life I had come up against the idea that when something seems too good to be true, it probably is.

And this is who I am: a complete Protestant with a decidedly ecumenical bent. I never got that rosary when I was seven, but a friend gave me one when I'd been a Benedictine oblate for nearly five years. I still value music and story over systematic theology—an understatement, given the fact that I was so dreamy as a child that I learned not from Sunday school but from a movie on television that Jesus dies. Either my Sunday school teachers had been too nice to tell me (this was the 1950s), or, as usual, I wasn't paying attention. I am just now beginning to recognize the truth of my original vision: we go to church in order to sing, and theology is secondary.

I remember very little about my confirmation class in a Congregational church in Waukegan, Illinois, except that it was easy because I was good at memorizing, and the minister was a kindly man. I was still singing in my dad's choir, and music still seemed like the real reason for church. In high school in Hawaii, my Methodist Youth Fellowship played volleyball with the Young Buddhist League.

My interest in religion deepened in adolescence, when my family joined a politically active United Church of Christ congregation, where adult classes were taught by professors of religion, one of them a German who had studied with Bultmann at Heidelberg. He was a good Lutheran, too; once, in his student days, he had a theological argument with his brother that got so bad the police had to be called.

I had a crush on him, and took a number of his classes, still totally innocent of both romance and theology; it's only with hindsight that I see I was on a disaster course. I was not yet a poet, but was destined to become one. I needed a teacher who would not have scorned Evelyn Underhill's *Mysticism,* a book I had found on my own, looking for some useful definition of religious experience. I needed liturgy and a solid grounding in the practice of prayer, not a demythologizing that left me feeling starved, thinking: If this is religion, I don't belong. Growing up and discovering who I was meant not going near a church again for nearly twenty years.

During that time I became a writer. I used to think that writing had substituted for religion in my life, but I've come to see that it has acted as a spiritual discipline, giving me the tools I needed to rediscover my religious heritage. It is my Christian inheritance that largely defines me, but for years I didn't know that.

In the early 1970s, when I was out of college, working in New York City and hovering on the fringe of the Andy Warhol scene, a question crept into my consciousness one day, seemingly out of the blue: "What is sin?" I thought I should know, but my mind was blank. I felt like the little boy in *The Snow Queen* who, as he's being carried off in the Queen's carriage, tries desperately to remember the Lord's Prayer but can think of nothing but the multiplication tables.

"What is sin?" It never occurred to me to go to a church for the answer. If the church hadn't taught me in my first twenty years what sin was, it probably never would. I now realize that the question was raised by the pious Protestant grandmother at my core. I had no idea she was there, and didn't know how to listen to her. I didn't realize it at the time, but my move in 1974 from New York to South Dakota was an attempt to hear her voice more clearly. It was a search for inheritance, her place. It was also a religious pilgrimage; on the ground of my grandmother's faith I would find both the means and the end of my search.

All of my grandparents lived out their faith on the Plains. My paternal grandparents, the Reverend John Luther Norris and his wife, Beatrice, served twelve Methodist churches in South Dakota and several more in Iowa. Prairie people have long memories, and they still tell stories about my grandfather's kindness. One man recalls that after his wife died, leaving him with several small children, he began drinking heavily. My grandfather came to his house one day to do the family's laundry, and though the man was drinking the whole time, my grandfather never preached about it; he just kept talking to him about his plans for the future, and, as he put it, "helped me straighten up my life." In his youth, my grandfather had been a black sheep in the Methodist fold, and he often exhibited more tolerance and flexibility than his wife, who clung to a rigid and often fierce fundamentalism.

My maternal grandfather, Frank Totten, was a doctor who practiced medicine in South Dakota for fifty-five years after moving from Kansas in 1909. He could be sentimental about religion but lacked faith; his wife, Charlotte, a former schoolteacher, was a quietly pious Presbyterian, renowned in her church for the excellent Bible studies she conducted for the women's group. She was just about the only adult who could make me mind when I was little, and it was to her house that I moved in 1974, shortly after her death. I'm convinced that her spirit visited me in her kitchen and taught me how to bake bread using her bowl, her old wooden spoon and bread board. And for a time I tried on her Presbyterian church, the way I wore her old jackets and used her furniture. I still enjoyed singing hymns, but found that church was an uneasy exercise in nostalgia, and soon stopped going.

When some ten years later I began going to church again because I felt I needed to, I wasn't prepared for the pain. The services felt like word bombardment—agony for a poet—and often exhausted me so much I'd have to sleep for three or four hours afterward. Doctrinal language slammed many a door in my face, and I became frustrated when I couldn't glimpse the Word behind the words. Ironically, it was the language about Jesus Christ, meant to be most inviting, that made me feel most left out. Sometimes I'd give up, deciding that I just wasn't religious. This elicited an interesting comment from a pastor friend who said, "I don't know too many people who are so serious about religion they can't even go to church."

Even as I exemplified the pain and anger of a feminist looking warily at a religion that has so often used a male savior to keep women in their place, I was drawn to the strong old women in the congregation. Their well-worn Bibles said to me, "there is more here than you know," and made me take more seriously the religion that had caused my grandmother Totten's Bible to be so well used that its spine broke. I also began, slowly, to make sense of our gathering together on Sunday morning, recognizing, however dimly, that church is to be participated in and not consumed. The point is not what one gets out of it, but the worship of God; the service takes place both because of and despite the needs, strengths, and frailties of the people present. How else could it be? Now, on the occasions when I am able to actually worship in church, I am deeply grateful.

But the question of inheritance still haunts me, and I sometimes have the radical notion that I'm a Christian the way a Jew is a Jew, by maternal lineage. Flannery O'Connor remarks in her letters that "most of us come to the church by a means the church does not allow," and I may have put on my grandmother Totten's religion until it became my own. But the currents of this female inheritance spring from deep waters. Mary is also my ancestor, as is Eve. As Emily Dickinson once said, "You know there is no account of her death in the Bible, and why am I not Eve?" Or, why not my two grandmothers, reflecting two very different strains of American Protestantism that exist in me as a continual tension between curse and blessing, pietism and piety, law and grace, the God of wrath and the God of love.

When I was very small my fundamentalist grandmother Norris, meaning well, told me about the personal experience I'd have with Jesus one day. She talked about Jesus coming and the world ending. It sounded a lot like a fairy tale when the prince comes, only scarier. Fundamentalism is about control more than grace, and in effect my grandmother implanted the seed of fundamentalism within me, a shadow in Jungian terms, that has been difficult to overcome. Among other things, it made of Christological language a stumbling block, and told me that as a feminist, as a thinking and questioning person, I had no business being in church. More insidiously, it imbedded in me an unconscious belief in a Monster God. For most of my life you could not have convinced me that, to quote a Quaker friend, "trust comes before belief and faith is a response to love more than an acceptance of dogma."

Trust is something abused children lack, and children raised with a Monster God inside them have a hard time regaining it. My uncle told me once about having his mother sit at the edge of his bed and tell him that Jesus might come as a thief in the night and tomorrow could be that great day when the world ends. "That sucks when you'd been planning a ball game and a rubber gun battle," he said. He would pull the covers over his head when she left, and try to shut out the sounds of Jesus sneaking around in the dark.

A few years ago when I was on retreat at a monastery a poem came boiling up out of me. Called "The Jesus They Made for Us," it is an exorcism of the Monster God:

> He was a boy who drank his mother's milk
> He was always kind to children
> He swallowed them like fish
> He drank up all his mother's milk

> He ate up stars like candy
> He swallowed the sea like a hungry whale

This last image came from a dream I'd had in which I lay on a beach unable to move as a giant whale swam toward me, meaning to rape and crush me. I suspected that this whale was my true image of God, a legacy of my childhood.

A few days later I happened to visit with a little girl who showed me her drawing journal. A recent entry was a big blue whale with three words printed underneath it in purple crayon: "God Is Love." Startled, I said, "That's a wonderful picture," and she replied dreamily, "I just love that whale." With no small sense of awe I realized that we had each partaken of a powerful image, and the difference in how we perceived it amounted to the difference between us. This taught me a new appreciation of what it means to approach the holy as a little child, and some of my trust was restored.

But trust in the religious sphere has been hard to come by. Like many Americans of my baby-boom generation. I had thought that religion was a constraint that I had overcome by dint of reason, learning, artistic creativity, sexual liberation. Church was for little kids or grandmas, a small-town phenomenon that one grew out of or left behind. It was a shock to realize that, to paraphrase Paul Simon, all the crap I learned in Sunday school was still alive and kicking inside me. I was also astonished to discover how ignorant I was about my own religion. Apart from a few Bible stories and hymns remembered from childhood I had little with which to start to build a mature faith. I was still that child in *The Snow Queen*, asking "what is sin?" but not knowing how to find out. Fortunately a Benedictine friend provided one answer: "Sin, in the New Testament," he told me, "is the failure to do concrete acts of love." That is something I can live with, a guide in my conversion. It's also a much better definition of sin than I learned as a child: sin as breaking rules.

Comprehensible, sensible sin is one of the unexpected gifts I've found in the monastic tradition. The fourth-century monks began to answer a question for me that the human potential movement of the late twentieth century never seemed to address: if I'm O.K. and you're O.K., and our friends (nice people and, like us, markedly middle class, if a bit bohemian) are O.K., why is the world definitely not O.K.? Blaming others wouldn't do. Only when I began to see the world's ills mirrored in myself did I begin to find an answer; only as I began to address that uncomfortable word, sin, did I see that I was not being handed a load of needless guilt so much as a useful tool for confronting the negative side of human behavior.

.   .   .

Religion is in my blood, and in my ghosts. My maternal grandmother Totten had a livable faith and a tolerance that allowed her to be open to the world. My grandmother Norris lived with the burden of a harder faith. She had married my grandfather—a divorced man whose wife had abandoned him and their two small children—after his conversion at a revival meeting. The older sister she revered became a medical missionary, but my grandmother found her mission in marriage and in raising seven children as the wife of a Plains pastor who served in seventeen churches in thirty-two years. Their first child born on the Plains, Kathleen Dakota, was born with rickets. While my grandmother was still nursing she conceived again; her doctor found her too exhausted and malnourished to sustain another pregnancy and performed an abortion. Early in their marriage her husband had rejected her affection in such a way that it was still fresh in her memory sixty years later. Long after he was dead she could calmly say, "You know, of course, he never loved me."

Her last child was born when she was in her forties, soon after her stepson, the eldest, died of meningitis. She prayed for another boy and promised the Lord that she would rear him to become a minister if her prayers were answered—Grandma Norris was nothing if not biblical. She had a son who tried and failed to live out her plans for him; only years later did she affirm him in his chosen vocation of teaching, reasoning that Jesus was a teacher, too. For most of her life she would ask of anyone she met: "Are you saved?"

It's this hard religion, adding fuel to an all-American mix of incest, rape, madness, and suicide, that nearly destroyed an entire generation in my family. My father's status as oldest remaining son, his musical talent, a sense of humor, and a solid marriage helped save him. But my aunts suffered terribly, and one was lost. I never met her; she died the year I was born. She died of lots of things: sex and fundamentalist religion and schizophrenia and postpartum despair. She was a good girl who became pregnant out of wedlock and could make no room for the bad girl in herself. She jumped out of a window at a state mental hospital a few days after she had her baby.

Looking at an old family photograph when I was twelve, I saw a face I didn't recognize. Asking who this was, I first heard her story. Suicides have a way of haunting the next generation, and adolescence is when most of us begin to know who we will be. I believe I became a writer in order to tell her story and possibly redeem it. This goes much deeper than anything I understand, but, in part, I also joined a church because of her. I needed to find that woman sacrificed to a savage god. I needed to make sure she was forgiven and at peace.

The first time I stayed at a monastery hermitage I surfaced one day for morning prayer with the community. My stomach was growling, anticipating breakfast, and I was restless. A monk read what I've since learned is a prayer they say every morning, that all their deceased confreres, oblates, relatives, benefactors, and friends may rest in the peace of the risen Christ. That morning, I knew it was done; I didn't have to worry about my aunt any more. They tell me this is Catholic theology, not Protestant; I couldn't care less. Her name was Mary, and she had good pitch. The church was music to her, and she sang all her life in church choirs.

THE OLD TESTAMENT/
THE NEW TESTAMENT

JAMES MCBRIDE

"God makes me happy," proclaims Ruth McBride Jordan in these paired chapters from her son James McBride's best-selling book, The Color of Water. *In this duet of remembrances, McBride, a composer and journalist, shares with us his remarkable mother, a Polish-born Jew, a rabbi's daughter run off to Harlem, married to a black Baptist minister, and reborn in Christ. To this, McBride adds his own voice, recalling the uproarious church life that sustained him and his eleven siblings.*

THE OLD TESTAMENT

MY FATHER *was a traveling preacher. He was just like any traveling preacher except he was a rabbi. He wasn't any different from the rest of those scoundrels you see on TV today except he preached in synagogues and he wasn't so smooth-talkin'. He was hard as a rock and it didn't take long before the Jewish congregations figured him out and sent him on his way, so we traveled a lot when I was a young girl. In those days any Orthodox Jew who said he was a rabbi could preach and go around singing like a cantor and such. That's all some of those Jews could do in those days, travel around and preach and* *sing. There weren't jobs out there like you know them today. Living. That was your job. Surviving. Reading the Old Testament and hoping it brought you something to eat, that's what you did.*

See, Orthodox Jews work with contracts. Or at least my family did. A contract to marry. A contract to preach. A contract for whatever. Money was part of their lives because they had nothing else, like a real home. At least we didn't. Tateh would sign a contract with a synagogue and after a year the synagogue wouldn't renew it, so we'd pack up and move to the next town. We lived in so many places I can't remember them. Glens Falls, New York; Belleville, New Jersey; Port Jervis, New York; Springfield, Massachusetts; someplace called Dover. I remember Belleville because someone was always giving us hand-me-down clothes there. That's how the members from the congregations would pay us, with food and a place to stay and their cast-off clothes. I remember Springfield, Massachusetts, because my sister Gladys was born there. We called her Dee-Dee. She was four years younger than me. Dee-Dee came into this world around 1924. Whether she is still in this world today I do not know. She would be the last of my mother's children still alive other than me.

We carted everything we had from town to town by bus—clothes, books, hats, and these huge quilts my mother had brought from Europe. They were full of goose feathers. You call them piezyna, in Jewish. They were warm as a house. My sister and I slept under them wherever we lived. We attracted a lot of attention when we traveled because we were poor and Jewish and my mother was handicapped. I was real conscious of that. Being Jewish and having a handicapped mother. I was ashamed of my mother, but see, love didn't come natural to me until I became a Christian.

For a while we lived above a Jewish store in Glens Falls, in upstate New York, and the kind Jewish people who ran it baked us pies and gave us apples. We went sledding and did things as a family and my parents seemed to get along. It wasn't bad up there really, but as usual Tateh's contract didn't get renewed and we had to leave. Luckily he got an offer to run a synagogue in Suffolk, Virginia. He told Mameh, "We're moving south." Mameh didn't want to go. She said, "Maybe we can get something up here," because her sisters and her mother were in New York City, but talking to him was like talking to that wall over there. He said, "We're moving," and we went to Suffolk, Virginia, around 1929. I was eight or nine at the time.

I still remember the smell of the South. It smelled like azaleas. And leaves. And peanuts. Peanuts everywhere. Planters peanuts had their headquarters in Suffolk. Mr. Obici ran it. He was a big deal in town. The big peanut man. He gave a lot of money out to people. He built a hospital. You could buy peanuts by the pound in Suffolk for nothing. There were farmers growing peanuts, haul-

ing peanuts, making peanut oil, peanut butter, even peanut soap. They called the high school yearbook The Peanut. *They even had a contest once to see who could make the best logo for Planters peanut company. Some lady won it. They gave her twenty-five dollars, which was a ton of money in those days.*

Suffolk was a one-horse town back then, one big Main Street, a couple of movie theaters—one for black folks, one for white folks—a few stores, a few farms nearby, and a set of railroad tracks that divided the black and white sections of town. The biggest event Suffolk had seen in years was a traveling sideshow that came through town on the railroad tracks, with a stuffed whale in a boxcar. The folks loved that. They loved anything different, or new, or from out of town, except for Jews. In school the kids called me "Christ killer" and "Jew baby." That name stuck with me for a long time. "Jew baby." You know it's so easy to hurt a child.

Tateh worked at the local synagogue, but he had his eye on this huge old barn-type building across the tracks on the so-called colored side of town with the aim of starting a grocery store there. Well, that upset some of the synagogue folks. They didn't want their holy rabbi going into business—and doing business with niggers, no less!—but Tateh said, "We're not moving anymore. I'm tired of moving." He knew they'd get rid of him eventually—let's face it, he was a lousy rabbi. He had a Jewish friend in town named Israel Levy who signed a bank note that allowed Tateh to get his hands on that old place. Tateh threw a counter and some shelves in there, an old cash register, tacked up a sign outside that said "Shilsky's Grocery Store" or something to that effect, and we were in business. The black folks called it "Old Man Shilsky's store." That's what they called him. Old Man Shilsky. They used to laugh at him and his old ragtag store behind his back, but over the years they made Old Man Shilsky rich and nobody was laughing then.

Our store was a rickety, odd, huge wooden structure that looked like it was held together with toothpicks and glue. It sat at the very edge of town, near the town jail and overlooking the wharf. On the first floor was the store, a storage area, an ice room, a kitchen with a kerosene stove, and the backyard. We slept upstairs. There was no living room, no dining room upstairs, just rooms. Me and Dee-Dee slept in one room under our big quilt. Mameh often slept in the same room as us, and my brother Sam and Tateh slept in the other. My parents didn't have the kind of warm relations that most parents had. Mameh was a very good wife and mother. Despite her overall poor health—she could barely see out of one eye, had severe pains in her stomach that grew more and more painful over the years—she could do more with one hand than I can do with two. She cooked matzoh balls, kneydlach, *gefilte fish,* kugl, *chopped liver, and more kosher dishes than I can remember. She would darn socks. I learned how* to chop fish, meat, and vegetables on a butcher-block cutting board from her. She kept the religious traditions of a Jewish housewife and was loyal to her husband, but Tateh had absolutely no love for her. He would call her by any name and make fun of her disability. He'd say, "I get sick to look at you," and, "Why do you bother trying to look pretty?" His marriage was a business deal for him. He only wanted money. That and to be an American. Those were the two things he wanted, and he got them too, but it cost him his family, which he ran into the ground and destroyed.

We had no family life. That store was our life. We worked in there from morning till night, except for school, and Tateh had us timed for that. He'd be standing in the road outside the store with his hands on his hips at three P.M. sharp, looking down the road for me and Sam, and later Dee-Dee, as we ran the six blocks home from school. Right to work we went. Homework was done between customers. We were the only store open in town on Sundays, because we celebrated our Sabbath from Friday to Saturday evening, so we did booming business on Sundays because the white folks would shop there as well as our normal customers.

We sold everything in that store: cigarettes, by the pack or loose—Camels, Lucky Strike, Chesterfields for a penny each, or Wings, two for a penny; we sold coal, lumber, firewood, kerosene, candy, Coca-Cola, BC powder, milk, cream, fruit, butter, canned goods, meat. Ice was a big product. It was put into the big wooden icebox in the back of the store and sold by the chunk or into smaller pieces that sold for fifteen cents each. That icebox was big enough for a person to walk in, which I never did. Anything that could close behind me, or trap me, I never liked. I'm claustrophobic. I can't stand feeling stuck or trapped in a place. I like to move. Even as a tiny girl I was like that. Hobbies? I had none. Running. That was my hobby. Sometimes when Tateh wasn't home, I'd tear out the door of the store and run. Just run anyplace. I would run down the back roads where the black folks lived, across the tracks to where the white folks were. I loved to sprint, just to feel the wind blowing on my face and see things and not be at home. I was always a running-type person.

Of course I had something to run from. My father did things to me when I was a young girl that I couldn't tell anyone about. Such as getting in bed with me at night and doing things to me sexually that I could not tell anyone about. When we'd go to the beach in Portsmouth, he'd get into the water with me, supposedly to teach me how to swim, and hold me real close to his body near his sexual parts and he'd have an erection. When we'd get back to the beach, Mameh would ask, "Are you getting better at swimming?" and I'd say, "Yes, Mameh," and he'd be standing there, glaring at me. God, I was scared of him.

Anytime he had a chance, he'd try to get close to me or crawl into bed with me *and molest me. I was afraid of Tateh and had no love for him at all. I dreaded him and was relieved anytime he left the house. But it affected me in a lot of ways, what he did to me. I had very low self-esteem as a child, which I kept with me for many, many years; and even now I don't want to be around anyone who is domineering or pushing me around because it makes me nervous. I'm only telling you this because you're my son and I want you to know the truth and nothing less. I did have low self-esteem as a child. I felt low.*

Folks will run with that, won't they? They'll say, "Oh, she felt low, so she went on and married a nigger." Well, I don't care. Your father changed my life. He taught me about a God who lifted me up and forgave me and made me new. I was lucky to meet him or I would've been a prostitute or dead. Who knows what would've happened to me. I was reborn in Christ. Had to be, after what I went through. Of course it wasn't torment twenty-four hours a day being a Jew. We had good times, especially with my mother. Like on Passover, where you had to clean that house spic-and-span. Not a crumb or speck of leavened bread could be found anywhere. We loved getting ready for it. You had to use Passover dishes and we had a big seder, where the family sat down and the table was set with matzoh and parsley, boiled eggs and other traditional Jewish food. We set an empty chair for the coming of Elijah—see, Jews think the real Messiah hasn't got here yet. The Haggadah had to be read and Tateh would ask us children questions about why we celebrated the feast of Passover. Well, you can believe we knew the answer rather than get smacked across the face by him, but to be honest with you, I used to see that empty chair we left for Elijah at the table and wish I could be gone to wherever Elijah was, eating over somebody else's house where your father didn't crawl into bed with you at night, interrupting your dreams so you don't know if it's really him or just the same nightmare happening over and over again.

THE NEW TESTAMENT

Mommy loved God. She went to church each and every Sunday, the only white person in sight, butchering the lovely hymns with a singing voice that sounded like a cross between a cold engine trying to crank on an October morning and a whining Maytag washer. My siblings and I would muffle our laughter as Mommy dug into hymns with verve and gusto: *"Leaning. . . oh, leannning. . . safe and secure on the—"* Up, up, and away she went, her shrill voice climbing higher and higher, reminding us of Curly of the Three Stooges. It sounded so horrible that I often thought Rev. Owens, our minister, would get up from his seat and stop the song. He'd sit behind his pulpit in a spiritual trance, his eyes closed, clad in a long blue robe with a white scarf and billowed sleeves, as if he were prepared to float away to heaven himself, until one of Mommy's clunker notes roused him. One eye would pop open with a jolt, as if someone had just poured cold water down his back. He'd coolly run the eye in a circle, gazing around at the congregation of forty-odd parishioners to see where the whirring noise was coming from. When his eye landed on Mommy, he'd nod as if to say, "Oh, it's just Sister Jordan"; then he'd slip back into his spiritual trance.

In the real world, Mommy was "Mrs. McBride" or "Mrs. Jordan," depending on whether she used my father's or stepfather's name, but in Rev. Owen's church, she was Sister Jordan. "Sister Jordan brought quite a few of her children today," Rev. Owens would marvel as Mommy stumbled in with six of us trailing her. "*Quite* a few." We thought he was hilarious. He was our Sunday schoolteacher and also the local barber who cut our hair once a month when we grew big enough to refuse Mommy's own efforts in that direction—she literally put a bowl on your head and cut around it. He was a thin man who wore polyester suits and styled his hair in the old slicked-back conk, combed to the back in rippling waves. He could not read very well—I could read better than he could when I was only twelve. He'd stand on the pulpit, handkerchief in hand, wrestling with the Bible verses like a man possessed. He'd begin with, "Our verse for today is. . . ahh, ummm, ahh. . . ." flipping through the pages of his Bible, finally finding the verse, putting his finger on it, and you could hear the clock going *tick, tock, tick, tock,* as he struggled with the words, moving his lips silently while the church waited on edge and my sister Helen, the church pianist, stifled her giggles and Mommy glared at her, shaking her fist and silently promising vengeance once church was over.

Rev. Owens's sermons started like a tiny choo-choo train and ended up like a roaring locomotive. He'd begin in a slow drawl, then get warmed up and jerk back and forth over the subject matter like a stutterer gone wild: "We. . . [silence]. . . know. . . today. . . arrhh. . . um. . . I said WEEEE. . . know. . . THAT [silence] ahhh. . . JESUS [church: "Amen!"]. . . ahhh, CAME DOWN. . . ["Yes! Amen!"] I said CAME DOWWWWNNNN! ["Go on!"] He CAME-ON-DOWN-AND-LED-THE-PEOPLE-OF-JERU-SALEM-AMEN!" Then he'd shift to a babbling "Amen" mode, where he spoke in fast motion and the words popped out of his mouth like artillery rounds. "Amens" fired across the room like bullets. "It's so good AMEN to know God AMEN and I tell you AMEN that if you AMEN only come AMEN to God yourself AMEN there will be AMEN no turning back AMEN AMEN AMEN! Can I get an AMEN?" (AMEN!")

And there we were in aisle 5, Sister Jordan in her church hat and blue dress, chuckling and smiling and occasionally waving her hands in the air like everyone else. Mommy loved church. Any church. Even Rev. Owens's Whosoever Baptist Church she loved, though he wasn't her favorite minister because he left his wife, or vice versa—we never knew. Mommy was a connoisseur of ministers; she knew them the way a French wine connoisseur knows Beaujolais red from Vouvray white. Rev. Owens, despite his preaching talents, wasn't even in the top five. That elite list included my late father, the late Rev. W. Abner Brown of Metropolitan Baptist in Harlem, our family friend Rev. Edward Belton, and a few others, all of whom were black, and with the exception of Rev. Belton, quite dead. She considered them old-timers, men of dignity and dedication who grew up in the South and remembered what life was like in the old days. They knew how to fire up a church the old-fashioned way, without talk of politics and bad mouthing and negativity but with real talk of God and genuine concern for its parishioners. "Your father," she often mused, "he'd give anybody his last dime." She did not like large churches with political preachers, nor Pentecostal churches that were too wild. And despite her slight dislike of Rev. Owens and his odd style—he once preached a sermon on the word "the"—T-H-E—she had respect for him because his church and preachings were close in style to that of her "home" church, New Brown Memorial. Unlike New Brown, however, Whosoever wasn't a storefront church. It was a tiny brick building that stood alone, about fifteen feet back from the sidewalk, with a sign above the door that was done by a painter who began his lettering without taking into account how little space he had. It read: WHOSOEVER BAPTIST CHURCH."

I never saw Mommy "get happy" at Whosoever Baptist, meaning "get the spirit" and lose control—thank God. When people got happy it was too much for me. They were mostly women, big mamas whom I knew and loved, but when the good Lord climbed into their bones and lifted them up toward Sweet Liberty, kind, gentle women who mussed my hair and kissed me on my cheek and gave me dimes would burst out of their seats like Pittsburgh Steeler linebackers. "Oh *yessss!*" they'd cry, arms outstretched, dancing in the aisles, slithering around with the agility of the Pink Panther, shuddering violently, purse flying one way, hat going another, while some poor old sober-looking deacon tried grimly to hang on to them to keep them from hurting themselves, only to be shaken off like a fly. Sometimes two or three people would physically hold the spirited person to keep her from hurting herself while we looked on in awe, the person convulsing and hollering, "Jesus, Jesus! Yes!" with Rev. Owens winging along with his spirited "AMEN'S" and "ah yes's!" I never understood why God would climb into these people with such fervor, until I became a grown man myself and came to understand the nature and power of God's many blessings, but even as a boy I knew God was all-powerful because of Mommy's utter deference to Him, and also because she would occasionally do something in church that I never saw her do at home or anywhere else: at some point in the service, usually when the congregation was singing one of her favorite songs, like "We've Come This Far by Faith" or "What a Friend We Have in Jesus," she would bow down her head and weep. It was the only time I ever saw her cry. "Why do you cry in church?" I asked her one afternoon after service.

"Because God makes me happy."

"Then why cry?"

"I'm crying 'cause I'm happy. Anything wrong with that?"

"No," I said, but there was, because happy people did not seem to cry like she did. Mommy's tears seemed to come from somewhere else, a place far away, a place inside her that she never let any of us children visit, and even as a boy I felt there was pain behind them. I thought it was because she wanted to be black like everyone else in church, because maybe God liked black people better, and one afternoon on the way home from church I asked her whether God was black or white.

A deep sigh. "Oh boy. . . God's not black. He's not white. He's a spirit."

"Does he like black or white people better?"

"He loves all people. He's a spirit."

"What's a spirit?"

"A spirit's a spirit."

"What color is God's spirit?"

"It doesn't have a color," she said. "God is the color of water. Water doesn't have a color."

I could buy that, and as I got older I still bought it, but my older brother Richie, who was the brother above me and the guy from whom

I took all my cues, did not. When Richie was fourteen he'd grown from a tittering, cackling torturer of me to a handsome, slick high school kid who was an outstanding tenor sax player. He got accepted at Music and Art High School in Manhattan and had reached a point in his life where jazz was the beginning, the end, and the middle. He took to wearing a leather jacket and a porkpie hat like legendary tenor man Lester Young, joined a neighborhood R&B band, and Ma had increasing difficulty in getting him to go to school. The dudes in the neighborhood called him "Hatt" and respected him. The girls loved him. He was bursting with creative talent and had ideas he acted upon independently without the approval of, or the knowledge of, Ma. A few blocks from our house was an eight-foot-high stone with a plaque on it that commemorated some civil historic event, and one morning on the way to the store, Mommy noticed that the rock had been painted the black-liberation colors, red, black, and green. "I wonder who did that," she remarked. I knew, but I couldn't say. Richie had done it.

All my siblings, myself included, had some sort of color confusion at one time or another, but Richie dealt with his in a unique way. As a boy, he believed he was neither black nor white but rather green like the comic book character the Incredible Hulk. He made up games about it and absorbed the character completely into his daily life: "I'm Dr. Bruce Banner," he'd say as he saw me eating the last of the bologna and cheese. "I need a piece of your sandwich. Please give it to me now or I'll get angry. I must have it! Please don't make me angry. Give me *that sandwich!!!* GIVE ME—Oh no! Wait. . . ARRHH-HHHHGGGHHHH!" and thereby he'd become the Hulk and if I hadn't gobbled my sandwich by then, well, the Hulk got it.

One morning in Sunday school Richie raised his hand and asked Rev. Owens, "Is Jesus white?"

Rev. Owens said no.

"Then how come they make him white here in this picture?" Richie said, and he held up our Sunday school Bible.

Rev. Owens said, "Jesus is all colors."

"Then why is he white? This looks like a white man to me." Richie held the picture high so everyone in the class could see it. "Don't he look white to you?" Nobody said anything.

Rev. Owens was stuck. He stood there, wiping his face with his handkerchief and making the same noise he made when he preached. "Wellll. . . ahh. Wellll. . . ahhh. . . ."

I was embarrassed. The rest of the kids stared at Richie like he was crazy. "Richie, forget it," I mumbled.

"Naw. If they put Jesus in this picture here, and He ain't white, and He ain't black, they should make Him gray. Jesus should be gray."

Richie stopped going to Sunday school after that, though he never stopped believing in God. Mommy tried and tried to make him go back, but he wouldn't.

Mommy took great pride in our relationship to God. Every Easter we had to perform at the New Brown Church, playing our instruments or reciting a story from the Bible for the entire church congregation. Mommy looked forward to this day with anticipation, while my siblings and I dreaded it like the plague, always waiting till the morning of the event before memorizing the Bible story we would recite. I never had problems with these memory-crunching sessions, but one year my older brother Billy, whose memory would later serve him well enough to take him through Yale University Medical School, marched to the front of the church wearing suit and tie, faced the congregation, started out, "When Jesus first came to. . ." then blanked out completely. He stood there, twitching nervously, dead in the water, while my siblings and I winced and held our breath to keep from laughing.

"Oh, that's all right now. . ." murmured my godfather, Deacon McNair, from his seat on the dais next to the minister, while Mommy twitched in her seat watching Billy, her face reddening. "Try it again," he said.

"Okay," Billy said, swallowing. "When Jesus first came to. . . No, wait. . . . Um. Jerusalem was. . . Wait a minute. . . ." He stood there, stalled, gazing at the ceiling, biting his lip, desperately trying to remember the Bible story he had memorized just a half hour before, while the church murmured, "Oh it's all right now. . . just keep trying," and Mommy glared at him, furious.

A few more embarrassing seconds passed. Finally Deacon McNair said, "Well, you don't have to tell us a Bible story, Billy. Just recite a verse from the Bible."

"Any verse?" Billy asked.

"Any verse you want," the deacon said.

"Okay." Billy faced the church again. Every face was silent, watching him.

"Jesus wept," he said. He took his seat.

Dead silence.

"Amen," said Deacon McNair.

After church, we followed Mommy as she stalked out, and my god-father met her at the door. "It's all right, Ruth," he said, chuckling.

"No it's not," Ma said.

When we got home, Mommy beat Billy's butt.

from *MEMORIES OF A CATHOLIC GIRLHOOD*

MARY McCARTHY

Mary McCarthy's parents died in the influenza epidemic of 1918 when she was just six years old, leaving her and her brothers orphaned. They were shuttled from relative to relative—Jewish, Catholic, and Protestant—each tradition vying for influence. This excerpt from McCarthy's Memories of a Catholic Girlhood *was her attempt to reconstruct her parochial school education and her sense of "mystery and wonder" in the Catholic Church. McCarthy, a prominent American novelist and critic who died in 1989, absorbed the vocabulary of saints and symbols that stayed with her through a love of literature and art, long after her allegiance to Catholic doctrine had dissipated.*

LOOKING BACK, I see that it was religion that saved me. Our ugly church and parochial school provided me with my only aesthetic outlet, in the words of the Mass and the litanies and the old Latin hymns, in the Easter lilies around the altar, rosaries, ornamented prayer books, votive lamps, holy cards stamped in gold and decorated with flower wreaths and a saint's picture. This side of Catholicism, much of it cheapened and debased by mass production, was for me, nevertheless, the equivalent of Gothic cathedrals and illuminated manuscripts and mystery plays. I threw myself into it with ardor, this sensuous life, and when I was not dreaming that I was going to grow up to marry the pretender to the throne of France and win back his crown with him, I was dreaming of being a Carmelite nun, cloistered and penitential; I was also much attracted by an order for fallen women called the Magdalens. A desire to excel governed all my thoughts, and this was quickened, if possible, by the parochial-school methods of education, which were based on the competitive principle. Everything was a contest; our schoolroom was divided into teams, with captains, for spelling bees and other feats of learning, and on the playground we organized ourselves in the same fashion. To win, to skip a grade, to get ahead—the nuns' methods were well adapted to the place and time, for most of the little Catholics of our neighborhood were children of poor immigrants, bent on bettering themselves and also on surpassing the Protestants, whose children went to Whittier, the public school. There was no idea of equality in the parochial school, and such an idea would have been abhorrent to me, if it had existed; equality, a sort of brutal cutting down to size, was what I was treated to at home. Equality was a species of unfairness which the good sisters of St. Joseph would not have tolerated.

I stood at the head of my class and I was also the best runner and the best performer on the turning poles in the schoolyard; I was the best actress and elocutionist and the second most devout, being surpassed in this by a blond boy with a face like a saint, who sat in front of me and whom I loved; his name, which sounds rather like a Polish saint's name, was John Klosick. No doubt, the standards of the school were not very high, and they gave me a false idea of myself; I have never excelled at athletics elsewhere. Nor have I ever been devout again. When I left the competitive atmosphere of the parochial school, my religion withered on the stalk.

But in St. Stephen's School, I was not devout just to show off; I felt my religion very intensely and longed to serve God better than anyone else. This, I thought, was what He asked of me. I lived in fear of making a poor confession or of not getting my tongue flat enough to receive the Host reverently. One of the great moral crises of my life occurred on the morning of my first Communion. I took a drink of water. Unthinkingly, of course, for had it not been drilled into me that the Host must be received fasting, on the penalty of mortal sin? It was only a sip, but that made no difference, I knew. A sip was as bad as a gallon; I *could not* take Communion. And yet I had to. My Communion dress and veil and prayer book were laid out for me, and I was supposed to lead the girls' procession; John Klosick, in a white suit, would be leading the boys'. It seemed to me that I would be failing the school and my class, if, after all the rehearsals, I had to confess what I had done and drop out. The sisters would be angry, my guardians would be angry, having paid for the dress and veil. I thought of the procession without me in it, and I could not bear it. To make my first Communion later, in ordinary clothes, would not be the same. On the other hand, if I took my first Communion in a state of mortal sin, God would never forgive me; it would be a fatal beginning. I went through a ferocious struggle with my conscience, and all the while, I think, I knew the devil was going to prevail: I was going to take Communion, and only God and I would know the real facts. So it came about: I received my first Communion in a state of outward holiness and inward horror, believing I was damned, for I could not imagine that I could make a true repentance—the time to repent was now, before committing the sacrilege; afterward, I could not be really sorry for I would have achieved what I had wanted.

I suppose I must have confessed this at my next confession, scarcely daring to breathe it, and the priest must have treated it lightly: my sins, as I slowly discovered, weighed heavier on me than they did on my confessors. Actually, it is quite common for children making their first Communion to have just such a mishap as mine: they are so excited on that long-awaited morning that they hardly know what they are doing, or possibly the very taboo on food and water and the importance of the occasion drive them into an unconscious resistance. . . . Yet the despair I felt that summer morning (I think it was Corpus Christi Day) was in a certain sense fully justified: I *knew myself,* how I was and would be forever; such dry self-knowledge is terrible. Every subsequent moral crisis of my life, moreover, has had precisely the pattern of this struggle over the first Communion; I have battled, usually without avail, against a temptation to do something which only I knew was bad, being swept on by a need to preserve outward appearances and to live up to other people's expectations of me. The heroine of one of my novels, who finds herself pregnant, possibly as the result of an infidelity, and is tempted to have the baby and say nothing to her husband, is in the same fix, morally, as I was at eight years old, with that drink of water inside me that only I knew was there. When I supposed I was damned, I was right—damned, that is, to a repetition or endless re-enactment of that conflict between excited scruples and inertia of will.

I am often asked whether I retain anything of my Catholic heritage. This is hard to answer, partly because my Catholic heritage consists of two distinct strains. There was the Catholicism I learned from my mother and from the simple parish priests and nuns in Minneapolis, which was, on the whole, a religion of beauty and goodness, however imperfectly realized. Then there was the Catholicism practiced in my grandmother McCarthy's parlor and in the home that was made for us down the street—a sour, baleful doctrine in which old hates and rancors had been stewing for generations, with ignorance proudly stirring the pot. The difference can be illustrated by an incident that took place when I stopped off in Minneapolis, on my way to Vassar as a freshman, in 1929. In honor of the occasion, my grandmother McCarthy invited the parish priest to her house; she wanted him to back up her opinion that Vassar was "a den of iniquity." The old priest, Father Cullen, declined to comply with her wishes and, ignoring his pewholder's angry interjections, spoke to me instead of the rare intellectual opportunities Vassar had in store for me.

Possibly Father Cullen was merely more tactful than his parishioner, but I cannot forget my gratitude to him. It was not only that he took my grandmother down a peg. He showed largeness of spirit—a quality rare among Catholics, at least in my experience, though *false* magnanimity is a common stock in trade with them. I have sometimes thought that Catholicism is a religion not suited to the laity, or not suited, at any rate, to the American laity, in whom it seems to bring out some of the worst traits in human nature and to lend them a sort of sanctification. In the course of publishing these memoirs in magazines, I have received a great many letters from the laity and also from priests and nuns. The letters from the laity—chiefly women— are all alike; they might almost have been penned by the same person; I have filed them under the head of "Correspondence, Scurrilous." They are frequently full of misspellings, though the writers claim to be educated, and they are all, without exception, menacing. "False," "misrepresentation," "lying," "bigotry," "hate," "poison," "filth," "trash," "cheap," "distortion"—this is the common vocabulary of them all. They threaten to cancel their subscriptions to the magazine that published the memoir; they speak of a "great many other people that you ought to know feel as I do," *i.e.,* they attempt to constitute themselves a pressure group. Some *demand* an answer. One lady writes: "I am under the impression that the Law forbids this sort of thing."

In contrast, the priests and nuns who have written me, apropos the same memoirs, strike a note that sounds almost heretical. They are touched, many of them say, by my "sincerity"; some of the nuns are praying for me, they write, and the priests are saying masses. One young Jesuit tells me that he has thought of me when he visited Forest Ridge Convent in Seattle and looked over the rows of girls: "I see that the startling brilliance of a slim orphan girl was fairly matched with fiery resolve and impetuous headlong drive. Nor was it easy for her those days. I suppose I should be thinking that technically you are an apostate, in bad standing, outside the gate. . . ." An older priest writes me that I am saved whether I know it or not: "I do not suggest to you where you will find your spiritual home—but that you will find it—of that I am certain—the Spirit will lead you to it. Indeed for me you have already found it, although you still must seek it." A Maryknoll nun invites me to visit her mission. None of these correspondents feels obliged to try to convert me; they seem to leave that to God to worry about. Some of them have passed through a period of doubt themselves and write me about that, to show their understanding and sympathy. Each of the letters has its own individuality. The only point of uniformity is that they all begin: "Dear Mary."

I am grateful to these priests and nuns, grateful to them for existing. They must be a minority, though they would probably deny it, even among the clergy. The idea that religion is supposed to teach you to be good, an idea that children have, seems to linger on, like a sweet treble, in their letters. Very few people appear to believe this any more, it is utterly out of style among fashionable neo-Protestants, and the average Catholic perceives no connection between religion and morality, unless it is a question of someone *else's* morality, that is, of the supposed pernicious influences of books, films, ideas, on someone else's conduct.

From what I have seen, I am driven to the conclusion that religion is only good for good people, and I do not mean this as a paradox, but simply as an observable fact. Only good people can afford to be religious. For the others, it is too great a temptation—a temptation to the deadly sins of pride and anger, chiefly, but one might also add sloth. My grandmother McCarthy, I am sure, would have been a better woman if she had been an atheist or an agnostic. The Catholic religion, I believe, is the most dangerous of all, morally (I do not know about the Moslem), because, with its claim to be the only true religion, it fosters that sense of privilege I spoke of earlier—the notion that not everyone is lucky enough to be a Catholic.

I am not sorry to have *been* a Catholic, first of all for practical reasons. It gave me a certain knowledge of the Latin language and of the saints and their stories which not everyone is lucky enough to have. Latin, when I came to study it, was easy for me and attractive, too, like an old friend; as for the saints, it is extremely useful to know them and the manner of their martyrdom when you are looking at Italian painting, to know, for instance, that a tooth is the emblem of Saint Apollonia, patron of dentistry, and that Saint Agnes is shown with a lamb, always, and Saint Catherine of Alexandria with a wheel. To read Dante and Chaucer or the English Metaphysicals or even T. S. Eliot, a Catholic education is more than a help. Having to learn a little theology as an adult in order to understand a poem of Donne or Crashaw is like being taught the Bible as Great Literature in a college humanities course; it does not stick to the ribs. Yet most students in America have no other recourse than to take these vitamin injections to make good the cultural deficiency.

If you are born and brought up a Catholic, you have absorbed a good deal of world history and the history of ideas before you are twelve, and it is like learning a language early; the effect is indelible. Nobody else in America, no other group, is in this fortunate position. Granted that Catholic history is biased, it is not dry or dead; its virtue for the student, indeed, is that it has been made to come alive by the violent partisanship which inflames it. This partisanship, moreover, acts as a magnet to attract stray pieces of information not ordinarily taught in American schools. While children in public schools were studying American history, we in the convent in the eighth grade were studying English history down to the time of Lord Palmerston; the reason for this was, of course, that English history, up to Henry VIII, was Catholic history, and, after that, with one or two interludes, it became anti-Catholic history. Naturally, we were taught to sympathize with Bloody Mary (never called that in the convent), Mary Queen of Scots, Philip of Spain, the martyr Jesuits, Charles I (married to a Catholic princess), James II (married first to a Protestant and then to Mary of Modena), the Old Pretender, Bonnie Prince Charlie; interest petered out with Peel and Catholic Emancipation. To me, it does not matter that this history was one-sided (this can always be remedied later); the important thing is to have learned the

battles and the sovereigns, their consorts, mistresses, and prime ministers, to know the past of a foreign country in such detail that it
becomes one's own. Had I stayed in the convent, we would have gone
on to French history, and today I would know the list of French kings
and their wives and ministers, because French history, up to the Revolution, was Catholic history, and Charlemagne, Joan of Arc, and
Napoleon were all prominent Catholics.

Nor is it only a matter of knowing more, at an earlier age, so that it
becomes a part of oneself; it is also a matter of feeling. To care for the
quarrels of the past, to identify oneself passionately with a cause that
became, politically speaking, a losing cause with the birth of the modern world, is to experience a kind of straining against reality, a rebellious nonconformity that, again, is rare in America, where children
are instructed in the virtues of the system they live under, as though
history had achieved a happy ending in American civics.

So much for the practical side. But it might be pointed out that to
an American educator, my Catholic training would appear to have no
utility whatever. What is the good, he would say, of hearing the drone
of a dead language every day or of knowing that Saint Ursula, a Bre-
ton princess, was martyred at Cologne, together with ten thousand
virgins? I have shown that such things proved to have a certain usefulness in later life—a usefulness that was not, however, intended at
the time, for we did not study the lives of the saints in order to look at
Italian painting or recite our catechism in order to read John Donne.
Such an idea would be atrocious blasphemy. We learned those things
for the glory of God, and the rest, so to speak, was added to us. Nor
would it have made us study any harder if we had been assured that
what we were learning was going to come in handy in later life, any
more than children study arithmetic harder if they are promised it
will help them later on in business. Nothing is more boring to a child
than the principle of utility. The final usefulness of my Catholic training was to teach me, together with much that proved to be practical, a
conception of something prior to and beyond utility ("Consider the
lilies of the field, they toil not, neither do they spin"), an idea of sheer
wastefulness that is always shocking to non-Catholics, who cannot
bear, for example, the contrast between the rich churches and the
poor people of southern Europe. Those churches, agreed, are a folly,
so is the life of a dirty anchorite or of a cloistered, non-teaching nun—
unprofitable for society and bad for the person concerned. But I prefer to think of them that way than to imagine them as an investment,

shares bought in future salvation. I never really liked the doctrine of Indulgences—the notion that you could say five Hail Marys and knock off a year in Purgatory. This seemed to me to belong to my grandmother McCarthy's kind of Catholicism. What I liked in the Church, and what I recall with gratitude, was the sense of mystery and wonder, ashes put on one's forehead on Ash Wednesday, the blessing of the throat with candles on St. Blaise's Day, the purple palls put on the statues after Passion Sunday, which meant they were hiding their faces in mourning because Christ was going to be crucified, the ringing of the bell at the Sanctus, the burst of lilies at Easter—all this ritual, seeming slightly strange and having no purpose (except the throat-blessing), beyond commemoration of a Person Who had died a long time ago. In these exalted moments of altruism the soul was fired with reverence.

Hence, as a lapsed Catholic, I do not trouble myself about the possibility that God may exist after all. If He exists (which seems to me more than doubtful), I am in for a bad time in the next world, but I am not going to bargain to believe in God in order to save my soul. Pascal's wager—the bet he took with himself that God existed, even though this could not be proved by reasoning—strikes me as too prudential. What had Pascal to lose by behaving as if God existed? Absolutely nothing, for there was no counter-Principle to damn him in case God didn't. For myself, I prefer not to play it so safe, and I shall never send for a priest or recite an Act of Contrition in my last moments. I do not mind if I lose my soul for all eternity. If the kind of God exists Who would damn me for not working out a deal with Him, then that is unfortunate. I should not care to spend eternity in the company of such a person.

from *HERETIC'S HEART: A JOURNEY THROUGH SPIRIT AND REVOLUTION*

MARGOT ADLER

Margot Adler, New York bureau chief for National Public Radio, grew up trying to make sense of the divergent worldviews of her divorced parents: her mother a flamboyant, Yiddish-speaking leftist radical, and her father an atheist, Marxist Jew raised Protestant by his father, the renowned psychiatrist, Alfred Adler. In these selections from her recent autobiography, Heretic's Heart: A Journey Through Spirit and Revolution, *Adler contemplates this complex lineage along with the roots of her own Pagan spirituality, fueled by the transformative tales of goddesses heard as a child, transporting her to other worlds with story and song.*

GROWING UP in the atheist, semi-Marxist, non-Jewish, Jewish home my parents created, it took me until I was about five to learn the name of our religion, and even then it was only because I finally asked. "We believe," I was told, "in the brotherhood of man." It was a statement that I knew had something to do with people being good and treating each other with respect, but many questions remained. What *was* the brotherhood of man, what did it *feel* like, and did it include *me?* Perhaps, I thought, it was like the word *mensch,* a word that on the surface simply meant a human being, but was tinged by the emotions of my family and friends to mean a real person, a good person, a person who is generous and loving—a progressive, a person that lives according to good values.

And my family did. Although during the middle of my teenage rebellion, and in my own anger at my parents' divorce, I would scream at my father—that he was a hypocrite, that he talked a good Marxist line but my mother had actually done more politically, that he spoke of a beautiful society while making a wreck of his own family—in actual fact, both my parents did live pretty much according to their principles.

And although, given his age and his era, my father had a tendency to expect his wives to cater to him, he preached gender equality before it was fashionable, and he was a talented therapist to a group of well-known feminist writers. His tastes were simple: he had no car, no credit cards, no country house, no assortment of those gismos and gadgets that most baby boomers today expect.

But our religion, the Brotherhood of Man, seemed pretty sterile, despite its high ethics, and I grew up believing that my Catholic friends had a better deal.

Then, in 1951, my mother had an experience of recognition and revelation that brought her back to her Jewish roots. It took place during that same trip to Europe that brought back the Eisler records with their Bach labels. She later told the story with such passion that it seemed almost sacrilegious to question any part of it.

"The family had arrived in Berlin," my mother recounted, "and we were waiting to change planes when a German official came up to us and said, 'Ihre Papiere, bitte!' [Your papers, please!] And suddenly, at that moment, I smelled the fires of Buchenwald in my nostrils." Then we entered the plane and my mother sat down with me next to a very old rabbi with a very long white beard. "You were sitting in my lap," she said to me, "and you began to play with his beard. You stuck out your tongue and began to lick his beard. I asked the rabbi if we were disturbing him, and he said, 'Nein.' Then he leaned over and whispered, 'Sind Sie eine Deutsche?' [German?] and I said, 'Nein.' And then he whispered, 'Sind Sie Jüden?' and I screamed, 'Yes! And what's more I speak Yiddish fluently!'" My mother said she spent the rest of the plane ride conversing in the Yiddish she had spoken as a child.

When we returned to New York my mother told me, "You're Jewish!" To which my father replied, "No she's not!" Both statements were true. My father was so totally assimilated he had not even been circumcised, much less been given two seconds' worth of Jewish education. But my mother said that not only was I Jewish because I was her daughter, but that anyone Hitler considered a Jew *was* a Jew, and therefore she and my father were equally Jewish, even if my father had no idea what being Jewish was about.

Now that my mother, who had once changed her name and invented stories of a partly French origin, had decided she was Jewish, she decided to embrace Jewish culture. So Freyda called up relatives with whom she had almost nothing in common and invited them—perhaps to their great embarrassment—to a party to celebrate her rapprochement with her heritage. To my father, who grew up with no such traditions, my mother's new enthusiasm seemed bizarre. By conviction an atheist, and brought up in an ostensibly Protestant home, Jewish religion and culture had no echo for him.

I have always believed, rightly or wrongly, that the seeds of my parents' disaffection began with that plane trip from Berlin, and in fact, within a year my father (not always the prince of tact) had said within my presence that he *liked* my mother, but he did not love her. Whatever the truth, the question of my Jewishness would forever in the future involve conflict. Was I in the box or outside it? Was I my mother's daughter or my father's? Being Jewish seemed to mean choosing, something I was determined not to do. And in the end, such religious discord, coupled with my clear love of ceremony and classical myths, propelled me toward a very different religious community.

•   •   •

... Just after I turned nine I began to travel to school by myself on the New York City subways. My mother trained me carefully, over a period of weeks, showing me how to enter the subway and where to change trains. Often I would stand mesmerized in the front car, looking out at the tracks speeding by below. Pushed and pummeled by rush-hour crowds, on one wintry day I found myself tightly pressed into the folds of a woman's luxurious fur coat. I let myself cuddle in the soft fur unobserved. At the Twelfth Street exit, I would climb up the stairs and walk less than a hundred yards to the doors of my school, City and Country. Almost everything that was eventually to dominate my life—music, ancient history, Pagan spirituality—began for me at this tiny Greenwich Village school.

.   .   .

What was this notion of song that floated in and out of all my years of education, and yet had little to do with the piano lessons I was given as a child, or the musical theory courses I later took in high school? Music, like books, became an integral part of my fantasy life. I would sit at the piano for hours, not practicing, but letting my hands stray through the keys, improvising, while my thoughts returned to far-off ages. I would dream of being historical figures gleaned from books, or new creations that emerged from novels but took on a life of their own, transformed in my head.

My memories of City and Country are infused with songs—folk songs, work songs, holiday songs, rounds, madrigals, songs in African and European languages. By the time I left the school, at the age of fourteen, I knew by heart at least half the songs in the *Fireside Book of Folk Songs,* as well as hundreds of others that were handed out on mimeographed sheets, handwritten in fading purple ink. I remember slipping unnoticed into the music room before graduation and rifling through the file cabinets, taking one copy of each song. I sorted and stapled the sheets together. When I was done, I had thirty-six sea chanteys, twenty-three work songs, forty carols, and fifty-six rounds.

.   .   .

What was it about singing that led me to feel such joy? As an only and lonely child, I found separation the constant theme of relationship, and music the binder and healer. Although I had always been able to put an end to my own feelings of estrangement by staring into a bonfire or entering nature, song was a doorway into an entirely new world. It was a group creation, a way into a shared state of ecstatic harmony.

.   .   .

City and Country not only allowed me to float in a river of song, when I was ten years old the school also introduced me to the power of ritual. At 4:00 A.M. on the first of May, 1957, my mother and I set out for school. We took the subway, joining riders who were already beginning their working day. I noticed bakers and painters, their overalls smeared with the white of paint and dough.

Before dawn our class was taken to the country, where we were led to gardens filled with pink and white and purple flowers. As the sky slowly reddened and the sun rose, we picked armfuls of budding branches. When we were laden with more than we could carry, we returned to school. We walked up the stairs, singing medieval May Day carols, our arms filled with blossoms. How simple and unexpected and joyous to give such gifts! Later we danced around the maypole, as we would every year.

Ever since that May morning I have understood that ritual has the power to end our alienation from the earth and from each other. It allows us to enter a world where we are at home with trees and stars and other beings, and even with the carefully hidden and protected parts of ourselves that we sometimes contact in dreams or in art. More gentle, but also more powerful than many a drug, ritual returns us to our always present but often unfelt, connected selves.

City and Country was also where I first met the Pagan gods. I resonated with the wildness of Artemis, her solitary ways in nature, but I also wanted Athena's strength, the wisdom and political savvy of the goddess of a great city. These two goddesses seemed so much more powerful than any of the images of women that surrounded me at home and school. The real women around me were shockingly vulnerable, even if they talked boldly and brazenly at times. I watched my own flamboyant, theatrical, and seemingly invincible mother fall into depression after her divorce. I looked at my mother's friends—all earthy, funny and wise, but they had all sacrificed careers for their husbands and children, and almost all of them were now divorced. The women around my mother were vibrant and original, but most had begun their creative work late in life and never quite lived up to their brilliance.

And so I secretly dreamed I was Athena or Artemis come down to earth, and spent hours creating fantastic adventures. Deep down, in my heretic's heart, I knew that I did not want to worship these goddesses, they were beings I desperately wanted to become.

Looking back at my years at City and Country, it doesn't seem odd to me that I adopted the ancient Greek religion as my own. Mythology and nature were the only real elements of religion I encountered, and they were powerful.

. . .

I'm riding on a bus through East Germany. It's 1973 and my revolutionary days are behind me, but somehow I have agreed to join a delegation of socialists and peace activists for a tour of the GDR. The bus is traveling between Potsdam and Dresden, and as I look out the window am I thinking about these historic cities and their fate in World War II? Or about communism? Not at all. I am debating about whether or not I am going to join a Witches' coven.

"You must be kidding," I think in my mother's tone of voice, although I then realize she would never condemn such a move. I remember the books on her shelves, *Zen and the Art of Archery* and *The Way of Zen* by Alan Watts. And I think to myself, "Once I almost joined the Communist Party, and once I thought the only honorable profession was to be a full-time revolutionary. Perhaps Marx was right, history first appears as tragedy, and then as farce. Here I am standing at the precipice once again, but this time I am asking: Shall I become a Witch?"

And then it hits me: if it doesn't work out, I could always leave! Why did such a simple thought never occur to me during my two other attempts to leap over the edge? Perhaps because in my family tradition Witches didn't even exist, so becoming a Witch couldn't have seemed like an act of commitment. Becoming a communist and ensuring yourself a large FBI file was far more serious, although the truth is that today both Wicca and communism can get you fired from a job, or give the other side in a divorce the ammunition it needs to win a custody battle.

My religious and political confusion had permeated my working life. I'd become sick of journalism, of reporting what the columnist Russell Baker dismissed as "olds": coups, tornadoes, disasters, crimes, political upheavals, wars. Like Baker, I sought "news": archeological finds, scientific discoveries, things we might actually care about in a hundred years or more. I desperately searched for the longer view, the more eternal.

. . .

It is 1996. I am walking on South Road, in Chilmark, back on Martha's Vineyard. I pass the Abel's Hill cemetery, where so many Mayhews, Flanderses, Pooles, Tiltons, Larsens, Nortons—the old names of this island community—are buried. Lillian Hellman is

buried here too, her small, thin black stone difficult to find, surrounded by shells. Most people come here to see the grave of John
Belushi, and to participate in a ritual as poignant in its own way as the
letters and flowers left at the Vietnam Wall. On the top of the rough
boulder that marks his grave is a constantly changing altar created by
people meditating on their addictions. This morning's collection is
small: a beer bottle, two pennies (a potent symbol for our culture's
greatest addiction), a cigarette butt, a piece of candy (ah, my own
addiction), a wild rose (attended by visiting yellow jackets), some
rocks, a clam shell. In the past, I've seen pills, rolling papers, a coke
spoon.

The human tendency to connect to others, to ancestors, and to the
cosmos through simple ritual, despite the stigma in our secular culture, amazes me. People create ceremony everywhere they go. Sometimes the occasions are obvious: the birthday parties, Thanksgiving
dinners, and religious celebrations. Others are more surprising—just
watch the thousands who hold up cigarette lighters in darkened
rock concert cathedrals. Or, in New York City, on the night before
Thanksgiving, when thousands gather in the streets to watch while
the floats for the Macy's parade are pumped up with helium. As at
some great Latin American festival, tiny children sit on their parents'
shoulders or are held up to watch in awe as Superman or Spiderman
or Snoopy begin to form from oblivion, a giant hand, a foot, a head,
appearing as once did the gods of old. We can mourn that our car-
toon gods seem lightweights in comparison to those of the Greeks,
but people make do; they create gods from what they are given. And,
as writer Patricia Monaghan once said, "Our culture doesn't
encounter the mysteries very well—we do birth, death, even marriage very badly."

As I sit by this graveyard I think about how ritual allows us to enter
a different realm, the timeless one.

The Old Left was so afraid of the irrational. Although many of my
parents' friends stood reverent as they watched artists paint, or listened to a symphony or a poem, most were afraid to enter the artistic,
dream realm themselves, and it is no wonder. My parents and their
generation understood the misuse of religion, the self-delusion that
leads to witchhunts. Dogmatists, many of them, they were also afraid
they would be taken over, subsumed, overwhelmed, because in their
world, everything is either/or. There is mysticism or rationality, good

or evil, male or female, light or dark, Christian or Pagan. I've come to realize those choices never made sense to me.

. . .

In our either/or obsessive world, people go from one totalistic belief to another, from one cult to another, from one religious or ideological war to another. Skepticism and mystery are sworn enemies. You are either a socialist or a capitalist, although the truth of the world is mostly mixed economies. You are either a skeptic or a believer, instead of having spiritual faith but being at home with constant doubt. This mentality works something like addiction—it's all or nothing. Either you think LSD will save the world, or you think everyone who takes it will lose his or her mind. But many people really can have a glass of wine without being alcoholics.

The world of the Old Left had great truths, but its principal failing was that it could not bridge these divisions. It was too afraid of the irrational and its pull, and it did not really understand the human need for the juice and mystery of ecstatic experience; it did not realize that one can enter the flow of the mysterious the non-ordinary reality known to all artists, poets, and indigenous peoples without losing one's intellectual integrity; that one can dance round a bonfire until dawn and still make one's living as a scientist or a computer programmer; that one can work to end poverty and exploitation but still embrace song and dance and dream. Like shamans of old, we can attempt to maintain our balance as we walk in different worlds.

In my own life, I still begin each project with the question, What can I do to turn the world upside down, to question assumptions, to undermine received wisdom?

. . .

My own evolution over the last twenty-five years, to embrace the earth traditions, the Pagan traditions, was partly a way to make my peace with the dreamer and doubter, this person who loved multiplicity, who would never be pleased with a single reality, truth, or map.

Though not for everyone, the earth traditions allow me a life of balance, and allow me to remain optimistic; they allow me the grace of perceiving the cup as always half full, never half empty. These traditions say that all is holy, the body, the mind, the imagination, birth, sex, death—and that the stuff of the sacred is all around us, right here, right now, in the material world. You don't have to die to get the good stuff—which doesn't mean that other worlds besides the material do not exist.

I know now that the mysteries are everywhere. It is not necessary to read a holy book, or hear a divine revelation; the mysteries are in seed and scarlet leaf, and in the *doing* which has very little to do with *believing*.

I am singing again, as I did as a child, and collecting rounds and chants. I have realized that chant and song is my pathway to the stars, and that I have a talent to bring others to share in ecstatic song, so that those who have been told they can't sing can throw caution to the wind and come into their own voice, to sing, to shout, to ululate, to listen, to explore, to experiment, to harmonize.

We sit in a circle and my friend Eclipse is drumming—the deep, sonorous sounds of the Jimbe, her arms strong and muscled from such continuous work. Others join with drums and bells and rattles. I am leading a circle of song. Then comes the lingering tone of a deep bell; then silence, candlelight, and sage. "It is time to remember," says Eclipse. And the women, and sometimes men as well, let imagination, fantasy, (or is it memory?) take them (forward? back?) to a magical place, and their voices call out to one another in the darkness:

"Bare feet on cool stone floors." "A canopy of stars." "A waterfall." "The sounds of crickets." "A procession of dancers with urns on their heads and snakes coiled around their arms." The voices continue to create a place for ceremony.

And then the chants—most of them from the various contemporary communities of women, Pagans, Witches, but also a sprinkling of songs from the East, and from indigenous people, all of them simple, so that it is easy to soar, to call and respond, to break into parts, to occasionally add drumming and dancing, and to learn, once again, what earth-based peoples have always known: that to sing something over and over for a very long time (long for us, that is, we who often grow uncomfortable when something lasts for more than fifteen minutes) stops the intolerable busyness of our culture, so that we can return to that eternal stream the ancients knew when they performed their ecstatic rites.

From coast to coast, the sons and daughters of immigrants are singing and drumming—in small groups and large, under trees, in churches, in living rooms. The sons and daughters of slaves are singing also. They are also reading, researching, writing, creating, rooting around in the ashes for something more. They know that their ancestors had rich traditions that were thrown away or destroyed by others. They also know some of these traditions were oppressive. Their work may seem silly to outsiders, but they have taken on a huge task—to create anew what was lost, a vibrant culture, filled with songs, ceremonies, dances, lullabies, myths. To create such a culture—one that is rich yet at home with notions of individual freedom and modern life—what a Herculean task!

But a possible one. And as the last flames flicker out and the last tone dissipates, each person returns to their ordinary life with some small remnant of the incredibly subversive notion that the world and we can be transformed and reborn, that "we are as gods and might as well get good at it."

Almost all initiatory journeys return to the beginning, and, as in the famous poem, the wanderer knows the place for the first time. The journey of his barefoot minstrel starts in the place where nature and music and mystery abound, and where talents and dreams flourish. Then, as in all such journeys, there is the exposure to fears and trials, and teachers both good and bad; there is the great toll that society and culture always extracts, the long time when dreams and talents and desires are submerged, and the ensuing struggle for freedom and values. At the end of my own journey there is a return to ritual and song.

I think back to that old school picture—the ten-year-old girl with the fake lute and the pageboy haircut, singing about a falcon's escape and yearning to be a minstrel, wishing to be like Constance Clume, giving courage to the troops as they prepare to fight for freedom. And I finally know to be true what I never believed before: that there really are minstrels in the world, perhaps millions. How lucky to finally claim my heritage as one of them.

from *AN ORPHAN IN HISTORY*

PAUL COWAN

Originally published in 1982, six years before his untimely death from leukemia, Village Voice *journalist Paul Cowan's* An Orphan in History *navigates the tension between observance and modernity in his search for his Jewish roots. Raised by highly assimilated, highly successful parents ambivalent about their Jewishness, Cowan was taught both the lure and the pain of "passing" in an elite WASP world. With the stark realization that his past had been "amputated," Cowan writes of his triumphant struggle to reclaim the traditions of his ancestors while remaining fully American.*

FOR MORE than four years now, I have been embarked on a wondrous, confusing voyage through time and culture. Until 1976, when I was thirty-six, I had always identified myself as an American Jew. Now I am an American and a Jew. I live at once in the years 1982 and 5743, the Jewish year in which I am publishing this book. I am Paul Cowan, the New York-bred son of Louis Cowan and Pauline Spiegel Cowan, Chicago-born, very American, very successful parents; and I am Saul Cohen, the descendant of rabbis in Germany and Lithuania. I am the grandson of Modie Spiegel, a mailorder magnate, who was born a Reform Jew, became a Christian Scientist, and died in his spacious house in the wealthy gentile suburb of Kenilworth, Illinois, with a picture of Jesus Christ in his breast pocket; and of Jacob

Cohen, a used-cement-bag dealer from Chicago, an Orthodox Jew, who lost everything he had—his wife, his son, his business, his self-esteem—except for the superstition-tinged faith that gave moments of structure and meaning to his last, lonely years.

As a child, growing up on Manhattan's East Side, I lived among Jewish WASPs. My father, an only child, had changed his name from Cohen to Cowan when he was twenty-one. He was so guarded about his youth that he never let my brother or sisters or me meet any of his father's relatives. I always thought of myself as a Cowan—the Welsh word for stonecutter—not a Cohen—a member of the Jewish priestly caste. My family celebrated Christmas and always gathered for an Easter dinner of ham and sweet potatoes. At Choate, the Episcopalian prep school to which my parents sent me, I was often stirred by the regal hymns we sang during the mandatory chapel service. In those years, I barely knew what a Passover seder was. I didn't know anyone who practiced archaic customs such as keeping kosher or lighting candles on Friday night. Neither my parents nor I ever mentioned the possibility of a bar mitzvah. In 1965, I fell in love with Rachel Brown, a New England Protestant whose ancestors came here in the seventeenth century. It didn't matter the least bit to her—or to me—that we were an interfaith marriage.

Now, at forty-two, I care more about Jewish holidays I'd never heard of back then, Shavuot or Simchat Torah, than about Christmas or Easter. In 1980, fifteen years after we were married, Rachel converted to Judaism, and is now program director of Ansche Chesed, a neighborhood synagogue we are trying to revitalize. Our family lights Friday night candles, and neither Rachel nor I work on the Sabbath. Since 1974, our children, Lisa and Matt, have gone to the Havurah School, a once-a-week Jewish school we started, and at fourteen and twelve they're more familiar with the Torah than I was five years ago. They are very thoughtful children, who have witnessed the changes in our family's life and are somewhat bemused and ambivalent about them. There is no telling whether they'll follow the path we have chosen. But that is true of all children. This past September, Lisa undertook the difficult task of learning enough Hebrew in six months to chant a full Haftorah (a prophetic text) at her bat mitzvah at Ansche Chesed. That day I was as happy as I've ever been in my life.

By now, I see the world through two sets of eyes, my American ones and my Jewish ones. That is enhanced, I suppose, by the fact that my father, who was once president of CBS-TV, who produced "The Quiz

Kids," "Stop the Music," and "The $64,000 Question," and my elegant mother, an ardent civil-rights activist, moved easily through all sorts of worlds. Even now, as a journalist, I want to be at once a versatile American writer like James Agee or John Dos Passos and an evocative Jewish one like Isaac Bashevis Singer or Chaim Potok. Sometimes it makes me feel deeply conflicted. Sometimes it makes my life seem wonderfully rich and varied. I do know this: that my mind is enfolded like a body in a prayer shawl, by my ancestral past and its increasingly strong hold on my present. Scores of experiences have caused me to re-create myself, to perceive a five-thousand-year-old tradition as a new, precious part of my life.

I am not alone. Indeed, I believe my story, with all its odd, buried, Old World family mysteries, with its poised tension between material wealth and the promise of spiritual wealth, is the story of much of my generation, Jew and gentile alike.

It is also, of course, the story of a faith—Judaism—which remained a powerful force in my family despite my parents' outwardly assimilated lives. I have a brother, Geoff, forty, and two sisters, Holly, thirty-eight, and Liza, thirty-four. Right now Holly and I are more religiously observant than Geoff or Liza. But the four of us all live lives whose Jewish flavor would have been unimaginable to us when we were young. I know that, for my part, I am reacting to the rootlessness I felt as a child—to the fact that for all the Cowan family's warmth, for all its intellectual vigor, for all its loyalty toward each other, our pasts had been amputated. We were orphans in history.

More important, I think, we were reacting to strong messages both our parents were sending—messages that made us feel a duty and a desire to find a way back home. When I was in grade school, my mother's ideas influenced me more directly than my father's. Polly was an active, attractive person—the only woman I've ever known who cared as much about elegance as she did about social justice. Her cool organizational style and dazzling smile left a lasting impression on everyone she met. But underneath it all, she felt a passionate turbulence about her background that left a deep impression on me.

Polly, whose German-Jewish family had come to America in 1848, was haunted by the Holocaust. Sometimes she became obsessed with small details that reminded her of that era. When I was a little boy, if my hair flopped down over my eyes, she would tell me I looked like Hitler and insist that I brush it back. Until I was in my mid-teens in the 1950s, she never permitted me to walk through the Yorkville section of New York, since the Nazis had once been strong in that German-American neighborhood. Those rather quirky attitudes blended in with the certainty—which she repeated as a litany—that even in America, even for wealthy Jewish merchants like the Spiegels or successful show business people like the Cowans, outward prosperity, apparent mobility, had nothing to do with real security. She and my father sent me to fine schools, which prepared me to become part of the American elite. She seemed to agree when my father urged me to get a Ph.D., but in quieter conversations, when we were shopping together or talking late at night, she'd insist that I learn a trade—not a profession, but a trade—since she secretly believed that one day we'd have to leave all our goods and money behind and flee to some strange foreign land, where my survival would be insured by a skill that didn't depend on language.

But her feelings about the Holocaust also imbued her—and us—with a secular messianism: a deep commitment to the belief that we had a lifelong debt to the six million dead. We could repay some of it, she always insisted, by fighting anti-Semitism wherever we encountered it. Furthermore, she believed that our history of oppression obliged us to combat all forms of injustice. Because of her influence, most of our family was involved in the civil-rights movement, particularly in the Mississippi Freedom Summer in 1964. Geoff and I registered voters in the Delta and Vicksburg. Polly organized groups of northern black and white women to spend time in the state's segregated communities, arranging covert integrated meetings. Holly sent out a newsletter about the Summer Project. Lou, frightened for us but proud, used all the influence he'd acquired as a television executive and confidant of politicians to keep us out of trouble and promote our causes.

There was no doubt in any of our minds that we were risking our lives to achieve the very American goal of integration because our kinsmen had been slaughtered in Lithuania, Poland, and Germany.

But it never occurred to me, back then, that my mother's intense, sometimes reverent, sometimes frightened feelings about the six million would leave me with a thirst for the inner details of the faith she knew nothing about, whose name she wanted me to defend.

In retrospect, I realize that my father must always have half hoped that I would develop that thirst. Indeed, he promoted it toward the end of his life, when he was in his sixties and I was in my thirties. But as I was growing up, I thought he wanted to divorce himself forever from the religious world he'd known as a boy in Chicago. He never talked very much about his father, Jake Cohen, but the few details he did divulge portrayed my grandfather as a cruel man: harsh and nasty toward his wife, Hetty Cohen (whom my father adored), subject to inexplicable rages that would occasionally cause Jake to order his son Lou to sleep on the kitchen floor. Sometimes Jake would leave his wife and child and work, with no explanation and no warning, so that he could attend a boxing match in Detroit or New Jersey. Incredibly, he seemed to begrudge his only son all his teenage triumphs. He never came to see Lou compete in track and field championships. When Lou was elected president of his high school student council, Jake looked at him mockingly and asked, "Why did they choose you?"

Lou felt that he had been saved from Jake Cohen by his mother's bachelor brother, his uncle Harry Smitz (whom Lou always called Holly). He liked to tell an anecdote that illustrated the contrast between those relationships. When Lou was a high school senior, his track team won a city championship. But Lou didn't receive any awards. When he came home that night, very upset, Jake Cohen asked him, "what made you think you deserved to win anything?" Holly Smitz had a medal he always wore on his watch. He gave it to his nephew and said, "That's your award."

Lou called or visited his mother almost every day of his adult life. I remember him weeping for hours when she died in 1949.

He rarely saw Jake Cohen. He did send him seventy-five dollars a week and I recall his telling us, with irritation in his voice, that Jake, destitute, was always nagging him for more. Jake died in 1950. I can't remember my father mentioning that fact.

Once, when I was a boy, my father told me that he recalled the Yom Kippurs he went to synagogue and watched Jake Cohen weep and beat his breast to atone for his sins. Then, after services, Lou would walk home with his parents and the rest of the huge Cohen clan and listen, appalled, as they fought over status and money; as they gossiped cruelly about siblings who weren't there. That wasn't religion, my father would tell me angrily. That was hypocrisy.

Now, though, as I review my childhood, I remember random words and gestures which hinted that my father had emotional roots in the world the Cohens inhabited—roots that flowered into ideas and activities late in his life.

He was a distinctly Jewish-looking man, while everyone else in our family was ethnically indistinguishable. He was about six foot two inches and always overweight. My mother would glance fondly at his slightly soft body, talk wryly about the incredible amount of worried attention he lavished on us, and tell her children that her husband was our real Jewish mother. He had a large nose (my mother would occasionally touch my small one and tell me she was glad it wasn't big like his), and a quick, ready smile, an eager way of listening, that made people realize at once that he was alert to every nuance of their mood. I have a childhood memory of watching my father move from table to table at the show business hangouts like Sardi's which he frequented because of his job, working the room like a skilled politician. He made everyone he met feel singularly important, looking at them continuously, never gazing off to see if a more powerful person was somewhere else in the room. He communicated warmth through his attentive silences, through his ability to reach out and touch people fondly, not sensuously or aggressively. And he was always ready with a compliment; when he introduced his friends to each other, he always seemed to be orchestrating what was best in them. He was protective, not threatening.

Sometimes, slightly self-mockingly, he'd use one of his few Yiddish words to describe his behavior to my mother. He had *shmeicheled* (buttered up) someone. But he was doing himself a slight injustice. For though he could be cunning about people's strengths and weaknesses, he rarely let himself dwell for long on their flaws. At dinner he'd often tell us that some friend, some colleague, was "a darling man"—that was his favorite expression. He wooed people, but rarely considered that they might have self-serving reasons for staying inside his orbit. He shmeicheled with love.

I have been writing about his public persona. But inside the family, there were other, more intimate ways that Louis Cohen's ethnic past revealed itself through Louis G. Cowan's cosmopolitan present. For example, I always knew that he didn't like to eat pork, but I believed my mother's teasing assertion that he was displaying a silly, endearing superstition akin to his belief that if you had bubbles in your coffee you'd get rich. But when I remember the involuntary look of disgust that sometimes passed over his face when we had pork chops for dinner, I think that his reflexive aversion to the meat that's forbidden to religiously observant Jews might have provided a glimpse of tangled, powerful feelings he was unable to express openly—unable, perhaps, to express to himself.

On Sundays, when I was a boy, he would often take the entire family down to the Lower East Side, which was still a predominantly Jewish neighborhood. Our ostensible mission would be to buy some bagels and lox and challah. But we could have gone around the corner to do that. He would spend delighted hours lingering on those crowded, noisy streets, exploring the small stores, watching the transactions, usually in Yiddish, between the shoppers and the storeowners, who wore yarmulkes and stroked long gray beards as they talked. Back then, I thought my father liked the neighborhood because it was quaint, or because he had an insatiable curiosity for new faces, new ideas. It never crossed my mind that the place might evoke memories for him. But now I recall that, as we walked back to the car, we'd pass signs with Hebrew letters and my father, whose verbal memories of his religious childhood were so sparse and bitter, would remark with pleased amazement that he hadn't studied Hebrew for thirty years but he still could read the language. Back then, it never occurred to me to ask him why he had studied Hebrew. Now I wonder what sort of associations were tumbling around in his brain.

When I told my parents I planned to marry Rachel, I regarded the fact that she wasn't Jewish as a casual, interesting detail. I was astonished to see how unsettled my father became. Later he came to love her so much that her background didn't matter to him at all. But the memory of the quick stab of pain that crossed my father's face when I told him my good news is one I'll always carry.

It helps me understand another scene that has troubled me. Christmas was an important event in our house. My mother used to start shopping in mid-November, working from the master list she composed each year of relatives, friends, and business associates who required presents. Geoff and I had an annual date to cavort up and down Fifth Avenue just before the holiday, caroling to startled passersby, buying our parents gifts like mynah birds or a long-stemmed Sherlock Holmes pipe when we couldn't think of any useful presents. Every Christmas Eve, my father would sit down in the small, cozy study where we gathered, open up *A Christmas Carol,* and try to sustain our interest in the story we all knew by heart. We drifted away, one by one, to wrap up our presents and put them under the tree. He would always laugh—our inattention was a family tradition—but with the tone of martyrdom in his voice, which suggested there was some emotional turbulence he was fighting to conceal. Now I realize that Christmas wasn't his holiday any more than pork was his food, though he loved the day as a chance to shower gifts on his wife and children. How could Jake Cohen's son have felt completely comfortable on Christmas Eve? The expression on his face must have reflected the sense that, on such occasions, there was a hidden but unbridgeable cultural gulf between him and the Jewish-WASP family he adored.

I don't want to make Louis Cohen sound like the passive victim of forces he could not control. On the contrary, when I was growing up he wanted nothing so much as to blend in with the cosmopolitan elite. I think that when he was president of CBS-TV, he felt he had found the assimilationist utopia he'd always been seeking right there in the boardroom.

He wanted me to go to Choate, especially when my teachers at the progressive Dalton School—which boys had to leave in eighth grade—told my parents that I'd never get into a good college unless I was forced to acquire decent study habits. Once I was rejected at Exeter, his persistence overrode my mother's feeling that, at a church school, I'd encounter a sustained psychological version of the physical dangers she feared when she told me not to walk through Yorkville. My father wanted me to become friends with upper-class WASPs so that I could function in their world with the kind of ease he wished he possessed. The strategy backfired completely.

For the first two years I was at Choate, 1954 and 1955, I felt I was walking through a human minefield of anti-Semitism. Later, when I was more self-possessed and poised, the bigotry that so many people there displayed disgusted me so much that I decided I never wanted to become part of their crowd. That attitude reinforced the voice that was already in me, urging me to identify as a Jew.

I entered Choate when I was thirteen, bar mitzvah age. If I didn't know much about synagogue life, I knew even less about church life. I remember the first few times I attended the mandatory nightly chapel services. All the worshipers knew what hymns to sing. Was there a sort of spiritual telepathy that united them? I was a very scared young boy—awed by the easy suburban grace of my classmates, who seemed far more self-assured than the wealthiest assimilated Jews I had known in New York. I certainly didn't want to betray my ignorance by asking dumb questions. So it took me a very bewildered week to realize that the numbers tacked onto the church's pillars referred to the little red hymnal in front of me.

Sometimes for me that Choate chapel was a magic place. I loved the musty smell of the old wooden pews, especially on rainy days. The hymns became so important to me that I memorized dozens of them. Perhaps some, like "Onward, Christian Soldiers" and "Glorious Things of Thee Are Spoken" (which had the same melody as "Deutschland Über Alles") should have bothered me. They didn't. They awed me. So did the sight of my classmates receiving confirmation from the bishop of Connecticut, who looked majestic in his white robe and deep purple stole, with a miter in his right hand. Once in a while, usually as exams approached, I would go down to chapel for morning services, which weren't mandatory. I'd drink the grape juice and eat the wafer that symbolized communion. In a way it was superstitious. Choate's God was the only one I knew, and I figured that if I appeased Him I'd get good grades on my exams. But I knew I was also a very lonely boy, who needed to believe in a Supreme Being to ease my relentless fear.

There were about twenty-five Jewish kids out of the five hundred students at Choate. Most of them had more religious training than I, and they experienced flashes of guilt, not moments of exhilaration, during the high points of the Episcopalian ritual. On Holy Days like Rosh Hashana and Yom Kippur—whose meaning I knew, but never connected to my own life—some of them would disappear from chapel—and often from school—to participate in ceremonies I couldn't quite imagine.

One of them, Joel Cassel, had spent his first thirteen years in a Jewish community in Waterbury, Connecticut. We were friends, but we never once discussed our backgrounds or our feelings while we were at Choate. Long after we had graduated he told me that his family had kept kosher back in Waterbury, that he had had a Conservative bar mitzvah, that he'd been president of his synagogue's youth group. His father, like mine, had sent him to Choate because the school seemed like the gateway to the American dream, but his father's ambition didn't ease Joel's sense of displacement. Outwardly, he was a tough, funny kid. I envied him his ability to win friends by making our classmates laugh. But inwardly he must have hurt terribly.

The chapel services were the focus of his pain. My favorite hymns, like "Onward, Christian Soldiers," offended him so much, he told me in later years, that every single night, while the rest of us were reciting the Lord's Prayer or the Episcopalian litany, he would ask God to forgive him for being in chapel at all. He'd promise God that "If I say Christ, I don't mean it—believe me."

Every night, as the service ended, the school's headmaster would bid us to pray "through Jesus Christ, our Lord." After Yom Kippur in our junior year, the Christian words seemed so offensive to Joel that he decided to push his mood of repentance into action and defy the blessing directly. He refused to bow his head in prayer. The small symbolic revolt excited all the Jews at Choate. We met once, decided that none of us would bow our heads, and called ourselves "the Wallingford Jew Boys." It was the kind of act that would have appealed to my mother—and did appeal to the moralistic, wrathful Polly Cowan in me. I remember holding my head high those nights, feeling an incredibly strong surge of tribal loyalty that I'd never before experienced.

Our action clearly threatened the Reverend Seymour St. John, the headmaster. One night he gave a sermon insisting that if he went to a mosque he'd take off his shoes; if he went to a synagogue he'd wear a skullcap. "When in Rome, do as the Romans do," he admonished us. (None of us had the knowledge or the wit to point out that his Anglican forebears hadn't exactly followed that advice.) In only slightly veiled terms, he threatened to expel anyone who insisted on keeping his head upright. Our revolt collapsed instantly. We were isolated and vulnerable once again. Since none of us had the courage to exchange stories of the anti-Semitism we had experienced, each of us felt we were being tormented because we were personally deficient.

Wade Pearson lived next door to me during my first year at Choate. Night after night he would come into my room and lecture me about how pushy and avaricious Jews are. Did I think the character Shylock came out of Shakespeare's imagination? Did I think Fagin was a pure invention of Dickens'? No, they were generic types. I—and my kind—were just like those forebears. During those sessions, Wade's friend Chip Thornton, a fat kid who was reputed to be a great wit, would add mirth to our literary talk by calling me "the traveling muzzy" because of my acne, or making jokes about "the mockies"—a term for Jews I had never heard before.

Lester Atkins, a loutish kid who sat behind me in junior year math class, used to clamp his feet so tightly against my jacket that if I leaned forward to answer a question I'd wind up with an unmendable rip. One day he snatched my geometry book. He gave it back to me at the end of class, though he didn't tell me he'd written me a message. That night I went to my teacher's apartment to ask for help with homework. The teacher pointed to a carefully-lettered sign that had been inscribed on the upper right hand corner of the page we had been working on that day. Had I written it myself? he asked. FUCK YOU, YOU KIKE, it said.

Then there was Ned the Gimp, as he called himself, who used to limp into the common room of the dorm where we all lived one summer, and greet me with the thick, mocking Yiddish accent he had lifted from Mr. Kitzel on the old Jack Benny show. The other kids thought the routine was a riot. I know that Joel Cassel, who had been toughened by the years he had spent as one of the few Jews in the public schools of Waterbury, Connecticut, would have found some way to neutralize the Gimp with banter. I couldn't do that. Usually I'd laugh nervously, hoping that my acquiescence would allow me to blend into the gang that seemed so menacing—until the next day when the Gimp's onslaught would resume. By then, I'd read *The Sun Also Rises*. I had the terrible feeling that I was the reincarnation of the long-suffering Robert Cohen. That was reinforced when a friend of mine asked me why I was so passive when the Gimp was around. Oddly, my friend's well-meaning question hurt me even more than the Gimp's insults. For it convinced me that all the kids at Choate saw me as Robert Cohen: helpless and weak-willed: a prototypical defenseless Jew.

I never told my parents about the anti-Semitism I experienced at Choate. I never told anyone. I felt guilty about it, as if I were personally responsible for my plight. Each autumn they had a Fathers' Weekend at the school. Lou, still rising in the media world, was his usual schmeicheling self, charming the teachers with his personality, trying to cement our relationship to the school by donating a complete set of Modern Library books. I felt very much in the shadow of this energetic, self-made, successful man. I didn't want to take the risk of describing my problems, for that might make him feel that his oldest son was a failure. Besides, what could he—or Polly—do about the anti-Semitism? Complain to the headmaster? I didn't want them—or anyone—to wage my fights for me. I was very impressionable back then. In sermon after sermon, the Reverend St. John told us that Choate was a place where you took responsibility for yourself. You went "the extra mile" if you had a problem. I accepted that view. It seemed unmanly to complain.

For nearly three years, I'd lie awake every night, fantasizing about ways to escape from the school. Then I realized I didn't want to leave in what I considered disgrace. So I'd fantasize ways to impress the bigots, ways to leave with dignity.

I actually did impress them. By senior year, I was a big shot on the newspaper, the literary magazine, the debate society. I'd found a special motley substratum of bright, wacky friends—my working-class Italian roommate, who was there on a science scholarship; the son of Spanish immigrants who lived in Wallingford, where Choate was located; a very poetic jazz musician; a brilliant, worldly exchange student from Switzerland. We created a fantasy world for ourselves which mocked the real world in which our classmates lived. For example, after vacations, dozens of kids would boast about visiting two New York whores, Gussie and Sally. My roommate and I named our goldfish Gussie and Sally. In New York we'd crash the society dances, and puzzle the serious preppy girls with questions about where we could stable the polo ponies we had just brought up from Panama. At Choate, one dance weekend, we organized a folk sing where my date—about whom I'd written a very romantic story in the school literary magazine—was the star. Our classmates flocked to that, not to the formal events which the school had organized. By senior year we were bright enough and lively enough to seem quite glamorous. We had succeeded on our own terms.

But those successes created a new set of problems. Now kids who wanted to befriend me often made a conscious effort to disassociate me from other Jews. Hans Peterson, a bookish lacrosse player, came from Long Island. The Jews were taking over his home town, he would inform me, and I should know their true nature. They were loud and money-minded, bad-mannered and aggressively sarcastic. Of course, I was different: I was soft-spoken, well-read, with a taste for parody and fantasy. At least, that was his explicit message. His implicit message was that I bore direct responsibility for his new neighbors.

In my senior year, Sidney Konig, a younger Jewish kid on my corridor, was the new target of abuse. I didn't really like him. He was so whiny, so defensive, so obviously Jewish-looking, that I secretly believed he deserved the treatment he was receiving. Still, I became his ally. As seniors, my Italian roommate and I wielded power over the other kids. We'd punish anyone who mistreated Sidney.

Why, I wonder now, could I debate Hans or defend Sidney with a degree of aggressiveness I could never display when the Gimp was teasing me? My answer makes me a little uncomfortable.

It stems from my mother's insistence that in the presence of anti-Semitism I should always announce I was a Jew. What a curiously mixed message that was! For years, I thought it simply contained the willed bravery of her *noblesse oblige*. But now I realize that there was an unmistakable, slightly disdainful pride in her sense that, with my Welsh name, my brown hair, my thin nose, I could "pass" for whatever I wanted. I could be free in America, not wed to any ghetto.

So, in her opinion, as a totally assimilated Jew—or, rather, as a Jew who could escape whenever I wanted—I was supposed to remember the Holocaust and defend my less fortunate kinsmen, the Sidneys, the Jews who were moving into Hans's town on Long Island, in just the same way as I was supposed to defend the blacks.

In grade school, it never occurred to Polly—or to me—that *I* might be the Jew who needed defending. I wasn't prepared for personal abuse. When it came I was paralyzed with confusion and surprise. And I was paralyzed with the feeling that it was both self-demeaning and gauche to fight back.

My four years at Choate shattered the illusion Polly had helped implant. And they reinforced her equally strong, completely contradictory assertion that a Jew in any profession, under any name, was subject to attack.

After the four years at Choate, I could never pretend that I was and wasn't Jewish: that I could be part of a family which fought oppression in the name of the six million, and yet remain personally unscarred by anti-Semitism. I couldn't hide, except by surrendering my Jewish identity completely. Neither Wade nor Lester the Lout nor Ned the Gimp cared at all whether my name was Paul or Saul, Cowan or Cohen; whether I went to chapel or synagogue on Yom Kippur; whether I bowed my head and said an Episcopalian litany or held it high and recited the Shema. Either way, I was a Shylock, a Mr. Kitzel, a kike.

Once I'd been through that experience, my mother's message about the six million became, perhaps, the single most important fact of my life. For, though I didn't begin to understand the consequences of my feelings for decades, I knew from then on that it was unthinkable that anyone would ever separate me from my tribe.

· · ·

It was at Choate that my fascination with my grandfather Jacob Cohen began. At Dalton where I lived in an assimilated world of liberal, tolerant peers, he seemed like an oddity, a cruel man who had caused my father great pain, but who bore little connection to me. But at Choate, where I was an outsider, my identity as Paul Cowan, the son of a TV producer and a mail-order heiress, sometimes seemed like a disguise.

As a result, I began to dwell on the fact that I was the grandson of someone named Cohen: an Orthodox Jew, an impoverished used-cement-bag dealer from Chicago. Of course, I had no idea of what an Orthodox Jew was or what a used-cement-bag dealer did. But I wanted very much to know. So gradually, imperceptibly, while my teachers at Choate praised me for adapting so well to the school's environment, I began to feel impelled to search for a link between Jake Cohen's world and mine.

My father was the only link, but he was rarely willing to talk about the past. So I remember very clearly the night he sat up with Geoff and me in the small, book-lined study of our apartment, eating ice cream while he reminisced. He began by describing his early days as a public relations man in Chicago, where he'd handled accounts like the Aragon and Trianon ballrooms, where he'd publicized bandleaders like Kay Kyser, Wayne King, and Ted Weems. I loved those stories, loved the gritty feel of the streets in Chicago's uptown section where he'd worked, loved the fact that my father, now so at home in the CBS boardroom, had once earned about half his money as the owner of Riverside Roller Rink in Chicago. In the shank of that intimate night, I asked him to tell us more about the Cohen family.

Where, in Eastern Europe, did the Cohen family come from? He said he didn't know. Then he added, "They weren't really Cohens anyway. I guess you boys don't know this, but Cohens are supposed to be part of the Jewish priestly caste. They had some other name in Europe, but they thought that America was one gigantic Jewish community, so they changed their names when they came here so that people would think they were important."

When Geoff was in college, he used the anecdote in one of his most important examinations to sum up the complete uprooting most immigrants underwent in America. When I heard Malcolm X say he'd dropped his original name because it was a slave name, I felt the angry black man was speaking for me. For America—or, at least, Americanization—had robbed my family of its name, its identity.

Geoff and I never discussed my father's story until we were in our thirties. Then we discovered that the rift between our ancestors in Europe and the Cohens in Chicago, between Jake Cohen and Lou Cowan, had been echoing in our psyches throughout our adult lives.

I tried to search for my grandfather's identity when I was in graduate school at the University of Chicago—in the Hyde Park area of the city, where the Cohens had lived. I often found myself chatting with elderly Jewish shopkeepers, asking them whether they had known Cohen, the used-cement-bag dealer. I think I imagined a wizened old man who carried used cement bags under one arm, a battered copy of *Ring Magazine* under another, and spoke with a faint Yiddish accent. I never met anyone who knew him.

By the time I was in my thirties, the Judaism that was the subtext of my childhood had emerged to form an increasingly close bond between my father and me. By then, I was a professional journalist, a staff writer for *The Village Voice*. In 1972, I set out to write a short nostalgia piece about the Jewish socialism that had once flourished on New York's Lower East Side, and discovered that there were tens of thousands of old, mostly Orthodox, Jews in the neighborhood, who lived at the poverty level of three thousand dollars a year. I wrote about them in a long article called "Jews Without Money, Revisited." More important, I felt an unexpected attraction to their world. In a way, of course, the project was a continuation of my search for Jake Cohen. I remember imagining him in the basement shuls where I spent some of my time.

A few years later I spent an afternoon in the Munkaczer tallis (prayer shawl) factory, a few blocks away from the stores and old synagogues that used to enthrall my father on those Sundays when we searched for bagels and lox on the Lower East Side. David Weiderman, seventy-two, born in Hungary, was weaving the garment on a clattering fifty-two-year-old mechanical loom. His father, who had taught him the trade, died in Hitler's Europe. Now Weiderman, isolated from his past in that small, noisy store, tried to uphold the tradition of careful religious craftsmanship he had learned as a boy. His prayer shawls were made out of pure Turkish wool. He was scornful of the cheap, mixed tallisim, imported from Israel, made of wool diluted with rayon. "Let the others do it the way they want," he said. "It's not my business. I'll do it the way it has always been done."

How proud he was of that ancient trade! For a moment I saw him as the guardian of an irrecoverable past.

That night I described David Weiderman to my father. I thought he would be mildly interested. To my astonishment, he was fascinated. The next morning he called me. He'd been thinking about the tallis maker all night. Why didn't I try to recover the past I had glimpsed in his store by writing about Orthodox Jewish craftsmen?

I couldn't, I said. The gray-bearded old sages I had seen on the Lower East Side seemed unapproachable. They reminded me of my assimilation, of my ignorance of the basic Hebrew blessings, of most holidays that marked the cycle of my ancestors' years. Besides, some were bound to know that I had married a gentile. I'd mentioned that fact in "Jews Without Money, Revisited." I didn't want to argue with them about my personal life. I feared they would treat me as an irretrievable outcast, or insist that I embrace their ways. No, I told my father. Their world was off limits to me.

But he was relentless. Every week or two he would remind me of the valuable spiritual adventure I was passing up. He would repeat his idea for a book with a greater degree of eagerness than I'd ever heard in his voice. I would recite my list of disabilities and change the subject.

If he was relentless about my Jewish present, I was relentless about his past. One night in 1975, when he was in his mid-sixties and I was in my mid-thirties, I spent an hour in the living room of the apartment of the Westbury Hotel, where he and my mother moved after all four of us children had left home, begging him to tell me the names of his Cohen kin. Grudgingly, he consented. To my surprise, he not only knew their names; he knew their occupations and the dates they had died.

He said I had one living great-uncle, Abraham Cohen, a former Republican alderman who had represented the district adjacent to the University of Chicago. The news excited me. I told him I wanted to meet this Abraham Cohen the next time I was in Chicago. I was sure I could protect my father by disguising my name and pretending I was a graduate student writing a Ph.D. thesis on Jews in American politics.

"No," he said, "don't do that. The Cohens will only hurt us. They'll ask us for money." His fear didn't make any sense to me. Our names were in the phone book. Besides, the Cowans weren't exactly a private family. If my mother and father weren't making news, my brother and I were writing it. Anyway, Jake Cohen had been dead for more than twenty years. How could one of his brothers hurt us?

Still, I obeyed my father's request. He'd had cancer and three heart attacks. I didn't want to risk stirring up memories that might kill him. But we did agree—tacitly at first, then quite openly—that when he died I'd do everything possible to uncover his missing past—and mine.

By 1976, Rachel and I were fasting on Yom Kippur. When I told my father that, he answered that were he in better health, he would join us. He had fasted every year until he was thirty, he said. I was thirty-six at the time. In all our conversations about Judaism, he had never told me that simple fact.

That Yom Kippur we talked of other Jewish traditions. A few weeks earlier I had heard of a Jewish law which says that all holy books must be buried, for to throw them out is to profane the name of the Lord. My father believed that all books were sacred. That day he told me a friend of his had searched through the Talmud and found the wording of that injunction. He planned to have it printed in specially designed letters. Then he wanted to frame it and hang it up in his office, next to his treasured copy of the First Amendment.

He never got to do that. Early in the morning of November 18, 1976, my parents' apartment at the Westbury Hotel caught on fire. They both died in their sleep.

The fire was headline news. So when I wasn't visiting the precincts of death—the police station, the funeral home, my parents' blackened apartment—I was answering condolence calls. Most were from friends. But one was very strange.

It came from a man named Bert Lazarus, who lived in Chicago but happened to be in New York on business. He said he was a cousin of my father's, on the Cohen side. In a soft, hesitant voice, he said that he had to catch a plane during the funeral. Could he come to the reception before it and pay his respects?

Lazarus was wearing a long black coat when he entered the reception room at Campbell's Funeral Home. He had chalk-gray hair and deep-set blue eyes.

Geoff and I were standing next to each other when he came in and introduced himself. After a brief, embarrassed pause, Geoff asked the question that haunted us both. What was our true family name?

Lazarus paused, surprised by the question, unsettled by Geoff's intensity.

"Why, it's Cohen, of course," he said in his soft voice. "Your great-great-grandfather Jacob Cohen was a rabbi in Lithuania."

"Where in Lithuania?" I asked.

"A town called Lidvinova. He must have been a very fine man. The oldest Orthodox synagogue in Chicago is named after him."

He hurried away a few minutes later. What a strange gift Lazarus had inadvertently brought. He had given us our identity at the moment of our parents' death.

In the weeks after the fire, I became determined to honor what had turned out to be my father's last wish—to write about Orthodox craftsmen. I was lucky to find a guide to their world—Rabbi Joseph Singer, sixty-four, born in Poland to a family of rabbis, the tenth-generation descendant of Gershon Kitover, brother-in-law of the Baal Shem Tov, the founder of the hasidic movement.

Did Lou guess that I'd find such richness in Rabbi Singer's world? Did he realize that, as I immersed myself in it, I would come to identify with the Jewish community—warm, quarrelsome, and difficult as it is, and claim its traditions as my inheritance?

As soon as I began to meet people who made that religion seem attractive, I was faced with a clear choice—a choice, indeed, about history, though I never knew how to articulate it until my sister Holly furnished the words. Should I explore Judaism, the real, living link with my ancestors and the six million? Or should I reject it, and be another conscious participant in the obliteration of five thousand years of history?

Put that way, of course, it wasn't really a choice. Maybe my parents' Judaism lacked content, maybe it was laced with ambivalence. But there was such a deep wellspring of pride at the core that everything else seemed relatively unimportant. I loved Polly's secular messianism. I missed the part of Lou that had perished in America. I have come to realize that my challenge is how to recover Saul Cohen, how to enter the religious world that would once have been his by inheritance, without relinquishing Paul Cowan and the America he loves.

from *MEMORIES, DREAMS, REFLECTIONS*

Carl Jung

A great deal of the work of Swiss psychiatrist Carl Gustav Jung, born in
1875, was devoted to analyzing images and themes of a religious nature
found in the vocabulary of the unconscious. In this excerpt from his
well-known autobiography, Memories, Dreams, Reflections, *Jung*
recounts the desultory preparation for his first Communion which he
received from his minister father. When he at last consumes the holy bread
and wine, an adolescent Jung experiences an initiation astonishingly
devoid of the terrifying mystery and transcendence he has already known
in his own secret spiritual encounters.

My father personally gave me my instruction for confirmation. It bored me to death. One day I was leafing through the catechism, hoping to find something besides the sentimental-sounding
and usually incomprehensible as well as uninteresting expatiations
on Lord Jesus. I came across the paragraph on the Trinity. Here was
something that challenged my interest: a oneness which was simultaneously a threeness. This was a problem that fascinated me because of
its inner contradiction. I waited longingly for the moment when we
would reach this question. But when we got that far, my father said,

"We now come to the Trinity, but we'll skip that, for I really understand nothing of it myself." I admired my father's honesty, but on the other hand I was profoundly disappointed and said to myself, "There we have it; they know nothing about it and don't give it a thought. Then how can I talk about my secret?"

I made vain, tentative attempts with certain of my school-fellows who struck me as reflective. I awakened no response, but, on the contrary, a stupefaction that warned me off.

In spite of the boredom, I made every effort to believe without understanding—an attitude which seemed to correspond with my father's—and prepared myself for Communion, on which I had set my last hopes. This was, I thought, merely a memorial meal, a kind of anniversary celebration for Lord Jesus who had died $1890 - 30 = 1860$ years ago. But still, he had let fall certain hints such as, "Take, eat, this is my body," meaning that we should eat the Communion bread as if it were his body, which after all had originally been flesh. Likewise we were to drink the wine which had originally been blood. It was clear to me that in this fashion we were to incorporate him into ourselves. This seemed to me so preposterous an impossibility that I was sure some great mystery must lie behind it, and that I would participate in this mystery in the course of Communion, on which my father seemed to place so high a value.

As was customary, a member of the church committee stood godfather to me. He was a nice, taciturn old man, a wheelwright in whose workshop I had often stood, watching his skill with lathe and adze. Now he came, solemnly transformed by frock coat and top hat, and took me to church, where my father in his familiar robes stood behind the altar and read prayers from the liturgy. On the white cloth covering the altar lay large trays filled with small pieces of bread. I could see that the bread came from our baker, whose baked goods were generally poor and flat in taste. From a pewter jug, wine was poured into a pewter cup. My father ate a piece of the bread, took a swallow of the wine—I knew the tavern from which it had come—and passed the cup to one of the old men. All were stiff, solemn, and, it seemed to me, uninterested. I looked on in suspense, but could not see or guess whether anything unusual was going on inside the old men. The atmosphere was the same as that of all other performances in church—baptisms, funerals, and so on. I had the impression that something was being performed here in the traditionally correct manner. My father, too, seemed to be chiefly concerned with going through it all according to rule, and it was part of this rule that the appropriate words were read or spoken with emphasis. There was no mention of the fact that it was now 1860 years since Jesus had died, whereas in all other memorial services the date was stressed. I saw no sadness and no joy, and felt that the feast was meager in every respect, considering the extraordinary importance of the person whose memory was being celebrated. It did not compare at all with secular festivals.

Suddenly my turn came. I ate the bread; it tasted flat, as I had expected. The wine, of which I took only the smallest sip, was thin and rather sour, plainly not of the best. Then came the final prayer, and the people went out, neither depressed nor illumined with joy, but with faces that said, "So that's that."

I walked home with my father, intensely conscious that I was wearing a new black felt hat and new black suit which was already beginning to turn into a frock coat. It was a kind of lengthened jacket that spread out into two little wings over the seat, and between these was a slit with a pocket into which I could tuck a handkerchief—which seemed to me a grown-up, manly gesture. I felt socially elevated and by implication accepted into the society of men. That day, too, Sunday dinner was an unusually good one. I would be able to stroll about in my new suit all day. But otherwise I was empty and did not know what I was feeling.

Only gradually, in the course of the following days, did it dawn on me that nothing had happened. I had reached the pinnacle of religious initiation, had expected something—I knew not what—to happen, and nothing at all had happened. I knew that God could do stupendous things to me, things of fire and unearthly light; but this ceremony contained no trace of God—not for me, at any rate. To be sure, there had been talk about Him, but it had all amounted to no more than words. Among the others I had noticed nothing of the vast despair, the overpowering elation and outpouring of grace which for me constituted the essence of God. I had observed no sign of "communion," of "union, becoming one with. . ." With whom? With Jesus? Yet he was only a man who had died 1860 years ago. Why should a person become one with him? He was called the "Son of God"—a demigod, therefore, like the Greek heroes: how then could an ordinary person become one with him? This was called the "Christian religion," but none of it had anything to do with God as I had experienced Him. On the other hand it was quite clear that Jesus, the man, did have to do with God; he had despaired in Gethsemane and on the cross, after having taught that God was a kind and loving father. He too, then, must have seen the fearfulness of God. That I could understand, but what was the purpose of this wretched memorial service with the flat bread and the sour wine? Slowly I came to understand that this communion had been a fatal experience for me. It had proved hollow; more than that, it had proved to be a total loss. I knew that I would never again be able to participate in this ceremony. "Why, that is not religion at all," I thought. "It is an absence of God; the church is a place I should not go to. It is not life which is there, but death."

I was seized with the most vehement pity for my father. All at once I understood the tragedy of his profession and his life. He was struggling with a death whose existence he could not admit. An abyss had opened between him and me, and I saw no possibility of ever bridging it, for it was infinite in extent. I could not plunge my dear and generous father, who in so many matters left me to myself and had never tyrannized over me, into that despair and sacrilege which were necessary for an experience of divine grace. Only God could do that. I had no right to; it would be inhuman. God is not human, I thought; that is His greatness, that nothing human impinges on Him. He is kind and terrible—both at once—and is therefore a great peril from which everyone naturally tries to save himself. People cling one-sidedly to His love and goodness, for fear they will fall victim to the tempter and destroyer. Jesus, too, had noticed that, and had therefore taught: "Lead us not into temptation."

My sense of union with the Church and with the human world, so far as I knew it, was shattered. I had, so it seemed to me, suffered the greatest defeat of my life. The religious outlook which I imagined constituted my sole meaningful relation with the universe had disintegrated; I could no longer participate in the general faith, but found myself involved in something inexpressible, in my secret, which I could share with no one. It was terrible and—this was the worst of it—vulgar and ridiculous also, a diabolical mockery.

I began to ponder: What must one think of God? . . . God alone was real—an annihilating fire and an indescribable grace.

What about the failure of Communion to affect me? Was that my own failure? I had prepared for it in all earnestness, had hoped for an experience of grace and illumination, and nothing had happened. God had been absent. For God's sake I now found myself cut off from the Church and from my father's and everybody else's faith. Insofar as they all represented the Christian religion, I was an outsider. This knowledge filled me with a sadness which was to overshadow all the years until the time I entered the university.

TAKING MARTHA WITH ME

BEVERLY COYLE

Fifth-generation Floridian Beverly Coyle grew up a "PK"—a preacher's kid—in the rural south of the 1950s, the daughter of a liberal Methodist minister and an elegant, educated mother. Now a professor of English at Vassar College and an acclaimed novelist, Coyle wrote this semi-fictionalized memoir as the opening to The Kneeling Bus, *her short story debut. Sensitive to her upper-crust social and religious heritage, Beverly/Carrie is scandalized when her father violates the precepts of Methodist "good taste" with an Easter sunrise baptism in the Atlantic Ocean instead of a proper "sprinkling" in church.*

MY FATHER was a Methodist minister, but since he was never a strong "pulpit man," he rose quite slowly in the hierarchy of Southern Methodism. I grew up in large renovated parsonages all over rural Florida in the fifties. There were no religious pictures on the walls of those old furnished houses; my mother would not hear of it; my mother, Caroline, had been president of her sorority; my father was a liberal with advanced degrees who'd smoked cigarettes in the Navy. And I was taken to New York the summer I turned nine, where I saw Patty McCormack burn up her red shoes in *The Bad Seed*.

So it was a shock for me to learn that spring when I was still nine that my father was going to immerse a woman named Mrs. Mollengarden in the Atlantic Ocean at the Easter Sunrise Service.

My parents must have had reasonable conversations about it: how it actually came about that Mrs. Mollengarden had set her mind to a low-church ceremony; how Dad had already agreed to something so beyond his congregation's notion of good taste. Now they were breaking the news to my sister Jeanie and me, rehearsing their story for the larger fold.

"You're going to do it in the *ocean?*" Jeanie asked. Neither of us could quite grasp just how bad the situation was. There was still hope in the room for a simple sprinkling on dry ground.

But when my father didn't answer, we almost saw the whole thing and turned at once to look at Mother. Her lids fluttered bravely. "She has requested it," my mother explained. "Your father will take Mrs. Mollengarden out to the sandbar where the water is calm."

She might as well have said that he would take Mrs. Mollengarden out to the sandbar to be hanged by the neck until she was dead. We were better prepared to hand down that sentence to the woman ourselves than to be told that apparently all you had to do was ask for an immersion and it would be immediately granted unto you.

I thought of Martha, the Baptist preacher's daughter, whom I tortured occasionally in the neglected mango grove that separated her family's parsonage from ours. Martha was something of a dirty yard girl with impetigo below the knees. She had the habit of pulling out her eyelashes, and from time to time I was observed bossing her around the properties. I knew my sister disapproved of even the simple convenience of this connection, and I feared her indictment of me now that we'd been told of Mrs. Mollengarden. And so I was surprised when, after an early supper, Jeanie invited me to leave the house with her. Jeanie could be counted on to sometimes love me in an emergency. We went to the town dump, where no children were supposed to go anymore since a man had exposed himself there to somebody in the high school.

My sister led me to a spot where she and her best friend, Celia, were planning to start a club. They had already cut windows in a refrigerator box and acquired orange crates. I knew I was never to come there again, but could sit inside for now if I was prepared to make fun of Mrs. Mollengarden, whom neither of us had ever met.

"She has big veins on one of her legs," I said. My kindlier self knew the woman was going to be merely doughy and hopeless, a woman without any make-up or good sense. But instead I invoked ugly details—crooked hips inside a sack dress, loose arms dangling down like monkey vine. Jeanie said none of it mattered; *she* wasn't going to the Easter Sunrise Service this year. No matter what.

I shifted my weight and thought about this challenge.

"I want to go," I admitted.

"So go," Jeanie said.

I looked at her. "I want to see how he'll do it."

"I'll show you how he'll do it, Carrie," and she grabbed me by my hair and pushed me under. I went down with a great gasp, screaming and laughing and kicking at the sides of the refrigerator box. ". . . in the name of the Father and the Son and John the Baptist," my sister said, "and when she comes up she'll be stinking . . ."

Jeanie didn't let go until she'd gotten in a terrific pull at the roots.

My father was out on the front lawn when I came up to report to him about Jeanie's clubhouse at the dump. He sighed and said we would all have to discuss this matter later, but for the moment did I want to come with him to Martha's house? He had asked Reverend Wenning if he could borrow a baptismal robe.

Of course I would come. I took up Dad's hand to lead him through the old mango grove. I was the only one in the family who had ever visited the Wennings on the other side, and besides the grove was full of hazards: old tires and tin cans and things I'd hauled in there myself. I made sure I led him over easy ground.

It was already twilight inside the big grove. The old trees had dropped blotched fruits of the day; mangos lay where they fell—split and exposed to flies. It was a freeze grove, and the still living trees were casting themselves away very slowly; they were dying in peace.

"Will you have her kneel down?" I asked. I steered him safely around the obstacles. He was making an effort to keep the deep, loose sand out of his shoes. I wouldn't have said anything in the world to hurt his feelings. I knew his family had been Assemblies of God, although it was not often mentioned, or them either. We had one photograph they'd taken of him in high-top shoes and a cotton dress with three starched flounces. He could have passed for some child on my mother's side, except that a detail in the picture gave everything away. There was no screen on the open window above my father's head.

"Dad! Will you have her kneel down?" I asked him softly.

"Who's that, sweetheart?" he said.

"Mrs. Mollengarden! When you get her out there will you have her kneel down or what?"

"Oh, I see what you mean," he said. "I suppose I could do that. To tell you the truth I haven't thought about it."

"You could take a pitcher out there with you," I said. "You could have her kneel down and then pour water on her head out of the pitcher." I already knew which of my mother's would be appropriate. A plain buff one with no stripes.

"Ummm," he said, "perhaps I could." And then we fell silent and I seemed to see the invisible path in front of us—the one I'd heard about, the one you traveled if you were a big enough person. It lay as the strait and narrow under my feet.

We marched formally up to the back screen door of the Wennings' rundown parsonage, where Martha was watching out for us. My father had telephoned ahead, and Martha held open the door to let us in. Reverend Wenning had the robe right there ready in the dark kitchen. It was a well-used, very plain maroon robe with lead sinkers sewn into the hem. He pointed these out to us in an offhand way while my father slipped the whole thing on. Mrs. Wenning murmured that it was a good fit, averting her eyes to the floor, where the robe fell in plumb lines above the tops of his shoes.

"I suppose I could fix up one of our choir robes this way," Dad said. I heard one of the sinkers crack against his ankle bone.

Reverend Wenning was already saying it was no trouble to let Dad borrow this one. "You take it on with you, Preacher," he said. "This is an extra." Mrs. Wenning asked Martha to get a sack.

"Well, I appreciate it." Dad said. He made a point of taking the robe off as slowly as he could. Mrs. Wenning smiled and folded it carefully inside a brown bag from Winn Dixie. We shuffled politely out the screen door to discover darkness had fallen over their back yard. Martha went barefoot a few steps with us beyond the porch stoop, then paused to watch until we came to the edge of the grove.

"Good-bye," my father called out. I was not sure what I heard in his voice—the unfamiliar neighborliness of it all; Reverend Wenning having the robe there in his kitchen like that. "Thank you!" he called.

The next day was Saturday and I found her watching for me from Habakkuk—the largest tree in the grove. She had all the trees named for books of the Old Testament. From this tree we could see the small road that ran past our houses and the two churches that sat three blocks apart. Even in daylight the grove was shaded and cool. But the sun had dried the fallen fruit and dispersed the heavy odors.

As I climbed to a favorite limb I'd staked out for myself, I was pleased to hear that Martha was curious about the robe. "You don't have a baptismal pool in your church," she said, though it was not a boast. Martha was not a swaggerer. The previous summer she'd grown quite bruised and yellow from a case of what they called mango poisoning. She and her brothers turned bright orange before it was over and they'd all had to stay out of the grove for months. I wondered that she never thought to brag about this episode in our uneventful days—a girl who'd been poisoned and lived.

I lay back on my limb and stretched my arms over my head. I had schemes for almost dying like that—going to the brink and returning safely. It was to be like a push from a swing—the seat brought up impossibly high and hurled with a snap to send me face up into the blue.

"My dad won't *need* a baptismal pool, Martha," I said.

I could rarely count on her to keep to the subject, even when she tried, as she did now after a little pause. "Do you want me to take you over to look at the pool in our church again?" Martha asked.

"No, thank you," I said, knowing she well remembered how I'd tricked her into letting me see their baptismal pool back behind the pulpit; we'd discovered it enclosed with a heavy curtain she said they tied to one side whenever there was a need. The sunken square was as dry as a culvert and had bounced our whispers around until we'd scared ourselves. I regretted my earlier interest in this facility now that immersion had come so legitimately and effortlessly into my own life.

"Don't forget, I'm getting baptized this summer," Martha said.

"I know," I said.

"Are you going to come? Did you ask your mom yet?"

"Yes."

I heard her sigh in contentment.

"But I can only come if you invite me, Martha. You have to send me an invitation."

"Why?"

"So that way my mom will know it's all right with your mom."

"My mom don't care."

I sat up. "Well, she has to care, Martha. Your mom has to care. Don't be so stupid."

Now, Martha was thoroughly confused and she looked off somewhere else with those frightening eyes of hers. My mother had told her she had such lovely eyes that she ought not to do that, pulling out her lashes like that. To me it was another exotic accomplishment completely wasted on her.

"My mom wants you to come," she finally said.

"Then all you have to do is send me an invitation."

"All right," Martha said. Of course she wasn't sure what it meant to send an invitation, and I knew that perfectly well. I saw her wipe her eyes with the back of her hand.

"Oh, now don't tune up and cry," I said. I climbed down off my limb and sat beside her on hers. "I'll tell you a secret if you won't tell anybody."

"I won't," Martha promised.

"Do you know why my dad borrowed your daddy's robe?"

"No," Martha whispered. "He don't know either."

"Because my dad is going to immerse a lady . . . in the *ocean.*"

And I was aware at that moment I had said sacred words—words that were miraculously joined with deed. I saw myself taking Martha by the hand and guiding her into the safety of my father's denomination, where she could be baptized any way she wanted now, where she would eat right and fill out, where her hair would thicken and her color would improve and she would go to college.

"What's the matter?" I said when I turned to find that she'd pulled back from me, as if of all times in her life she would choose this one in which to press her advantage. But it was a look of helpless dismay. Poor Martha was seeing bathing suits and inner tubes; she was smelling hot dogs and suntan oil.

"You mean," she whispered, "he's going to do it at the *beach?*"

Sunday was Palm Sunday, the immersion a week away, and upstairs in the parsonage I poured powder in my shoes and watched the street filling up with cars. We Methodists had an oyster shell parking lot behind the new educational plant. But the Baptists just pulled up anywhere. From the bathroom window I could see Reverend Wenning's congregation parking, on grassy littorals, pickup trucks and station wagons. They stood around talking with Bibles pressed against their chests, calling out encouragements to their children, who shouted back at them from the trees in the grove. As a rule I never saw Martha on Sundays, but I wanted to find her that morning to show her something, to set her straight about the matter of the beach. I slipped out the back door and sneaked up unobserved to my edge of the grove, where I could watch for her. I had never done this before and knew instantly that Martha never had either. The mango trees were full of boys.

In church that morning, we all stood at the end of the service and sang an Easter hymn. A very tall man behind me bellowed out over my head and into the reds in the windows, which shone bright cherry. "Up from the grave He arose, / With a mighty triumph o'er His foes." I counted all the straw purses strewn in the pews in front of me. Somewhere in the church was a straw purse that belonged to Mrs. Mollengarden. It would be decorated in shell flowers with bits of wire stem like all the other ladies' purses, but it suddenly came to me that she was a very large woman, and that when my father took her in his arms, lowering her down, leaning over her, supporting her, raising her up again, surely—for there was no other possibility—surely one of his arms, his *left* arm in fact, would touch Mrs. Mollengarden's front. I rehearsed it all in a large arena just inside my head. I stood hip-deep in early April waters and silently curved my father's man's arms around enormous spheres of space. There just wasn't a question in my mind but that his left arm was going to touch Mrs. Mollengarden's breast.

After church I told my mother in the kitchen that I thought he ought to have her kneel down.

"I hardly think that's necessary," Mom said, thrusting a set of napkins and silverware at me. She thought I was trying to dramatize the whole affair.

"But you see, if Mrs. Mollengarden would just kneel down," I began, but my mother simply turned away, repeating that she thought such a thing would not be at all necessary. She lowered her voice and whispered it. We children were not to worry.

And yet when the Sunday meal began, as we all sat and watched Dad carve up a roast chicken, my mother reasoned aloud. The air would be cold next Sunday morning, she said, and after the immersion she wondered if he and Mrs. Mollengarden wouldn't need to jump immediately into the car and out of the wind, which would be coming up fast with the tide change. She'd been thinking how he'd need to have on something old and plenty warm under Reverend Wenning's robe. No one would see because it would be best if he simply arrived at the service wearing the robe.

Jeanie sat and stared at the chicken. Dad arranged the meat with some deliberation, as if he heard nothing. Every time he lifted a little slice and delivered it to its proper spot, the movement carried the easy suggestion that he was merely taking the bird apart and putting it back together again. My mother might as well have been speaking in tongues.

Well, there was no place to change except in the public bathhouse, she continued, and that was way up behind the dunes. No one would want to stand around waiting for him to change. If the air was unusually still there'd be sand flies.

"This looks delicious, doesn't it, girls?" my father said.

And we would have to remember to put towels in the car. None of us was to forget to remind her about the *towels*.

Had she let her imagination have full play, it would have probably involved that lovely Northern couple, Mr. and Mrs. Deaton, standing well dressed and dignified in the early morning light, watching Noel Willis, their favorite pastor, leading that large woman out to where Mom hoped the sandbar would be—not so far out so that nothing could be heard, but far enough to silhouette them demurely against the rising sun. Beyond that she could not go.

That afternoon I found my friend up in old Habakkuk.

"Get down," I said. "I want to show you something."

I waited with some impatience as she took special care to ease herself out of that tree, wipe her hands carefully on her print dress, then take from me the illustration I'd torn from one of my old Sunday school books. It showed John the Baptist standing beside Jesus in what was without question the *Sea* of Galilee.

"There you are, Martha," I said.

Martha studied it a long time; she was immediately in love with the illustration, and I saw her bite her bottom lip as she silently named for herself all the principals.

"You see? Even Jesus was baptized in the ocean."

Martha nodded her head. It was the River Jordan, she said, though she continued to nod that she took my point to heart. I saw then she'd never been my adversary in this matter of the beach. She'd simply had a fleeting image of the place as she knew it in Florida—ice cream wrappers poking up in the sand and very loud Yankees.

I pointed out to her some of the details of the illustration which interested me: John the Baptist stood somewhat behind Jesus and had his hands folded in prayer. The dove, descending from heaven inside a sun ray, dominated the scene, and, if one looked closely, it did look more as though Jesus had simply had water poured on his head. He didn't look especially wet.

"That's the Holy Ghost," she said, pointing to the dove.

"The Holy Spirit," I corrected her softly.

"Yes," Martha said.

"You can keep this," I said.

She blinked at me. "I got lots of pictures, but I don't have this here one."

"You keep it," I said.

"And you can have it back whenever you get lonesome for it," she said.

We were quiet for some time before I spoke again.

"Martha, when you get baptized this summer, are you going to kneel down in the water or what?"

"Grown-ups kneel down," she said. "Children stand up."

"Why is that?" I said. I was starting to feel better already. Martha had a way of looking far off to a place where things were supremely uncomplicated.

"I could find out from my daddy," she said.

"No, that's okay," I said. "I was just wondering."

Then Martha sat right down in the sandy grove and put the picture in her lap. I walked around behind her and leaned myself against a trunk.

"It's real quick, isn't it?" I said.

"What?" Martha said.

"Getting baptized. It doesn't take long, does it?"

"No," Martha said, "but it lasts forever."

She pushed her fine blond hair out of her eyes and turned to look at me. "You don't remember it, do you?" she suddenly said. "You was just a baby, wasn't you?"

"That's right." I looked her straight in the eye. "I was christened by a bishop."

Martha's eyes widened.

"You don't have bishops, do you?" I said, offhand.

"No!" she said. "What was he *like?*"

"He looked nice," I said.

"Did they take any pictures of you?"

She could not have done a nicer thing than ask to see photos. The Methodist ministers, posing in their creamy white suits, impressed Martha the most, I thought. Without my telling her, she saw that my christening had been an occasion. Those were district superintendents wearing the fashionable white suits of the day, and that was me in the white center, lying in the bishop's arms. I decided I could press her for more information while she studied the rest of the family album.

"And so when they kneel down, what happens then?"

Martha looked up. And I remember now how she must have looked, that Renaissance angels had no eyelashes. Michelangelo's Mary had no eyelashes. Martha could have been carved from pink marble. She got up slowly from the edge of my bed, knelt down on the floor, and crossed her arms over the front of her chest. Then she held her nose and leaned back as far as she could. Finally she pulled herself up and let her sweet breath out again. There was not a sound anywhere in the house. I could hear the waves flapping gently on the shore, and, while I knew everything would be all right, I knew they wouldn't be the same either.

"Martha?" I suddenly asked. "Do you want to come with us?"

"Where?"

"Do you think your mom would mind if you came next week to our Easter Sunrise Service?"

Martha blinked and looked far off.

"I'll ask her," she said.

I don't remember the long week that followed. I do remember sleeping rather lightly the night before in my blue-papered room down the hall from Jeanie, who'd wangled a sleep-over at Celia's so she could ride out to the sunrise service with Celia's family. Unfortunately, after the service Celia's family assumed Jeanie would return to town with us and we assumed she would return with them. And so, twenty minutes after my father had tried to immerse Mrs. Mollengarden in the Atlantic Ocean—all of us piling into the car to get them out of the knifing cold—Jeanie was left stranded at Boynton Beach. And when the poor child was finally rescued, she was in hysterics because she'd had no dime and had been afraid to ask a stranger for one.

My mother blamed it on all our confusion and worry. Things had been so eventful. My father and Mrs. Mollengarden had actually stepped in a hole on their way out to the sandbar. For a moment there, with only a few seagulls scolding and dipping frantically over the water, there had been no sign of them. Then a few moments later they had both come up again a bit farther out, where their feet found the edge of the sandbar which we'd always taken for granted, little children paddling out to it six days of the week. When we saw the two grown-ups standing tall at last, the water out there only came a little above their knees. Dad and Mrs. Mollengarden appeared merely to be wading in the sunrise. And so finally the ceremony had begun. No one was able to hear a word he said because people were still stunned at the near drowning they'd just witnessed before he could get the deed done and lead the woman, quite shaken, back to shore; whereupon my mother gave up all decorum and rushed to meet them with bundles of towels, which fell in the water everywhere as Dad searched around his feet in the vain hope that his glasses might have washed up somehow at that very point.

I was the only one who was not mortified by the interminable flailing moments before they reached the sandbar safely, and so fortunately remembered forever and ever exactly the way he did it. His right arm went around her shoulders as I had imagined and his left arm swung gracefully and firmly over Mrs. Mollengarden's large bosom as he lowered her down and said the words and raised her up again while Martha and I stood waiting with the small congregation. We held hands the whole time and Martha talked softly but a great deal, which I had not expected of her.

"This is right before the dove comes down," she said first of all when the two of them stood face to face and prepared to make that lovely embrace. And while Mrs. Mollengarden was under, Martha said amen and nudged me so that I said it too, quite involuntarily. But when they stepped silently apart there on the sandbar, and when they waded cautiously back to shore in light that scorched the waters, Martha told me frankly that she'd seen the Holy Spirit out there with them and that the Holy Spirit had kept them aloft.

THE EPISTLE OF PAUL THE APOSTLE
TO THE EPHESIANS

RITA DOVE

In this lyrical, "painterly" reflection on a New Testament epistle, Pulitzer Prize-winning poet Rita Dove contrasts Saul/Paul's sun-drenched land-scape from Damascus to Ephesus to that of black middle-class Akron, Ohio, where Dove came of age in the African Methodist Episcopal Zion Church. America's former Poet Laureate, Dove recalls light and vision, sin and salvation, but most of all the ongoing mystery of grace visited upon all her diverse ancestors in faith.

ON THE mysteries of vision, H.D. writes: "We begin with sympathy of thought." One of the last great modern mystics, H.D. scribbled her *Notes on Thoughts and Vision* in a notebook marked "July, Scilly Islands" in 1919, when she retreated to these islands off the coast of Cornwall in order to recuperate—from war, from illness and the breakup of her marriage, from the death of her brother and the hazardous birth of her daughter Perdita. Sea air and salt light to heal a wounded spirit: "The doctor prescribes rest."

I am reading H.D. on a grassy knoll overlooking the grounds of the Villa Serbelloni, the "Study and Conference Center" of the Rocke-feller Foundation on Lake Como in northern Italy, trying to ignore a niggling restlessness I've had ever since my arrival. Do I feel dis-placed in the serenity of this splendid retreat, high above the tourist traffic of the village of Bellagio, here where terraced hills plunge into clear waters and cypresses slope into the mists at evening? Five weeks of hydrangeas and tiger lilies, white-coated butlers and silver candle-sticks—what sumptuous reward for all the hours spent hunched in a sixty-watt circle of light, smudging my way through a wilderness of words! At last no meals to cook or phones to answer; little mail, no children; a room of one's own, a study in the woods, and all around, beauty . . . but I'm not writing.

I've told myself it takes time to unwind, and I try to relax by read-ing afternoons when the *breva* sweeps the fog from the lake, freshen-ing the shore. I read sprawled in a rattan chair set up outside, next to my study, hoping the sun will burn off the stress and fill the emptiness with magic.

While browsing in the villa library this morning I talked with a poet from Canada; he was convinced that the jewellike medieval painting of Saul on the way to Damascus that's mounted near the dictionaries is an unsigned Bono. Unsure who Bono was but unwilling to show my ignorance, I scrutinized the canvas for a signature—nothing in the tufted grass, the parched and rutted road, no scrawls in the sur-real blue heaven or bright curls of the seraphim—and before I remembered to put on my museum demeanor I was captivated by the wistful sincerity of the scene before me. Saul looked utterly terri-fied, his horse rearing and his fellow travelers baffled by such strange behavior on an ordinary day. How devastating an experience for a man so certain of his convictions! No wonder he spent three days in darkness afterward, emptied of himself, until Ananias came to claim him in the name of Christianity. No wonder his name changed, the same sound but a different beginning.

H.D.'s *Notes* drop to the grass. A few yards away, three goldfish hid-den under the lily pads send up their perky semaphores: I hear this infinitesimal percolation even as wild birds overhead belt out Italian chorales and a speedboat growls across the lake. So that's what's been bothering me: the germ of a poem dealing with religion. But, as if I were a Jewish dyer trading in royal purple, I struggle against the notion of Christianity acquiring a poem from me—just as I struggle against the ideologue who has haunted me since adolescence, whose stony gaze I still feel whenever I rail against the strictures of institu-tional belief.

· · ·

Life before Paul was milk and honey, grapes and warm bread, card-board-and glitter crèches. In those early Sunday-school years we were fed on floods and famines, raining toads and babies in baskets. Come twelve and the age of accountability, Christ appeared in the Temple and there followed a progression of sun-drenched miracles— Lazarus rising from his shroud, fish gleaming on proliferating hunks of bread. We loved the repetition of blessings, the palms fanning above the stolid head of a donkey, even the thirty pieces of silver. Blood and vinegar on the cross was swept over quickly, and Sunrise Services emphasized the rock rolled away, shining wings, astonish-ment, and His Glorious Resurrection. That was what a miracle was, after all: absence and light.

I was thirteen when the man who would introduce me to the apos-tle Paul walked into our senior Sunday-school class. He was tall, dark, and hellishly handsome, severely dressed in a matte-black narrow suit and black shirt from which rose a ring of shocking white, like a slipped halo. Never before had I seen a clerical collar (our minister wore standard suits with striped ties which peeked from his velvet-trimmed "preaching" robe); I thought the collar was his own inven-tion, a kind of symbolic leash worn as a token of his service to God. He was the new assistant minister, straight out of theological school in the South (an exotic country to us in Akron, Ohio), and would take over the twelve-to-fifteen-year-olds, leaving our former teacher with the less unruly high schoolers.

Of course all the girls developed an immediate crush on him. We followed him breathlessly across the hall to a smaller, pale green class-room and without being asked formed a semicircle around the table he leaned against, like a male model from *Ebony* magazine, pinstriped trousers draping elegantly just above the buffed black wing-tips. On his left hand glinted, to our disappointment, a large wedding band.

"What do you know of mortal sin?" he asked.

We goggled at him and tittered nervously. "Mortal" sounded all right to us. He frowned, straightening the crease in his pant leg, then patiently unveiled to us the concepts of irretrievable error and pur-gatory. Since we were past the age of twelve, he explained, we were accountable for our sins against the Ten Commandments, which were inviolable. And out transgressions against any of those laws—whether actual or committed *in thought only*—were unforgivable except through Jesus Christ.

We barely heard the Jesus Christ part. We were doomed, for we had just coveted another woman's husband; we had also disobeyed our parents, stolen, lied, cursed—and if one counted thinking (how can you control your thoughts?) as well, then we committed these transgressions all the time. In an instant, flirting had changed from harmless entertainment to hellfire.

Our church was A.M.E. Zion. The acronym stands for African Methodist Episcopal, an appellation that contains all the contradictions and acclimatizations black Americans have gone through to accommodate both the African memory and the American dream. Basically Methodist, our church believed in a moderate liturgy (responsive readings) but did not tolerate kneeling or chanting; the "Episcopal" distinguished us from the Baptists not only in decorum—we baptized with a few drops of water on a baby's forehead—but in class. Determinedly of the bourgeoisie ("boojy" we called our parents, among them dentists, general practitioners, dry-cleaning moguls), we did not approve of hee-hawing sermons, though the minister was permitted to shout out the last sixth of his text.

"African" meant many things. Sometimes it was the license to wear proud colors and hats piled high, as extravagant as platters—unlike the drab skirt-and-blouse attire of the white Lutherans one street over. "African" also referred to our intimate relationship with God and Christ, the permission to wipe Christ's sweat from our brows and talk to him like a brother, to identify our lot with that of the Israelites under Pharaoh. Martin Luther King, Jr. was our Moses, charged with delivering his people across the Selma bridge. "African" bore the very cadences of nostalgia for our lost homeland, wherever it may have been—though in those turbulent years of Miriam Makeba and Malcolm X there was an edge to that nostalgia as well, a defiant hope from those who wished for mercy but just might choose, if pressed, to prevail by whatever means necessary.

But "African" always meant righteous singing. I particularly loved the "old hundred" hymns, standard oldies sung during the formal catechism of the service, before the sermon, as well as the choral outbursts from the white-clad women in the front pew.

Ah, the deaconesses! Mostly widows with massive bosoms, all ancient, these women put their blinding white shirtwaists, their chalky nylons, and Shinola-white shoes every Sunday. Some wore tiny starched bonnets, very much like nurses or pilgrims, and others preferred the pure ornament of a scrubbed dark face lifted to the Lord. They were the self-appointed brides of Christ and the acknowledged mothers of the church, the arbiters of the Holy Spirit, and they disapproved of flash and frivolity and black militancy. (Though they never complained about Afros, since several of them had let their hair "go back" to furry halos.) The deaconesses were already seated when the rest of the congregation trickled in. Usually they were bent in prayer, humming vigorously to the mumbled supplications of a deacon, usually the oldest male, who by virtue of his sex and age was permitted to kneel on the first step leading to the altar.

The deaconesses were also intimate with what W. E. B. Du Bois called the Sorrow Songs—older hymns, prehistoric canons that resembled nothing familiar or comforting. They had very few words and were frightening in their near-inarticulate misery. For at least a half hour before the processional signaled the official start of the service, the old women hummed, rocked, wailed these chants as parishioners arrived and drifted into the pews. Unlike gospel, "big/with all the wrongs done done," these songs reeked with unappeasable loss and pain. They were the moans of slavery, the rhythms of an existence dulled by rote and brutality and hopelessness, an isolation so complete there could be no words.

The deaconesses led the congregation in that complex courtship between the Holy Spirit and mortal endeavor; the give and take, the surge and ebb between the minister's sermon and their shouted counterpoint was our clue to how well the minister was doing in bringing us closer to holiness, indeed, bringing us *in Christ*, in Paul's complex, mystical phrase, until heat and pinching waistbands dropped away and the message from the pulpit entered us directly, like an injection.

What is the mystery of grace? What does it mean to be *in* Christ? I watched the older women of the church "get happy"; I could see them gathering steam, pushing out the seams of their composure until it dropped down, the Holy Spirit, falling upon them like a hatchet from heaven. Instead of crumbling they rose up, incandescent, to perform amazing feats—they tightroped the backs of pews, skipped along the aisles, threw off ushers and a half-dozen able-bodied men with every shout. (Men rarely got happy; when they did, theirs was a decorous performance, hardly an experience at all.) A woman "full of the Spirit" was indomitable; one could almost see sunbeams glancing off the breastplate of righteousness, the white wings twinkling on the sandals of faith. And when it was over, they were not diminished but serene, as if they'd been given a tonic.

Why couldn't I be filled, transfused with glory? The most I'd experienced was a "quickening"—a mini-transformation characterized by shortened breath and an intense longing for the indefinite . . . what? I was tongue-tied, hopelessly guilt-ridden and self-conscious to boot. The most I could do was get teary-eyed. In the face of those bolder ecstasies, I'd fall back into my own ashes, quenched.

Witnessing these transformations usually made me churlish for the rest of the day. I decided God didn't like intelligence. And though we hadn't been meant to sample the Tree of Knowledge, surely we couldn't be blamed for the intelligence we'd been saddled with.

Sunday evenings after "60 Minutes" my father would push off his slippers and shrug into his overcoat, keys jangling. We knew the signal: another trip to Grandma's on the East Side. It was a long way through town, along the gorge and then the slow climb up Market Street, past the defunct oats silos and the Fir Hill Conservatory of Music, then down Arlington and into the purgatorial Furnace Street, where the smoke and brimstone miraculously began, spewing from Plant One of the Goodyear Rubber Company and the smaller infernos of Mohawk and General Tire. This was the part of the journey I waited for. The backlit plumes of smoke and murky variations of exhaust and light were exciting, a negative snapshot of power and hope; the mere sight of a belching smokestack at night made me think of evening gowns and diamond lavaliers.

All across town the accompaniment was radio—the staid ministerial admonitions of a local Presbyterian congregation on the way, and afterward the surging gospels of Shiloh Baptist, my grandmother's own church, whose evening service she attended faithfully via the airwaves, rocking in her armchair in the back bedroom. I was awed by so much fervor: that one could go to church on Sunday morning and still have ardor left over to attend an evening service seemed strange, yet weirdly desirable. How simple life would be if one could believe that much! Later, in bed, I'd tuck my transistor radio under the pillow and tune into the Catholic broadcast at ten—after Shiloh Baptist's creaking ship of lamentations what a relief, a balm, *Hail Mary full of grace Blessed art thou among women and blessed is the fruit of thy womb Jesus* whispered over and over until I dozed off, safe for another night.

Into the intact world of childhood, Paul had introduced Doubt, and I resisted. As far as I was concerned, Saul/Paul was altogether too fervent—his persecution of the Christians too single-minded, his conversion too spectacular, his teachings too humorless. It wasn't the gaudiness of his martyr's life I distrusted (John's vision of the Apocalypse, in contrast, seemed absolute to me and vividly *correct*); rather, it was the contradiction between his life and his words. "Do as I say, not as I do"—we'd learned in Sunday school to nod, straight-faced, when reciting the commandments but to watch as scandals erupted in that orchestrated adult world: a senior usher ogling a pair of fine hips rolling under orange shantung, the occasional girl burgeoning under her choir robes. We waited for public recriminations, but all went on as before. We had a saying: Saints can backslide, but never trust a person who can't dance. Paul couldn't dance, but he shore could talk. Our assistant minister felt it his duty to initiate us into the world of words, the irretrievability of a vow.

I also distrusted the name change, from the Jew Saul to the astringent New Age Paul. Paul—a name without history. Somehow I suspected him of abandoning with his born name the Old Testament, where Sauls and Jeremiahs flourished, and his desert treks and prison tenure had no aura. He was a traveling salesman, his epistles little more than shtick.

And Paul had no music; neither did he make a joyful noise before the Lord. He despised pageantry and silver ornament. His was a ministry of noon—no shadows or respite from the all-reaching rays of righteousness. I could not think of Paul without imagining parched mesas and the emblazoned killing ground of a Colosseum. Even the olives he preferred must have been sharp with rosemary, chewy and bitter.

But the god I knew understood the value of a wink. He was nothing like this Paul with his blind stare, his frozen faith burning in his eyes. Leave such clenched fervor to human beings; gods and angels are casual. No wonder he saw life in terms of architecture, and the body become church, a sacred building you entered silently and where you'd better not spit. And farther up the wine-dark aisle, the path of blood transfixed, this sacrificial artery leading to the plateau where no body lived but Thought reigned, gold and wax and velvet, paltry adornment designed to render palpable to the congregation the ineffable integrity of the spirit. This, then, was Christ presiding over the church, and Man presiding over Wife.

The mystery of Paul's ideology is revealed through his metaphors: comparing the church to a marriage. To be saved, to establish a mystical and *ongoing* spiritual strength, one does not try to become Christ or to identify with Christ; instead, one develops a *relationship to* him.

This is a "primitive" concept: the ancient Greeks mingled freely with their gods and goddesses, with sometimes disastrous (poor Leda), sometimes beneficent (Odysseus guided to Ithaca by Pallas Athene) results. African slaves in America transferred their attitudes toward divinities to the abstract figures of Christianity, telling Mary not to weep, exhorting Jonah not to despair, and rejoicing that Christ had personally reached down to lift them up. Black worshipers sat down to talk with God as with an old friend. When I was in my early teens, black disc jockeys favored a popular song that went: "I had a talk with my man last night; / He reassured me everything was all right." It was years before I heard the gospel song that had been its inspiration: "I had a talk with God last night." I was not as shocked by this discovery as perhaps I should have been; I was already on the way to secular humanism. After all, I had been talking to God for several years, bargaining and wheedling from the cave of my pillow, protesting my good intentions.

Human agency. I rolled the phrase around in my mouth as I perched on the curved lip of the pew, willing myself to remember the words through the sermon's climax and the preacher's ecstatic Call to Altar so that I might carry them home and find a use for them. *Human agency* was the key I'd been looking for in the rigid latticework the New Testament had raised around my daily living. Obedient though I was, I could not believe the thoughts that entered my daydreams so easily were forbidden. To hold the mind accountable—surely this wasn't what God had meant. Surely he did not want robots as children; surely a doll's house would be a bore for such a mighty spectator.

The world is protean. Every adolescent knows this, lives this . . . and is astonished at adults' ability to fasten onto the order of things with smug attentions. How can they skim the surface of such stormy oceans? Mother snapping her facial compact shut with a satisfied click, Father Turtle-waxing the Ford on Saturday afternoon: where is the pleasure to be located in these routines when the ultimate pleasure (as every adolescent discovers) is sexual—the disintegrating joy of a French kiss, the utterly selfish desire of the body to *know more?* Of course, we didn't understand the concept of guilt, major guilt—the kind that can't be erased from heart and mind, that distresses even ten, fifteen years later, whenever buried incidents float unbidden to the surface. How could we? We hadn't lived very much.

Saul watched as Stephen was stoned to death; Paul was celibate in order to serve his Christ more ardently. Aren't these flip sides of the same coin? And if not, where did Saul go? Who, if anyone, was in the body that sat three days in darkness in Damascus, who spoke before the crowds, who crouched in that dark prison cell and built up the body of Christian thought into a white and pillared building? Did he remember Saul at all—or had he, as Paul, burned away his past self so completely that with it fled the childhood words for stone and bread? What initially fills the void when the old self is struck down and out—what rushes in before the light, what rides the arrow tip of redemption into the benighted soul?

In the rattan chair beside the lily pond, far above the unspeakable blue waters of Lake Como, the poem for Paul takes shape:

On the Road to Damascus

They say I was struck down by the voice of an angel:
    flames poured through the radiant fabric of heaven
as I cried out and fell to my knees.

My first recollection was of Unbroken Blue,
    but two of the guards have already sworn by
the tip of my tongue set ablaze. As an official,

I recognize the lure of a good story:
    useless to suggest that my mount
had stumbled, that I was pitched into a clump

of wild chamomile, its familiar stink
    soothing even as my palms sprang blisters
under the nicked leaves. I heard shouts,

the horse pissing in terror—but my eyes
    had dropped to my knees, and I saw nothing.
I was a Roman and had my business

among the clouded towers of Damascus.
    I had not counted on earth rearing,
honey streaming down a parched sky,

a spear skewering me to the dust of the road
    on the way to the city I would never
enter now, her markets streaming with vendors

and compatriots in careless armor lifting a hand
    in greeting as they call out my name,
only to find no one home.

Paul's first visit to Ephesus lasted over two years, during which time he argued in the synagogue and converted "divers souls." Afterward he made for Jerusalem, sending back to Ephesus two disciples to keep the flame burning. In Paul's absence, the disciples met resistance from the silversmiths, who had a hefty business in shrines to the goddess Diana and naturally resented the loss in trade the new icon-less religion would occasion. Led by the silversmith Demetrius, the people rose up in defense of their goddess; when the disciples tried to speak, the crowd outshouted them, for two hours chanting "Great *is* Diana of the Ephesians." Forced to retreat, the disciples were recalled by Paul, who "embraced them" and set out himself for Ephesus, where he gave the heretics "much exhortation" (Acts 20:1–2).

Did Paul's harsh words succeed at Ephesus, or did Diana prevail? The Bible is curiously silent on this point. In fact, the authorship of the Epistle to the Ephesians is heavily disputed among theological scholars—and it was almost certainly not written for the Ephesians, though of course we have other testimonies of his ministry there. It hardly matters whether Paul wrote this epistle or not—the spirit of his thought is still intact. We know from Acts that Paul appeared at Ephesus with a bag of tricks, handkerchiefs emerging from his sleeves to heal the sick and raise the dead . . . and yet the artisans with their silver statuettes of Diana were still able to rouse the people: We want Diana, thousand-breasted deity, they told Paul's disciples, who were forced to retreat. Was the light in Paul's eyes too empty? Or was it simply that two mysticisms—the matriarchal vision of fertility and wholeness, the patriarchal vision of order and clarity—were insisting on their separate paths to glory?

When I was a teenager Paul seemed to be a hard man with an unreal-istically severe code of sacrifice, a fanatic who devised silly laws of diet, dress codes, and impossible rules of behavior; an ideologue who equated belief with ethics and transformation with institutional rhetoric. This was the worldview our assistant minister promulgated; Paul was his boogeyman.

I see now that Paul's proclamations were demanded of him. At that time Christianity was still a heresy within a larger tradition; Saul's persecution of Christians, his conversion, and his consequent wran-gles with the priests of the Temple—these events were all in the fam-ily, so to speak. At the time when the Pauline Epistles were written, the biggest question for the new religion was whether or not to accept

Gentiles; once that quandary was settled, more mundane issues (Can they remain uncircumcised? Must they obey the Judaic rules of diet?) were the order of the day. The disciples attempted to thread a path through the existing Old Testament laws; they sought an extension, and fulfillment, of Judaism. Paul's public needed concrete rules, so he gave them restrictions to hold on to: Wife, obey your husband; husband, love your wife—just as you obey Christ and He loves you. Children, obey your parents. Servants (this is the tricky one), obey your masters—followed by a telling conditional: "according to the flesh, with fear and trembling, in singleness of your heart, as unto Christ" (Ephesians 6:5–6). And because pictures are worth a thousand words, he gave them metaphors: the Church as a bride, Christ as bridegroom, and martial imagery sure to delight a city devoted to the huntress Diana. Gird the loins with truth, slip the feet into the Gospel of peace, take up the breastplate of righteousness and the shield of faith! Blatant theatrics, but it worked.

Yet Paul *was* a mystic. Only a mystic would address the newly converted with "And you *hath he quickened,* who were dead in trespasses and sins." Or: "the fulness of him that filleth all in all." Devising a system for connecting and reflection, a guide for conducting a life of energized joy—this is Paul's abiding light.

Whenever I move to a new place, the first thing I usually do is "cozy up" my study; I throw down rugs, mount marionettes on the walls, place a crystal or a hand-carved elephant on a shelf where my fidgety gaze might fall for a moment and rest. This time, though, it was different. After leaving the Rockefeller Study and Conference Center in Bellagio, I moved into what was easily the most nondescript room I have ever written poetry in—white brick, gray industrial-strength carpet—and yet, six months later I still could not bear to tack up so much as a single poster.

It was as if the photographs and paintings that used to provide companionship in my solitary hours of composition had ceased to serve as windows and begun to block the view. It seemed I required no distraction from the void. To put it less negatively: I no longer felt the need to focus in on an object in order to allow my thoughts free rein, unsupervised—a window had opened in me.

I was nearly finished writing "On the Road to Damascus" before I understood what about the gold-leaf-and-lapis universe in the painting the Canadian poet attributed to Bono had so moved me that morning in the Villa Serbelloni. Saul was terrified because the eyes that had studied the Law and looked calmly on at the slaying of another man had for the first time failed their owner. The Roman world, once as compact and manageable as the toylike apparition of the city of Damascus hovering on the horizon, had split apart, and he was falling into a mystery, bottomless and widening.

Paul's account of his conversion, on the other hand, is essentially the story of a seduction. He has been entered by Christ the Bridegroom and remade in the image of his Love. Then, as in any marriage, one must work at redemption; one must learn to forgive oneself.

H.D. writes: "We must be 'in love' before we can understand the mysteries of vision." This does not mean penetrating the mysterious, nor does it mean being taken by storm. Grace is a state of being, not an assault; and enlightenment, unlike epiphany, is neither brief nor particularly felicitous. The Saul in the painting knew better. Anyone who feels the need to connect the outside world with an interior presence must *absorb* the mysterious into the tangle of contradictions and longings that form each one of us. That's hard, ongoing work, and it never ends.

THE GENERATION OF FAITH

RANDALL BALMER

Professor of religious studies at Barnard College, Columbia University, Randall Balmer is the author of highly praised books including Mine Eyes Have Seen the Glory: A Journey into the Evangelical Subculture of America, *serialized by PBS television. In this essay, published here for the first time, Balmer details his own strict Christian fundamentalist upbringing in Minnesota followed by years of intellectual restlessness and doubt. Struggling with—and separating from—certainty, Balmer manages to hold on to faith in God, the thrill of the world's beauty, and the comfort of grace, no matter how fleeting.*

And Jacob was left alone; and a man wrestled with him until the breaking of the day. When the man saw that he did not prevail against Jacob, he touched the hollow of his thigh; and Jacob's thigh was put out of joint as he wrestled with him. Then he said, "let me go, for the day is breaking." But Jacob said, "I will not let you go, unless you bless me." And he said to him, "What is your name?" And he said, "Jacob." Then he said, "Your name shall no longer be called Jacob, but Israel, for you have striven with God and with men, and have prevailed." Then Jacob asked him, "Tell me, I pray, your name." But he said, "Why is it that you ask my name?" And there he blessed him. So Jacob called the name of the place Peniel, saying, "For I have seen God face to face, and yet my life is preserved." The sun rose upon him as he passed Peniel, limping because of his thigh.

—Genesis 32:24–31 (RSV)

I ENVIED them in a way—their ease and self-confidence, the way they glided smartly across campus, their new American Tourister briefcases in tow. Moving from class to class, they knew—almost instinctively, it seemed—when to laugh at the professor's remarks. They asked all the right questions; they learned all the right answers. They were clean-cut and well groomed and athletic and earnest and attentive. They smiled most of the time. They socialized effortlessly among themselves, guffawing at inside jokes. More than anything else they exuded an air of confidence and self-assurance.

These were men of God, studying for the ministry at a fundamentalist seminary, and I was supposed to be among them. For as long as I can remember I had been groomed for the ministry, which is to say that my devout parents expected great things of me. My Christmas present following my sixth birthday was a three-foot-high replica of my father's pulpit, and family lore abounds with recollections of me as a six-year-old stemwinding preacher. I sang "Jesus loves me, this I know" in Sunday school, and "The B-I-B-L-E, yes, that's the book for me" and "Jesus wants me for a sunbeam."

I was "saved" at the age of three at the kitchen table in the back of a parsonage overlooking the Minnesota prairie. After breakfast and our family devotions my father asked if I was ready to ask Jesus into my heart. For some reason, I have a vivid mental image of the toaster, its brown fabric-covered cord trailing off the table. Yes, of course I would renounce my sinfulness and ask Jesus into my heart, and from that moment on I was saved. I had been born again.

I grew up in the secure cocoon of fundamentalist faith, society, and dogma. I was a quick study and learned from an early age to detect who was saved and who wasn't. The Lutherans up the road were a bit suspect, what with all their vestments and dead liturgy. Baptists were pretty much okay, though God knows they could get cantankerous at times. Roman Catholics, of course, were beyond the pale. I knew, for example, that I could never pursue the crush I had on Mary Kay Zimmer at school because she was Catholic, and my parents had informed me gently, but in no uncertain terms that if I married anyone other than a *Christian* girl I would be disowned.

There were, I soon learned, other ways to tell who was saved and who wasn't. Smokers were non-Christians because they defiled their bodies, and our body was a temple of the Lord. Drinking was also a sign of wickedness, and when my dad served Holy Communion at church it was grape juice, not wine, and it came in tiny glass containers barely larger than a thimble. Dancing was also a sign of "worldliness"; the Apostle Paul had admonished us to be separate from the world, to be *in* the world but not *of* the world. As Christians, we were called out of the world; our real citizenship lay in heaven, not on this earth, and this world, after all, was doomed and transitory. Jesus was coming back at any moment, and we had better be ready. Don't let Jesus catch you on the dance floor or in a movie theater.

I learned my lessons well. Rarely did I slip my fundamentalist moorings, and when I did I stayed pretty close to shore, even during the perilous years of adolescence. I shuffled off to Bible camp in the summer, where I swam and hiked and braided lanyards and fell in love and rededicated my life to Jesus at the campfire a couple of dozen times.

What's it like to grow up fundamentalist? I hear that question a lot, along with the corollaries: Is it true your parents didn't let you play cards? Did you really have to bring a note excusing you from square dancing in gym class? Your parents made you go to church more than once a week? What about sex? No sex before marriage, really?

I've always detected an undercurrent of voyeurism in these questions, but, for the record, the answer is yes to all of the above. No cards, no dancing, church three or four days a week and at least twice on Sunday. And no premarital sex. I had to sneak off to my first motion picture at the age of sixteen, feeling dreadfully guilty the whole time. We didn't have a television until I was nearly ten, although I'm not sure if that was because of religious conviction or relative poverty. Probably a bit of both.

Growing up fundamentalist meant living in a tiny world whose every question had an answer. It was a world inebriated with rhetoric about authority and obsessed with chains of command—the authority of the Bible, the authority of the church, the pastor, the husband, the father—and all of it dominated by authoritarian preachers, too many of them sporting egos the size of Montana.

It was a world marked by pious rhetoric, a kind of cloying God-talk. Did you get that promotion? Well, praise the Lord! My heart was really challenged by that message. God has been so good to me; I don't deserve his favors. The Lord has given me a real heart for the unsaved. I just wanna' do God's will.

Growing up fundamentalist meant growing up profoundly alienated from my own body, especially my sexuality. I recall my mother remarking to a friend that, even when I was ill, I never complained. The tone in her voice suggested admiration, so I sought to sustain that stoicism, subscribing to the aw-shut-up-and-it'll-get-better school of medicine.

There was comfort in that world, I'll not deny it. There's a certain appeal to being cosseted in a subculture with little room for ambiguity, where my destiny, both heavenly and earthly, had already been determined. Yet here I was watching these seminarians armed with their briefcases and their self-assurance. They had stuck with the program. They had solved the riddle of faith, which for them was really no riddle at all. Ask them a question, any question, and they could supply you with an answer. They could recite the cosmological and the ontological arguments backwards and forward, along with an airtight case for biblical inerrancy, the virgin birth, and the premillennial return of Jesus. Belief for them was effortless and easy, and yes, I envied them.

I was twenty-two at the time, a year out of college, and unemployed. After extensive deliberation I had turned down a career as an underwriter for Allstate Insurance Company, and as I looked for gainful employment I knew I was searching for something else: I was searching for the certainty I saw on the scrubbed faces of the seminarians. I knew I hadn't become the sunbeam Jesus apparently wanted. In the argot of the evangelical subculture, I was "willful" and "wayward"; I had slipped my moorings and was drifting in doubt and uncertainty.

A kind of intellectual restlessness had overtaken me. I was enamored of the world of ideas, so for a time I thought the way to reclaim the faith lay in rational argumentation, intellectual respectability. I was embarrassed by the simple piety of my parents, so I tried to dress up evangelical convictions in Enlightenment finery. Phrases like "reasoned belief" and the "integration of faith and learning" tripped off my tongue and became a kind of mantra. The theological discipline of apologetics seemed like the right course. If only we fundamentalists could come up with a reasonable defense of the faith then we could hold our heads high in the marketplace of ideas. More important, we could distance ourselves from those loopy charismatics and pentecostals, who gave us all a bad name with their naïve reliance on religious experience.

Attending church at that juncture of my life was excruciating, so painful that I rarely tried. The sentiments I acknowledged at the time were anger and betrayal, but the subculture still had enough of a hold on me that I felt embarrassed as well, ashamed that the faith had not taken hold of me—or had I not taken hold of the faith?—the way I thought it should. When guilt overtook me and I did show up at church I heard vapid and self-congratulatory sermons about the goodness of God and the rewards of living a "good Christian life." I heard admonitions about avoiding the perils of worldliness and triumphal assurances that God would eventually vanquish his adversaries, if not in this world then assuredly in the next. This God struck me as austere and demanding; he seemed to be big on rules, to hear the preachers tell it.

After a couple of decades steeped in fundamentalism I found the whole business rather nauseating—the megalomaniac preachers, the cloying God-talk, the overweening moralism—and so I trotted off to graduate school and immersed myself further in the life of the mind. Fundamentalism, with its petty squabbles over doctrinal minutiae and its taboos about beer and hair length and motion pictures, couldn't have been farther from my consciousness. I was busy building a career of my own, and I couldn't care less about the smug seminarians with their self-righteous patter about God's will and sanctification and all their hoary theological schemes.

Despite my satisfaction with the life of the mind, however, the life of the Spirit still beckoned, and I count this as a remarkable working of grace. Shortly after settling into my first academic appointment, I decided, in effect, to revisit my past, although I didn't recognize that I was doing so at the time. I set out on a journey into the evangelical subculture in America with the idea of lending some perspective to the televangelist scandals then titillating the media in the mid-1980s. I visited churches and camp meetings and seminaries and Bible camps. I heard plenty of bad sermons in the course of my travels and more renditions of "Shine, Jesus, Shine" than I care to count, but I also started hearing the gospel. I heard the gospel in the strains of "Amazing Grace, How Sweet the Sound" and in the simple expressions of piety of folks with their arms upraised to Jesus. I heard the gospel in an old friend's lament that fundamentalists had taken the gracious, beckoning words of Jesus and twisted them into demands, threats, and moral imperatives.

I don't think I heard much of the gospel during my visit to a fundamentalist Bible camp in the Adirondack Mountains of upstate New York, but there, as the flames of the campfire licked the darkness, my life began to make sense to me. I saw how desperately my parents wanted to rear me in the faith, how they wanted me to have the same conversion to fundamentalist Christianity that had so profoundly shaped their own lives. At the same time, however, as I listened to teenagers around the campfire talk about their own spiritual lives, I saw how difficult it was for me to appropriate my parents' faith. They had socialized me in the church since infancy—Sunday school, sermons, family devotions, Bible camp—and yet they expected that my moment of conversion would have the same transformative power as theirs. That, I concluded, was unrealistic because my "conversion" at age three was, at best, a ratification of the beliefs and the regimen that had been drilled into me since birth.

I saw myself in the adolescent faces around the campfire that night. I recognized the urge, under the extraordinary pressure of parents and peers, to give my life to Jesus, to conjure the right religious emotions, and then to declare my readiness to live a "good Christian life" and abide by all the fundamentalist strictures. I also recognized myself in those who, choking back tears, were "rededicating" their lives to Jesus, those whose conversions hadn't generated the emotion or the transformation they thought was expected of them, so they were revisiting the moment yet again as the flames danced and the embers glowed.

My experience at the Bible camp prompted me to reconsider my own struggle with faith. With the encouragement of a fellow pilgrim, I discarded my image of the self-confident seminarians and the triumphalist preachers. I even set aside the imposing specter of God the Father, who had been portrayed to me as demanding and authoritarian. I found Jesus a much more sympathetic figure. Jesus, I suspected, wouldn't have felt very comfortable with the briefcase crowd either. As nearly as I could tell, he hung around with ne'er-do-wells, people on the margins of society—fishermen and tax collectors; adulterers and lepers.

In time, it occurred to me that the entire Bible was populated with scoundrels. Paul certainly fits that description, both before and after his conversion. Peter didn't score too well on the loyalty test. David could not have become a member of any fundamentalist church that I'm aware of; he was hardly the poster boy for "traditional family values."

And yet the Bible seems to celebrate these characters. God chooses Paul—irascible old Paul, who had graduated at the top of his class at the persecution academy, to be the conduit for spreading the gospel. Jesus surely must have given Peter his nickname, The Rock, with his tongue at least partially in cheek, to call attention to the fact that, with his spineless dithering, Peter was anything but solid. David, the Scriptures tell us, was a man after God's own heart.

Then there's Jacob. He heads the list of scoundrels. Jacob, you'll recall, was the guy who, disguised beneath a goatskin, cadges his brother's rightful inheritance while Esau is out fetching supper. Jacob gets his comeuppance a bit when, after working seven years for the woman he loves, his devious father-in-law delivers the wrong woman to Jacob's marriage bed. Jacob works another seven years and finally secures Rachel for his second wife. He succeeds pretty well in the ranching business and then one day, camped out in the hill country, word arrives that Esau and his entourage are about to drop by. Jacob, all alone and sweating bullets, finally beds down by the Jabbok River and, in the course of a fitful night, grapples with a phantom—a man or an angel, perhaps, or even God—a wrestling match that leaves him with a bum leg.

Whatever else you care to say about these characters, they strike me as quintessentially human—Jacob and Paul and David and Peter and a hundred others whose images flicker before us in the Bible, however briefly. They are three-dimensional beings with a substance to them that I found lacking in the role models of my fundamentalist past. The religion of my childhood, not to mention the seminarians who so unnerved me, had taken the stories of these wonderfully complex and textured characters and reduced them to morality plays— abject sinners who suddenly are transformed into good, rule-abiding Christians.

Through some unaccountable working of grace, I began to see them not so much as saints but as fellow pilgrims. Like me, they are flawed. They trudge along, step by step, just like most of us mortals. What they share in common, I think, is a sense that the call of God is the call to be human, to embrace our humanity in all of its ambiguity. They see that the call of God is a summons to embark upon a journey of faith whose destiny is not always apparent. The Letter to the Hebrews in the New Testament tells us that when Abraham, another character with a checkered past, answered the call of God, "he went out, not knowing where he was to go."

In David James Duncan's novel *The River Why*, Gus Orviston, the central character, is a maniacal fisherman—like those first followers of Jesus—who unwittingly finds himself on a spiritual quest. After hours of debate and conversation, Gus's spiritual adviser, an aspiring fisherman himself, finally cuts to the chase. "I'm not sane, Gus. I believe in the rivers of living water; I believe our souls swim in that water; I believe Jesus and Buddha and Krishna are the savour in that water; I believe in the Garden World and its Queen. I love the ol' Whopper."

The path of faith is not tidy. For many, belief in itself is an affront to intelligence and even to sanity, especially when you can explain the spiritual quest in psychological or sociological or physiological terms. But, like Gus Orviston's interlocutor, like Paul and David, I believe in the rivers of living water, and those rivers sustain me in my pilgrimage. For me, the path to faith has been rocky and my steps uneven. I am plagued by doubts and fears and anxieties. I feel desolate, at times, and my cries to God meet with silence. I have been locked in a lovers' quarrel with my father, the preacher, for the better part of three decades, a quarrel over faith and belief and theology that has not so much abated as it has taken a different form since his sudden passing a few months ago. Like Abraham, I'm not always certain where I'm going on this pilgrimage, and my progress is slowed, I'm sure, whenever I pause to wrestle with God—or someone—lurking there in the darkness. My trajectory is rarely straight and not always upward. It resembles at times the woven, brown cord of a toaster trailing off the table. . . .

And yet what sustains me is a sense, or at least the hope, of divine presence, that I am not alone on this pilgrimage, but I am in the company of friends who will pick me up from time to time and point me in the right direction. What sustains me is a suspicion that there is still enchantment in the natural world. What sustains me is the laughter of my sons. What sustains me is the delight of love and companionship and making love. What sustains me is the conviction that the journey brings its own rewards, regardless of the destination, that holiness somehow is imbedded in the process itself.

I believe because of the epiphanies, small and large, that have intersected my path—small, discrete moments of grace when I have sensed a kind of superintending presence outside of myself. I believe because these moments—a kind word, an insight, an anthem on Easter morning, a chill in the spine—are too precious to discard, and I choose not to trivialize them by reducing them to rational explanation. I believe because, for me, the alternative to belief is far too daunting. I believe because, in the waning decades of the twentieth century, belief itself is an act of defiance in a society still enthralled by the blandishments of Enlightenment rationalism.

I no longer envy the seminarians I knew twenty years ago, even though I'm sure those spiritual athletes are far ahead of me on the journey. I congratulate them on their self-confidence. They figured out all of their answers before I even knew the questions, and I will never be able to match their strides.

But perhaps you, too, are a pilgrim, and if you look for me check somewhere toward the back of the pack. Like Jacob, I'm the guy with a limp.

IN SEARCH OF THE THIN PLACE

ALBERT JORDY RABOTEAU

A highly respected professor of American religious history at Princeton University, Albert Raboteau faced a crisis as he neared his fiftieth year. Rebelling against his need to always be responsible and "perfect," he overturns his life in search of his spiritual self. Raised Roman Catholic but recently converted to Eastern Orthodoxy, Raboteau finally comes to terms with the oppositions that have haunted him for years—the monastery or the world, the communal or the solitary, the holy or the mundane—when he journeys to the bleak, northern English isle of his spiritual ancestor Cuthbert, a seventh-century monk and bishop who also struggled with service and solitude.

STANDING IN church alone, I intone the opening of the vespers service, a "readers" vespers, meaning "without a priest." No one else has come this August Saturday evening except me—and the angels. Should I continue or should I wait? The light streams through the western windows. I've lit all the candles and it is ten minutes after the time we normally start. I chant tentatively:

Bless the Lord, O my soul! O Lord my God, You are very great; You are clothed with honor and majesty. You cover Yourself with light as with a garment. You stretch out the heavens like a curtain. You lay the beams of Your chambers in the waters. You walk on the wings of the wind. You

make Your angels spirits, Your ministers a flaming fire. You laid the
foundation of the earth, that it should never be moved.

The door opens and my wife, Julia, enters, followed by four more
women. We are six. I continue now more confidently:

The sun knows its time for setting. You make darkness, and it is night. O
Lord, how manifold are Your works! In wisdom have You have made
them all.

This is a mission of the Orthodox Church, five months old, counting from our first liturgy in March. The church we gather in is small,
as is our congregation . . . a handful of families and a continually surprising group of visitors. We chose to dedicate the mission to the
Mother of God "Joy of All Who Sorrow" as a sign of our desire to minister to those who suffer and are in need. The church building that we
are in now used to be a Roman Catholic mission before the congregation grew too large and moved elsewhere. When we first saw this
church, we felt that it was special. It felt prayed in and so we rented it
from the Catholic parish that outgrew it, trusting that we, too, would
grow in this place.

From the start, I have been the lay coordinator for our church, the
person responsible for organizing the week-by-week and day-by-day
details. So I feel responsible, and, at the same time, I resist feeling
responsible, since it is, as I constantly say, "in God's hands." The tension between wanting the mission to grow and trying to be detached
is taut within me. At each liturgy we sing the words "Lay aside all
cares; lay aside all earthly cares." And I try, but I keep worrying about
charcoal for the censer, soap in the bathroom, monthly rent pay-
ments, Sunday offering deposits, weekly Bible Study, and hardest of
all, conflicts that occasionally arise in such a small group. Sometimes I
wake at four A.M., worried about the mission and its future. I feel that
people depend on me. Since I was a child, I have always felt that
people depended on me. A burden full of responsibility that led me,
in mid-life, to kick over the traces: to stop trying to be perfect; to be
for a while disastrously irresponsible. How can I learn to manage this
inner balancing act of responsible non-responsibility?

I try to connect this theme that runs through my life to a constella-
tion of more recent events that I ponder still. Three years ago I had a
dream: I am on the northeast coast of England, with Julia, facing an

island. Our access to it depends upon the tide which has receded, allowing us to walk to the island by stepping on a series of wooden pylons and rocks. Beyond the large island is a smaller one which I realize is "my island." The larger island is deserted and treeless but the land is a yellow-green that glows and I know that if we can find the door we will discover the entrance to the underground cloister of a monastery.

Several days later I told this dream to a friend, who said "There is such a place. It's called Lindisfarne." I had not read or heard about Lindisfarne, other than the Lindisfarne gospels, but my dream accurately depicted it, as I learned later—a tidal island with another smaller island lying off its southern coast like "my island," almost exactly as I dreamed it. A year later, Julia and I took a trip, a pilgrimage to Lindisfarne. When we arrived, I was disappointed at the crowdedness and development of "Holy Island," as it's known. What drew my eye was a small island off the coast which I took to be the same small island of my dream and which is known as "St. Cuthbert's island," the site of his first hermitage.

Cuthbert (c. 634–687), one of the most popular saints of England, was a monk who became prior of Lindisfarne. He was widely known for preaching to the surrounding people of Northumbria and for reports of miracles in answer to his prayers. After serving as prior for several years, he retired to a hermitage, first on the little island close to Lindisfarne and then, in search of greater solitude, to Inner Farne, an island about seven miles distant. He was chosen bishop, refused, but reluctantly yielded to the repeated requests of the king and clergy. After two years, sensing his death, he resigned the bishopric to return to Inner Farne where he died. His body was first buried at Lindisfarne, but then removed because of the threat of Viking raids and, after years of wandering, ended up in Durham Cathedral. The feast day of the translation of his relics is September 4—my birthday.

When we saw St. Cuthbert's island—"my" island—I felt strongly that this was the goal of my pilgrimage, that this was, for me, the holy place, not Cuthbert's tomb in Durham Cathedral and not Lindisfarne itself. It was this small rocky place that I felt I needed to reach. The tide, however, wasn't yet fully out, so it was impossible to walk to the isle without getting our feet soaked with cold North Atlantic sea water. As Julia and I tried to figure out how to get there, we met two women who struck up a conversation with us. The older one, wearing babushka, overcoat, and carrying a cane, introduced herself as Doris..

She was especially friendly and talkative. Doris told us that she and her friend were part of a group of oblates of the Sisters of Mary Immaculate, an Anglican religious order, and that they and several others were accompanying their spiritual director, Sister Deidre, on pilgrimage to Lindisfarne. She said she had been to Iona, another place of Christian pilgrimage, but found Lindisfarne more spiritual. "It is what we call a 'thin place,'" she told me, "a place where the distance between heaven and earth is very thin."

The other, younger woman had been trying to reach the isle but the water was too deep, and sharp shells as well as slippery stones made the footing risky. I decided I had to get there anyway and began to walk over using an old iron pipe as a staff to steady my steps on the rocks, seaweed, and mud. Julia came, too. Once on the isle, she considerately wandered off to give me space to be alone. I walked out to an edge of rock that faced away from Lindisfarne toward the sea and sat down. This was indeed an "absolute" place, a place for facing the awesome presence of God. I felt for a few moments a sense of being alone and at peace with the rocks, the sea, the gulls skimming the sunlit water, the shimmering waves, and the low gray clouds. A stark beauty. I thought of how cold and stormy it must be in wintertime. Behind me, the ruins of a stone chapel encircled a tall wooden cross and I wondered what it would have been like to dwell there in a cell of rock.

Suddenly my solitude was broken by a woman walking nearby, so I ended my contemplation and started looking for rocks to take back home from this holy island. I waved to Julia who came over to join me and take some photographs. Gradually, by twos and threes, a group had assembled . . . perhaps eleven or twelve people in all, now sitting on the circle of stones where Cuthbert's hermitage had once stood. It was the oblates and their spiritual guide, Sister Deirdre, and they asked if we would like to join them in prayer. One by one, they began to read prayers from Celtic prayer books, several of which I recognized from a collection of prayers I had been using. They read them slowly, meditatively. Then Sister Deirdre asked me if I'd like to pray. I closed my eyes: "Dear God thank you for the beauty of this day and the wonderful providence of our fellowship. Thank you for bringing us together from such far distances, over so many miles to this place that resonates with the holiness of your saints. Preserve in us that resonance so that we may take with us some of the holiness we feel here. Thank you for your love which sustains us at each moment and each breath." When the circle reached Julia, she prayed "I am grateful for the beauty that surrounds us and for the birds and animals who are completely pure and innocent. May we learn from them and take their purity and innocence back into our world of cities and traffic." As we continued to pray around the circle, my eyes filled with tears at the tangible, gratuitous love that had brought us all to Cuthbert's island.

Later, thinking back, I was struck by the connection between solitude and community that I encountered in this "thin place"—how it was manifested in what I knew of Cuthbert's own life, and its apparent meaning for my own life. Perhaps this is what the dream and the trip were about; the absolute and fearful aloneness of solitude before God coming together with the loving regard and kindness of community. Learning that they aren't antithetical but contrapuntal.

From the time I was twelve I wanted to be a monk. I had read Thomas Merton's books and dreamed of the beauty of the contemplative life. But I didn't enter a monastery; I got married and had four children. I never got over the desire for solitude though, and the notion of being a monk lingered like a shadow vocation over my life, the path not taken, the heroic ideal that stood in contrast to the disappointment of ordinary life. It took me a long time, and the failure of my first marriage, for me to be able to understand that the holy is, in fact, to be found in the ordinary. I kept searching for it elsewhere by teaching and writing instead of in my family until I came to realize, at age forty-nine, that my life seemed no longer to be my own. I no longer even knew what I wanted but only what other people wanted of me. I was worn away by the desire to be perfect, to live up to expectations. And then a huge hole opened up in my life and I walked into it. I left my wife, hurting her and my children deeply. I resigned from a prestigious position in the university where I teach. And I traveled abroad, ostensibly to attend an academic conference, but actually searching for my lost self.

I visited an Orthodox monastery in England where I talked to a kind monk about the disintegration of my life. I visited churches in Paris and Florence. I went to Assisi and prayed before the cross of San Damiano that spoke to St. Francis but did not tell me what to do. I lectured at the conference and returned home knowing that my life had been overturned. I had failed the most important relationships of my life and I had done so in search of some spurious form of sanctity.

Is this, perhaps, the meaning that Lindisfarne and Cuthbert's life offer for my own life? That I was mistaken to identify monastic solitude as the place of holiness, and community as the place of ordinary, hum-drum responsibility? I think of what I've read about Cuthbert, how he spent his nights in prayer, up to his waist in the cold waters of the North Atlantic. When he came out, the sea otters warmed his chilled feet. By day, he did his duties as prior or bishop, preaching among the peoples of Northumbria. All the while, he longed for solitude with God. I wonder: how did he make peace with this desire for solitude and the burden of his responsibilities?

We claim that the saints are our ancestors in the faith and we believe that they are windows between this world and heaven, between the known and the unknown, between the time of dreaming and the time of waking. Guides to the holy, they beckon us to embrace the tension and antimonies that stretch our lives, sometimes close to the breaking point. As a wise friend advised me, there is no "holy island," every moment is an island of holiness. If we but perceived it, "the thin place" where God can be apprehended is all around. Grace is everywhere, if we submit to God, not to our ideas of sanctity.

I would encounter Cuthbert again.

Two years after our pilgrimage to Lindisfarne, Julia and I went back to England, this time to visit the St. John the Baptist Orthodox monastery in Essex that I had visited alone four years earlier during my time of darkness and soul searching. The monk I had met and spoken with then was still there. He asked what had happened since he saw me last. I told him that I had gone through a painful divorce. I had become Orthodox. And I had remarried. I told him of the new mission church that Julia and I had helped to start and asked for his prayers. In our conversation, I mentioned the trip to Lindisfarne and my connection to Cuthbert, and his eyes lit up. He said "Just think of it. That huge cathedral in Durham is built on the relics of this one man." Then he told me a story about St. Cuthbert's body being exhumed in the nineteenth century and how an Anglican rector had taken some relics of Cuthbert and that some of them had wound up in his hands. He asked if I would like a relic of St. Cuthbert. Deeply touched and amazed, I thanked him over and over again. The next day he handed me a small silver reliquary cross containing a relic of St. Cuthbert. Immediately I put it on the chain around my neck, next to the Jerusalem cross that I wear.

On the last day of our visit, Divine Liturgy was crowded with Sunday visitors from London. A woman pushed her paralyzed son forward through the crowd in his wheelchair to receive Holy Communion, and as I watched, I felt a strong urge to touch St. Cuthbert's relic to his head. I didn't, but then I became aware of the compassion that not only I, but all those around me, felt for this boy and his mother. I realized it was a very old feeling and suddenly it was transformed into an overwhelming experience of how much God loves all of us, each of us, at every instant, and that it was God's love certainly, not our perfection, that matters.

As we got ready to leave, I went to say good-bye to my monk friend, but couldn't find him. On the train ride to London, I opened my briefcase and noticed a small red box. I asked Julia if it was hers and she said no. I opened it and found a copy of St. Cuthbert's pectoral cross. My friend had slipped it into my bag.

Back at home, another task awaits me. Someone noticed that the church ceiling is leaking. Sure enough, there is a small puddle of brown, sticky liquid on the floor. I wipe it up and next day there it is again. I figure it is stagnant rain water that collected on a flat section of the roof and slowly seeped in. But it turns out that I am mistaken. A colony of bees has built a hive inside the church walls. Our church drips honey.

III

FLESH

and

SPIRIT

MY FATHER'S HOUSE

DON BELTON

Novelist Don Belton grew up in the early 1960s in Philadelphia's black community, yearning for an unnamable kind of love and tenderness between men. But in the "hard Eden" of his father's house rigid boundaries clearly separated right from wrong, male from female, black folks from white—except for the dominant image of a very "feminine-looking" white Jesus that confused the categories and laced Belton's spiritual longings with homoerotic desire.

As FAR back as I can remember, back to my earliest childhood, I have been pulled by the power of homoeroticism, perceived as a kind of life of the body, and pulled as well by the life of the spirit. Both have been mystical forces for me, alluring as fate, calling me to bear witness to something larger than time. Religion was, in my early life, the flaming sword that lay stretched between these two attractions, colonizing desire and reproducing man's fall from pleasure.

When I was a child everything in my father's house had a name and everything had a place. If something wasn't given a place or a name in my father's house, it didn't exist. I grew up yearning for the unnameable, the unplaceable. Later, I would learn names for what was missing, but back then I lived in a hard Eden, sensing something was buried in the kingdom of my father's house, something hot and unspeakable.

There was a way to speak to adults, my father taught me. A way to ask. A way to speak on the telephone. A way to eat. To be excused from the table. To stand. To sit. To behave when company came. A way to play so as not to disrupt the entire house. So as not to get my clothes dirty. Not a right and wrong way. There was one way: the way my father taught me. I was constantly corrected and reproved. I was rehearsed in his rules. I was policed and inspected. This color socks only goes with that color trousers. Use this fork for salad and that fork for meat. Only girls laugh: tee hee. Boys must laugh: ha ha. I took my rest at my precise bedtime, and my day began at exactly the same hour each morning. My evening and morning prayers were meticulously recited like incantations for an easy sentence in the prison of my father's house. I was not allowed to break a rule—ever. There was always something to say I was sorry for, something for which I knew I would never be entirely forgiven. Even at an early age, I learned to keep my sins a secret.

My father's Bible sat, big as the Book of Life in a DeMille epic, on the glass-topped coffee table in our living room. His Bible was bigger than the TV screen in the cabinet Magnavox he owned until the late '60s (when the civil-rights movement, riots, and the murder of Martin Luther King, Jr., had won consumer credit in giant downtown appliance stores for upstanding members of the negro middle class like my father. It took all that before a nineteen-inch color television set, full of the mass cultural phantasmagoria, was installed in our North Philadelphia row home). But back in the late '50s and early '60s, when I was a baby and toddler, the Bible lay, as if in state, as the presiding shrine and oracle of my father's house.

As far back as I can remember, I was carried back and forth to church, by my father and various other relatives. I was taken back and forth as though I were receiving treatments for a persistent ailment. During my childhood, we attended various churches, all of them Black and all of them Sanctified Holiness. Although there were often prayer meetings in our home, where the Black saints would gather, transforming themselves as they sang and spoke their quiet supplications to God, church provided a mode of expression that was forbidden in my father's house. Church was a spectacle. The members of the congregation not only prayed and sang. They "shouted." They danced the holy dance and walked the floor of the church in otherworldly syncopation. They beat their hands and jangled tambourines in double time. They screamed and cried. They fainted. The services at these churches were emotional extravaganzas so feverish that a small battalion of white-gloved ushers were dispatched to administer fanning, blankets, and smelling salts to soul-struck worshipers.

I learned about the Bible in the churches we attended. When I was two or three years old I started Sunday school, where I was indelibly imprinted with religion, indoctrinated through songs and stories. I sang with the children's Sunday school choir: "The B-I-B-L-E/That is the book for me/I'll stand alone/on the word of God/the B-I-B-L-E." My favorite song, however, was "Jesus loves me/this I know/for the Bible/tells me so." I sang it in and out of church. I sang it with the plaintive sincerity and hunger to be transported that children possess.

Perhaps I was so wrapped up in this song because even then it seemed to offer a paradigm that could subvert the power of my father's religion, his house, even as I used it to make a show of submitting to its power.

I was obsessed with Jesus, though, truly, I had no idea who or what Jesus was. Perhaps my obsession stemmed from my early recognition that Jesus was a sign of ambiguity in a house where everything else seemed hard and fast. The images of Jesus available to me were of a beautiful young white man, adapted, I now realize, from the Christ images of Italian Renaissance paintings. Recently I made a brief tour of museums and cathedrals in Italy. I was struck by the homoerotic force of the Christs painted by Giotto, Michelangelo, and da Vinci. The images of Christ that emerged during the Renaissance celebrated spiritual principles at the same time that they celebrated the male body.

The Christ images of *my* early childhood were the earliest images I can remember where there was the clear association of maleness with beauty. The depictions were from a standard repertoire and many quoted one another: Christ crucified, the Last Supper, the Good Shepherd, Christ praying in the Garden, Christ expelling the money lenders from the Temple, Christ with the bleeding heart. Of course the Christs of my early childhood, unlike the Christs from the Italian Renaissance, were two-dimensional, for the most part; the work of hack colorists and copyists. Still, they retained some of the flavor of their sources and passed along intimations of the power of those sources to me. I recall, very early, being fascinated by a drawing in a book my father owned of Samson straining his perfect body between two pillars, toppling the palace of the Philistines. This picture was like a door for me into which I escaped for hours from the resoluteness of my father's house. I lived in a suspended state of enchantment, poring over that picture, captivated by its tricks of proportion and light, its representation of the beauty of harmony in the male body. I assumed, until I learned to read well enough, that this was merely another picture of Jesus.

What these pictures of Jesus bore in common was the picture of an at once consequential and pregnable male youth—a god—wearing scant, diaphanous clothes, clothing that parted strategically to provide voyeuristic focus on beautiful limbs, a naked heart. The only thing I had to compare these pictures to back then was the provocative, but by today's standards tame, pinup girl calendar photos hanging in the office of an uncle's gas station and the neighborhood barber shop, where my father and I went for our weekly haircuts—both aggressively male and secular spaces.

The calendar pictures of thinly clothed young women were profane, not sacred. They were visual confections. But so, in a sense, were the pictures of Jesus I knew from my Sunday school textbooks, the illustrations in my father's Bible, funeral parlor fans, and decorative household notions. This seemed especially true of pictures of the crucified Christ wearing nothing more than a loin covering. Even as a child, the image of the exposed, undressed Christ made these pictures available to me for erotic readings. Both the image of the pinup girl and the image of Jesus were sentimental, populist cultural productions. Both were idealized and eroticized through their vulnerability to the gaze of the viewer.

I remember once looking at a picture of Jesus, painted on a plate, that hung on the wall in our kitchen and asking my father, "Is Jesus a man or a woman?" The picture showed Jesus standing outside a small house knocking at the door. He was holding a shepherd's hook, which I recognized since it had been identified for me by my father in another picture where Jesus was among the lambs, The Good Shepherd. If he was a man, I had no idea what sort of man. Certainly, no man I knew had long hair. My father had told me many times that the Bible maintained that it was a shame for a man to wear his hair long, and so he and I went ritualistically to the barber each week to have our heads shorn and sprinkled with bay rum. It was not only the hair, however, that made me suspect Jesus might be a woman. It seemed he was always doing something a woman rather than a man did in terms of the gender vocabulary I understood then. He suffered. He healed. He wept. He provided care. He was a kind of male mother, I thought.

In the picture in our kitchen, I was told in response to my questions, Jesus was knocking at the door of my heart, asking to come in. But I could plainly see Jesus was *not* knocking at the door of a heart. He was knocking at the door of a house, my father's house. This was even stranger, because Jesus was white.

In the neighborhood where I lived, whites did not socialize with blacks, though we had one or two white neighbors and there were several white merchants along our avenue. No white person ever entered our home when I was very young. When a caterer came, or a carpenter, or the florist or a furniture delivery man, these were negro men. In those days, we lived and socialized in an authentic black community. Moreover, images of white men in my father's house were rare and exotic. Television, newspapers, and magazines had not yet come to dominate our virtual lives. And we didn't know any white men, though at the family New Year's Eve party held annually in our home the gathered men told white man stories. In these stories, white man embodied evil and power. The white man was worse than the Devil, because, according to my father's religion, the Devil had been put under the subjection of God. The white man was godless and was subject to nothing and no one. The white man lied and seduced, jailed, ravaged, and lynched.

Yet, for all the white man's evil deeds since time immemorial, I knew that my uncles and my father smiled in the faces of white merchants and white policemen. They were gracious when a white man summoned them to a counter or a desk in a downtown bank. They deferred to white men on the sidewalk, especially at night on dark streets far from home, and spoke to no negro or family person in the same tones of high regard reserved for a white man: "Yes, sir," and "No, sir," and "Thank you, sir." My mother bore my father's children, kept his house, cooked for him, and he never once thanked *her*. These black men loved their wives and children. I knew this. I knew they were good men. They dreamed, worked, and sacrificed. Through my childhood and adolescence, each of them exhausted themselves to build a legacy out of their bodies in factories, shipyards, metal yards and, rarely, office buildings—selling second-hand, driving trucks, shining shoes, hauling, hammering, and serving. Many of them worked two or three jobs concurrently. In their time, each would destroy his body with work and strain. Once or twice a year, he might seem to weep as he prayed a desperate prayer in church. Or take down a guitar in a living room and sing a song that was like a letter from "down home." Or sit among each other in a kitchen laughing, telling drawn-out, mercurial stories. I always suspected their public deference and private hatred for white men belied a preoccupation with a white man's power to subvert or corroborate their own claim to Western manhood.

And there were the pictures of Jesus, white, lordly, and ravishing, on the walls of my father's house. It is a simple matter to say that my father, in his persistence in "white" Christianity, was only a victim of the histories of colonialism and slavery. But that version denies my father's agency and his subjectivity. After all, my father was a man, thinking and willing. *He* put that Bible in a place of prominence in his house. *He* framed and hammered those pictures to his walls.

I never asked why Jesus was white. Perhaps his "shameful" hair balanced out the social currency of his racial whiteness. I *wanted* him to be white. He needed to be white. I read Jesus' whiteness as a queerness, like the whiteness of a ghost or the queerness of the white peacock I'd once seen at the Philadelphia Zoo—a manifestation of the world's erratic side that had not yet been spoken. This whiteness was strange, not hateful. Something strange was at the gate of my father's house, knocking.

I had to wait to become a man myself to understand that my father's coldness was his gift to me. By teaching me to become regimental and unbreakable, my father taught me to safeguard my heart from the same world that would, so shortly after the announcement of President Johnson's New Society, mock my father's dreams and destroy the neighborhood that had been his Canaan, the son of Georgia peasants. My father would work himself to death by the time I reached the age at which he fathered me.

Jesus was a queer token between my father and me, a sign of paradox. The paradox, I now understand, is that love is its own safeguard. When I reached adolescence, our house had grown noisy with phantom TV, stereo, and radio voices. My father's house was heavy with things. Fine, secondhand furniture and the carpenter's handiwork were replaced by plastic-covered creations from giant factories. We hid away from one another inside that house. I, in my room, listening to music and reading books. He, in the basement, alone down there for hours, when he wasn't hiding in sleep on the living room sofa before the ghoulish light of the TV. The community outside my father's house was no longer the model black community of the late '50s that had been his pride. The neighborhood was under siege. A chapter of the Black Panther Party had moved in down the street from us in 1969, and with the Panther headquarters had come a heavy and menacing police presence on our avenue. In 1970, Philadelphia police raided the Panther house. My father's neighborhood awoke to gunfire. By the late afternoon, the Philadelphia police chief strode down our avenue, declaring through a megaphone that all the dirty bastards living in this hellhole should be shot. Only a decade earlier, John Fitzgerald Kennedy had flashed by our sycamore-shaded house, smiling and waving in a motorcade on his way to the presidency of the United States, trailing hope.

In 1970, I was attending a Quaker boys' day school on an academic scholarship. There, I was isolated and admired in a world of affluent white boys. At home, I missed my father terribly, although I could not ever remember being close to him or hearing him tell me he loved me. I was lonely for my father. At the same time I hid from my father, I began to track him. I sneaked and went through his chest of drawers. I looked in his closets, his shoe boxes, fishing tackle boxes and toolboxes for the secrets of his heart. I went behind him, fingering the filters of the cigarettes he had smoked and left in ashtrays, hoping to finger some secret thought. Once I steamed open and read a letter he had written to the grandmother who had raised him, hoping I would learn my father's true identity.

One day when I was eleven or twelve years old, and my father was out of the house on an errand, I made a fine, strange discovery. I found, hidden beneath a floorboard in our basement, his money box. The box was unlocked. There were several rolls of half dollars and dimes, and twenty dollars or so in old bills. Beneath the money box, however, there was a bundle of photographs wrapped in a brown silk scarf. The photographs were male physique photos—a series of white male nudes, well-made men standing in a sun-washed forest. I looked at each photograph of each man, carefully, as if each picture was a letter from some distant homeplace of the soul. My hands felt as if they were vibrating. When I was done looking at the photographs, I wrapped them as I had found them and replaced everything beneath the floorboard. I never mentioned the pictures to my father or anyone. Still, I always felt he knew I'd seen them after that day and that even before I'd seen them I'd felt them buried in his house. At times, I thought he left them there for me to find. Perhaps I am wrong, but I believe my father died waiting for me to unearth his softness. Somewhere inside the furnace of work he turned himself into, my father was a man crying for love between men, love that risked and healed the contradictions.

from *IN THE WILDERNESS*

KIM BARNES

Poet and writer Kim Barnes's autobiography, In the Wilderness, *a finalist for the 1997 Pulitzer Prize, takes us to the impoverished logging community in rural Idaho where she was raised in a strict Pentecostal church. In this selection, Barnes is a gawky, devout girl approaching puberty, pulled between holiness and desire, her body stirred as much by prayer as by the forbidden warmth of a young boy's touch.*

Between dogpath and Pierce lies Cardif Spur, a cluster of faded trailers and creosote-stained shacks named after a sawmill operator. One of those shacks was the parsonage, which shared a large open space between the road and Trail Creek with the Cardiff Spur Mission, the Pentecostal church my parents had chosen for us to attend. Our first meetings were around a potbelly stove, scooted so close the preacher was made to circle behind us, calling on us to confess our latest sin.

The men who attended were loggers and mill hands, men who blended easily with the small population of the area. On Sundays, they wore freshly pressed shirts, suitcoats and trousers; other days, they were distinguished only by their profession: black boots and stagged pants cut to mid-calf, out of the way of saws and snags. The women who attended our church, however, with their long skirts, plain faces

217

and coiled hair were easily identified as holy-rollers. I became aware of the fact that I, as a girl approaching adolescence, was being dressed accordingly—no shorts, short-sleeved blouses, blush or pierced ears—only when we made our visits to Lewiston, where Nan would shorten my dresses and trim my hair, clucking all the while about never having seen such nonsense. She believed I could be a beauty queen: how was that to happen if people's only notice of me was the simple curiousness of a girl dressed like a dowager?

I signed the church's youth pledge and carried a white waxy card listing the regulations governing my behavior. I promised never to dance, drink, smoke, or swear. I would not go to movie theaters, frequent bowling alleys, swim with the opposite sex or dance except under the Spirit. The hem of my dresses would measure two inches below my knees, and I would refrain from wearing pants. I would wear no jewelry, makeup or other adornment that might draw attention to my physical self and cause another to lust after me in an unholy way. I would pray daily, fast frequently and believe always in the Lord as my Savior. I embraced these commandments, thrilled to have in my new purse a card bearing the large script of my signed name. When I made my commitment public, my parents and the other adults beamed with approval and prayed with hands on my shoulders that I forever follow the path of righteousness and turn not from the hard road onto the wider path of wickedness leading only to Hell.

I don't remember the name of our first preacher at Cardiff, thumping his Bible behind my head, taking great leaps around the room, agile beyond his years. He is a presence, a bellowing exhortation. Nor do I remember the day he left, the Sunday our new pastor, Brother Lang, took his place at the podium.

Joseph Lang was short and stocky, ruddy complected, with thick black hair that glistened like patent leather. His wife, Mona, was shorter still, burdened with enormous breasts that she shrugged and shifted into balance. She sat ramrod straight at the piano, hair the color of granite brushing the bench behind her. Their children were all ahead of me in school—Sarah, the eldest, then the two boys, Matthew and Luke.

They seemed always happy, singing separately or as a family, teasing with affection, catching us up in their enthusiasm for God. We often gathered at the personage for long hours of music: Brother Lang on his banjo, my father strumming along on the guitar my mother had bought him for Christmas—a Gibson arch-top f-hole—playing the simple chords he had learned as a boy. Brother Lang was originally from Texas and knew many of the bluegrass songs my parents loved, and when not playing gospel they filled the small room with the loud and vibrant twang of country.

Perhaps my father saw in Brother Lang the man he might become—a preacher, a husband whose family followed the path he laid out without question. My mother found in Sister Lang something her own life had never offered: a role model of Christian womanhood. And I found the same in Sarah, nearly a woman herself but willing to treat me with kindness, teaching me the art of modest behavior: keep your legs together, your skirt pulled over the caps of your knees; don't chew gum; run the water when you use the bathroom to mask the noise. Her long blond hair and virtuous demeanor brought her the attention of an eighteen-year-old boy from downriver, a trapper and wilderness guide, red-headed and easily embarrassed. At sixteen her parents believed her more than ready to marry, and before the year was out she and her new husband, Terry, had taken up matrimonial residence in her upstairs bedroom.

But there was one stipulation to their union: Terry could marry their daughter, but he must agree to never take her away from the family. Brother and Sister Lang believed that Sarah and Matthew had a singing ministry to fulfill, a calling that might bring them recognition and success in the process of spreading the Gospel. At some point during each service, Matthew and Sarah would take the stage. Matthew strummed his twelve-string and sang with his eyes closed while Sarah crossed her hands in front of her and focused on something just above the heads of the congregation. If Terry were to separate the family, their dreams would die.

At fifteen Matthew was impish and quiet. He loved hunting nearly as much as Bible study, and his mature approach to both impressed everyone. He delivered the Sunday sermon when his father was away, unmoving behind the podium, attempting only occasional and solemn glances at his attentive audience. His brother, Luke, a year younger, had high cheekbones touched by his father's coloring, full lips, startling blue eyes, a James Dean swagger. Cocky and intelligent, less serious than Matthew, he sometimes gave me the gift of his gaze, and I found myself shuffling the awkward corners of my elbows into a more presentable picture.

Along with my desire for his attention came an awareness of the failings of my eleven-year-old body—the skinny legs and ridiculously large feet, the heavy glasses that constantly slid down my nose. In his presence I jumbled my words and tripped for no reason. His smug grin humiliated me, and I came to realize that my best self lay in stillness. When around him, I moved only when I had to and spoke only when addressed, answering in clipped phrases, but no matter how I held myself in, wrapping my arms about my waist, double-crossing my legs, something escaped to betray me: I stuttered out the wrong chapter and verse when asked to recite Scripture; my stomach growled in the quiet between prayers; sweat pooled in my palms and beneath my arms. Surely he and everyone else could see how imperfect I was.

Sometimes after church, after the foyer had emptied and the adults had gone to the parsonage to drink coffee, he'd teach me the chords of a forbidden song—"Hey Jude" or "House of the Rising Sun"—and I'd plunk along on the old upright, filled the sanctuary with wanton rhythms. When he lowered his eyes and sang, I felt dizzy with a feeling I could no more identify than the taste of sugarcane. It was a tingling in my belly, a lightness in my bones. It felt like sin and I knew it.

What I did not know, could not foresee, none of us could, was how the church would cleave, how the congregation would be divided by the new preacher, this man of God come to the wilderness to save us. Then our numbers would grow, drawing converts from the camps and near towns until the pews filled with believers. The building itself would be torn down, a new one built. The old woodstove would be hauled across the creek and dumped; a new oil furnace would blow its warmth into the church. Our circle would once again tighten, drawn together by the Langs until our lives—theirs and the lives of my family—became meshed, inseparable. We rocked in the comfort of their ministry until those last few months when one died, another dreamed of demons so horrible he purged his body of food and trembled in his wife's arms to stand and sing God's praises and another locked himself in an earthen cell with only a few jugs of water and a Bible, praying for a sign, deliverance for us all.

Tuesday night, Pathlighters. Wednesday night, prayer meeting. Thursday, men's Bible study, women's Aglow. Sunday school, church, choir practice, evening service. In between we gathered informally, sharing dreams and Scripture, passing out tracts in town, witnessing to our few and patient neighbors. And every few months, *revival*.

The revivalist would arrive, bringing with him an air of excitement, the anticipation of a circus or carnival. We held meetings in our church, in the grange halls of other small towns or, most memorably, in huge tents set up in mown fields and vacant lots. If a creek were close by, we had full-immersion baptisms, sometimes so spontaneous the women had no time to don double slips beneath their dresses. When they surfaced, hands raised to heaven and speaking in tongues, translucent pink showed through the wet cloth. Their skirts floated up like lilies.

Meetings lasted for hours, every night, beginning with the opening prayer, a few answering amens, then singing. As our voices rose, people began to clap, then sway, palms raised to the ceiling. When the missionary took the podium, we were primed for his outpouring of God-given wisdom and spiritual insight. By the time the sermon ended, the pitch of our praise had built to the point of drowning out his closing words, and he called on us to confess and be reborn in loud outbursts that sounded more like commands than entreaties. Finally, the entire congregation shouted and stomped, those gifted in tongues adding their heavenly language to the booming chorus.

Each preacher was different. One might holler and wave his arms; another pounded the pulpit with his Bible until the spine broke and pages flew. The missionary from down south danced in the aisles, twirling with his arms outstretched, head thrown back, heels clicking the wooden floor in the measured beat of flamenco. The first man to prophesy my future was a grandfatherly missionary with hair the color of new dimes, who sold us beautiful wooden boxes carved by the natives of Haiti. In our second week of revival, two people had been healed: one of an ulcer, the other of a slow-knitting rib, cracked when his saw kicked off a limb and knocked him flat. It was this preacher who called me out one night after the sermon, after Sister Baxter had prophesied in tongues and Sister Johnson had interpreted God's message, a message of warning lest Satan rally his army, jealous of our praise. Several women had fallen under the Spirit and lay on the floor weeping—others less stunned draped the women's legs with lap cloths to ensure modesty.

He found me, head bowed, a little sleepy, muttering my prayers and unprepared for his attention. The voices quieted as he called me to the altar. I stepped away from my seat and made my way toward the front, weaving through the prostrated bodies. His eyes were serious and piercing, as though there was something I was hiding, as though he could read in my face what had roused in him the need to clasp my head between his sweaty palms and drive me to my knees.

I felt no fear. I felt the roughness of his hands and the eyes of the church upon me, but I believed in this man of the Lord. I had seen him heal the Paxson boy, seen the short leg lengthen in the preacher's cupped hand. What wound or fault he might find in me I could not discern, but I waited calmly to be free of it, to be made newly whole.

"What is your name, child?"

"Kim," I whispered.

"Sister Kim, God has brought us here together tonight for a very special reason. Do you know what that is?" He let his gaze sweep the room. "Sister Kim walks among you with a gift. Sister Kim, do you know what that gift is?"

I heard the voices behind me: "Yes, Lord!" "Thank you, Jesus!" I thought I heard my mother crying. I shook my head, filled with a growing curiosity as though a stranger were about to read my palm, uncover a family secret. I steadied myself against the weight of his hands.

"You, my daughter, have the gift of healing. You are a healer!" Behind me the praise grew louder. The room felt suddenly hot and I wished for an open door, a window letting in the cool night air. His hands were heavier than my legs could stand and I fell, sweat trickling down my sides.

Sister Lang pounded out chords on the upright. I don't remember the hymn or what other hands came to bless me. I only remember my knees on the cold wood floor and wondering what my father thought then, what would be expected of me in the days to come. I wondered if Luke had witnessed my anointing. I wondered what part of him I might touch.

The next Sunday I sat at the table of Brother and Sister Baxter. They ran cattle outside of Weippe, an even smaller town than Pierce, twenty miles southwest. There were others there my age, children still wobbly in their manners at the table's far end, eating silently while the adults pondered the day's sermon and praised the wife's fried chicken. If there was a lull in the conversation, if the discussion had turned to the past week's revival, I don't recall. I only know I felt a sudden pain, as though a nail were being driven into my ear. I whimpered and my fork clattered to my plate.

I had never had an ear infection, had never felt the kind of pain I now felt, both throbbing and sharp. I remembered the missionary's words, and with absolute certainty stood up and announced, "Someone here has an earache."

Looking from one unperceiving face to another, I pressed my hand to the right side of my head.

"Someone's ear hurts."

I stood with my neck bent to ease the pressure. At the other end of the table a woman let out a single sob. It was Sister Baxter.

I moved from my child's place and walked to her chair. She bowed her head, softly crying, and I placed my hand on her right ear. I could feel the heat there, the drumming pain. Others joined me, clasping my shoulders, touching my back.

"Dear Lord, our sister has a need. She needs you, Jesus." My words were met with a chorus of *amens* and *hallelujahs*. I drew a breath. My eleven-year-old awkwardness was gone. The words flowed.

"We ask that you take this pain from her. Heal her, Lord! In God's name we pray."

The chorus grew loud and encompassing, until the body I touched and the hands touching me melded. I floated in a swell of sound, a humming of breath and blood.

"You will be healed!" I demanded it, surprised by the volume of my voice. The woman shuddered and groaned. The heat from her ear spread from my fingers into my arm and shoulder—my neck and face flushed with it. I opened my eyes and found myself in that room, the chicken half-eaten, gravy scumming the plates. The woman shivered in my hands.

Later, I played with the other children in the barn. The woman's one daughter and I hid from the boys in the stubble, giggling with pleasure at their blindness. We rooted tadpoles from the shallows and stabbed them onto rusty hooks. The creek held catfish and we bobbed for them in the manure-silted water. Each one we pulled from the muddy stream seemed a miracle, so different from the blazing trout I caught in the clear runoff of Reeds Creek. I held their sleek black bodies in my hands, smothering the spiny backs, careful of their poison.

We trapped the big green frogs that huddled beneath the over-hanging grass, and while the girls swaddled them in the hems of their skirts the boys got a hammer from the barn and made little crosses of split barnwood. Holding the struggling frogs by their tiny wrists and ankles, we drove small nails through each webbed foot, then studied them for a while. Their white bellies spasmed, their mouths opened and closed. They looked like rotund little men with their legs stretched straight. Someone suggested making miniature crowns of nettles but no one wanted to be stung.

We planted them in the muddy creek bottom, three frogs hanging above the water, arranged to mimic the painting we had seen of the crosses on Golgotha: Christ, the largest frog, in the middle, the two thieves on either side. Something about the symmetry of the mar-tyred frogs seemed targetlike and the boys ran to the house and came back with their BB guns. Bulls-eye was the belly, and we all took turns until the frogs sagged on their crosses and we lost interest in the game.

That night, after evening service, Sister Baxter slipped into bed beside her already sleeping husband. When she woke the next morn-ing her pillow was sticky with pus. The fever was gone. Whether it would have been so had I not touched her, I didn't know. I can explain the progress of illness and infection but not the moment when her pain took hold of me as though it were my own affliction.

She testified at church that a miracle had been wrought, and only then did I feel the weight of expectation fall upon me, heavy as the missionary's hands. My parents allowed me to walk in front of them. The other children began to resent the way the adults nodded when-ever I spoke. The attention made me aware of how seriously every-one looked upon my gift, yet I wasn't sure I could do it again. If I failed to discern an illness, or if I prayed for someone to be healed and nothing happened, would it mean I had sinned, that I was unworthy?

And then there was Luke. How did he fit into the maze my life was becoming? Somewhere between a child's innocent cruelty and her coming initiation into the world. When I thought of Luke's hands, how they touched me accidentally or on purpose but always in a way I remembered for days, I was filled with more emotion than I had ever experienced crucifying frogs or healing the sick.

Many Sunday afternoons my family spent at the parsonage. While the women made stew or fried venison dusted with flour, Matthew,

Luke and I hunched together on the narrow stairway leading upstairs, sharing the dirty jokes we had heard at school, guessing what went on in the bed of their sister.

It was always dark there, and we spoke in whispers. The closeness of our bodies took my breath away. When Luke's leg rested against mine I could no longer hear what was being said. When he put his hand on my knee, the sweet shock traveled to the bone and began a fire that spread its warmth to my crotch, a feeling so pleasurable I shuddered with the sure sin of it.

When we returned to the company of our parents, I could still feel the heat of his hand. Even if I could not articulate what I was feeling, I understood that what we were doing fell into the category of sin called "petting"—touching between young men and women that brought on our elders' direst warnings. I burned with shame to have given myself so easily to his caress. I prayed for forgiveness, for strength, for whatever temptation this was to leave me. But even in sleep I remembered his palm pressed against bare skin beneath the hem of my skirt.

The more I tried to forget the pleasure of being close to Luke, the more I longed for it. This was a symptom of Satan's influence I recognized: the greatest sin was desire for anything other than God. Desire for money, whiskey, the touch of another without the marriage blessing—any possession or worldly place—was lust and must be controlled, purged and destroyed.

I saw that something had begun its slow possession. How could I be both healer and sinner? How could I close my eyes in prayer when all I could see was the face of the preacher's son? I was lost, no language to describe how I savored this sin, no one to prophesy my salvation or damnation. I huddled beneath the covers of my bed, hearing the wind rise, the pinecones tacking the ground. Surely God would cause a tree to fall, send it crashing through the roof. I imagined Luke's kiss, then the slide of his hand between my legs. The night held still. I could dream of no more.

IF ONLY I'D BEEN BORN
A KOSHER CHICKEN

JYL LYNN FELMAN

Thighs, breasts, wings: are we talking about a kosher chicken or a girl? In this multi-layered essay, performance artist, attorney, and award-winning writer Jyl Lynn Felman uses her mother's attentive, loving preparation of the centerpiece of the Sabbath meal as the touchstone for her own female self. Why can't she be a bubelah, *a nice, compliant Jewish girl, instead of a* vilde chaye, *a wild animal, and a woman who loves women?*

THE PROBLEM with my mother's dying is not so much that she died but that she died without telling me how to make a chicken. If I could make a chicken the way my mother did, I could have her with me always, or so I imagine. In my fantasy, whenever I want to talk to my mother, I go to the kosher butcher or buy Empire frozen if I'm in a hurry, and I cook that chicken until my mother appears alive and well before me. So strong is the smell of the roasting chicken in my mind that I feel my mother coming into the room this very minute. Before sitting down, without even looking, she automatically reaches toward the table I have set so carefully. She arranges the silverware slightly—moving the napkin away from the fork. And then she sits upright and healthy at my own kitchen table. So vivid is the picture that I am smiling, full of our shared presence. As though my mother and I had just spent the afternoon together, talking as we always did. And searching for a way into each other's lives.

Fortunately, both my mother and the roasted kosher chicken live now in my imagination. But I simply cannot cook. I broil. I grill. I set the table nicely. But I cannot cook at all. Instead, I search everywhere for the perfectly cooked, tender and moist, crisp but not dry roasted chicken. Yet the fantasy is important to me. How could I let my mother die without learning how to cook her chicken? It seems improbable that the thought never occurred to me before she died a year ago. Didn't I know that I would miss her most through the food I eat and the food she cooked? It seems so obvious that I do not know how to cook because I gave up at an early age. I felt for sure that I had to make a choice about my Jewish female future before my future was made for me. Only now, at age forty, my mother gone from me forever by a year, and my Jewish female future made, do I understand how large a mistake I made and how much of the mistake was a product of both my mother's story and my own. For it is in poultry, legs and thighs, breasts and wings, where my mother and I mapped out the fragile borders of our femaleness and made whole the permanent expression of our Jewishness.

My mother washed us both in the same kitchen sink. Only I don't know who came first, the baby or the bird. First I am on the counter watching, then I am in the sink splashing. My mother washes me the way she washes her kosher Shabbas chicken breasts. Slow and methodical, as though praying, she lifts my small right arm; she lifts the wings of the chicken; and scrubs all the way up to where she cannot scrub anymore, to where the wing is attached to the body, the arm to the shoulder. Plucking feathers from the freshly slaughtered bird, she washes in between my fingers; toes by toe. Gently she returns my short stubby arms to the sides of my plump body which remains propped upright in the large kitchen sink. I am unusually silent throughout the duration of this ancient cleansing ritual. Automatically my arms extend outward, eternally and forever reaching for her.

The cold wet chicken, washed and scrubbed, sits next to us on the counter. I weigh more than the chicken, but as far as I'm concerned we're identical, the chicken and I. Except for our heads and the feathers. The chicken has no head and I have no feathers. But I will have hair. Lots of body hair on this nice Jewish girl that my mother will religiously teach to pluck and to shave until my adolescent body resembles a perfectly plucked pale young bird waiting to be cooked to a hot crisp, golden brown and served on the same sacred platter as my mother herself was before me.

At thirteen I stand on the *bimah** waiting to address the entire congregation. I am also upstairs in the bathroom, alone in the terrifying wilderness of my adolescent femaleness. But I stand on the *bimah* and prepare to chant. On my head is a white silk yarmulke held in place by two invisible bobby pins. For the first time in my life, I prepare my female self the exact same way she taught me in her kosher kitchen sink. *Borachu et Adoni hamivorach.* I look out at the congregation of Beit Avraham. My mother is crying. I look in the mirror; I inspect my face, my eyebrows are dark brown and very thick. *Baruch atah Adoni hamivorach laolam voed.* I place the tweezers as close to the skin as possible to catch the root, so the hair won't ever grow back. *Baruch atah Adoni, Elhaynu melach haolam . . .*† My parents are holding hands as I recite the third blessing in honor of being called to the Torah. And then I begin. Although my *haftarah*‡ portion is long and difficult I want it to last forever because I love the sonorous sounds of the mystical Hebrew letters. But I am surprised at how much it hurts to pull out a single hair from under my pale young skin. When I reach the closing blessings my voice is strong and full and I do not want to stop.

The rabbi asks my parents to stand. They are kissing me, their youngest baby girl. But I am surprised at how much it hurts to shape my thick Ashkenazi eyebrows into small elegant, anglo female arches. Then I remember the ice cubes that she soaks the chickens in, to keep them fresh and cold before the plucking and how I used to watch her pluck out a long, particularly difficult feather without a single break. She had special *fleishig*§ tweezers, for use in the kitchen only. The congregation sings, *"Mi chamocha boalim Adoni."* I go to the kitchen for ice cubes wrapped in terry cloth, which I hold diligently up to my adolescent brow. *Michamomcha Adoni nadar bakodesh . . . "Who is like unto thee, O most High revered and praised, doing wonders?"* I have no feeling above my eyes, but the frozen skin is finally ready for plucking.

These first female rituals have no prayers as I stand before the rabbi utterly proud of what I have accomplished. He places his hands above my head. *"Yivorech et Adoni . . ."* He blesses my youthful passage into the adult community of Jews. When I stand alone in the bathroom, my eyes water as I watch the furrowed brow of my beloved

---

*See note, page 84.
†The beginning words of a Hebrew blessing: *Blessed are you, Lord our God, King of the Universe . . .*
‡A selection from the Prophets, often chanted by the bat/bar mitzvah.
§For use with meat.

ancestors disappear from my face forever. At the exact same moment that I become a bat mitzvah I begin the complex process of preparing myself for rebirth into gentility. I complete these first female rites in silence, without the comfort of my mother or a single Hebrew *brocha*.* The congregation rises, and together we say, *"Yiskadel, Viskadesh sh'ma rabo."* Today I am permitted to mourn publicly. I have become a beloved daughter of the covenant, only the covenant is confusing. *Shema Yisrael Adoni echad,* I love my people Israel, but I loathe my female self. Is this what my mother wanted for me? On the occasion of my bat mitzvah my body splits apart and my head becomes severed from the rest of my body, a chicken without a head, a head without a body.

I am balanced precariously between the sink, the toilet, and the cold tile floor. I use my father's shaving cream to hide all traces of the hair growing up and down my legs. I stand with my legs in a wide inverted V and smother my right leg with white foam. My left leg supports my young body while my right leg straddles the sink. Slow and methodical, I scrape the hair off each leg. I have to concentrate very hard so I don't cut myself. Every two minutes I stop to rinse the thick tufts of hair stuck out of the razor. Then I inspect the quality of my work. The finished skin has to be completely smooth, as though there never was any thick brown hair covering my body. Convinced that the right leg is smooth enough, I lower it to the floor. When I am finished shaving my legs, I raise my right arm and stare into the mirror. The hair under my arms is soft, and there isn't very much of it. At thirteen, I do not understand why I have to remove this hair too. As I glide the razor back and forth, I am aware of how tender my skin is and how raw it feels once all the hair is removed. Rinsing off the now clean space, I notice that the skin is turning red. And when I roll on the sticky, sweet-scented deodorant, it burns. But I lower my right arm, lift my left one, and begin again, continuing until I am fully plucked and have become my mother's chicken.

She shows me how to remove all traces of blood from the body. After soaking, there is salting. But the blood of the chicken accumulates under the wings and does not drain out, into her spotless kosher sink. She roasts each chicken for hours, turning the thighs over and over, checking for unclean spots that do not disappear even in the stifling oven heat. With a single stroke of the hand and a silver spoon,

*Blessing.

she removes a spot of blood from the yolk of an imperfect egg. First she cracks each one separately into a glass bowl; if the yolk is clear, luminous, she adds it to another bowl. But whenever the blood spreads like tiny veins into the center of the bright yellow ball, she throws out the whole egg.

For my turn, I roll the egg slowly in between my palms; I learn to feel the blood pulsating right inside the center so I don't ever have to break it open. I learn that the sight of red blood on the food Jews eat is disgusting. Red juice from an undercooked chicken always makes me gag. I stop eating red meat. I eat all my food well done. I do not tell her when I start to bleed. Instinctively I keep my femaleness to myself. I watch her throw out a dozen eggs, one at a time, crying at the waste. To spill a drop of blood is to waste an entire life.

When I start to bleed, I keep my femaleness to myself. When she finds out, she is furious. How long? I cannot remember. She is hurt. When was the first time? I do not remember. She is almost hysterical, but I cannot remember. I remember only that all signs of blood on the body must be removed. I do not tell my mother when I begin to bleed. Instead I wrap wads of cotton in toilet paper so thick that no one will ever guess what's inside. I clean myself the exact same way she cleans blood from the chickens in her sink. I soak and I salt. I soak and I salt. For hours at a time. For years I will away my own femaleness. I do not spill for months in a row and then, when I do, it's just a spot, a small speck, easily removed like the red spot floating in my mother's yolk.

Before I am born I float in my mother's yolk and I am never hungry. Soon after I am born the hunger begins. By seventeen I am so hungry I do not know what to do with myself. All I can think about is food and how I cannot get enough.

At seventeen I leave the States for Israel. I have to leave. When I arrive *b'eretz** I cannot stop eating. I stuff myself the way my mother stuffs her kosher Shabbas chicken breasts. I stuff myself with grilled lamb shaved right off a hot rotating skewer and stuffed into warm, fresh pita with sautéed onions and lemon juice. In Jerusalem I cannot stop eating as I wait for the bus to take me to the Turkish Bath House where I crouch in the corner on a low stool, sip steaming Turkish coffee, suck on floating orange peels, and stare at all the naked bodies.

I cannot stop eating halvah laced with green pistachios while Miz-

*In the land of Israel.

rachi women with olive skin soak in pools of turquoise water. Slowly, as though praying, they unbraid each other's long, thick dark hair. Standing in water up to their waists, they comb out the knots. They knead their scalps and foreheads gently, washing their hair in the juice of fresh lemons. The women soak in silence. Large round bodies move from pool to sacred pool; hot then cold, tepid, and cool. Back and forth. Tall and thin. Brown skin. Torsos dip and soak in swirls of foaming water. Surrounded by the scent of eucalyptus they soak their feet in burning crystals. Bodies in water float through steam.

I want to take my clothes off, but I cannot stop eating whole figs with date jam spread on fresh Syrian bread while Sephardic women lie on heated marble slabs and close their eyes. Their breasts sag; sunlight doesn't filter in. Bodies in steam float through air. But I am never full. They drink chilled yellow papaya juice from thin paper cups while cooling their sweating foreheads. I want to take my clothes off, but I cannot stop eating. Wings and thighs. Breasts and legs. They soak and they salt in pools of blue water. With avocado soap they wash each other's spines and massage their aching muscles. Jewish women bathe in ancient cleansing waters. Wrapped in soft terry cloth they climb the steps to the roof and begin to eat: plates of hummus lined with purple olives, smooth baba ganhouj and almond macaroons. I can almost touch the sky, sitting on the roof; the Jerusalem sun is hot and strong.

Down below I see the streets of Meah Shearim.* Narrow sidewalks and small shops. Women concealed within their bodies. Safely covered from head to toe. Orthodox men in black. Praying as they walk. Their eyes never meet. On the street. Their hands never touch. On the street. Women are covered from head to toe.

On the rooftop women eat, naked in the sun—mothers and daughters, sisters. They lounge on cement slabs, laugh among themselves, and feed each other grape leaves. But I cannot stop eating, staring at the street below. Women with children; live chickens squawking. Preparing for Shabbat. Men in black hats. Long beards. Everything ordered and prearranged. *Ani Adoni Elochechah.* I am the Lord thy God. The Torah is absolute. I love my people Israel. (I loathe my female self.) I cannot stop eating, caught between the roof and the street below. I dream that I am falling, falling to the ground. But I never land. I stay caught forever, hanging limb by limb. Caught for-

*An ultra-Orthodox neighborhood in Jerusalem.

ever, limb by limb. The Jerusalem sun is hot and strong. Burning me at seventeen. Suspended as I am. Between my people and myself.

The suspension makes me crazy as I wander the biblical streets. Where do I belong? The suspension is intolerable. I have no place to go. Every week I visit Meah Shearim. Searching not just for my head but for my body too. Every Friday I stay with an Orthodox family and light Shabbas candles as the sun sets. When I'm in my head my body disappears and then I cannot find my Jewish female self. At night I wander back alone from the center of the city to where I live on Har Hatzofim. I search as I walk, staring in the dark, peering into windows, looking for my soul.

In the States, I'm in my body, but I cannot find my head. At home *b'eretz* I eat my way through the city longing to be whole. With my bus fare I buy a kilo of jelly cookies. I eat as I walk in the dark through villages and urban streets. All I do in Israel at seventeen is eat. I tap a hunger so wide that I do not know what to do. I know that I will have to leave the country. There is no one to tell how hungry I have become, because a hunger like this is forbidden.

I have no place to go. I do not know it yet completely. But I fall in love with Israel the way I will fall in love with a woman for the first time. With all my heart and with all my soul. I want to return to the land forever. To live in Meah Shearim. That will save me from my hunger, or so I think and pray. At seventeen I wander the streets of Jerusalem, terrified at what I know I will grow up to be. But there is no one to tell how hungry I have become because a hunger like this is forbidden. I swallow my passion whole; my body swells until I am so enormous that I have to leave the land I love.

Alone, my mother flies to rescue me on an El Al jumbo jet. But I do not say a word. I have become a knaidel, a dumpling, floating in the soup: a nice Jewish girl who doesn't say a word. But stuffed inside my mother's dumpling, swimming just below the surface is a *vilde chaye** waiting to jump out. A wild beast waiting to get out. My mother takes the window seat, staring hard at me, her fat baby girl, drowning in the soup.

As we fly back together, I know that I have failed. She doesn't ask and I cannot tell her what exactly happened. That I fell in love. With Sarah and Hagar, and with Lot's wife the moment she looked back. She doesn't ask and I cannot tell her what exactly happened. That I

*A wild animal.

tapped a hunger I did not know I had. I have watched my mother eat and never gain a pound. She can eat and eat and eat, devour anything in sight, but I never see her body change. I never know what happens to all the food that she consumes. Mine shows on my body, right outside for everyone to see; but the food that she consumes disappears and is impossible to see. My hunger is outside; hers is never seen. Yes, the country's beautiful . . . I did not ever want to leave. And I do not want to cry. Even though I know right inside my mother's dreams for me we can no longer speak.

When we arrive in the States, our covenant begins to break—mother to daughter, daughter to mother. We do not speak the words, but they float between us, growing larger day by day. Right after Pesach*, like the first signs of spring, I start to grow all my body hair back again. A *vilde chaye*. She is mortified. It is so soft. She is horrified. I can't believe I ever shaved it off. A wild beast. I run my hands up and down my legs. And when I lift my arms, she turns her head away. She tells me that my body is disgusting. Not a nice Jewish girl, never seen or heard, who does not say a word. I thought my body was my own. More than her knaidel† floating in the soup.

The covenant is broken; I've claimed my body as my own. But the silence floats between us, growing larger day by day. What my mother always feared is true. I grow up to be a stunning, raging, wild, forbidden *vilde chaye*. I did not ever want to leave my mother's Shabbas table; but in my twenties, she cannot set a place for me. I learn to close my eyes, light the candles, say the kiddush‡ and the *motzi*§ by myself. But I cannot cook her chicken so I cannot bring her home to me. And without my mother present, I cannot bear to eat her food.

I become a vegetarian, even though the food tastes strange and never smells the same. With other *vilde chayes*, I make a seder of my own. We become the red beets sprouting green leaves, sitting where the shank bones belong. We wash each other's hands as we pass the bowl around. But we cannot taste our mothers in the soup, and in their absence we grow lame. How can I have my mother and myself? For years we barely speak, and in her absence I grow tame. Only later do I know that her silence is her shame that she gave birth to me, who let my hair grow back. But I did not ever want to choose my mother

*The festival of Passover.
†Dumpling.
‡The blessing recited over wine.
§The blessing recited over bread.

or myself. And when we, *d'vilde chayes,* call forth our mothers' names: *ematanu, Sarah, Rivkah, Rachel v' Leah,* it is the first time I say my mother's name out loud.

We know that we have been cast out, that our hunger is the shame of both our mothers and our people. Our grief is overwhelming that we have no place to go. Either we are heard among the women but never fully seen or we are seen among our people but never ever heard. There is no language we can speak as we shake our heads in sorrow that we are not counted too.

But I continue to look back, to remember who I am. *Im eshcahac yerushalayim, t'shchah y'menie.* If I forget [Thee O] Jerusalem, may my right hand lose its cunning. I know my mother's waiting and looking back herself. Through her silence she is praying that I will reappear. Through my silence I am praying for my mother to appear. But to reappear is difficult, not knowing what I'll find. At the seder table with other *vilde chayes* my voice grows strong and clear. I learn that I must speak the words to those who do not want to hear. To my mother and my people it's hard to speak what they have always feared. That we are your daughters too and cannot be forgotten or erased.

We are the stories that were never told. We are Shifrah and Purah, the midwives giving birth. We are Ruth and Naomi and Boaz's sister Dina. And Sarah and Hagar whom she sent away. We are Deborah the judge, leading the troops, fighting on the front. We are Miriam in the bulrushes saving her brother, Moses. And Rachel and Leah when they are betrayed. We are Vashti who refused and Esther who agreed. We are all of this and more. This was my mother's fear. That I was all of this and more. We are the unplucked chickens squawking in the yard. That the neighbors always see. And at the weddings and bar mitzvahs we are either not invited or told to come alone, to be quiet and blend in. But we are your daughters and cannot be forgotten or erased.

Sometimes we do not look the same; this was my mother's shame. She did not understand, for as long as she lived, why I could not look just a little more like her and a lot less like me. I never understood, until the day she died, why my mother couldn't be a little more like me and a lot less like her. My mother too was betrayed. For there was no one she could tell about her young *vilde chaye* whom she had to love in secret and never celebrate. The rabbis turned their heads away and fathers followed suit. The mothers did not talk, or even whisper by themselves. My mother would not even tell her younger sister because she was afraid of what the neighbors always say: What will the goyim think? That we are your daughters. Your sisters and your aunts. And the cousins in the pictures, standing side by side. *A shunda for d'goyim**. No one says a word. Instead, they keep the family secret and only mouth the words. Like how and why and when?

The truth is, I always was just like I am today, only I didn't know. It wasn't possible as I was growing up to see any other way. For the longest time I floated in the soup and didn't say a word. Then one day I had to choose to leap right out of the bowl. I came to understand that there are those of us who lead the way and those who like to follow. My mother was a follower who gave birth to a leader. This was not easy for my mother or for me. I did not choose to be a leader; it was chosen for me. But what I do not know is if my mother ever felt constrained, as I always did, if it was her choice to follow or if she felt that she had no choice. Perhaps she was afraid to lead—this I'll never know. Yet this is how the cycle flows. In every generation, from follower to leader, *l'dor v dor†*. From leader to follower.

All her life my mother didn't understand what it meant to birth a *vilde chaye*. This was my aching disappointment. Before she died, I never had a chance to tell her that to lead, like Moses or Deborah, is to risk the people's wrath. That to be a *vilde chaye* is to live forever on the edge with your life often at stake. I never had the chance to say out loud that I always needed her. My mother's grief at who I am is my deepest sorrow. I wanted her, more than anyone else on earth, to understand and not to be afraid. But this simply wasn't possible; just like me, she didn't know any other way. Sometimes, late at night, when I feel my people's wrath, I wonder, was she right? Is it better not to be seen or heard? A dumpling floating in the soup? Sometimes, late at night, with my life out on the edge, I wonder, was my mother right? Is it better just to be a *bubelah,* a nice Jewish girl, rather than a *vilde chaye?* I always loved my mother and I know that she loved me. The mistake I made is in her chicken that I never learned to cook. From the plucking to the soaking, from the salting to the stuffing to the removal of the blood, we are bound to language and a common history. From the laws of kashruth to the sacred

---

*Something shameful that Jews believe compromises their image in the eyes of non-Jews.
†From generation to generation.

washing of the hands, it is in poultry that we are bound eternal in our femaleness.

In my fantasy I am born a kosher chicken with my mother's hands holding me. She washes me forever in her large kitchen sink. Cleaning my wings, she tells me not to change a thing, that she loves me just the way I am. On Friday afternoons all her Shabbas friends come to see the baby soaking in the sink. They pinch and they poke, laughing at my teeny tiny *polkies**. As a kosher chicken I'd be blessed by the shochet† and served on a sacred silver platter with squares of kugel‡ by my side to keep me warm. If only I'd been born a chicken rather than a *vilde chaye,* there would be no painful separation from my mother or my people. I'd be plucked and stuffed, then roasted to a crisp golden brown. Sprinkled with paprika, I'd look gorgeous all the time.

Near the end I washed my mother's hands and feet. She couldn't talk, but she let me in that close. As I washed her legs and thighs, we made a silent, fragile peace; she the perfect *balabosta§*, and I, the stunning *vilde chaye.* But in my fantasy I am born a kosher chicken. I sit forever plump and round in the center of my mother's Shabbas table. When she lights the candles and closes her eyes, I am there forever by my mother's side. She is there forever by her daughter's side. We are together, at the Shabbas table, sitting side by side.

---

*Yiddish, "Chicken legs."
†Kosher butcher; ritual slaughterer.
‡A cake or pudding made from noodles or potatoes.
§A proud Jewish homemaker.

from *VISIONS OF GLORY*

BARBARA GRIZZUTI HARRISON

In Visions of Glory, *her now out-of-print history and memoir of the Jehovah's Witnesses, noted journalist, critic, and novelist Barbara Grizzuti Harrison remembers her years as a child convert and Witness proselytizer. In this excerpt, a teenage Barbara is preoccupied with her developing, mysterious female body and her fear of impurity and sin.*

⟶⟶**I**N 1944, when I . . . was 9 years old, I became one of Jehovah's Witnesses. . . . After my baptism at a nation convention of 25,000 Witnesses in Buffalo, New York, in the summer of 1944, I became an ardent proselytizer, distributing *The Watchtower* and *Awake!* magazines on street corners and from door to door, spending as much as 150 hours a month in the service of my newly found God—under the directives of the Watchtower Bible and Tract Society, the legal and corporate arm of Jehovah's Witnesses.

As I had been immersed in water to symbolize my "dedication to do God's will," I became, also, drenched in the dark blood-poetry of a religion whose adherents drew joy from the prospect of the imminent end of the world. I preached sweet doom; I believed that Armageddon would come in my lifetime, with a great shaking and rending and tearing of unbelieving flesh, with unsanctified babies swimming in blood, torrents of blood. I believed also that after the slaughter Jehovah had arranged for His enemies at Armageddon, this quintessen-

tially masculine God—vengeful in battle and benevolent to sur-
vivors—would turn the earth into an Eden for true believers.

Coincidentally with my conversion, I got my first period. We used
to sing this hymn: "Here is He who comes from Eden/All His raiments stained with blood." My raiments were stained with blood too.
But the blood of the Son of Man was purifying, redemptive, cleansing, sacrificial. Mine was proof of my having inherited the curse
placed upon the seductress Eve. Mine was filthy. I examined my dis-
charges with horror and fascination, as if the secret of life—or a har-
binger of death—were to be found in that dull, mysterious effluence.

I was, in equal measure, guilt-ridden and—supposing myself to be
in on the secrets of the cosmos—self-righteous and smug. I grew up
awaiting the final, orgasmic burst of violence after which all things
would come together in a cosmic ecstasy of joy—this in a religion that
was totally antierotic, that expressed disgust and contempt for the
world.

My ignorance of sexual matters was so profound that it frequently
led to comedies of error. Nothing I've ever read has inclined me to
believe that Jehovah has a sense of humor; and I must say that I consider it a strike against Him that He wouldn't find this story funny:

One night shortly after my conversion, a visiting elder of the congregation, as he was avuncularly tucking me into bed, asked me if I
was guilty of performing evil practices with my hands under the covers at night. I was puzzled. He was persistent. Finally, I thought I
understood. And I burst into wild tears of self-recrimination. Under
the covers at night, I bit my cuticles—a practice which, in fact, did
afford me a kind of sensual pleasure. (I didn't learn about masturba-
tion—which the Witnesses call "idolatry," because "the masturbator's
affection is diverted away from the Creator and is bestowed upon a
coveted object" [*TW*, Sept. 15, 1973, p. 568]—until much later.)

So, having confessed to a sin I hadn't known existed, I was advised
of the necessity for keeping one's body pure from sin; cold baths were
recommended. I couldn't see the connection, but one never questioned the imperatives of an elder, so I subjected my impure body to
so many icy baths in midwinter that I began to look like a bleached
prune. My mother thought I was demented. But I couldn't tell *her*
that I'd been biting my cuticles, because to have incurred God's
wrath—and to see the beady eye of the elder steadfastly upon me at
every religious meeting I went to—was torment enough.

I used to preach, from door to door, that an increase in the number of rapes was one of the signs heralding the end of the world; but I didn't know what rape was. I knew that good Christians didn't commit "unnatural acts"; but I didn't know what "unnatural acts" were. (And I couldn't ask anybody, because all the Witnesses I knew began immediately to resemble Edith Sitwell eating an unripe persimmon when these abominations were spoken of.) Consequently, I spent a lot of time praying that I was not committing unnatural acts or rape.

Once, having heard that Hitler had a mistress, I asked my mother what a mistress was. (I had an inkling that it might be some kind of sinister super-housekeeper, like Judith Anderson in *Rebecca*.) I knew from my mother's silence, and from her cold, hard, and frightened face, that the question was somehow a grievous offense. I knew that I had done something wrong, but as usual, I didn't know what.

The fact was that I never knew how to buy God's—or my mother's—approval. There were sins I consciously and knowingly committed. That was bad, but it was bearable. I could always pray to God to forgive me, say, for reading the Bible for its "dirty parts"; for preferring the Song of Solomon to all the *begats* of Genesis. But the offenses that made me most horribly guilty were those I had committed unconsciously; as an imperfect being descended from the wretched Eve, I was bound, so I had been taught, to offend Jehovah seventy-seven times a day without my even knowing what I was doing wrong.

There was guilt, and there was glory: I walked a spiritual tightrope.

I feel now that for the twelve years I spent as one of Jehovah's Witnesses, three of them as a member of the Watchtower Society's headquarters staff, I was living out a vivid dream, hallucinating within the closed system of logic and private reality of a religion that relished disaster; rejoiced in the evil of human nature; lusted for certitude; ordered its members to disdain the painful present in exchange for the glorious future; corrupted ritual, ethics, and doctrine into ritualism, legalism, and dogmatism.

I was convinced that 1914 marked "the beginning of the times of the end." So firmly did Jehovah's Witnesses believe this to be true that there were those who, in 1944, refused to get their teeth filled, postponing all care of their bodies until God saw to their regeneration in His New World. (One zealous Witness I knew carried a supply of cloves to alleviate the pain of an aching molar which she did not wish to have treated by her dentist, since the time was so short till Jehovah would provide a new and perfect one. To this day, I associate the fragrance of cloves with the imminence of disaster.)

More than thirty years have passed, but though their hopes have not been fulfilled, the Witnesses have persevered with increased fervor and conviction. Their attitude toward the world remains the same: because all their longing is for the future, they are bound to hate the present—the material, the sexual, the fleshly. It's impossible to savor and enjoy the present, or to bend one's energies to shape and mold the world into the form of goodness, if you are waiting only for it to be smashed by God. There is a kind of ruthless glee in the way Jehovah's Witnesses point to earthquakes, race riots, heroin addiction, the failure of the United Nations, divorce, famine (and liberalized abortion laws) as proof of the nearness of Armageddon.

The God I worshipped was not the God before whom one swoons in ecstasy, or with whom one contends: He was an awesome and awful judge, whom one approached through his "channel," the "divinely appointed Theocratic organization"—the Watchtower Bible and Tract Society. The Christ in whose name I prayed was not a social reformer, nor was he God incarnate, the embodiment of the world's most thrilling mystery, God-made-man. He was, rather, merely a legal instrument (albeit the most important one) in God's wrangles with the Devil. All the history of the world is seen, by Jehovah's Witnesses, as a contest between Jehovah and Satan.

·   ·   ·

I rehearse, I jealously preserve preconversion memories; they flash before my mind like magical slides. I treasure a series of intense, isolated moments. I hoard happy images that are pure, unsullied by values assigned to them by others. Afterward, there was nothing in the world to which I was permitted to give my own meaning; afterward, when the world began to turn for me on the axis of God's displeasure, I was obliged to regard all events as part of God's plan for the universe as understood only by Jehovah's Witnesses. Afterward, meanings were assigned to all things. The world was flattened out into right and wrong; all experience was sealed into compartments marked Good and Evil. Before my conversion, each beloved object and event had the luminosity and purity of a thing complete in itself, a thing to which no significance is attributed other than that which it chooses to reveal.

Images of innocence: dark, cool, sweet rooms and a mulberry bush; fevers, delirium and clean sheets and chicken soup and mustard plasters; summer dusk and hide-and-seek; Hershey Kisses in cut-glass bowls; Brooklyn stoops; sunlight in a large kitchen, the Sunday gravy cooking; the Andrews Sisters singing "I'll Be with You in Apple Blossom Time."

Saturdays I played with the beautiful twins Barbara and Violet, who mirrored each other's loveliness, like Snow White and Rose Red. I thought it was impossible that they should ever be lonely or frightened. I wanted the half of me that had escaped to come back, so that I could be whole, like Barbara-and-Violet.

Sunday afternoons I went to my father's mother's house. I sat at Grandma's vanity table—pink-and-white, muslined and taffetaed, skirted and ribboned—and played with antique Italian jewelry in velvet-lined leather boxes and held small bottles of perfume with mysterious amber residues. From the trellised grape arbor of the roof garden Grandpa had built I imagined I saw Coney Island and the parachute ride. One day, in an attic cupboard, I found a pearl-handled revolver; it belonged, they said, to the distant cousin who smelled of herbs and spices and soap—the old lady who cried when Little Augie Stefano was shot in a barber's chair.

The house of my mother's family, near the Brooklyn Navy Yard, always smelled of fermenting wine and of incense to the saints; its walls and tin ceilings were poverty-brown and -green; but there was always a store-bought chocolate cake waiting in the icebox for my visit. And my grandfather sang me the Italian Fascist Youth Anthem as he hoed his Victory Garden: Mussolini had made the trains run on time, but the good soil of Brooklyn yielded better tomatoes than the harsh soil of Calabria.

These are the fragments I jealously preserve like the crèche from Italy (sweet Mary, humble Joseph, and tiny Jesus—always perfect and new) that adorned each Christmas morning.

After my conversion, I began immediately to have a dream, which recurred until I released myself from bondage to that religion twelve years later, when I was 21. In the dream, I am standing in my grandmother's walled garden. At the far corner of the garden, where the climbing red roses shine like bright blood against the whitewashed wall, stands a creature icy, resplendent, of indeterminate sex. The creature calls to me. In my dream its voice is tactile; I feel it flow through my veins like molten silver. I am rendered bloodless, will-less; the creature extends its arms in a gesture that is at once magisterial and maternal, entreating and commanding. I walk toward its embrace, fearful but glad, unable not to abandon myself to a splendid doom. The creature seizes me in its arms and I am hurled out of the garden, a ravaged Humpty-Dumpty flying through dark and hostile space, alone.

I understand that dream to have been telling me my truest feelings, which my conscious, waking mind censored for long hard years: I understand it to be my soul's perception that my religion had isolated and alienated me from the world, which it perceived as evil and menacing, and which I regarded, at the bedrock level of my being, as imperfect but not un-good; my religion savaged those to whom it offered salvation. For twelve years I lived in fear.

from *THE STORY OF MY EXPERIMENTS WITH TRUTH*

MOHANDAS GANDHI

As a son in a devout Hindu family, Mohandas Gandhi, born in 1869, was duty-bound to comply with child marriage when he was only thirteen, a practice he was to severely oppose later in life. In his lengthy autobiography, The Story of My Experiments with Truth, *Gandhi, who became known as the father of India, recalls with great anguish the newly married lust which kept him away from his own father's deathbed, and the shame which haunted him for years to come. Though faithful to his wife and not yet fifty, ever seeking after God and truth, Gandhi ultimately sought to curb his significant carnal appetites by embracing the Brahmacharya vows of celibacy and renunciation, controlling his senses in "thought, word, and deed."*

THE TIME of which I am now speaking is my sixteenth year. My father . . . was bed-ridden, suffering from a fistula. My mother, an old servant of the house, and I were his principal attendants. I had the duties of a nurse, which mainly consisted in dressing the wound, giving my father his medicine, and compounding drugs whenever they had to be made up at home. Every night I massaged his legs and retired only when he asked me to do so or after he had fallen asleep. I loved to do this service. I do not remember ever having neglected it.

243

All the time at my disposal, after the performance of the daily duties, was divided between school and attending on my father. I would only go out for an evening walk either when he permitted me or when he was feeling well.

This was also the time when my wife was expecting a baby—a circumstance which, as I can see today, meant a double shame for me. For one thing I did not restrain myself, as I should have done, whilst I was yet a student. And secondly, this carnal lust got the better of what I regarded as my duty to study, and of what was even a greater duty, my devotion to my parents. . . . Every night whilst my hands were busy massaging my father's legs, my mind was hovering about the bed-room—and that too at a time when religion, medical science and commonsense alike forbade sexual intercourse. I was always glad to be relieved from my duty, and went straight to the bed-room after doing obeisance to my father.

. . .

The dreadful night came. My uncle was then in Rajkot. I have a faint recollection that he came to Rajkot having had news that my father was getting worse. The brothers were deeply attached to each other. My uncle would sit near my father's bed the whole day, and would insist on sleeping by his bed-side after sending us all to sleep. No one had dreamt that this was to be the fateful night. The danger of course was there.

It was 10:30 or 11 P.M. I was giving the massage. My uncle offered to relieve me. I was glad and went straight to the bed-room. My wife, poor thing, was fast asleep. But how could she sleep when I was there? I woke her up. In five or six minutes, however, the servant knocked at the door. I started with alarm. "Get up," he said, "Father is very ill." I knew of course that he was very ill, and so I guessed what "very ill" meant at that moment. I sprang out of bed.

"What is the matter? Do tell me!"

"Father is no more."

So all was over! I had but to wring my hands. I felt deeply ashamed and miserable. I ran to my father's room. I saw that, if animal passion had not blinded me, I should have been spared the torture of separation from my father during his last moments. I should have been massaging him, and he would have died in my arms. But now it was my uncle who had this privilege. He was so deeply devoted to his elder brother that he had earned the honour of doing him the last services! My father had forebodings of the coming event. He had made a sign for pen and paper, and written: "Prepare for the last rites." He had then snapped the amulet off his arm and also his gold necklace of *tulasi*-beads and flung them aside. A moment after this he was no more.

The shame, to which I have referred in a foregoing chapter, was this shame of my carnal desire even at the critical hour of my father's death, which demanded wakeful service. It is a blot I have never been able to efface or forget, and I have always thought that, although my devotion to my parents knew no bounds and I would have given up anything for it, yet it was weighed and found unpardonably wanting because my mind was at the same moment in the grip of lust. I have therefore always regarded myself as a lustful, though a faithful, husband. It took me long to get free from the shackles of lust, and I had to pass through many ordeals before I could overcome it.

Before I close this chapter of my double shame, I may mention that the poor mite that was born to my wife scarcely breathed for more than three or four days. Nothing else could be expected. Let all those who are married be warned by my example.

.   .   .

We now reach the stage in this story when I began seriously to think of taking the *brahmacharya* vow. I had been wedded to a monogamous ideal ever since my marriage, faithfulness to my wife being part of the love of truth. But it was in South Africa that I came to realize the importance of observing *brahmacharya* even with respect to my wife. I cannot definitely say what circumstance or what book it was, that set my thoughts in that direction, . . .

.   .   .

What then, I asked myself, should be my relation with my wife? Did my faithfulness consist in making my wife the instrument of my lust? So long as I was the slave of lust, my faithfulness was worth nothing. To be fair to my wife, I must say that she was never the temptress. It was therefore the easiest thing for me to take the vow of *brahmacharya*, if only I willed it. It was my weak will or lustful attachment that was the obstacle.

Even after my conscience had been roused in the matter, I failed twice. I failed because the motive that actuated the effort was none the highest. My main object was to escape having more children.

.   .   .

Seeing, therefore, that I did not desire more children I began to
strive after self-control. There was endless difficulty in the task. We
began to sleep in separate beds. I decided to retire to bed only after
the day's work had left me completely exhausted. All these efforts did
not seem to bear much fruit, but when I look back upon the past, I
feel that the final resolution was the cumulative effect of those unsuccessful strivings.

.   .   .

The importance of vows grew upon me more clearly than ever
before. I realized that a vow, far from closing the door to real freedom, opened it. Up to this time I had not met with success because
the will had been lacking, because I had had no faith in myself, no
faith in the grace of God, and therefore, my mind had been tossed on
the boisterous sea of doubt. I realized that in refusing to take a vow
man was drawn into temptation, and that to be bound by a vow was
like a passage from libertinism to a real monogamous marriage. "I
believe in effort, I do not want to bind myself with vows," is the mentality of weakness and betrays a subtle desire for the thing to be
avoided. Or where can be the difficulty in making a final decision? I
vow to flee from the serpent which I know will bite me, I do not simply make an effort to flee from him. I know that mere effort may
mean certain death. Mere effort means ignorance of the certain fact
that the serpent is bound to kill me. The fact, therefore, that I could
rest content with an effort only, means that I have not yet clearly realized the necessity of definite action. "But supposing my views are
changed in the future, how can I bind myself by a vow?" Such a doubt
often deters us. But that doubt also betrays a lack of clear perception
that a particular thing must be renounced. That is why Nishkulanand
has sung:

"Renunciation without aversion is not lasting."

Where therefore the desire is gone, a vow of renunciation is the natural and inevitable fruit.

from *THE BOOK OF MARGERY KEMPE*

MARGERY KEMPE

The Book of Margery Kempe *is the earliest surviving autobiographical writing in English. Born in 1373, Kempe was a married, middle-class woman in Norfolk, England, who could neither read nor write, and so dictated her spiritual travails, referring to herself as "this creature." Kempe experienced madness and highly intimate visions of Jesus Christ after the birth of her first child, and then despair following the failure of her own business. Bewailing her wretchedness with public outbursts of uncontrollable sobbing, Kempe was regarded by some as an attention-seeking hypocrite. Yet she was shriven—made confession—several times a day, and endeavored to live a life devoted to prayer, fasting, pilgrimage, mortification of the flesh, and a rejection of worldly things. After bearing fourteen children by the age of forty, she desired to commune only with Jesus in heaven, and thus, wishing to live chastely, engaged in a wrestling of wills with her husband—with God on her side.*

ONE NIGHT, as this creature lay in her bed with her husband, she heard a melodious sound so sweet and delectable that she thought she had been in paradise. And immediately she jumped out of bed and said, "Alas that ever I sinned! It is fully merry in heaven." This melody was so sweet that it surpassed all the melody that might be heard in this world, without any comparison, and it caused this creature when she afterwards heard any mirth or melody to shed

very plentiful and abundant tears of high devotion, with great sob-
bings and sighings for the bliss of heaven, not fearing the shames and
contempt of this wretched world. And ever after her being drawn
towards God in this way, she kept in mind the joy and the melody that
there was in heaven, so much so that she could not very well restrain
herself from speaking of it. For when she was in company with any
people she would often say, "It is full merry in heaven!"

And those who knew of her behavior previously and now heard her
talk so much of the bliss of heaven said to her, "Why do you talk so of
the joy that is in heaven? You don't know it, and you haven't been
there any more than we have." And they were angry with her because
she would not hear or talk of worldly things as they did, and as she
did previously.

And after this time she never had any desire to have sexual intercourse with her husband, for paying the debt of matrimony was so
abominable to her that she would rather, she thought, have eaten and
drunk the ooze and muck in the gutter than consent to intercourse,
except out of obedience.

And so she said to her husband, "I may not deny you my body, but
all the love and affection of my heart is withdrawn from all earthly
creatures and set on God alone." But he would have his will with her,
and she obeyed with much weeping and sorrowing because she could
not live in chastity. And often this creature advised her husband to
live chaste and said that they had often (she well knew) displeased
God by their inordinate love, and the great delight that each of them
had in using the other's body, and now it would be a good thing if by
mutual consent they punished and chastised themselves by abstain-
ing from the lust of their bodies. Her husband said it was good to do
so, but he might not yet—he would do so when God willed. And so he
used her as he had done before, he would not desist. And all the time
she prayed to God that she might live chaste, and three or four years
afterwards, when it pleased our Lord, her husband made a vow of
chastity, as shall be written afterwards, by Jesus's leave.

And also, after this creature heard this heavenly melody, she did
great bodily penance. She was sometimes shriven two or three times
on the same day especially of that sin which she had so long concealed
and covered up, as is written at the beginning of this book. She gave
herself up to much fasting and keeping of vigils; she rose at two or
three of the clock and went to church, and was there at her prayers
until midday and also the whole afternoon. And then she was slan-

dered and reproved by many people because she led so strict a life. She got herself a hair-cloth from a kiln—the sort that malt is dried on—and put it inside her gown as discreetly and secretly as she could, so that her husband should not notice it. And nor did he, although she lay beside him every night in bed and wore the hair-shirt every day, and bore him children during that time.

Then she had three years of great difficulty with temptations, which she bore as meekly as she could, thanking our Lord for all his gifts, and she was as merry when she was reproved, scorned or ridiculed for our Lord's love, and much more merry than she was before amongst the dignities of this world. For she knew very well that she had sinned greatly against God and that she deserved far more shame and sorrow than any man could cause her, and contempt in this world was the right way heavenwards, for Christ himself chose that way. All his apostles, martyrs, confessors and virgins, and all those who ever came to heaven, passed by the way of tribulation, and she desired nothing as much as heaven. Then she was glad in her conscience when she believed that she was entering upon the way which would lead her to the place that she most desired.

And this creature had contrition and great compunction, with plentiful tears and much loud and violent sobbing, for her sins and for her unkindness towards her maker. She reflected on her unkindness since her childhood, as our Lord would put it into her mind, very many times. And then when she contemplated her own wickedness, she could only sorrow and weep and ever pray for mercy and forgiveness. Her weeping was so plentiful and so continual that many people thought that she could weep and leave off when she wanted, and therefore many people said she was a false hypocrite, and wept when in company for advantage and profit. And then very many people who loved her before while she was in the world abandoned her and would not know her, and all the while she thanked God for everything, desiring nothing but mercy and forgiveness of sin.

.   .   .

For the first two years when this creature was thus drawn to our Lord she had great quiet of spirit from any temptations. She could well endure fasting—it did not trouble her. She hated the joys of the world. She felt no rebellion in her flesh. She was so strong—as she thought—that she feared no devil in hell, for she performed such great bodily penance. She thought that she loved God more than he loved her. She was smitten with the deadly wound of vainglory and felt it not, for she desired many times that the crucifix should loosen his hands from the cross and embrace her in token of love. Our merciful Lord Christ Jesus, seeing this creature's presumption, sent her—as is written before—three years of great temptations, of one of the hardest of which I intend to write, as an example to those who come after that they should not trust in themselves nor have joy in themselves as this creature had—for undoubtedly our spiritual enemy does not sleep but busily probes our temperament and attitudes, and wherever he finds us most frail, there, by our Lord's sufferance, he lays his snare, which no one may escape by his own power.

And so he laid before this creature the snare of lechery, when she thought that all physical desire had been wholly quenched in her. And so she was tempted for a long time with the sin of lechery, in spite of anything she might do. Yet she was often shriven, she wore her hair-shirt, and did great bodily penance and wept many a bitter tear, and often prayed to our Lord that he should preserve her and keep her so that she should not fall into temptation, for she thought she would rather have been dead than consent to that. And in all this time she had no desire to have intercourse with her husband, and it was very painful and horrible to her.

In the second year of her temptations it so happened that a man whom she liked said to her on St. Margaret's Eve before evensong that, for anything, he would sleep with her and enjoy the lust of his body, and that she should not withstand him, for if he might not have his desire that time, he said, he would have it another time instead—she should not choose. And he did it to test what she would do, but she imagined that he meant it in earnest and said very little in reply. So they parted then and both went to hear evensong, for her church was dedicated to St. Margaret. This woman was so troubled with the man's words that she could not listen to evensong, nor say her paternoster, nor think any other good thought, but was more troubled than she ever was before.

The devil put it into her mind that God had forsaken her, or else she would not be so tempted. She believed the devil's persuasions, and began to consent because she could not think any good thought. Therefore she believed that God had forsaken her. And when evensong was over, she went to the said man, in order that he should have his will of her, as she believed he desired, but he put forward such a pretense that she could not understand his intent, and so they parted for that night. This creature was so troubled and vexed all that night that she did not know what she could do. She lay beside her husband, and to have intercourse with him was so abominable to her that she could not bear it, and yet it was permissible for her and a rightful time if she had wished it. But all the time she was tormented to sin with the other man because he had spoken to her. At last—through the importunings of temptation and a lack of discretion—she was overcome and consented in her mind, and went to the man to know if he would then consent to have her. And he said he would not for all the wealth in this world; he would rather be chopped up as small as meat for the pot.

She went away all ashamed and confused in herself, seeing his steadfastness and her own instability. Then she thought about the grace that God had given her before, of how she had two years of great quiet in her soul, of repentance for her sins with many bitter tears of compunction, and a perfect will never again to turn to sin but rather, she thought, to be dead. And now she saw how she had consented to her will to sin. Then she half fell into despair. She thought herself in hell, such was the sorrow that she had. She thought she was worthy of no mercy because her consenting to sin was so wilfully done, nor ever worthy to serve God, because she was so false to him.

Nevertheless she was shriven many times and often, and did whatever penance her confessor would enjoin her to do, and was governed according to the rules of the Church. That grace God gave this creature—blessed may he be—but he did not withdraw her temptation, but rather increased it, as she thought.

And therefore she thought that he had forsaken her, and dared not trust to his mercy, but was troubled with horrible temptations to lechery and despair nearly all the following year, except that our Lord in his mercy, as she said to herself, gave her every day for the most part two hours of compunction for her sins, with many bitter tears. And afterwards she was troubled with temptations to despair as she was before, and was as far from feelings of grace as those who never felt any. And that she could not bear, and so she continued to despair. Except for the time that she felt grace, her trials were so amazing that she could not cope very well with them, but always mourned and sorrowed as though God had forsaken her.

.   .   .

Then on a Friday before Christmas Day, as this creature was kneeling in a chapel of St. John, within a church of St. Margaret in N., weeping a very great deal and asking mercy and forgiveness for her sins and her trespasses, our merciful Lord Christ Jesus—blessed may he be—ravished her spirit and said to her, "Daughter, why are you weeping so sorely? I have come to you, Jesus Christ, who died on the cross suffering bitter pains and passion for you. I, the same God, forgive you your sins to the uttermost point. And you shall never come into hell nor into purgatory, but when you pass out of this world, within the twinkling of an eye, you shall have the bliss of heaven, for I am the same God who has brought your sins to your mind and caused you to be shriven of them. And I grant you contrition until your life's end.

"Therefore, I command you, boldly call me Jesus, your love, for I am your love and shall be your love without end. And, daughter, you have a hair-shirt on your back. I want you to leave off wearing it, and I shall give you a hair-shirt in your heart which shall please me much more than all the hair-shirts in the world. But also, my beloved daughter, you must give up that which you love best in this world, and that is the eating of meat. And instead of meat you shall eat my flesh and my blood, that is the true body of Christ in the sacrament of the altar. This is my will, daughter, that you receive my body every Sunday, and I shall cause so much grace to flow into you that everyone shall marvel at it.

"You shall be eaten and gnawed by the people of the world just as any rat gnaws the stockfish. Don't be afraid, daughter, for you shall be victorious over all your enemies. I shall give you grace enough to answer every cleric in the love of God. I swear to you by my majesty that I shall never forsake you whether in happiness or in sorrow. I shall help you and protect you, so that no devil in hell shall ever part you from me, nor angel in heaven, nor man on earth—for devils in hell may not, nor angels in heaven will not, nor man on earth shall not.

"And daughter, I want you to give up your praying of many beads, and think such thoughts as I shall put into your mind. I shall give you leave to pray until six o'clock to say what you wish. Then you shall lie still and speak to me in thought, and I shall give you high meditation and true contemplation. And I command you to go to the anchorite at the Preaching Friars and tell him my confidences and counsels which I reveal to you, and do as he advises, for my spirit shall speak in him to you."

Then this creature went off to see the anchorite as she was commanded, and revealed to him the revelations that had been shown to her. Then the anchorite, with great reverence and weeping, thanking God, said, "Daughter, you are sucking even at Christ's breast, and you have received a pledge of paradise. I charge you to receive such thoughts—when God will give them—as meekly and devoutly as you can, and then come and tell me what they are, and I shall, by the leave of our Lord Jesus Christ, tell you whether they are from the Holy Ghost or else from your enemy the devil."

.   .   .

It happened one Friday, Midsummer Eve, in very hot weather—as this creature was coming from York carrying a bottle of beer in her hand, and her husband a cake tucked inside his clothes against his chest—that her husband asked his wife this question: "Margery, if there came a man with a sword who would strike off my head unless I made love with you as I used to do before, tell me on your conscience—for you say you will not lie—whether you would allow my head to be cut off, or else allow me to make love with you again, as I did at one time?"

"Alas, sir," she said, "why are you raising this matter, when we have been chaste for these past eight weeks?"

"Because I want to know the truth of your heart."

And then she said with great sorrow, "Truly, I would rather see you being killed, than that we should turn back to our uncleanness."

And he replied, "You are no good wife."

And then she asked her husband what was the reason that he had not made love to her for the last eight weeks, since she lay with him every night in his bed. And he said that he was made so afraid when he would have touched her, that he dared do no more.

"Now, good sir, mend your ways and ask God's mercy, for I told you nearly three years ago that you[r desire for sex] would suddenly be slain—and this is now the third year, and I hope yet that I shall have my wish. Good sir, I pray you to grant what I shall ask, and I shall pray for you to be saved through the mercy of our Lord Jesus Christ, and you shall have more reward in heaven than if you wore a hair-shirt or wore a coat of mail as a penance. I pray you, allow me to make a vow of chastity at whichever bishop's hand that God wills."

"No," he said, "I won't allow you to do that, because now I can make love to you without mortal sin, and then I wouldn't be able to."

Then she replied, "If it be the will of the Holy Ghost to fulfill what I have said, I pray God that you may consent to this; and if it be not the will of the Holy Ghost, I pray God that you never consent."

Then they went on towards Bridlington and the weather was extremely hot, this creature all the time having great sorrow and great fear for her chastity. And as they came by a cross her husband sat down under the cross, calling his wife to him and saying these words to her: "Margery, grant me my desire, and I shall grant you your desire. My first desire is that we shall still lie together in one bed as we have done before; the second, that you shall pay my debts before you go to Jerusalem; and the third, that you shall eat and drink with me on Fridays as you used to do."

"No, sir," she said, "I will never agree to break my Friday fast as long as I live."

"Well," he said, "then I'm going to have sex with you again."

She begged him to allow her to say her prayers, and he kindly allowed it. Then she knelt down beside a cross in the field and prayed in this way, with a great abundance of tears: "Lord God, you know all things. You know what sorrow I have had to be chaste for you in my body all these three years, and now I might have my will and I dare not, for love of you. For if I were to break that custom of fasting from meat and drink on Fridays which you commanded me, I should now have my desire. But, blessed Lord, you know I will not go against your will, and great is my sorrow now unless I find comfort in you. Now, blessed Jesus, make your will known to my unworthy self, so that I may afterwards follow and fulfill it with all my might."

And then our Lord Jesus Christ with great sweetness spoke to this creature, commanding her to go again to her husband and pray him to grant her what she desired: "And he shall have what he desires. For, my beloved daughter, this was the reason why I ordered you to fast, so that you should be the sooner obtain your desire, and now it is granted to you. I no longer wish you to fast, and therefore I command you in the name of Jesus to eat and drink as your husband does."

Then this creature thanked our Lord Jesus Christ for his grace and his goodness, and afterwards got up and went to her husband, saying to him, "Sir, if you please, you shall grant me my desire, and you shall have your desire. Grant me that you will not come into my bed, and I grant you that I will pay your debts before I go to Jerusalem. And make my body free to God, so that you never make any claim on me requesting any conjugal debt after this day as long as you live—and I shall eat and drink on Fridays at your bidding."

Then her husband replied to her, "May your body be as freely available to God as it has been to me."

This creature thanked God greatly, rejoicing that she had her desire, praying her husband that they should say three paternosters in worship of the Trinity for the great grace that had been granted them. And so they did, kneeling under a cross, and afterwards they ate and drank together in great gladness of spirit. This was on a Friday, on Midsummer's Eve.

Then they went on to Bridlington and also to many other places, and spoke with God's servants, both anchorites and recluses, and many other of our Lord's lovers, with many worthy clerics, doctors and bachelors of divinity as well, in many different places. And to various people amongst them this creature revealed her feelings and her contemplations, as she was commanded to do, to find out if there were any deception in her feelings.

from *THE LONG LONELINESS*

DOROTHY DAY

In these selections from The Long Loneliness, *first published in the early 1950s, Dorothy Day, a life-long social activist and co-founder of* The Catholic Worker, *grapples with her profound love for Forster, her common-law husband, and her growing desire to become a Catholic as she prepares to give birth to their child. Day, born at the turn of the century, maintained that it was through the love she shared with Forster that she came to know God's love. Yet it was his antipathy toward religion that finally forced her to choose between their relationship and the covenant of baptism.*

I WAS SURPRISED that I found myself beginning to pray daily. I could not get down on my knees, but I could pray while I was walking. If I got down on my knees I thought, "Do I really believe? Whom am I praying to?" A terrible doubt came over me, and a sense of shame, and I wondered if I was praying because I was lonely, because I was unhappy.

But when I walked to the village for the mail, I found myself praying again, holding in my pocket the rosary that Mary Gordon gave me in New Orleans some years before. Maybe I did not say it correctly but I kept on saying it because it made me happy.

Then I thought suddenly, scornfully, "Here you are in a stupor of content. You are biological. Like a cow. Prayer with you is like the opiate of the people." And over and over again in my mind that phrase was repeated jeeringly, "Religion is the opiate of the people."

"But," I reasoned with myself, "I am praying because I am happy, not because I am unhappy. I did not turn to God in unhappiness, in grief, in despair—to get consolation, to get something from Him."

And encouraged that I was praying because I wanted to thank Him, I went on praying. No matter how dull the day, how long the walk seemed, if I felt sluggish at the beginning of the walk, the words I had been saying insinuated themselves into my heart before I had finished, so that on the trip back I neither prayed nor thought but was filled with exultation.

Along the beach I found it appropriate to say the *Te Deum*. When I worked about the house, I found myself addressing the Blessed Virgin and turning toward her statue.

It is so hard to say how this delight in prayer grew on me. The year before, I was saying as I planted seeds in the garden, "I *must* believe in these seeds, that they fall into the earth and grow into flowers and radishes and beans. It is a miracle to me because I do not understand it. Neither do naturalists understand it. The very fact that they use glib technical phrases does not make it any less of a miracle, and a miracle we all accept. Then why not accept God's mysteries?"

I began to go to Mass regularly on Sunday mornings.

When Freda went into town, I was alone. Forster was in the city all week, only coming out week ends. I finished the writing I was doing and felt at loose ends, thinking enviously of my friends going gaily about the city, about their work, with plenty of companionship.

.   .   .

In spite of my desire for a sociable week in town, in spite of a desire to pick up and flee from my solitude, I took joy in thinking of the idiocy of the pleasures I would indulge in if I were there. Cocktail parties, with prohibition drinks, dinners, the conversation or lack of it, dancing in a smoky crowded room when one might be walking on the beach, the dull, restless cogitations which come after dissipating one's energies—things which struck me with renewed force every time I spent days in the city. My virtuous resolutions to indulge in such pleasure no more were succeeded by a hideous depression when neither my new-found sense of religion, my family life, my work nor my surroundings were sufficient to console me. I thought of death and was overwhelmed by the terror and the blackness of both life and death. And I longed for a church near at hand where I could go and lift up my soul.

It was pleasant rowing about in the calm bay with Forster. The oyster boats were all out, and far on the horizon, off Sandy Hook, there was a four-masted vessel. I had the curious delusion that several huge holes had been stove in her side, through which you could see the blue sky. The other vessels seemed sailing in the air, quite indifferent to the horizon on which they should properly have been resting. Forster tried to explain to me scientific facts about mirages and atmospheric conditions, and, on the other hand, I pointed out to him how our senses lie to us.

But it was impossible to talk about religion or faith to him. A wall immediately separated us. The very love of nature, and the study of her secrets which was bringing me to faith, cut Forster off from religion.

I had known Forster a long time before we contracted our common-law relationship, and I have always felt that it was life with him that brought me natural happiness, that brought me to God.

His ardent love of creation brought me to the Creator of all things. But when I cried out to him, "How can there be no God, when there are all these beautiful things," he turned from me uneasily and complained that I was never satisfied. We loved each other so strongly that he wanted to remain in the love of the moment; he wanted me to rest in that love. He cried out against my attitude that there would be nothing left of that love without a faith.

.   .   .

I could not see that love between man and woman was incompatible with love of God. God is the Creator, and the very fact that we were begetting a child made me have a sense that we were made in the image and likeness of God, co-creators with him.

.   .   .

Because I was grateful for love, I was grateful for life, and living with Forster made me appreciate it and even reverence it still more. He had introduced me to so much that was beautiful and good that I felt I owed to him too this renewed interest in the things of the spirit.

.   .   .

Our child was born in March at the end of a harsh winter. In December I had come in from the country and taken an apartment in town. My sister came to stay with me, to help me over the last hard months. It was good to be there, close to friends, close to a church where I could pray. I read the *Imitation of Christ* a great deal during those months. I knew that I was going to have my child baptized, cost what it may. I knew that I was not going to have her floundering through many years as I had done, doubting and hesitating, undisciplined and amoral. I felt it was the greatest thing I could do for my child. For myself, I prayed for the gift of faith. I was sure, yet not sure. I postponed the day of decision.

A woman does not want to be alone at such a time. Even the most hardened, the most irreverent, is awed by the stupendous fact of creation. Becoming a Catholic would mean facing life alone and I clung to family life. It was hard to contemplate giving up a mate in order that my child and I could become members of the Church. Forster would have nothing to do with religion or with me if I embraced it. So I waited.

from *BONE BLACK*

BELL HOOKS

Reminiscent of the erotic sensuality found in centuries of religious mystical poetry, feminist theorist and prolific writer bell hooks, in her memoir, Bone Black (see also page 89), presents this dream-like passage of holy longing, her preparation for the baptismal rite of passage into the church.

WHEN SHE gave herself to god she was not afraid. She was so sure he wanted her, had lain awake nights wondering when this soul like a ripened plum would wet his holy bed with unforgivable sweetness. She was sure that there was joy to be found in being wanted long before her mama decided that it was time she and her brother joined the church. She knew she was ready to be the bride of god, ready to shed her blood in his honor and for his name. Mama gave them their instructions. They were not to join during the morning services. When the preacher asked in that tender voice for all those souls longing for god, needing him, to come, to give them themselves—they were not to answer. They were to wait for revival, for the special week when a new preacher comes to do the service, when children and grown-ups walk down the aisle night after night saying yes, yes, yes—they wanted to be saved. In her bed at night she moved restlessly to the sound of their chanting yes, yes, yes—she wanted to be saved.

When their turn came, she sat next to her brother, slowly becoming the little sister he and the grown-ups had always wanted her to be. She had never liked crowds. She had never faced a crowd waiting to hear her confess secrets, to tell of her personal rendezvous with god. Her legs shook as she followed her brother down the aisle, her heart beat fast, loud, so loud that not even the preacher's smile—as he placed his hand in her hand, asking her did she love the lord, did she want him for her personal savior, did she want salvation—could give her speech. All the lines she had rehearsed, the pretty words that would describe her nightly meeting with god, their walks in the garden, the waiting for him near bushes of pink and white baby roses, the moist dew that sometimes caught in her hair, the way he warmed her hands with breath that smelled of honeysuckle and jasmine—all the words would not come. In place of words she gave them tears, the same tears that had wet his wounds, that like warm summer rain had caressed his flesh with everlasting love. Later, when her mama asked why she stood there crying like a baby, saying nothing, not opening her big mouth, she still refused to speak. She did not say they were holy tears, water that will heal and renew. She was waiting to tell him all.

They were to wear white, all white, gown, slip, panties, cap. She wanted god to see her as he had always seen her, naked, brown, her flesh moving in the darkness like dusk, like the moment before the call to morning prayer. She was afraid he would not know her in white. She felt ashamed to meet him this one time in so public a place. She was sure it meant an end to all the private love they shared, the secret meetings. She entered the dark church slowly. Seeing no one yet, hearing their voices sing of water that will be troubled, of wading in the water. She searched the night for some sign of his face. The cold water held her trembling flesh, took away her ability to wander aimlessly, searching. She was no longer free to seek, to come and go whenever she chose, he had dropped a net in the water, to capture her, to hold her, to make her holiness his own.

The brown hands of John the Baptist were about her—John, beheaded friend and lover. He spoke with the voice of a stranger. His words an alien tongue. Taking this his sister, he baptized her in the name of the father, the son, and the holy ghost. Only her anguished cry pierced the dark with knowledge of his betrayal.

from *THE SEVEN STOREY MOUNTAIN*

THOMAS MERTON

Born in 1915 of Protestant parents, Thomas Merton had an adventurous youth at Columbia University, clinging to his atheism and a love of endless talk and drink. But in 1938, when he was twenty-three, Merton first experienced the conversion of his intellect, followed by the surrender of his heart to God. In these excerpts from The Seven Storey Mountain, *which, along with his many other volumes, have inspired countless religious vocations, Merton is prompted by an insistent inner urging to go to Mass in the Roman Catholic church. Yearning toward baptism, his "happy execution and rebirth," he soon feels compelled to dedicate himself wholly to God and turn away from the things of this world.*

BY THE time I was ready to begin the actual writing of my thesis, that is, around the beginning of September 1938, the groundwork of conversion was more or less complete. And how easily and sweetly it had all been done, with all the external graces that had been arranged, along my path, by the kind Providence of God! It had taken little more than a year and a half, counting from the time I read Gilson's *The Spirit of Medieval Philosophy* to bring me up from an "atheist"—as I considered myself—to one who accepted all the full range and possibilities of religious experience right up to the highest degree of glory.

I not only accepted all this, intellectually, but now I began to desire it. And not only did I begin to desire it, but I began to do so efficaciously: I began to want to take the necessary means to achieve this union, this peace. I began to desire to dedicate my life to God, to His service. The notion was still vague and obscure, and it was ludicrously impractical in the sense that I was already dreaming of mystical union when I did not even keep the simplest rudiments of the moral law. But nevertheless I was convinced of the reality of the goal, and confident that it could be achieved: and whatever element of presumption was in this confidence I am sure God excused, in His mercy, because of my stupidity and helplessness, and because I was really beginning to be ready to do whatever I thought He wanted me to do to bring me to Him.

But, oh, how blind and weak and sick I was, although I thought I saw where I was going, and half understood the way! How deluded we sometimes are by the clear notions we get out of books. They make us think that we really understand things of which we have no practical knowledge at all. I remember how learnedly and enthusiastically I could talk for hours about mysticism and the experimental knowledge of God, and all the while I was stoking the fires of the argument with Scotch and soda.

That was the way it turned out that Labor Day, for instance. I went to Philadelphia with Joe Roberts, who had a room in the same house as I, and who had been through all the battles on the Fourth Floor of John Jay for the past four years. He had graduated and was working on some trade magazine about women's hats. All one night we sat, with a friend of his, in a big dark roadhouse outside of Philadelphia, arguing and arguing about mysticism, and smoking more and more cigarettes and gradually getting drunk. Eventually, filled with enthusiasm for the purity of heart which begets the vision of God, I went on with them into the city, after the closing of the bars, to a big speakeasy where we completed the work of getting plastered.

My internal contradictions were resolving themselves out, indeed, but still only on the plane of theory, not of practice: not for lack of good-will, but because I was still so completely chained and fettered by my sins and my attachments.

I think that if there is one truth that people need to learn, in the world, especially today, it is this: the intellect is only theoretically independent of desire and appetite in ordinary, actual practice. It is constantly being blinded and perverted by the ends and aims of passion, and the evidence it presents to us with such a show of impartiality and objectivity is fraught with interest and propaganda. We have become marvelous at self-delusion; all the more so, because we have gone to such trouble to convince ourselves of our own absolute infallibility. The desires of the flesh—and by that I mean not only sinful desires, but even the ordinary, normal appetites for comfort and ease and human respect, are fruitful sources of every kind of error and misjudgment, and because we have these yearnings in us, our intellects (which, if they operated all alone in a vacuum, would indeed, register with pure impartiality what they saw) present to us everything distorted and accommodated to the norms of our desire.

And therefore, even when we are acting with the best of intentions, and imagine that we are doing great good, we may be actually doing tremendous material harm and contradicting all our good intentions. There are ways that seem to men to be good, the end whereof is the depths of hell.

The only answer to the problem is grace, grace, docility to grace. I was still in the precarious position of being my own guide and my own interpreter of grace. It is a wonder I ever got to the harbor at all!

Sometime in August, I finally answered an impulsion that had been working on me for a long time. Every Sunday, I had been going out on Long Island to spend the day with the same girl who had brought me back in such a hurry from Lax's town Olean. But every week, as Sunday came around, I was filled with a growing desire to stay in the city and go to some kind of a church.

At first I had vaguely thought I might try to find some Quakers, and go and sit with them. There still remained in me something of the favorable notion about Quakers that I had picked up as a child, and which the reading of William Penn had not been able to overcome.

But, naturally enough, with the work I was doing in the library, a stronger drive began to assert itself, and I was drawn much more imperatively to the Catholic Church. Finally the urge became so strong that I could not resist it. I called up my girl and told her that I was not coming out that week-end, and made up my mind to go to Mass for the first time in my life.

The first time in my life! That was true. I had lived for several years on the continent, I had been to Rome, I had been in and out of a thousand Catholic cathedrals and churches, and yet I had never heard Mass. If anything had ever been going on in the churches I visited, I had always fled, in wild Protestant panic.

I will not easily forget how I felt that day. First, there was this sweet, strong, gentle, clean urge in me which said: "Go to Mass! Go to Mass!" It was something quite new and strange, this voice that seemed to prompt me, this firm, growing interior conviction of what I needed to do. It had a suavity, a simplicity about it that I could not easily account for. And when I gave in to it, it did not exult over me, and trample me down in its raging haste to land on its prey, but it carried me forward serenely and with purposeful direction.

That does not mean that my emotions yielded to it altogether quietly. I was really still a little afraid to go to a Catholic church, of set purpose, with all the other people, and dispose myself in a pew, and lay myself open to the mysterious perils of that strange and powerful thing they called their "Mass."

God made it a very beautiful Sunday. And since it was the first time I had ever really spent a sober Sunday in New York, I was surprised at the clean, quiet atmosphere of the empty streets uptown. The sun was blazing bright. At the end of the street, as I came out the front door, I could see a burst of green, and the blue river and the hills of Jersey on the other side.

Broadway was empty. A solitary trolley came speeding down in front of Barnard College and past the School of Journalism. Then, from the high, gray, expensive tower of the Rockefeller Church, huge bells began to boom. It served very well for the eleven o'clock Mass at the little brick Church of Corpus Christi, hidden behind Teachers College on 121st Street.

How bright the little building seemed. Indeed, it was quite new. The sun shone on the clean bricks. People were going in the wide open door, into the cool darkness and, all at once, all the churches of Italy and France came back to me. The richness and fulness of the atmosphere of Catholicism that I had not been able to avoid apprehending and loving as a child, came back to me with a rush: but now I was to enter into it fully for the first time. So far, I had known nothing but the outward surface.

It was a gay, clean church, with big plain windows and white columns and pilasters and a well-lighted, simple sanctuary. Its style was a trifle eclectic, but much less perverted with incongruities than the average

Catholic church in America. It had a kind of a seventeenth-century, oratorian character about it, though with a sort of American colonial tinge of simplicity. The blend was effective and original: but although all this affected me, without my thinking about it, the thing that impressed me most was that the place was full, absolutely full. It was full not only of old ladies and broken-down gentlemen with one foot in the grave, but of men and women and children young and old— especially young: people of all classes, and all ranks on a solid foundation of workingmen and -women and their families.

I found a place that I hoped would be obscure, over on one side, in the back, and went to it without genuflecting, and knelt down. As I knelt, the first thing I noticed was a young girl, very pretty too, perhaps fifteen or sixteen, kneeling straight up and praying quite seriously. I was very much impressed to see that someone who was young and beautiful could with such simplicity make prayer the real and serious and principal reason for going to church. She was clearly kneeling that way because she meant it, not in order to show off, and she was praying with an absorption which, though not the deep recollection of a saint, was serious enough to show that she was not thinking at all about the other people who were there.

What a revelation it was, to discover so many ordinary people in a place together, more conscious of God than of one another: not there to show off their hats or their clothes, but to pray, or at least to fulfil a religious obligation, not a human one. For even those who might have been there for no better motive than that they were obliged to be, were at least free from any of the self-conscious and human constraint which is never absent from a Protestant church where people are definitely gathered together as people, as neighbors, and always have at least half an eye for one another, if not all of both eyes.

Since it was summer time, the eleven o'clock Mass was a Low Mass: but I had not come expecting to hear music. Before I knew it, the priest was in the sanctuary with the two altar boys, and was busy at the altar with something or other which I could not see very well, but the people were praying by themselves, and I was engrossed and absorbed in the thing as a whole: the business at the altar and the presence of the people. And still I had not got rid of my fear. Seeing the late-comers hastily genuflecting before entering the pew, I realized my omission, and got the idea that people had spotted me for a pagan and were just waiting for me to miss a few more genuflections before throwing me out or, at least, giving me looks of reproof.

Soon we all stood up. I did not know what it was for. The priest was at the other end of the altar, and, as I afterwards learned, he was reading the Gospel. And then the next thing I knew there was someone in the pulpit.

It was a young priest, perhaps not much over thirty-three or -four years old. His face was rather ascetic and thin, and its asceticism was heightened with a note of intellectuality by his horn-rimmed glasses, although he was only one of the assistants, and he did not consider himself an intellectual, nor did anyone else apparently consider him so. But anyway, that was the impression he made on me: and his sermon, which was simple enough, did not belie it.

It was not long: but to me it was very interesting to hear this young man quietly telling the people in language that was plain, yet tinged with scholastic terminology, about a point in Catholic Doctrine. How clear and solid the doctrine was: for behind those words you felt the full force not only of Scripture but of centuries of a unified and continuous and consistent tradition. And above all, it was a vital tradition: there was nothing studied or antique about it. These words, this terminology, this doctrine, and these convictions fell from the lips of the young priest as something that were most intimately part of his own life. What was more, I sensed that the people were familiar with it all, and that it was also, in due proportion, part of their life also: it was just as much integrated into their spiritual organism as the air they breathed or the food they ate worked in to their blood and flesh.

What was he saying? That Christ was the Son of God. That, in Him, the Second Person of the Holy Trinity, God, had assumed a Human Nature, a Human Body and Soul, and had taken Flesh and dwelt amongst us, full of grace and truth: and that this Man, Whom men called the Christ, was God. He was both Man and God: two Natures hypostatically united in one Person or suppositum, one individual Who was a Divine Person, having assumed to Himself a Human Nature. And His works were the works of God: His acts were the acts of God. He loved us: God, and walked among us: God, and died for us on the Cross, God of God, Light of Light, True God of True God.

Jesus Christ was not simply a man, a good man, a great man, the greatest prophet, a wonderful healer, a saint: He was something that made all such trivial words pale into irrelevance. He was God. But nevertheless He was not merely a spirit without a true body, God hiding under a visionary body: He was also truly a Man, born of the Flesh of the Most Pure Virgin, formed of her Flesh by the Holy Spirit.

And what He did, in that Flesh, on earth, He did not only as Man but as God. He loved us as God, He suffered and died for us, God.

And how did we know? Because it was revealed to us in the Scriptures and confirmed by the teaching of the Church and of the powerful unanimity of Catholic Tradition from the First Apostles, from the first Popes and the early Fathers, on down through the Doctors of the Church and the great scholastics, to our own day. *De Fide Divina*. If you believed it, you would receive light to grasp it, to understand it in some measure. If you did not believe it, you would never understand: it would never be anything but scandal or folly.

And no one can believe these things merely by wanting to, of his own volition. Unless he receive grace, an actual light and impulsion of the mind and will from God, he cannot even make an act of living faith. It is God Who gives us faith, and no one cometh to Christ unless the Father draweth him.

I wonder what would have happened in my life if I had been given this grace in the days when I had almost discovered the Divinity of Christ in the ancient mosaics of the churches of Rome. What scores of self-murdering and Christ-murdering sins would have been avoided—all the filth I had plastered upon His image in my soul during those last five years that I had been scourging and crucifying God within me?

It is easy to say, after it all, that God had probably foreseen my infidelities and had never given me the grace in those days because He saw how I would waste and despise it: and perhaps that rejection would have been my ruin. For there is no doubt that one of the reasons why grace is not given to souls is because they have so hardened their wills in greed and cruelty and selfishness that their refusal of it would only harden them more. . . . But now I had been beaten into the semblance of some kind of humility by misery and confusion and perplexity and secret, interior fear, and my ploughed soul was better ground for the reception of good seed.

The sermon was what I most needed to hear that day. When the Mass of the Catechumens was over, I, who was not even a catechumen, but only a blind and deaf and dumb pagan as weak and dirty as anything that ever came out of the darkness of Imperial Rome or Corinth or Ephesus, was not able to understand anything else.

It all became completely mysterious when the attention was refocussed on the altar. When the silence grew more and more profound, and little bells began to ring, I got scared again and, finally, genuflecting hastily on my left knee, I hurried out of the church in the middle of the most important part of the Mass. But it was just as well. In a way, I suppose I was responding to a kind of liturgical instinct that told me I did not belong there for the celebration of the Mysteries as such. I had no idea what took place in them: but the fact was that Christ, God, would be visibly present on the altar in the Sacred Species. And although He was there, yes, for love of me: yet He was there in His power and His might, and what was I? What was on my soul? What was I in His sight?

It was liturgically fitting that I should kick myself out at the end of the Mass of the Catechumens, when the ordained *ostiarii* should have been there to do it. Anyway, it was done.

Now I walked leisurely down Broadway in the sun, and my eyes looked about me at a new world. I could not understand what it was that had happened to make me so happy, why I was so much at peace, so content with life for I was not yet used to the clean savor that comes with an actual grace—indeed, there was no impossibility in a person's hearing and believing such a sermon and being justified, that is, receiving sanctifying grace in his soul as a habit, and beginning, from that moment, to live the divine and supernatural life for good and all. But that is something I will not speculate about.

All I know is that I walked in a new world. Even the ugly buildings of Columbia were transfigured in it, and everywhere was peace in these streets designed for violence and noise. Sitting outside the gloomy little Childs restaurant of 111th Street, behind the dirty, boxed bushes, and eating breakfast, was like sitting in the Elysian Fields.

. . .

Yet with all this, I was not yet ready to stand beside the font. There was not even any interior debate as to whether I ought to become a Catholic. I was content to stand by and admire. For the rest, I remember one afternoon, when my girl had come in to town to see me, and we were walking around the streets·uptown, I subjected her to the rather disappointing entertainment of going to Union Theological Seminary, and asking for a catalogue of their courses which I proceeded to read while we were walking around on Riverside Drive. She was not openly irritated by it: she was a very good and patient girl anyway. But still you could see she was a little bored, walking around with a man who was not sure whether he ought to enter a theological seminary.

There was nothing very attractive in that catalogue. I was to get much more excited by the article on the Jesuits in the *Catholic Encyclopaedia*—breathless with the thought of so many novitiates and tertianships and what not—so much scrutiny, so much training. What monsters of efficiency they must be, these Jesuits, I kept thinking to myself, as I read and reread the article. And perhaps, from time to time, I tried to picture myself with my face sharpened by asceticism, its pallor intensified by contrast with a black cassock, and every line of it proclaiming a Jesuit saint, a Jesuit master-mind. And I think the master-mind element was one of the strongest features of this obscure attraction.

Apart from this foolishness, I came no nearer to the Church, in practice, than adding a "Hail Mary" to my night prayers. I did not even go to Mass again, at once. . . . It took something that belongs to history to form and vitalize these resolutions that were still only vague and floating entities in my mind and will.

One of those hot evenings at the end of summer the atmosphere of the city suddenly became terribly tense with some news that came out of the radios. Before I knew what the news was, I began to feel the tension. For I was suddenly aware that the quiet, disparate murmurs of different radios in different houses had imperceptibly merged into one big, ominous unified voice, that moved at you from different directions and followed you down the street, and came to you from another angle as soon as you began to recede from any one of its particular sources.

I heard "Germany—Hitler—at six o'clock this morning the German Army . . . the Nazis . . . " What had they done?

Then Joe Roberts came in and said there was about to be a war. The Germans had occupied Czechoslovakia, and there was bound to be a war.

The city felt as if one of the doors of hell had been half opened, and a blast of its breath had flared out to wither up the spirits of men. And people were loitering around the newsstands in misery.

Joe Roberts and I sat in my room, where there was no radio, until long after midnight, drinking canned beer and smoking cigarettes, and making silly and excited jokes but, within a couple of days, the

English Prime Minister had flown in a big hurry to see Hitler and had made a nice new alliance at Munich that cancelled everything that might have caused a war, and returned to England. He alighted at Croydon and came stumbling out of the plane saying "Peace in our time!"

I was very depressed. I was beyond thinking about the intricate and filthy political tangle that underlay the mess. I had given up politics as more or less hopeless, by this time. I was no longer interested in having any opinion about the movement and interplay of forces which were all more or less iniquitous and corrupt, and it was far too laborious and uncertain a business to try and find out some degree of truth and justice in all the loud, artificial claims that were put forward by the various sides.

All I could see was a world in which everybody said they hated war, and in which we were all being rushed into a war with a momentum that was at last getting dizzy enough to affect my stomach. All the internal contradictions of the society in which I lived were at last beginning to converge upon its heart. There could not be much more of a delay in its dismembering. Where would it end? In those days, the future was obscured, blanked out by war as by a dead-end wall. Nobody knew if anyone at all would come out of it alive. Who would be worse off, the civilians or the soldiers? The distinction between their fates was to be abolished, in most countries, by aerial warfare, by all the new planes, by all the marvelous new bombs. What would the end of it be?

I knew that I myself hated war, and all the motives that led to war and were behind wars. But I could see that now my likes or dislikes, beliefs or disbeliefs meant absolutely nothing in the external, political order. I was just an individual, and the individual had ceased to count. I meant nothing, in this world, except that I would probably soon become a number on the list of those to be drafted. I would get a piece of metal with my number on it, to hang around my neck, so as to help out the circulation of red-tape that would necessarily follow the disposal of my remains, and that would be the last eddy of mental activity that would close over my lost identity.

The whole business was so completely unthinkable that my mind, like almost all the other minds that were in the same situation, simply stopped trying to cope with it, and refixed its focus on the ordinary routine of life.

I had my thesis to type out, and a lot of books to read, and I was thinking of preparing an article in Crashaw which perhaps I would send to T. S. Eliot for his *Criterion*. I did not know that *Criterion* had printed its last issue, and that Eliot's reaction to the situation that so depressed me was to fold up his magazine.

The days went on and the radios returned to their separate and individual murmuring, not to be regimented back into their appalling shout for yet another year. September, as I think, must have been more than half gone.

I borrowed Father Leahy's life of Hopkins from the library. It was a rainy day. I had been working in the library in the morning. I had gone to buy a thirty-five-cent lunch at one of those little pious kitchens on Broadway—the one where Professor Gerig, of the graduate school of French, sat daily in silence with his ancient, ailing mother, over a very small table, eating his Brussels sprouts. Later in the afternoon, perhaps about four, I would have to go down to Central Park West and give a Latin lesson to a youth who was sick in bed, and who ordinarily came to the tutoring school run by my landlord, on the ground floor of the house where I lived.

I walked back to my room. The rain was falling gently on the empty tennis courts across the street, and the huge old domed library stood entrenched in its own dreary grayness, arching a cyclops eyebrow at South Field.

I took up the book about Gerard Manley Hopkins. The chapter told of Hopkins at Balliol, at Oxford. He was thinking of becoming a Catholic. He was writing letters to Cardinal Newman (not yet a cardinal) about becoming a Catholic.

All of a sudden, something began to stir within me, something began to push me, to prompt me. It was a movement that spoke like a voice.

"What are you waiting for?" it said. "Why are you sitting here? Why do you still hesitate? You know what you ought to do? Why don't you do it?"

I stirred in the chair, I lit a cigarette, looked out the window at the rain, tried to shut the voice up. "Don't act on impulses," I thought. "This is crazy. This is not rational. Read your book."

Hopkins was writing to Newman, at Birmingham, about his indecision.

"What are you waiting for?" said the voice within me again. "Why are you sitting there? It is useless to hesitate any longer. Why don't you get up and go?"

I got up and walked restlessly around the room. "It's absurd," I thought. "Anyway, Father Ford would not be there at this time of day. I would only be wasting time."

Hopkins had written to Newman, and Newman had replied to him, telling him to come and see him at Birmingham.

Suddenly, I could bear it no longer. I put down the book, and got into my raincoat, and started down the stairs. I went out into the street. I crossed over, and walked along by the gray wooden fence, towards Broadway, in the light rain.

And then everything inside me began to sing—to sing with peace, to sing with strength and to sing with conviction.

I had nine blocks to walk. Then I turned the corner of 121st Street, and the brick church and presbytery were before me. I stood in the doorway and rang the bell and waited.

When the maid opened the door, I said:

"May I see Father Ford, please?"

"But Father Ford is out."

I thought: well, it is not a waste of time, anyway. And I asked when she expected him back. I would come back later, I thought.

The maid closed the door. I stepped back into the street. And then I saw Father Ford coming around the corner from Broadway. He approached, with his head down, in a rapid, thoughtful walk. I went to meet him and said:

"Father, may I speak to you about something?"

"Yes," he said, looking up, surprised. "Yes, sure, come into the house."

We sat in the little parlor by the door. And I said: "Father, I want to become a Catholic."

.   .   .

As November began, my mind was taken up with this one thought: of getting baptized and entering at last into the supernatural life of the Church. In spite of all my studying and all my reading and all my talking, I was still infinitely poor and wretched in my appreciation of what was about to take place within me. I was about to set foot on the shore at the foot of the high, seven-circled mountain of a Purgatory steeper and more arduous than I was able to imagine, and I was not at all aware of the climbing I was about to have to do.

The essential thing was to begin the climb. Baptism was that beginning, and a most generous one, on the part of God, For, although I was baptized conditionally, I hoped that His mercy swallowed up all the guilt and temporal punishment of my twenty-three black years of sin in the waters of the font, and allowed me a new start. But my human nature, my weakness, and the cast of my evil habits still remained to be fought and overcome.

Towards the end of the first week in November, Father Moore told me I would be baptized on the sixteenth. I walked out of the rectory that evening happier and more contented than I had ever been in my life. I looked at a calendar to see what saint had that day for a feast, and it was marked for St. Gertrude.

It was only in the last days before being liberated from my slavery to death, that I had the grace to feel something of my own weakness and helplessness. It was not a very vivid light that was given to me on the subject: but I was really aware, at last, of what a poor and miserable thing I was. On the night of the fifteenth of November, the eve of my Baptism and First Communion, I lay in my bed awake and timorous for fear that something might go wrong the next day. And to humiliate me still further, as I lay there, fear came over me that I might not be able to keep the eucharistic fast. It only meant going from midnight to ten o'clock without any drinking water or taking any food, yet all of a sudden this little act of self-denial which amounts to no more, in reality, than a sort of an abstract token, a gesture of good-will, grew in my imagination until it seemed to be utterly beyond my strength—as if I were about to go without food and drink for ten days, instead of ten hours. I had enough sense left to realize that this was one of those curious psychological reactions with which our nature, not without help from the devil, tries to confuse us and avoid what reason and our will demand of it, and so I forgot about it all and went to sleep.

In the morning, when I got up, having forgotten to ask Father Moore if washing your teeth was against the eucharistic fast or not, I did not wash them, and, facing a similar problem about cigarettes, I resisted the temptation to smoke.

I went downstairs and out into the street to go to my happy execution and rebirth.

The sky was bright and cold. The river glittered like steel. There was a clean wind in the street. It was one of those fall days full of life and triumph, made for great beginnings, and yet I was not altogether exalted: for there were still in my mind these vague, half animal apprehensions about the externals of what was to happen in the church—would my mouth be so dry that I could not swallow the Host? If that happened, what would I do? I did not know.

Gerdy joined me as I was turning in to Broadway. I do not remember whether Ed Rice caught up with us on Broadway or not. Lax and Seymour came after we were in church.

Ed Rice was my godfather. He was the only Catholic among us—the only Catholic among all my close friends. Lax, Seymour, and Gerdy were Jews. They were very quiet, and so was I. Rice was the only one who was not cowed or embarrassed or shy.

The whole thing was very simple. First of all, I knelt at the altar of Our Lady where Father Moore received my abjuration of heresy and schism. Then we went to the baptistery, in a little dark corner by the main door.

I stood at the threshold.

"Quid Petis ab ecclesia Dei?" asked Father Moore.

"Fidem!"

"Fides quid tibi praestat?"

"Vitam aeternam."

Then the young priest began to pray in Latin, looking earnestly and calmly at the page of the *Rituale* through the lenses of his glasses. And I, who was asking for eternal life, stood and watched him, catching a word of the Latin here and there.

He turned to me:

"Abrenuntias Satanae?"

In a triple vow I renounced Satan and his pomps and his works.

"Dost thou believe in God the Father almighty, Creator of heaven and earth?"

"Credo!"

"Dost thou believe in Jesus Christ His only Son, Who was born, and suffered?"

"Credo!"

"Dost thou believe in the Holy Spirit, in the Holy Catholic Church, the Communion of saints, the remission of sins, the resurrection of the body and eternal life?"

"Credo!"

What mountains were falling from my shoulders! What scales of dark night were peeling off my intellect, to let in the inward vision of God and His truth! But I was absorbed in the liturgy, and waiting for the next ceremony. It had been one of the things that had rather frightened me—or rather, which frightened the legion that had been living in me for twenty-three years.

Now the priest blew into my face. He said: *"Exi ab eo, spiritus immunde:* Depart from him, thou impure spirit, and give place to the Holy Spirit, the Paraclete."

It was the exorcism. I did not see them leaving, but there must have been more than seven of them. I had never been able to count them. Would they ever come back? Would that terrible threat of Christ be fulfilled, that threat about the man whose house was clean and garnished, only to be reoccupied by the first devil and many other worse than himself?

The priest, and Christ in him—for it was Christ that was doing these things through his visible ministry, in the Sacrament of my purification—breathed again into my face.

"Thomas, receive the good Spirit through this breathing, and receive the Blessing of God. Peace be with thee."

Then he began again to pray, and sign me with Crosses, and presently came the salt which he put on my tongue—the salt of wisdom, that I might have the savor of divine things, and finally he poured the water on my head, and named me Thomas, "if thou be not already baptized."

After that, I went into the confessional, where one of the other assistants was waiting for me. I knelt in the shadows. Through the dark, close-meshed wire of the grille between us, I saw Father McGough, his head bowed, and resting on his hand, inclining his ear towards me. "Poor man," I thought. He seemed very young and he had always looked so innocent to me that I wondered how he was going to identify and understand the things I was about to tell him.

But one by one, that is, species by species, as best I could, I tore out all those sins by their roots, like teeth. Some of them were hard, but I did it quickly, doing the best I could to approximate the number of times all these things had happened—there was no counting them, only guessing.

I did not have any time to feel how relieved I was when I came stumbling out, as I had to go down to the front of the church where Father Moore would see me and come out to begin his—and my— Mass. But ever since that day, I have loved confessionals.

Now he was at the altar, in his white vestments, opening the book.

I was kneeling right at the altar rail. The bright sanctuary was all mine. I could hear the murmur of the priest's voice, and the responses of the server, and it did not matter that I had no one to look at, so that I could tell when to stand up and kneel down again, for I was still not very sure of these ordinary ceremonies. But when the little bells were rung I knew what was happening. And I saw the raised Host—the silence and simplicity with which Christ once again triumphed, raised up, drawing all things to Himself—drawing me to Himself.

Presently the priest's voice was louder, saying the *Pater Noster.* Then, soon, the server was running through the *Confiteor* in a rapid murmur. That was for me. Father Moore turned around and made a big cross in absolution, and held up the little Host.

"Behold the Lamb of God: behold Him Who taketh away the sins of the world."

And my First Communion began to come towards me, down the steps. I was the only one at the altar rail. Heaven was entirely mine— that Heaven in which sharing makes no division or diminution. But this solitariness was a kind of reminder of the singleness with which this Christ, hidden in the small Host, was giving Himself for me, and to me, and, with Himself, the entire Godhead and Trinity—a great new increase of the power and grasp of their indwelling that had begun only a few minutes before at the font.

I left the altar rail and went back to the pew where the others were kneeling like four shadows, four unrealities, and I hid my face in my hands.

In the Temple of God that I had just become, the One Eternal and Pure Sacrifice was offered up to the God dwelling in me: the sacrifice of God to God, and me sacrificed together with God, incorporated in His Incarnation. Christ born in me, a new Bethlehem, and sacrificed in me, His new Calvary, and risen in me: offering me to the Father, in Himself, asking the Father, my Father and His, to receive me into His infinite and special love—not the love He has for all things that exist—for mere existence is a token of God's love, but the love of those creatures who are drawn to Him in and with the power of His own love for Himself.

For now I had entered into the everlasting movement of that gravitation which is the very life and spirit of God: God's own gravitation towards the depths of His own infinite nature, His goodness without end. And God, the center Who is everywhere, and whose circumference is nowhere, finding me, through incorporation with Christ, incorporated into this immense and tremendous gravitational movement which is love, which is the Holy Spirit, loved me.

And He called out to me from His own immense depths.

from *THE CONFESSIONS*

St. Augustine

Born in the middle of the fourth century C.E. in North Africa of a Pagan father and a Christian mother, St. Augustine was attracted, in turn, by Manichean gnosticism, skepticism, and the mystical philosophy of Plotinus, all in his quest for meaning and truth. In The Confessions, *written when he was already a highly respected bishop in his forties, Augustine provides a detailed account of his torturous struggle to surrender his will and his life fully to God. Plagued by the strength of his sexual desire and ambition for worldly success, these excerpts first recall Augustine's early years, followed by his now-classic conversion in a garden in Milan, an event that was to significantly alter the course of Christianity in the West.*

"You are great, Lord, and highly to be praised" (Ps. 47:2): "great is your power and your wisdom is immeasurable" (Ps. 146:5). Man, a little piece of your creation, desires to praise you, a human being "bearing his mortality with him" (2 Cor. 4:10), carrying with him the witness of his sin and the witness that you "resist the proud" (I Pet. 5:5). Nevertheless, to praise you is the desire of man, a little piece of your creation. You stir man to take pleasure in praising you, because you have made us for yourself, and our heart is restless until it rests in you.

.   .   .

Who will enable me to find rest in you? Who will grant me that you come to my heart and intoxicate it, so that I forget my evils and embrace my one and only good, yourself? What are you to me? Have mercy so that I may find words. What am I to do that you command me to love you, and that, if I fail to love you, you are angry with me and threaten me with vast miseries? If I do not love you, is that but a little misery? What a wretch I am! In your mercies, Lord God, tell me what you are to me. "Say to my soul, I am your salvation" (Ps. 34:3). Speak to me so that I may hear. See the ears of my heart are before you, Lord. Open them and "say to my soul, I am your salvation." After that utterance I will run and lay hold on you. Do not hide your face from me (cf. Ps. 26:9). Lest I die, let me die so that I may see it.

．　．　．

Our lodging had a garden. We had the use of it as well as of the entire house, for our host, the owner of the house, was not living there. The tumult of my heart took me out into the garden where no one could interfere with the burning struggle with myself in which I was engaged, until the matter could be settled. You knew, but I did not, what the outcome would be. But my madness with myself was part of the process of recovering health, and in the agony of death I was coming to life. I was aware how ill I was, unaware how well I was soon to be. So I went out into the garden. Alypius followed me step after step. Although he was present, I felt no intrusion on my solitude. How could he abandon me in such a state? We sat down as far as we could from the buildings. I was deeply disturbed in spirit, angry with indignation and distress that I was not entering into my pact and covenant with you, my God, when all my bones (Ps. 34:10) were crying out that I should enter into it and were exalting it to heaven with praises. But to reach that destination one does not use ships or chariots or feet. It was not even necessary to go the distance I had come from the house to where we were sitting. The one necessary condition, which meant not only going but at once arriving there, was to have the will to go—provided only that the will was strong and unqualified, not the turning and twisting first this way, then that, of a will half-wounded, struggling with one part rising up and the other part falling down.

．　．　．

In my own case, as I deliberated about serving my Lord God (Jer. 30:9) which I had long been disposed to do, the self which willed to serve was identical with the self which was unwilling. It was I. I was neither wholly willing nor wholly unwilling. So I was in conflict with myself and was dissociated from myself. The dissociation came about against my will. Yet this was not a manifestation of the nature of an alien mind but the punishment suffered in my own mind. And so it was "not I" that brought this about "but sin which dwelt in me" (Rom. 7:17, 20), sin resulting from the punishment of a more freely chosen sin, because I was a son of Adam.

·   ·   ·

Such was my sickness and my torture, as I accused myself even more bitterly than usual. I was twisting and turning in my chain until it would break completely: I was now only a little bit held by it, but I was still held. You, Lord, put pressure on me in my hidden depths with a severe mercy wielding the double whip of fear and shame, lest I should again succumb, and lest that tiny and tenuous bond which still remained should not be broken, but once more regain strength and bind me even more firmly. Inwardly I said to myself: Let it be now, let it be now. And by this phrase I was already moving towards a decision; I had almost taken it, and then I did not do so. Yet I did not relapse into my original condition, but stood my ground very close to the point of deciding and recovered my breath. Once more I made the attempt and came only a little short of my goal; only a little short of it—yet I did not touch it or hold on to it. I was hesitating whether to die to death and to live to life. Ingrained evil had more hold over me than unaccustomed good. The nearer approached the moment of time when I would become different, the greater the horror of it struck me. But it did not thrust me back nor turn me away, but left me in a state of suspense.

Vain trifles and the triviality of the empty-headed, my old loves, held me back. They tugged at the garment of my flesh and whispered: "Are you getting rid of us?" And "from this moment we shall never be with you again, not for ever and ever." And "from this moment this and that are forbidden to you for ever and ever." What they were suggesting in what I have called "this and that"—what they were suggesting, my God, may your mercy avert from the soul of your servant! What filth, what disgraceful things they were suggesting! I was listening to them with much less than half my attention. They were not frankly confronting me face to face on the road, but as it were whispering behind my back, as if they were furtively tugging at me as I was going away, trying to persuade me to look back. Nevertheless they held me back. I hesitated to detach myself, to be rid of them, to make the leap to where I was being called. Meanwhile the overwhelming force of habit was saying to me: "Do you think you can live without them?"

Nevertheless it was now putting the question very half-heartedly. For from that direction where I had set my face and towards which I was afraid to move, there appeared the dignified and chaste Lady Continence, serene and cheerful without coquetry, enticing me in an honourable manner to come and not to hesitate. To receive and embrace me she stretched out pious hands, filled with numerous good examples for me to follow. There were large numbers of boys and girls, a multitude of all ages, young adults and grave widows and elderly virgins. In every one of them was Continence herself, in no sense barren but "the fruitful mother of children" (Ps. 112: 9), the joys born of you, Lord, her husband. And she smiled on me with a smile of encouragement as if to say: "Are you incapable of doing what these men and women have done? Do you think them capable of achieving this by their own resources and not by the Lord their God? Their Lord God gave me to them. Why are you relying on yourself, only to find yourself unreliable? Cast yourself upon him, do not be afraid. He will not withdraw himself so that you fall. Make the leap without anxiety; he will catch you and heal you."

I blushed with embarrassment because I was still listening to the mutterings of those vanities, and racked by hesitations I remained undecided. But once more it was as if she said: "'Stop your ears to your impure members on earth and mortify them' (Col. 3:5). They declare delights to you, but 'not in accord with the law of the Lord your God'" (Ps. 118: 85). This debate in my heart was a struggle of myself against myself. Alypius stood quite still at my side, and waited in silence for the outcome of my unprecedented state of agitation.

From a hidden depth a profound self-examination had dredged up a heap of all my misery and set it "in the sight of my heart" (Ps. 18:15). That precipitated a vast storm bearing a massive downpour of tears. To pour it all out with the accompanying groans, I got up from beside Alypius (solitude seemed to me more appropriate for the business of weeping), and I moved further away to ensure that even his presence put no inhibition upon me. He sensed that this was my condition at that moment. I think I may have said something which made it clear that the sound of my voice was already choking with tears. So I stood up while in profound astonishment he remained where we were sitting. I threw myself down somehow under a certain figtree, and let my tears flow freely. Rivers streamed from my eyes, a sacrifice acceptable to you (Ps. 50:19), and (though not in these words, yet in this sense) I repeatedly said to you: "How long, O Lord? How long, Lord, will you be angry to the uttermost? Do not be mindful of our old iniquities." (Ps. 6:4). For I felt my past to have a grip on me. It uttered wretched cries: "How long, how long is it to be?" "Tomorrow, tomorrow." "Why not now? Why not an end to my impure life in this very hour?"

As I was saying this and weeping in the bitter agony of my heart, suddenly I heard a voice from the nearby house chanting as if it might be a boy or a girl (I do not know which), saying and repeating over and over again "Pick up and read, pick up and read." At once my countenance changed, and I began to think intently whether there might be some sort of children's game in which such a chant is used. But I could not remember having heard of one. I checked the flood of tears and stood up. I interpreted it solely as a divine command to me to open the book and read the first chapter I might find. For I had heard how Antony happened to be present at the gospel reading, and took it as an admonition addressed to himself when the words were read: "Go, sell all you have, give to the poor, and you shall have treasure in heaven; and come, follow me" (Matt. 19:21). By such an inspired utterance he was immediately "converted to you" (Ps. 50:15). So I hurried back to the place where Alypius was sitting. There I had put down the book of the apostle when I got up. I seized it, opened it and in silence read the first passage on which my eyes lit: "Not in riots and drunken parties, not in eroticism and indecencies, not in strife and rivalry, but put on the Lord Jesus Christ and make no provision for the flesh in its lusts" (Rom. 13:13-14).

I neither wished nor needed to read further. At once, with the last words of this sentence, it was as if a light of relief from all anxiety flooded into my heart. All the shadows of doubt were dispelled.

from *FAITH, SEX, MYSTERY*

RICHARD GILMAN

When he was nearing thirty in the early 1950s, seeking transcendence while struggling with his own disturbing erotic desires, Richard Gilman, a "militantly atheistic Jew," converted to Roman Catholicism. In Faith, Sex, Mystery, *his complex confession of finding and then losing his faith, Gilman, an eminent drama critic, Yale professor, and prolific author, remembers his difficulty embracing the teachings of the Church.*

At the age of nearly thirty an erstwhile militantly atheistic Jew, a boy who had been brought up in a home where the letter of religion was observed if not always the full spirit, an intermittently kosher household, depending on whether his maternal grandparents were living there at particular times, grandparents who spoke Yiddish much more easily and more often than they did English and, particularly his grandmother, had gestures that included a wide sighing shrug in reaction to what fate dealt them and a frequent clapping (or klopping) of hand to forehead when destiny seemed especially bitter, and who engaged from time to time in a mysterious and unpleasant ritual connected to death called "sitting shivah"; the boy who had been sent on roller skates to Hebrew school three afternoons a week and had held the speed-reading record there for some years (or until it was broken by a laser-eyed boy whom, he was later told, everyone hated because he was fat and sweated a lot and was so smart); had been bar mitzvahed with as much panoply as the Depression years would allow, the gifts including the usual fountain pens and a most unusual biography of Admiral Byrd, he of the South Pole; had eaten gefilte fish, which he disliked, for the sake of the horseradish that went with it; had been filled with nausea at the sight of his mother or grandmother eviscerating a chicken, arm plunged to the elbow into the pale yellow creature's bowels, and could not eat that meat for years afterward; was familiar with, even though he had an aversion to using, such words as "goyim" and "shiksa" and even "Gentile"; had regarded as terrifying apparitions the nuns he would occasionally see going in and out of—*scuttling* in and out of—the Catholic church a few blocks away from his home in the Flatbush section of Brooklyn, a church from which an endless and similarly terrifying procession of coffins seemed to emerge; who had been pleased that his parents had given him the name Richard and not Seymour or Irwin or Myron and felt slightly ashamed of that; who had thought of the names "Christ" and "Jesus" as suffused with death, verbal coffins; and who late into his twenties had thought of himself as an exemplary product of a rational age, keen on art but on science too, especially humanistic science—this person had become a Catholic, which everyone will surely agree is considerably more problematic and consequential than becoming a fitness buff or subscribing dreamily to some Eastern cult.

There I was, a couple of days before Christmas of 1953, in the cathedral of Colorado Springs (the building was a big nondescript pile for which the designation "cathedral" meant that it was the seat of the diocese in that area), a six-foot, hundred-and-fifty-pound infant being bent backward by a priest over the baptismal font in lieu of being held in some gigantic godparent's arms.

The warm, no doubt stale, water trickled from my forehead into my hair and some fell on my cheeks, where it mingled with my sudden and embarrassing tears. But the embarrassment came after the fact. At the time, stricken and amazed, I had no thought that there were others watching. I was aware only of the soft voice of the priest intoning "In nomine patris et filii et spiritus sancti" and of the light touch of his fingers tracing the sign of the cross on my brow.

I felt like a tourist who has abruptly and unaccountably been made a citizen of some distant and enigmatic country, more remote than

Nepal, without having had time to do more than sketchily learn some of the language and the laws. I felt like I was on a kind of Ellis Island of the spirit and saw (or much later did) my forebears sorrowfully or reproachfully passing in the other direction.

Just before the ceremony the priest had asked me what baptismal name or names I wanted to take, what patron saints I wished to have. These are saints you ally yourself with at baptism—in the vast majority of cases of course they're assigned by parents—so that you're supposed to come under their wings and have special access to them. You can also choose the Virgin Mary or one of the angels like Gabriel, but you don't choose Christ; I wouldn't have called myself or thought of myself as Richard Jesus Gilman, though for some reason people from Spanish cultures have always liked to take that name.

But Richard Joan Thomas Gilman was permissible. I hadn't thought about it before that evening and had to decide quickly. But I knew at once whom I wanted: Joan of Arc and Thomas More. Two "secular" saints, one could say, two from the world and therefore not nearly as remote from me as the more usual kind, the ones that struck me as nothing but saints, nothing but Catholic. Thomas More, a writer and statesman and intellectual, a valorous lovely man; I had recently read a biography of him. And Joan, the "astounding virgin," as a contemporary chronicler had called her, yes Joan (a man can take a woman's name in this matter and vice versa) had along with Amelia Earhart been the Beatrice of my youth.

An hour or so later as I was driving back to the rooming house where I was staying, through the deserted snow-covered streets and the frosty air, I pulled to a stop in the middle of an intersection and burst into a flood of tears. They came from relief, fear of the unknown life that awaited me, the sense of having done something irrevocable that was at once alarming and potentially full of solace.

A prowl car pulled up and the cop got out, walked over to my car in the shambling yet wary way they do it, bent down, looking in at me and asked if there was any trouble. Through my tears I told him that I had just come from being baptized as a Catholic, wanting crazily to add, "I've just been made the property of God."

.   .   .

My life in the quotidian world, my "civilian" life as I'd come to regard it, went on very much as before. But inside the Church, within those visible and invisible walls, there are many new things I had to do, and together they brought about a turbulence in me that was very complicated, so that I have a hard time sorting it out after all these years.

I was an insider now. When I knelt in church to pray or went up to the altar rail to take Communion I did it as a bona fide member of the congregation, one of "them." I was taking part in their ceremony, the Mass, at which up to now I'd sat as a spectator.

. . .

Although I was never to become wholly adept at all the moves and pieces of timing that were second nature to my fellow worshipers I quite quickly mastered the basic tactics and procedures of the ceremony. I remember following the Mass in my missal a couple of weeks after my baptism and thinking that now I was doing it with near veteran or "professional" ease. Before that my missal, a handsome leatherbound one that had been given to me by Ruth, had at first seemed to be thoroughly alien and impenetrable and then, after she'd patiently gone through it with me, had begun to be comprehensible. Still it remained a disturbing object. Doubtless it could be a source of power and of liberating secrets, I thought, but there was also something adolescently arcane and even mumbo jumbo about it, as though it were a handbook for Masons or a Boy Scout manual.

Now I had learned to decipher it more or less, and felt more at ease, more like an initiate. Besides, I remember thinking, the Church *was* rather like the Masons or the Boy Scouts, if only in the sense that it too was a society or community with rules, precepts, ceremonies and stated values; the missal was then the handbook for this community's central ceremony and for its liturgical year. And yet there were times when the book's alien quality would strike my eyes again when I turned a page.

. . .

I remember how the typography often puzzled me and I remember too how the constant cross-references kept me frantically riffling back and forth. Nearly twenty-five years after I last used the missal I've forgotten most of its words, which are really the words of the Mass: Collect, Common, Veni sponsa. What do they mean? I sit here and think. Some fragments of meaning float back and then it all sinks again into the recesses of my memory.

At the time, though, knowing how to use the missal was one of the ways in which I had begun to fit in. And this produced complex feelings in me, ranging from sly pleasure at possessing a type of new semisecret identity to a sense of being an interloper despite the way I had taken my place among the faithful, or rather just because of that. I was fitting in, but this implied that I had come from elsewhere, had *been* someone else, and had arrived trailing differences which I would have to work in a strange, uncomfortable fashion to obliterate.

Yet why? What could I have expected in this regard? I was a convert and how would it be possible for me to erase the things that made me different from born Catholics for whom the Church was at the same time religion, background, community and, for better or worse, a chief principle of identity? And did I really want to erase these differences? To begin with I surely didn't want to erase my Jewishness. I had accepted the Church's argument that Catholicism was the fulfillment of Judaism, not its negation, and I didn't feel guilty of having "betrayed" anything. Besides, I'd become a Catholic from a stance of pure atheism, and hard as it might be to separate the ethnic and spiritual aspects of Judaism I'd already done it.

So I would remain Jewish, ethnically, or in the eyes of others. Which was just the point. For centuries being Jewish was regarded as both a religious and a racial matter, until the rise of secularism brought about a widespread abandonment of religious practice by Jews. How were they then to be identified except by their background? Frenchmen, Spaniards, Italians, Mexicans, and so on, have also in large numbers relinquished their religion in the modern age, but they're not stuck with being called Catholic; the religious term slides off them. One of the attractions of Catholicism had been its promise of an internationalism of the spirit, a loyalty surpassing race and culture, and I thought I could vault over ethnic differences on the wings of a transcendence; I thought I could adopt the Church as my true motherland.

For a while it worked. Beyond question it was a good thing that I began my life as a Catholic where I did. For the fact was that my fellow worshipers during this time were so unlike me racially and culturally, from such a different caste and world, that I felt relieved. I didn't have any need to compare myself to them the way I had to the secretaries and washerwomen and FBI types who made up nearly all the Catholics I had ever seen and who, because they were from *my* society, my race and culture, lent themselves to my snobbery, my sense of intellectual superiority.

The truth was that I thought of these Mexican women and the few men who came to the church as being exotic in a way and I could accept them and even envy them their simplicity and what I took to be their innocence, qualities I wanted, with immense naïveté as it naturally turned out, to engender in myself. I felt inferior to them spiritually, and this had the odd result of putting me in the way of my feelings of being an interloper or impostor. I too was a believer now, all right, but I hadn't been one before, and so it was as if I had come uninvited by these people into their house, as the result of a whim for all they knew, into the house where they had always lived; God or the Holy Ghost may have asked me in, but *they* hadn't.

The central element of the Mass, the high point of its "drama" and purpose, is the Eucharist, Communion, and this was rather a problem for me from the start. During the months when I was looking on but hadn't yet become a Catholic I used to watch with fascination the people who went up to take Communion when that part of the service came round. I remember often thinking how heterogeneous they were, especially on Sundays.

.   .   .

I would see well-dressed couples, teenagers, a few children, shabby old women, cops, who knows maybe a doctor or a dentist or a construction worker here and there. And I would think about how the act of taking Communion seemed to fulfill its name by bringing them into an affinity and common identity, their differences of sex, age and class momentarily obliterated. I don't mean anything politically, or sociologically or even metaphysically romantic by this, their sharing, let's say, in some splendid principle of equality of a kind that operates nowhere else and so might be a model. Or it may be I thought something like this abstractly but it wasn't what I saw.

I would look at the faces of these people and watch the way they moved as they went toward the altar rail and again when they came back. There wasn't much difference between the way they looked on these two little journeys, except that everything was more pronounced on the return trip.

Almost all of them had roughly the same expression on their faces and almost all moved in one of only two ways. Usually their eyes were half closed or they stared straight ahead or at the floor. Their mouths were nearly always closed, but self-consciously so, especially as they walked back to their pews with the Communion wafers dissolving on their tongues. It gave them a somewhat grim or pursed appearance. They moved either stiffly, slowly, very much like sleepwalkers, or else they scurried, but abstractedly, as if they were hurrying through a landscape of which they took no notice.

It was as if they had all been stricken suddenly with the same, probably fatal, disease, or had witnessed the same grave or awful event, a sight that had made them dreamy or thoughtful or tense, because their responsibilities had been increased. They were *carrying* themselves, I remember thinking, which really meant that they were carrying, self-importantly or, more often, humbly, the wafer or the anticipation of it or the sense of it if they'd already swallowed. They were treating themselves as reliquaries. I couldn't imagine myself ever acting like them, looking as they did.

But when it came my turn I must have acted like them. During the first week after my baptism the day arrived when I would take Communion for the first time. Such a trivial physical act, I told myself as the moment drew near: a papery, ecru-colored wafer deposited on your tongue by a priest who often had to conduct the whole operation as though on an assembly line, moving mechanically down the row of kneeling worshipers, placing the Host in the successively opened mouths, and intoning the accompanying little prayer, "May the body and blood of our Lord Jesus Christ lead you to life everlasting," or something like that.

I told myself that it wasn't complicated, that it was simply food for the soul, but I was apprehensive anyway. I can't remember which of two extreme conditions I was in as I moved for the first time from my pew to the aisle and then down to the altar rail. Either I was in complete turmoil or, more likely, I had emptied myself of all thought and emotion and moved down the aisle, knelt at the altar like the others (there were perhaps a dozen women and a few men), heard without registering the priest's words—but now, abruptly, I remember them precisely: "May the body of our Lord Jesus Christ preserve thy soul to life everlasting"—and received the thing in my mouth in a state of near catatonia.

I have just called the Host a "thing," which at the very least is disrespectful. But all the time I was a believer I was never able to call it anything else, certainly not "Host," for that was a word that puzzled and for some reason irritated me, as a number of other Catholic words and phrases did, simply as language: Sacred Heart, sodality, novena, Offertory. More fundamentally I could never wholly get over a deep mistrust of this central aspect of Catholic belief and practice, a mistrust to which was added a strain of embarrassment. I could never really accept, no matter how hard I tried (and I did try; I worked at it furiously), that what I was swallowing was in fact the "body" and by implication the "blood" of Christ.

If it had simply been a matter of symbolic substance and action, as I'm sure most open-minded people outside the Church consider it to be, if it had been a matter of representation, I could have managed it without difficulty. After all, I knew about symbolic modes and actions, from literature most comfortably; I knew about metaphor. But "transubstantiation," the word that describes the phenomenon of the Eucharist, the consumption of the Host and its subsequent effect, isn't a metaphor; it doesn't refer to something *standing for* something else, but to a materialization in another form or appearance, literally a "crossing-over" of substance.

And so this is what I faced: what I took in and ingested was and wasn't the body and blood of Christ. It wasn't, because all that was in your mouth was this papery object that dissolved very quickly and left scarcely any taste. And it was, because the Faith held it to be and you weren't supposed to rely on your senses or your reason in a matter such as this. It was a mystery, one of the many that resided at the center of belief, from which indeed belief hung; they would strain your mind to the breaking point if you chased after them, or they would induce humility and acceptance if you gave up the need for thoroughly rational explanation and simply let them be.

As long as I was an active Catholic I wavered or shuttled between these two opposing attitudes toward the Host and Communion and was more often in the condition of beleaguered doubt, my brain thumping with the effort to understand how this bizarre notion could be true and to learn the proper spirit in which it ought to be accepted. I spoke earlier of wanting mystery, and I stand by that. But in this case, as in some others, the mystery seemed too literal, if I can put it that way; unlike the idea of eternal happiness in God's bosom or Christ's redemptive sacrifice, its mysteriousness was confined to a physical fact, a thing being said to be another thing.

I remember at first making a grotesque attempt to cut round the perplexity by imagining literal flesh and blood in my mouth, which naturally disgusted me and made me realize that whatever else was going on here the Church was civilized enough not to ask us to pretend to be cannibals.

After that I went back to the idea of symbolic representation, knowing that this wasn't it either. But at least here I was helped by the fact that once I started to receive Communion the act and process immediately connected itself to the idea of the Mystical Body, which, with Christ at the center, was composed of all believers and which you entered or joined as soon as you had swallowed the wafer. Or so I understood the notion at the time.

The idea of a *body* of mankind, a close unity of all human beings, was familiar enough as a secular metaphor, a political one, for example. And so I didn't have all that much difficulty in taking the next mental step, accepting the unity that common belief in Christ forged and seeing it as something more than an idea. It was a *mystical* body, after all, I remember telling myself, it wasn't to be thought of in literal ways. Even so I would find myself trying to imagine it as somehow palpable, alternately envisaging it as a gigantic skin in which we were all encased or as a warm Jell-O-like sea in which we floated side by side, all of us, men, women, children, babies, along with the peaceful dead.

And so I had trouble from the beginning. There were times, though, when doubt would drop away and I would feel myself yielding to the sacrament and even feeling, or thinking that I did, its efficacy spreading through me. And always, however clumsily or heatedly I struggled with the idea of the Eucharist and other dogmas or beliefs—the Immaculate Conception, the Virgin Birth, Original Sin, the Trinity, Papal Infallibility and so on—all the doctrines and propositions that anti-Catholics can't stomach and that I too once couldn't abide—I understood and welcomed the way in which they made Catholicism different from any other religion I knew about. (Later I learned that the Episcopal and Lutheran churches accept most of these doctrines too.) Most important of all, I relied on the manner in which these dogmas and teachings separated the Faith from the nonreligious, untranscendent, rationalistic approaches to our lives and the world that I had previously explored and to which at times had committed myself.

I remember that after I had begun to be interested in Catholicism I came upon Saint Paul's definition of faith as "the evidence of things unseen" and thought the contradiction ought to be especially appealing to those who loved literature. In the same vein I remember being excited by Charles Péguy's description of the "bourgeois mind" as that which, whatever the person's social or economic class, invariably "preferred the visible to the invisible." I thought this the most acute and witty indictment of the materialist I'd ever seen, unless it was Baudelaire's epithet: "fanatics of utensils, enemies of perfume."

In the realm of aesthetics I had loved art in both particular works and as a category, because I had always wanted to believe in the invisible, to be in touch with a reality beyond the actual. When, in Kierkegaard's sense, I moved from a world of aesthetic truth to one of religion I of course wanted such a reality too. It was in fact one of the sources of my difficulty with so many practices of the Church that in them the attempt was always being made to convert the invisible into the visible, an action I thought resulted in a loss of mystery together with a plague of vulgarity: the Sacred Hearts, the Shroud of Turin, weeping Madonnas and all the relics.

Yet I had been guilty of that myself (the sea of Jell-O!) as an act of rebellion against the transcendence I otherwise craved and as something more: a periodic desire for specificity, the tangible in a world of abstraction. I had been attracted to Catholicism in part because of its efforts to bridge such gaps and fuse such antinomies and, in a more accepting mood, I could see that Communion, for example, was a way of bringing together physical and spiritual realities in an attempt to assuage what many people, religiously inclined or not, have always felt to be an intolerable space between facts and values.

In the midst of my rapacious purity of mental desire . . . I could see that for the Church to try to make certain aspects of the spirit and its operations palpable, or give them a visual correlative, wasn't necessarily to be vulgar or dim-witted or bourgeois . . . but to offer a concession to our limitations. It was a way of dealing with our inability ever truly to grasp the spiritual except as somehow incarnate, clothed. Christ, who was God but also man, might be thought of as the supreme example of that concession.

Later I would again rebel against the literalism of Catholic cults and popular practices but for now I went on the understanding that if anything distinguished Catholicism it was that it had never rested on abstractions, certainly not simple ethical ones, the way much of Protestantism does, but continually sank the realm of values back into the living bodies and textures of the world. So I swallowed my doubts along with the wafer and went to Communion nearly every day for several months and then two or three times a week, and after that once a week or so for a year or two and then less and less frequently as my faith dwindled. Never wholly able to give myself over to the sacrament, I managed, I thought, to fit within its spirit.

IV

SUFFERING

and

MORTALITY

CATHERINE MEANS PURE

KATHRYN HARRISON

Kathryn Harrison, novelist and author of the controversial memoir, The
Kiss, *reveals that her first Trinity was "Mother, Death, and God." In this
graphic yet finely wrought reflection on the connections between her life
and that of another Catherine—the fourteenth-century saint of Siena,
Harrison meditates on her own self-inflicted suffering toward redemption, following the path of her namesake.*

MY MOTHER died of breast cancer when I was twenty-
four. I took care of her while she died. I gave her her morphine, her
Halcion, her Darvocet, Percocet, Demerol, Zantac, and Prednisone. I
bathed her and I dressed her bedsores. Though I had to force myself
into such communion with disease, I kissed her each morning when
she woke and each evening as she fell asleep. Then I went into the
bathroom, took a cotton pad soaked with rubbing alcohol, and
scrubbed my lips with it until they burned and bled. Sometimes as I
did this I thought of Saint Catherine of Siena, who, in 1373, collected
into a bowl the pus from a woman's open breast cancer lesions. The
woman was Andrea, an older member of the Mantellate lay order to
which Catherine belonged. Previously, Andrea had caused Catherine
much trouble and public censure when she had implied that the
saint's infamous raptures and fasts were a pretense rather than any
manifestation of holiness. The bowl's foul contents stank and made

Catherine retch, and both in penance for her disgust and in determination to love her enemy, Catherine drank the old nun's pus. "Daughter! Daughter!" cried Andrea, tears of contrition wetting her cheeks. "Do not kill yourself!"

That night, Catherine had a vision of Christ. Her Holy Bridegroom bade her to his side, and she drank the blood of life that flowed from his wounds.

"You were named for saints and queens," my mother told me, when I was young enough that a halo and a crown seemed interchangeable. We were not Catholics yet. Judaism was our birthright, but we had early strayed and now we were members of the First Church of Christ, Scientist. Above my bed was a plaque bearing these words from its founder, Mary Baker Eddy: "Father–Mother Good, lovingly thee I seek, patient, meek. In the way thou hast, be it slow or fast, up to thee." The little prayer, which I was taught to recite as I fell asleep, worried me. I did not want to die fast. I had asthma, and each attack seemed capable of killing me, so when I was not thinking of my mother, whom I loved without measure, I thought of death and of God. They made my first trinity: Mother, Death, God.

I might have remained immune to the mind-over-matter doctrines of Mrs. Eddy, and to the subsequent seduction of the saints, had I not, when I was five, suffered an accident which occasioned a visit to a Christian Science "practitioner," or healer. The circumstances were these: My mother, divorced when I was not yet a year old, and when she was not yet twenty, had recently moved out of her parents' house in Los Angeles, a house where I continued to live, as an only child with my grandparents. It was the first of my mother's attempts to make a separate life for herself—a life which did not seem possible to her unless motherhood was left behind—and so now it was my grandfather who drove me to school each day. The egocentric logic of the small child damned me to a belief that my mother had left me with her parents because of my unworthiness. I knew already that my birth had interrupted her education; now I learned that my continued existence somehow distracted her from her paralegal job and, worse, chased off romantic prospects. The shiny, pink stretch marks which pregnancy had traced over her stomach seemed emblematic of the greater damage I had done, and each time my mother undressed before me, my eyes were drawn to this record of my first transgression. Each afternoon, I sat in the closet of her old room, inhaling her perfume from what dresses remained; each morning I woke newly disappointed at the sight of her empty bed in the room next to mine. So, despite my grandfather's determined cheer, it was a glum ride to school that was interrupted, dramatically, the day the old Lincoln's brakes failed.

Pumping the useless pedal, my grandfather turned off the road in order to avoid rear-ending the car ahead of us. We went down a short embankment, picked up speed, crossed a ditch, and hit one of the stately eucalyptus trees that form the boundary between Sunset Boulevard and the UCLA campus. On impact, the glove compartment popped open; and, not wearing my seat belt, I sailed forward and split my chin on its lock mechanism, cracking my jawbone.

My grandfather was not hurt. He got me out of the wrecked, smoking car and pressed a folded handkerchief to my face. Blood was pouring out of my mouth and chin, and I started to cry, from fear more than pain. I was struggling against the makeshift compress when, by a strange coincidence, my mother, en route to work, saw us from the street and pulled over. Her sudden materialization, the way she sprang nimbly out of her blue car, seemed to me angelic, magical, an impression enhanced by the dress she was wearing that morning, one with a tight bodice and a full crimson skirt embroidered all over with music notes. Whenever she wore this dress I was unable to resist touching the fabric of the skirt. I found the notes evocative, mysterious; and if she let me, I would trace my finger over the spiral of a treble clef or feel the stitched dots of the notes, as if they represented a different code, like that of Braille or Morse, a message that I might in time decipher.

My mother was unusually patient and gentle as she helped me into her car. We left my grandfather waiting for a tow truck and drove to UCLA's nearby medical center, where I was X-rayed and prepared for suturing. I lay under a light so bright that it almost forced me to close my eyes, while a blue, disposable cloth with a hole cut out for my chin descended over my face like a shroud, blocking my view of my mother. I held her hand tightly, too tightly perhaps, for after a moment she pried my fingers off and lay my hand on the side of the gurney. She had to make a phone call, she said; she had to explain why she hadn't shown up at work.

I tried to be brave, but when I heard my mother's heels clicking away from me on the floor, I succumbed to an animal terror and tried to kick and claw my way after her. All I had understood of what she said was that she was leaving me again—this time with strangers—and it took both the doctor and his nurse to restrain me. Once they had, I was tranquilized before I was stitched and then finally taken home asleep.

Later that afternoon, I woke up screaming, in a panic which had been interrupted, not assuaged, by the drug. My mother, soon exhausted by my relentless crying and clinging to her neck, her legs, her fingers—to whatever she would let me hold—took me to a practitioner, whose name she picked at random from the First Church of Christ, Scientist's directory.

The practitioner was a woman with gray hair and a woolly, nubby sweater which I touched as she prayed over me, my head in her lap and one of her hands on my forehead, the other over my heart. Under those hands, which I remember as cool and calm, even sparing in their movements, I felt my fear drain away. Then, the top of my skull seemed to be opened by a sudden, revelatory blow, and a searing light filled me. Mysteriously, unexpectedly, this stranger had ushered me into an experience of something I cannot help but call rapture. I felt myself separated from my flesh, and from all earthly things. I felt myself no more corporeal than the tremble in the air over a fire. I had no words for what happened—I have few now, almost thirty years later—and in astonishment I stopped crying. My mother sighed in relief; and I learned, at five, a truth dangerous to someone so young and lovelorn. I saw that transcendence was possible: that spirit could conquer matter, and that therefore I could overcome whatever obstacles prevented my mother's loving me. I could overcome myself.

In the years following the accident I became increasingly determined to return to whatever it was I had visited in the practitioner's lap, and I thought the path to this place might be discovered in Sunday school. Around the wood laminate table I was the only child who had done the previous week's assignment, who had marked my white vinyl-covered Bible with the special blue-chalk pencil and had read the corresponding snippet from Mary Baker Eddy's *Science and Health, with Key to the Scriptures*. The other children lolled and dozed in clip-on neckties and pastel sashed dresses while I sat up straight. The teacher had barely finished asking a question before my hand, in its white cotton glove buttoned tight at the wrist, shot up. Sometimes I would see the teacher looking at me with what seemed, even then, like consternation. The lassitude of the other children, their carelessly incorrect answers, which proceeded from lips still bearing traces of hastily consumed cold cereal, were clearly what she expected. What was disconcerting was my fierce recital of verses, my vigilant posture on the edge of the red plastic kindergarten chair.

The arena of faith was the only one in which I had a chance of securing my mother's attention. Since she was not around during the week to answer to more grubby requirements, and because she was always someone who preferred the choice morsel, it was to my mother rather than to my grandparents that the guidance of my soul had been entrusted. On Sundays, we went to church in Westwood and afterward to a nearby patio restaurant, where we sat in curlicued wrought-iron chairs and reviewed my Sunday-school lesson while eating club sandwiches held together with fancy toothpicks. The waiters flirted with my mother, and men at neighboring tables smiled in her direction. They looked at her left hand without any ring; they seemed to share my helpless longing. Through the awful calculus of mortal love, my mother—who already embodied for me the beauty of youth, who had the shiny-haired, smooth-cheeked vitality my grandparents did not, who could do backbends and cartwheels, and owned high-heeled shoes in fifteen colors—became ever more precious for her elusiveness, her withholding absence.

In order to reexperience the ecstatic rise that had for an instant made me an attractive child and that had come through the experience of pain, I began secretly—and long before I had the example of any saint—to practice the mortification of my flesh. At my grandfather's workbench I turned his vise on my finger joints. When my grandmother brought home ice cream from Baskin-Robbins and discarded the dry ice with which it was packed, I used the salad tongs to retrieve the small smoking slab from the trash can. In the privacy of the upstairs bathroom I touched my tongue to the dry ice's surface and left a little of its skin there. I looked in the mirror at the blood coming out of my mouth, at the same magic flow that had once summoned my mother from the impossibly wide world of grown-ups and traffic and delivered her to my side. Now I was fully ensnared in the wishful, initiating mistake that was to confuse and pervert my spiritual growth: from the beginning I viewed whatever power God represented as a means toward my mother's love. Through those transformations made possible by faith, I would become worthy of her loving me. Either that, or faith would make me feel no more pain from my mother's rejection than I had from my jaw while lying in the practitioner's lap. So I looked in the mirror at my tongue, I tasted my blood, and I practiced not hurting.

My mother converted to Catholicism when I was ten, and I followed in her wake, seeking her even as she sought whatever it was that she had not found in Christian Science. We had failed at even the most basic of Mrs. Eddy's tenets, for by then we routinely sought the care of medical doctors. At first we went only for emergencies like the accident to my chin, but then my mother developed an ulcer, and I, never inoculated, got tetanus from a scrape, physical collapses both stubbornly unaffected by our attempts to disbelieve in them.

In preparation for my first Communion, I was catechized by a priest named Father Dove. Despite this felicitous name, Father Dove was not the Holy Spirit incarnate: he chain-smoked and his face over his white collar had a worldly, sanguine hue. Worse, I suspected that my mother was in love with him. She fell in love easily. One Saturday, I made my first confession (that I had been rude to my grandmother and had taken three dollars from her purse), and the next day, I took Communion with eleven other little girls dressed in white; and from that time forward I attended church in a marble sanctuary filled with gilt angels, rather than in a gray-and-blue auditorium. Light came through the stained-glass windows and splashed colors over everything. A red circle fell on my mother's white throat. Incense roiled around us, and I looked down to compare the shiny toes of my black patent-leather shoes to those of hers. When we left, lining up to shake Father Dove's hand, I was able to study the faces around me and confirm that my mother's wide hazel eyes, her long nose, and high, white forehead indeed made hers more beautiful than anyone else's.

For Christmas the following year I received, in my stocking, a boxed set of four volumes of *Lives of the Saints*, intended for children. There were two volumes of male saints, which I read once, flipping through the onionskin pages, and then left in my dresser drawer, and two of female saints, which I studied and slept with. The books contained color plates, illustrations adapted from works of the masters. Blinded Lucy. Maimed Agatha, her breasts on a platter. Beheaded Agnes. Margaret pressed to death under a door piled high with stones. Perpetua and Felicity mauled by beasts. Well-born Clare, barefoot and wearing rags. Maria Maddalena de' Pazzi lying on the bed of splinters she made for herself in the woodshed. Veronica washing the floors with her tongue, and Angela drinking water used to bathe a leper's sores. I saw that there were those who were tortured, and those who needed no persecutors—they were enemies to their own flesh.

Saint Catherine of Siena began by saying Hail Marys on every step she climbed. Soon she slept on a board, with a brick for a pillow. She did not like her hair shirt because it smelled, so she took to wearing a little belt of nails that bit into her waist. As Catherine's *Dialogues* (dictated years later, while she was in a sustained ecstasy, which lasted weeks, even months) make clear, she believed earthly suffering was the only way to correct the intrinsic baseness of mankind.

My mother, also, held forth an ideal of perfection, an ideal for which she would suffer, but hers was beauty. For beauty she endured the small tortures of plucking and peel-off face masks, of girdles and pinched toes, of sleep sacrificed to hair rollers and meals reduced to cottage cheese. I knew, from my mother's enthusiastic response to certain pictures in magazines, to particular waifs in the movies, that the child who would best complement her vanity was dark-haired and slender and balanced on point shoes. I was blond, robust, and given to tree-climbing. By the time I was thirteen, all of what was wrong with me—the very fact of me, my presence—settled in an unavoidably obvious issue between my mother and me: how much I weighed. How much there was of me. As my conception had been accidental, as I ought not to have been there at all, it must have struck my mother as an act of defiance that I was so large a child, taller and sturdier than any other girl in my class.

I wished myself smaller. I began to dream at night of Beyond-the-Looking-Glass potions, little bottles bearing draughts that shrank me to nothing; the bit of mushroom which let me disappear between grass blades. I began, too, to dread Sunday lunches taken with my mother, who fastidiously observed my fork in its ascension to my mouth.

Saint Catherine was fourteen when her older sister Bonaventura died in childbirth. Bonaventura was the only member of Catherine's family with whom she shared any real sympathy, and Catherine blamed herself for her sister's death. She believed God had punished her and Bonaventura because Catherine had let her big sister tempt her into using cosmetics and curling her hair. She had let Bonaventura's example convince her, briefly, that a woman could embrace both heavenly and earthly desires.

Whatever buoyancy, whatever youthful resilience Saint Catherine had had, disappeared when she lost her sister. She became uncompromising in turning away from all worldly things: from food, from sleep, from men. Their mother, Lapa, a volatile woman whose choleric screams were reputedly so loud that they frightened passersby on Siena's Via dei Tintori, redoubled her efforts to marry off her uncooperative twenty-fourth child. Some accounts hold that Catherine's intended groom was Bonaventura's widowed husband, a foultongued and occasionally brutish man. Catherine refused; she had long ago promised herself to Christ. She cut off her hair and she fasted, eating only bread and uncooked vegetables. She began to experience ecstasies, and it is recorded that when she did, she suffered a tetanic rigor in her limbs. Then Lapa would take her daughter up from the floor where she'd fallen and almost break her bones as she tried to bend the girl's stiff arms and legs.

Though it had been ten years since my mother moved out, she had yet to find a place that suited her for any length of time, and so she received her mail at the more permanent address of her parents, and would stop by after work to pick it up. She came in the back door, cool and perfumed and impeccably dressed, and she drifted into the kitchen to find me in my rumpled school uniform, standing before the open refrigerator. One day, I turned around with a cold chicken leg in my hand. My mother had tossed her unopened bills on the counter and was slowly rereading the message inside a greeting card decorated with a drawing of two lovesick rabbits locked in a dizzy embrace. She smiled slightly—a small and self-consciously mysterious smile—and kept the content of the card averted from my eyes. When she had had her fill of it, she looked up at me. She said nothing but let her eyes rest for a moment on the meat in my hand; then she looked away, from it, from me. She did not need to speak to tell me of her disapproval, and by now my habitual response to my mother had become one of despair: muffled, mute, and stumbling. But in that moment when she looked away from me, hopelessness gave way before a sudden, visionary elation. I dropped the drumstick into the garbage can. The mouthful I had swallowed stopped in its descent, and I felt it, gelid and vile inside me as I washed the sheen of grease from my fingers. At dinnertime, after my mother had left for her apartment, I pleaded too much homework to allow time to eat at the table, and I took my plate from the kitchen to my bedroom and opened the window, dropping the food into the dark foliage of the bushes below.

Among saints, Catherine is remarkable for her will more than for her humility. One of the two women in all of history named a Doctor of the Church (the other is Saint Teresa of Ávila), she, too, confused crowns with halos, and presumed to direct the affairs of popes and kings. Even in her reports of self-flagellation, readers find the pride of the absolutist. No one believed more firmly in Catherine's baseness than did Catherine. Determined that she be the least among mortals, so also—by the topsy-turvy logic of Christian salvation—would she be assured of being the greatest. In her visions of Christ, it is Catherine alone who stands beside Him as His bride.

To earn that place was exhausting beyond mortal ability. Even as the saint tirelessly cared for plague victims, even as she exhorted thousands to convert and lobbied effectively for the return of the papacy from Avignon to Rome, she criticized, scourged, and starved herself. She allowed herself not one mortal pleasure: not food or rest, not beauty, not wealth, not marriage or children. Categorically, she rejected the very things that a mother hopes a daughter's life will hold. And reading accounts of her life, one senses how Catherine enjoyed thwarting her mother, Lapa, enjoyed refusing the life her mother gave her. Biographers record that Catherine tried to eat—she wanted to do so in order to dispel accusations of demonic possession—but vomited if so much as a mouthful remained in her stomach. "She lived for years on one lettuce leaf!" was how my mother introduced me to Saint Catherine, as if she were revealing the teachings of a new diet guru.

Holiness. The idea of being consecrated, set apart. And of being whole, pure, untainted by anything. There are different kinds of purity, just as there are many reasons for rejecting life. But, no matter the motive, to the ascetic the rejection always looks the same: like salvation. Catherine would guide me to the salvation I sought. Inhumanly, she had triumphed over mortal limitations, over hunger, fatigue, and despair. She had seen demons and fought them off. And I would use her to fashion my solitary and sinful faith. Sin. A term long ago borrowed from archery: to miss the mark.

During the celebration of the Eucharist, the priest would place the Communion wafer on my tongue. I withdrew it into my mouth carefully, making the sign of the cross over myself. Back in the pew I kneeled and lay my head in my arms in a semblance of devotion, stuck out my tongue, and pushed the damp wafer into my sleeve. I was a little afraid of going to hell, very afraid of swallowing bread. My rules had grown more inexorable than the Church's; they alone could save me. But the host was the host, and I could not bring myself to throw it away. So I kept it in my sock drawer with my other relics: a small fetish of my mother's hair, stolen strand by strand from the hairbrush she kept in her purse. An eye pencil from that same source. Two tiny cookies from a Christmas stocking long past, a gingerbread boy and girl, no taller than an inch. A red leather collar from my cat which had died. The trinity in my sock drawer: Mother, Death, and God in the form of weeks' worth of accumulated bits of the body of Christ which I would not eat. Despite Christian Science's early announcements to me, despite mind over matter, I remained enslaved to the material world. In my confused struggle with corporeality I clung to these bits of rubbish, a collection that would look more at home in a trash can than in a drawer, and resisted what might better save me: food.

I still had my little books of the female saints. I looked at them before bed some nights, stared at their little portraits, at bleeding hands and feet, at exultant faces tipped up to heaven. But I read longer hagiographies now, grown-up ones. When Catherine was twenty-four she experienced a mystical death. "My soul was loosed from the body for those four hours," she told her confessor, who recorded that her heart stopped beating for that long. Though she did not want to return to her flesh, Jesus bade her go back. But henceforth, she was not as other mortals; her flesh was changed and unfit for worldly living. From that time forward she swallowed nothing she did not vomit. Her happiness was so intense that she laughed in her fits of ecstasy, she wept and laughed at the same time.

As I lost weight I watched with exultation as my bones emerged, believing that what I saw would irresistibly lure my mother's love. By the time they had failed to do that—those unlovely angles and hollows—I had so thoroughly confused the sight of them with the happiness I had hoped they would bring that I had created a satisfying, if perverse, system of rewards, one that did not require my mother's participation. I had replaced her with the bait I had hoped would entice her. I loved my transformed self. I could not look at myself enough, and I never went into the bathroom that I did not find myself helplessly undressing before the mirror. I touched myself, too. At night I lay in bed and felt each jutting rib, felt sternum and hipbone, felt my sharp jaw, and with my finger traced the orbit of my eye. Like Catherine's, mine was not a happiness that others understood, for it was the joy of power, of a private, inhuman triumph. Of a universe—my body—utterly subjugated to my will.

My life was solitary, as befits a religious. Too much of human fellowship was dictated by hunger, by taking meals in company, and what I did and did not consume separated me from others. Since I had not yet weaned myself completely from human needs, I drank coffee, tea, and Tab. I ate raw vegetables, multivitamins, No-Doz, and, when I felt very weak, tuna canned in water. When I climbed stairs, I saw stars. And when forced to eat with my grandparents, I did so, but the mask of compliance was temporary, and upstairs in my bathroom, I vomited what I had eaten. Afterward, I would lift my shirt and examine my ribs in the mirror, wanting to be sure that there was no evidence of my brief defilement.

After meals, Catherine drank cold water and gagged herself with a stalk of fennel or a quill pen. It hurt her, and she was glad. She wanted to do all her suffering on earth so that she would be spared purgatory. *This will make you pure,* I used to think when I made myself throw up. I used ipecac, the emetic kept in first-aid kits, a poison to be taken against poisons. It was worse than using my finger, perhaps even worse than a quill; at least that had to have been quick in its mechanical approach. Ipecac was suffering; it seemed to take forever and caused a reeling, sweaty nausea that made me wish I were dead. The retching was violent, but then, I intended it to be punishment.

My grandmother and grandfather, sixty-two and seventy-one at my birth, were now so old that their failing senses granted me freedom unusual for a teenager. Going blind, they did not see my thinness. Deaf, they never heard me in my bathroom. By the time I was sixteen, they depended on my driver's license for their groceries; and en route to the supermarket, I would stop at the mall. "Where did you go, Kalamazoo?" my grandmother would ask when I returned, trying to understand why I was hours late. Sometimes she accused me of secretly meeting boys; she used the word "assignation." But I had always spent my time alone. In the department stores and I went from rack to rack, garment to garment: size two, size two, size two. Each like a rosary bead: another recitation, another confirmation of my size, one more turn of the key in the lock of safety.

Having conquered hunger, I began on sleep, and one night, in my room, very late, and in the delusional frenzy of having remained awake for nearly seventy-three hours, I began to weep with what I thought was joy. It seemed to me that I had almost gotten there: my flesh was almost utterly turned to spirit. Soon I would not be mortal, soon I would be as invulnerable as someone who could drink pus and see God. The next day, however, I fainted and suffered a seizure that left me unable for a day to move the fingers on my right hand. In the same hospital where I had long ago attacked the ER nurse with my fingernails, I had an electroencephalogram and a number of other tests which proved inconclusive. A different nurse, a different doctor, a different wing of the hospital. But nothing had changed: my mother was making a phone call in the corridor, and I lay on a table trying not to scream, far less able to articulate the danger I sensed than when I was five.

When college gave me the opportunity to leave home, I recovered partially. At heart, I wanted to believe in a different life, and I stopped going to mass and gained a little weight—not too much, because I began taking speed and still made myself throw up sometimes. I wore my mother's clothing, castoffs and whatever I could steal from her, articles that filled the reliquary of my peculiar faith. I zipped and buttoned myself into her garments as if they could cloak me with the love I wanted from her. Like miracle seekers who would tear hair, fingers—whatever they could—from a holy person's body, I was desperate, and one September I took my mother's favorite skirt from under the dry-cleaning bag hanging in the backseat of her car. It was purple, long and narrow. I packed it in my suitcase and took it to school with me. She called me on the phone a week later. "Send it back," she said. I denied having taken it. "You're lying," she said.

Lapa did not want Catherine to scourge herself, so, although her daughter was a grown woman, Lapa took away her private bedroom and forced Catherine to sleep in bed with her. Not to be denied the mortification of her flesh, the saint dragged a plank into the bed after Lapa had fallen asleep, and she laid it between her mother's body and her own. On Lapa's side was smooth wood; on Catherine's, spikes.

I wore the skirt twice, and when it fell from the hanger, I let it remain on the dark, dirty floor of my closet. When my mother called me again, I decided to return it, but there was a stain on the waistband that the dry cleaner could not remove. For an hour I sat on my dorm bed with the skirt in my lap, considering. Finally I washed it with Woolite, and ruined it. I returned the skirt to my mother's closet when invited, during spring break, for dinner at her apartment. *Please,* I begged silently, tucking it between two other skirts. *Please don't say anything more about it. Please.* When she called me late that night at my grandparents' house, I hung up on her. Then I went into the bathroom and I sat on the floor and wept: too late, too many hours past the dinner she had fed me to make myself throw up.

Kathryn, Katherine, Catherine. All the spellings proceed from the Greek, *Katharos,* or "pure one."

Did Lapa know who her daughter would be? Did my mother know me before she named me? Did we announce ourselves to our mothers in the intimacy of the womb, flesh whispering to flesh?

Or did they make us to fit our names?

I still believe in purity, and I believe that suffering must at least prepare the way for redemption. I believe, too, in love's ability to conquer. I believe in every kiss I gave my mother, even those I scrubbed away in fear. At the end of her life, I waited for my mother to tell me how much she loved me and how good a daughter I had always been. I had faith that my mother was waiting until the end to tell me that all along she had known I had performed impossible feats of self-alchemy.

She did not, but, as faith admits no end, mine continued beyond her death. After the funeral, I packed up her apartment and looked through all her papers for a note, a letter left for me and sealed in an envelope. I closed my eyes and saw it: a meticulous, fountain-pen rendition of *Kathryn* on creamy stationery. When I didn't find that, I looked for clues to her affection. I read what correspondence she had saved. I reviewed check registers dating back ten years. I learned how much she had spent on dry-cleaning her clothes, on her cats' flea baths, and on having her car radio repaired.

The death of my mother left me with a complex religious apparatus that now lacked its object, and I expected, then, to become an atheist. I frankly looked forward to the sterile sanity of it, to what relief it would bring. But I could not do it; I could not not believe. The habit of faith, though long focused misguidedly on a mortal object, persisted; and after a few years, I found myself returning to the Church. Sporadically, helplessly, I attended mass. Having relearned to eat earthly food, now I practiced swallowing the Eucharist. Often I found myself crying out of a happiness I did not understand and which mysteriously accompanied the sense that my heart was breaking.

Rapture, too, returned. Long after I had stopped expecting it, it overcame me on a number of otherwise unnoteworthy occasions. I excused this as a fancy born of longing, as an endorphin effect brought on by exercise or pain, as craziness, pure and simple. But none of these described the experience, that same searing, light-filled, ecstatic rise, neither pleasant nor unpleasant, for no human measure applied to what I felt: transcendence.

My prayers, too, were helpless. I mouthed them in spite of myself. *Make me good. Love me. Please make me good and please love me.* For the first time, I entrusted my spiritual evolution to some power outside my self and my will; I entrusted it to God's grace. If I were going to reach any new plane, my enlightenment, it would have to be God who transported me.

In the last months of her life, Catherine lost the use of her legs. Her biographers record that for years she had lived on little more than water and what sustenance she got from chewing, not swallowing, bitter herbs. In church one night, when she was too weak to approach the altar, the Communion bread came to her. Witnesses saw bread move through the air unassisted. Catherine saw it carried by the hand of Christ.

She died at thirty-three, the same age as her Bridegroom at his death. She died in Rome, and her body was venerated from behind an iron grille in a chapel of the Church of the Minerva, so that the throngs who came would not tear her to bits, each trying to secure a wonder-working relic.

All I have left of my mother are a box of books, a china dog, two cashmere sweaters with holes in the elbows, a few photographs, and her medical records. Among the last of these is her final chest X-ray, and just over the shadow of her heart is the bright white circle cast by the saint's medal she wore on a thin gold chain. No matter how many times the technicians asked her to remove it, she would not. Not long ago, I unpacked the box of medical records, and retrieved the X ray. I held it before a light once more, trying to see the image more clearly, but of course I could make out nothing. Just a small, white circle of brightest light. A circle blocking the view of the chambers of her heart. A circle too bright to allow any vision.

I will never know, but I have decided that the medal, now with my mother in her coffin, bears a likeness of Saint Jude. I have given my mother to this saint—the patron of lost causes, the patron of last resort—just as long ago she gave me to the saint of her choosing.

MEDITATIONS ON A SHADOW

BRADFORD MORROW

Award-winning novelist Bradford Morrow brings us, in these seven med-
itations, to the brink of his death and back again. Awash in a pure,
enveloping pain and unlikely to recover, Morrow ponders his life's choices
and regrets. Yet, as the cherished gift of language slowly slips away, the
music and religion of Morrow's childhood church stream back from mem-
ory's depths. The simple verses of the shepherd psalm, heard as if for the
first time, interwoven with hymn tunes and chorales, abide and inspire
Morrow as he begins the difficult ascent from the valley of the shadow of
death.

INTO THE DARK

I AM ON the road, dying. Wrapped in sheets and a thermal blanket, I am lying on my back, my knees up and arms at my sides. A woman holds my hand, my left hand. I don't know her, but my eyes are locked on her face. Walnut hair in waves frames an almond shape, pale with hazel eyes; the white blouse of a nurse, with buttons yellow as antique ivory; a strong upcountry woman younger a few years than her patient. Her hands broad, grip firm. She radiates natural com- passion, and talks to me. Beyond the kind temper of her words I

311

don't understand what she says. And I keep forgetting her name, however much I would like to remember. She is the last person I will ever see. This is what I have come to believe.

Chilled with fever, now a hundred and five, the infection in my belly has made me swollen like a barrel, and hard as an oak cask to the touch. No one can touch me, because of the severity of the pain. I do my best not to writhe. The Demerol does little to alleviate it, the antibiotics have failed to stem the tide of rot and venom. My white blood cell count has climbed above eighteen thousand toward twenty. My fingers and feet are frozen stiff, as if with frostbite. We are traveling very quickly in the ambulance on the road which is sometimes smooth, often not. When—if—we make it the hundred miles to the hospital in the city, they will open me up to find my sigmoid colon has ruptured, the breach no greater than a penny-nail head, so that in my peritoneum there exists a small, potent cesspool and my blood has become a river of filth. Peritonitis. I am jaundiced, my hands are yellow with hepatitis. For two days I have been septic, languishing in a small country hospital, misdiagnosed with classic acute diverticulitis. Would that it were, bad as that is.

I do not struggle to maintain consciousness; am terribly awake. This woman holding my hands is a nurse—I remember her name now—and yes, we are on the road in an ambulance. It is August and the high branches of maples and willows and ash, which I can see falling behind out the square windows, are lush auspicious green. I know this road well. The Hudson River is a few hundred yards to the east, rolling along at the base of sheer red cliffs.

My question is, Which goes into shock first, the liver or brain? And if I do survive will it be in a coma? My question is, Do the comatose dream? I must believe they do. And would a coma relieve me from this intimate torture? I doubt it would. My question is, Would these questions come to an end were I locked inside a coma?

The pain is difficult to pinpoint. That is, when they ask me, Where is the pain? I can answer with a wave of my hand over my middle, but it is now no longer the truth, no longer exact. The pain has grown toward completion. It embraces and envelops me so that it and I are becoming indistinguishable. Neither enemy nor perverse friend, the agony is me and none other. In my visual scape occasional corpuscle-shaped, fist-sized gray-black holes now and then float across the world inside the little silver room that journeys down the parkway.

The nausea is persistent, and I am stiff as if rigor mortis had already set in. Bursts of quaking continue to surge through me from head down, or beginning in the shoulders and splitting outward into the arms. Each ripple, every seam and pothole, produces a thick searing sensation.

The driver has asked would I mind if he plays country music on the radio. I don't want to hear country music, but say nothing. Despite myself, I hearten to the singing, the Dobro, the classic country base line. Then, the music is forgotten. This dark room must be where the coma comes, is what I think, or thought.

Never learned to dance the fandango. Never read *Don Quixote*, failed to see the Parthenon, somehow never found time to visit my grandparents' graves in Blue Hill, Nebraska, and Decatur, Alabama. The unfinished work, the unsaid apologies, the unstated affections. Never had children, failed at marriage but not at the friendships. Here on the gibbet swung high, confessionless and solitary.

Thoughts, some clichéd and some not, cascade, then center again—a distinct passage, that manner of thought—what I might have done and didn't, what I should have said but hadn't, where I could have gone and never did—all these just ceased. Regret gone, I am back with the woman who sits beside me on a steel bench. The plastic bag hung on a corkscrew silver finger above jigs, drips into the vial that feeds the tube which snakes down to the needle in my forearm. Saline and Cipro. We pass under a stone bridge, pink granite and shiny gray. What a gentle, beautiful arch.

SECOND MEDITATION

Then I am in a new sphere of reflection.

What is fascinating is that I am fascinated by what fascinates me, here in this—can it possibly be called?—predicament. What fascinates me is that all these bodily doings are the source of a kind of objective interest to me. Is this evidence of mind-body duality? The mind is sharp and quick and has, I swear, withdrawn to the back of my skull, there in the lower right quadrant. That is where it has established itself. The body is going down as the imagination remains steadier than ever, and marvelously engaged. White noise impedes sometimes—the radio now bothers me and I think to ask the driver to turn it down, but then reconsider: maybe the music, which he loves, will help him get us there quicker—but for the most part, it is my imagination that may be keeping me alive now. And that fascination is, to me, fascinating.

Plato found that both pleasure and pain "arising in the soul are a kind of motion" and that an intermediate state between the two exists, which he termed "quietude." My imagination was operative, I believe, in this median realm, paradoxical as that might seem. It burst forth moment to moment, in agreement with a physical burst of agony, but generally held to quietude. It watched, as best it could, horrified and entranced. Because it harbored in quietude, language and imagery could move over its surface with fresh ease, and without my having to work at it. The imagery was dark and cast in a deep red the color of old rose hips. The words came, it seemed, in random ensembles, from memory. And it, my imagination, gathered these phrases like an herbalist rare, curative flora. I thought they were bits of verse from different books of the Bible, plaited with passages from hymns my mother taught me. But it had been so long since I read the Bible, I no longer could be sure even if they were biblical, let alone what book of the Bible they might be from. If they were debris from hymns I once sang in the children's choir, I couldn't remember which hymns were which. I had been away from the church for more than half my life. The sources were forgotten.

Still, like that herbalist, I collected the phrases against the prospect I might survive this journey. If so, it would be valuable to return to them in health and look at them in a stronger light. I wait and listen.

IN WHICH MUSIC LIFTS LIKE FIRM HANDS

The Lord was my shepherd, then the Lord was not. Once, I was made to lie beside still waters, guided perhaps with a staff veiled from my youthful eye, a rod and a staff that promised—in the perfect silence of fluid tranquility—something. Promised comfort, and promised peace. Peace, repose, serenity. Yet, my wars lay ahead of me, and peace was nothing that I might logically have yearned for back then. Of what use is repose to a wild boy growing up on the westernmost margin of high plains where the earth suddenly surges into mountains? I who could see the snow-hatted range of the Continental

Divide from my bedroom window, who was far more likely to plunge into the slow, rich-brown irrigation canal near our house from a tire swing strung from a cottonwood, and make the cannonball splash as my friends howled and shrieked and raced back and forth on the dusty bank, than lie beside any still waters—what did I want with serenity, repose, peace? But yet the Lord was my shepherd, back then, and I was in the fold.

The family Bible lies opened on the kitchen table. My mother sits across the table from me as I recite. Wrote, rote; writ, rite. The words are learned by sound, as this is the only way I can hang on to them. Meaning seeps in later, or not at all. On the piano I can vault through Bach and Mozart, but these words are more slippery and difficult for me. The pure nonsense of naming the books of the Bible I find as easy as stringing together in memory consequent words such as those that make up a short psalm. Genesis, Exodus, Leviticus have the rhythm of Morse Code: dit-dah-dah, dit-dah-dah, dah-dit-dah-dah. Easy enough. But if there is meaning, already I want to remold, revise. The Lord is a shepherd, I push Him away. The Lord is your shepherd, have Him yourself. The tiniest verb changes everything, including the expression on my mother's face as she pours herself more coffee and urges me to try again.

She was the organist at the First Methodist Church. She also directed the choir. Too poor for baby-sitters, she brought me and my sister along with her to the church when she practiced. We played hide-and-seek in the sanctuary, raced the aisles between pews in end-less games of tag, as the church reverberated with oratorios and hymns from the huge pipe organ. Massive ramparts of organ sound, the pedal bass so heavy it pommeled my bony chest, the carillon tin-kling, the reedy oboesque and French horn notes made deliciously wavery through the speaker in the choir loft.

Religion was twofold for me. It was that swelling in my heart which I adored as I crouched in a dark niche on the altar, hiding from my sister—that swelling that was the natural response to my mother's music on the church organ. And it was that fought-for psalm that began with the words, *The Lord is my shepherd, I shall not want.*

Sermons were lost on me. I more clearly remember the scent of the Wrigley's Spearmint gum my grandfather was apt quietly to chew throughout the course of the service on Sunday mornings than any sermon. That, and my father's aftershave. Somehow, however, I got it into my head that I would grow up to be a preacher. This beanpole who survived Sunday mornings because of what that organ aroused in his narrow breast and little unto nothing else, a preacher? My early desire was eclipsed soon enough by the conviction I would grow up to compose religious music for the organ. In my head, in bed at night, I would improvise music for fantastic thousand-voiced choirs and impossible pipe organs. Violins, cellos, bassoons, timpani—the orchestras were vast, seated on hillsides, and responsive to the universal and unpredictable directions in which their mighty, if small, maker saw fit to take them.

Music *was* religion, in other words. And Psalm 23 became my whole and exclusive Bible, because it was music more than any other passage I read, its meanings almost (almost) secondary to its melody and measure. It has always been, like my impromptu, private cantatas and konzertes, subject to improvisational reshuffling. Even now, after glancing at the text, I see I have remodeled Psalm 23:2. *He maketh me to lie down in green pastures: he leadeth me beside the still waters,* it reads. And here I remembered it so clearly that He would have had me to walk with Him in green pastures and lie down beside still waters—the ponderous muddy waters of our dear canal.

FOURTH MEDITATION

Words, then, from the old psalm streamed into my scalded consciousness and as I shored them against my ruin, my little personal apocalypse settling so naturally in on me, I recognized that "these fragments I have shored against my ruins" was itself a fragment. One learned later in life and not quite as basic, because shoring against one's ruin was an adult act and involved a strength and knowledge I sensed I might not have available to me. Shoring things, anything—timbers, the ideas of others—against one's ruin was work only accomplished by an able defender, wasn't it? If so, this was, for me, an absurdity. How might I be able to stave off catastrophe? There was no shoring against this ruin, I thought. I hardly knew where I was. Or what were my chances. Shantih, the peace which passeth all understanding.

This was me clambering outside the process of this death, which was what my body was experiencing that August evening, peritonitic, hepatitic, and gangrenous, the contents of my colon awash in me. I would find out some days later that I should not have survived.

But survival is another story. In the quiet chrysalis of the ambulance, the line from Eliot's *The Wasteland* helped define what was transpiring, while the other fragments were building materials borne into remembrance—and they were *borne,* very much so, special and somehow aloft. They were from the first book I ever read.

Yea though I walk through the valley of the shadow of death thy rod and thy staff they comfort me.

No, it was not prayer. Was it a deflection, a warding off, an inept vesper service conducted in helpless freefall? *I will fear no evil,* more words manifest as if by their own will, and though they didn't form themselves into prayer it would be untruthful to declare they didn't comfort me. There was a warmth and luxury of childhood carried with them, less psychic Dilaudid than the solace of familiarity and the reminder of times that were not like the present time, times that were so plentiful with the energy of simply being alive that the squalor, torture, flesh-sadness, the inarguable defeat of life by death was not so much as a fleck of a dark star on the horizon of possibility. Yahweh understood the power of language, and by giving Adam the task of naming all the beasts and plants on the earth, He gave Adam the opportunity of understanding this power. As I lay there dying, these few simple verses learned so early in my life came back charged with similar ineffable power. That is, their weight was irrationally meaningful, indeed they exceeded meaning.

As the words angled, pitched by, I was able to wonder at them. *The valley of the shadow of death,* now why not just the valley of death? What was the shadow of death? And in that wondering another fragment emerged, *leadeth me beside still waters,* which I placed in the geography of this reverie in the synclinal furrow of the valley.

He leadeth me beside the still waters. He restoreth my soul. All was better when the patient accepted his fate and gave up the critical enquiry and whatever regret would pool like so much worthless sludge, making the fragmentary remembrances darkened. *He restoreth my soul,* the chain of thoughts continued as if guided by their own imperatives. And, of course, I couldn't resist asking that question that had made religion all but impossible for me throughout the course of my life: Yes, all right, but what He? And where? And why?

So, what happened that summer afternoon was not an objective review of childhood passages from the book, a revered book, but a revival of remembered images prompted by an imagination that had become all but sure it was about to experience the death of the body that had always housed it. Or, through which it had garnered its knowledge. That is: the death of the hands that held the book in the first place; death of the eyes that read those lines and mouth that spoke the words. The pain was serious flame, a golden scorching ingot placed in my gut. With the psalm I hoped to lift the ingot away, wrest it in tendrils of word and phrase out of me.

FIFTH MEDITATION

The shepherd psalm is not without human frailties and vice. King David is a biblical figure I cherish for the very reason he is so deliciously riven by mortal defect.

"Thou preparest a table before me in the presence of mine enemies," we read. As one scholar has noted, without comment: "A petty ruler of the fourteenth century B.C. addressed the following request to the Pharaoh: 'May he give gifts to his servants while our enemies look on.'" (El Amarna, 100: 33-35). Isn't it enough to be beloved of a powerful benefactor, and blessed with the various gifts such a Lord would lay upon your table? Must you pray for an envious audience of rivals to watch you eat, drink, and be merry?

Nor is there much largesse in the comfort that is conjured by the shepherd's rod, since the rod would be used to bash in the head of some hungry predator—a wolf or lioness who needs to feed her young, say—who has the bad judgment and rotten luck to come skulking around this particular flock. Better thee than me, poor starving wolf! Hardly the most selfless doctrine ever contrived by the ethicist or priest.

But still, self-sacrifice does not come easily, even to the most magnanimous. The spirit is willing but the flesh is weak, as Jesus well understood at Gethsemane. Indeed, all four evangelists concur that when it came time for Him to fulfill scripture and make His sacrifice, He did not go quietly into that good night, but let out a cry so anguished that even the centurion was moved to believe.

DEEDS

Just as the naming of the beasts of the field and fowl of the air was the first act of man (Genesis 2:19), perhaps a gradual loss of language is one of his last.

She told me her name, and I looked up at her, when we began to cross the bridge into the city and, as I say, I could not remember. The rigging and silver tower and the long graceful curve of the main suspension cables, lit now with white beams, the afternoon having drowned in evening dark, was visible out the windows in the back. I could not remember the name of the bridge. Words were being left behind, replaced by the visible. Words, which above all human inventions I had loved most, began to leave me. Adam had named the birds, and though I had worked hard to learn their names they were not with me anymore. Out the windows I saw a (seagull) drift through vertical cables of (the bridge), and was horrified to see I couldn't touch those simple, specific words. I saw faces and forms, hue and shading and movement, but the names that signed what they were, identified them, were shimmery and evanescent.

This is why the phrase *Yea, though I walk through the valley of the shadow of death* struck me with such power. The normal clamor in my head having abated, these earliest memorized words advanced with resonance and import that shook me with the thrill of discovery. It was as if I myself had invented the phrase. *My cup runneth over, for His name's sake*—what did that mean? Because there was some One Named, named and therefore somehow comprehensible or kin, I was rich and even here in this difficulty there was abundance, something to be earned, or fulfilled.

But still, I wasn't so delirious that I claimed for myself full authorship of any of this. It was shared, but I couldn't tell with whom. These were sweet old Bible phrases, I thought, and more the pity I could never bring myself to accept any savior, take a leap of faith into the invisible arms that promised me that *surely goodness and mercy shall follow me all the days of my life.*

I will fear no evil, that comes next. And I didn't fear evil or death or much of anything, not even the ugly continuous pain, nor did I hope to make some deathbed covenant—ah, how American to die in a car—strike some deal, also so American, the usual business of "Please, God, I know I have not believed and know I could have done more and could have done better, please if you can see your way clear to letting me live through this I will, promise promise, cross my heart or hope to . . . I will do more and better in the future, will follow the rules and . . ."—no, that never happened. *I will fear no evil, for thou art with me,* and it would be dishonorable and a lie to claim that I felt altogether alone. As we crossed the bridge a thread of hope must have woven through some of these thoughts and staggered remembrances. After all, I was fighting for my life.

The river, the wide river, the murky light-lined river whose waters were never still, the river beside which I hoped not to lie, we crossed that river and made it to the hospital and within an hour I was anesthetized into oblivion while they opened me right from breastbone down to pubis, heart to loins, and saved me. All the way into the operating room I carried these jumbled fragments, like votive candles, like uncomprehended offerings against my ruin.

SEVENTH MEDITATION: RETROSPECT

The valley of the shadow of death is, when one stands just there, in it, not much different from the valley of the shadow of death one imagined as a child reader, memorizing the psalm for Sunday school, haunted by it at night alone in bed. The comfort, plain and sweet, promised to the vulnerable child by the majestic, mysterious, benevolent shepherd of the psalm is attractive—no matter how resistant we can be—to the dying adult. But beyond the message, the language of the poem remains of the same surety. There are laws upheld in its construction, laws of wisdom and serenity, and yes of common sense as well. What this psalm offers the child it offers the adult in equal measure. Therein lies the genius.

"In my beginning is my end," Eliot once more rewords the Bible,

> Now the light falls
> Across an open field, leaving the deep lane
> Shuttered with branches, dark in the afternoon
> Where you lean against a bank while a van passes.

Life is music, death the pedal point. Life is the dance. Death the stamped earthen dance floor. The pedal point grounds the variation, the ground must be impressed. The shepherd psalm has been my C major scale, my Do-Re-Me. A place to begin, to move from the dominant to the next note, the D, or Re—king, beam of light, the dee of death—and thence up the scale until the octave is reached and repetition is possible. Bring us back to Do—the dough of food, the dew of drink, the do of accomplishment. Bring us back to the end which was again a new beginning for me. Back to the dark in that afternoon, where the van passed through the valley.

from *THE EARTH HOUSE*

JEANNE DUPRAU

The Buddhist tradition has a great deal to say about the causes and cessation of suffering. The more you resist, the more it overwhelms you, observes Bay Area writer and meditation practitioner, Jeanne DuPrau, mourning the death of Sylvia, her life-partner. In this austere yet deeply moving excerpt from The Earth House, *DuPrau's account of their years of involvement in a Zen community, DuPrau surrenders to her suffering in order to move through to the other side of pain and loss.*

THE NEXT three months were a long nightfall, winter and death sifting slowly down like twilight. Each day had more darkness in it than the one before, darkness that seemed to gather at both ends of the day, so that the light between grew briefer and dimmer.

At first Sylvia felt strangely well, for someone so ill. She was a little short of breath, a little weak; that was all. We continued our custom of taking a walk around two blocks in the evenings after dinner. But as time passed, her breath came harder, her strength diminished, and we walked more and more slowly. We had to stop often and rest, standing arm in arm under the streetlamps, looking at the black leafless trees with stars glittering coldly among their branches. After a while we shortened our walk to one block instead of two, and later we went only halfway down the street, then turned and came back. Her world was shrinking. After the beginning of November, when the radiation treatments ended, she did not leave the house again; by December, I could no longer persuade her even to take a turn around the living room.

The doctor ordered her an oxygen machine. It sat in the middle room, behind the closed door, which muffled a little the constant roar and thump it made as it sucked oxygen out of the air. A transparent plastic tube snaked under the door and down the hall, into Sylvia's bedroom, and up to a circle of tube that looped over her ears like glasses and blew air gently into her nose. All day, the machine chugged like an angry heart. You could feel it in the soles of your feet.

Her appetite waned. Only certain kinds of things appealed, white things and bland smooth sweet things. I made a list of them—pancakes, cottage cheese, canned peaches, mashed potatoes, custard. I carried the white tray with fold-down legs back and forth, bringing breakfast, lunch, and dinner, my old faith in the power of food sticking unreasonably with me. One by one, she stopped liking all the things on the list. She would sit with the plate in front of her on which I had arranged two soda crackers, a dab of cottage cheese, and two peach slices, and every five minutes or so she would take a tiny bite and then rest from the exertion of overcoming her repugnance. One day in mid-January she pushed the plate away and said, "No more solid food, ever again," and this turned out to be not just a wish but a statement of fact.

She didn't feel much pain—every now and then a twinge, somewhere in her left side. But the pain wasn't as bad as taking the pills against it. Better to have a pain than to risk the nausea that washed through her when she took the pills, or smelled ordinary food, or coughed too hard.

In the daytime she sat against a thick bolster of pillows, with a blue electric blanket over her legs. I read to her sometimes: *The Borrowers* and *The Cat Who Went to Heaven*. The Guide came, and she read to her, too—the *Heart Sutra*, and the *Tibetan Book of the Dead*. Sometimes Sylvia watched the soap operas and the talk shows on TV, and when she tired of that she looked out the window at the yellow daisies bobbing in the rain. The sky was always gray. Robins hurled themselves at the pyracantha bush next to the glass door, squawking and shrieking, the impact of their bodies thumping the clumps of berries against the wall. In the afternoons, Sylvia slept, and as time went on her sleeps grew longer and deeper. She fell into sleeps that were like ocean abysses, from which she clawed her way back up into daylight, groaning. At night I listened for the sound of coughing down the hall from my room.

Death closed in from all directions, like the shutter of a camera. One day she said her legs felt as if they no longer belonged to her. They lay there on the bed in their gray sweatpants and white socks, and she looked at them with detachment, as if they were stuffed legs that someone had sewed on.

I asked her if she thought back over her life, and she said she did not. It was far away from her. It was not interesting. Only the moment in which she found herself held her attention.

She grew thin, but not terribly thin. She never looked ghastly, not even right at the end. Her skin tightened over her high cheekbones and her fine collarbones; her eyes looked larger, her forehead higher. She was not changed by the disease into a different person, only distilled by it down to her essence. No delirium scrambled her mind; she had no pain severe enough to require the drugs that would make her groggy and dull. She was herself until one Monday night, when a bad cough brought the pain stabbing into her lungs and the nurse came with a morphine device that attached to the bedside table and dripped fluid steadily from a tube into a needle in her arm. She lay on her back, her eyes open a slit, only the whites showing, and for three days she breathed through liquid as her lungs filled. Once she floated up into an otherworldly sort of consciousness. Her eyes opened and focused slightly, but not on us, and she spoke in a faraway voice. We bent to hear, holding our breath, and she said, with spaces between the words, "It's wonderful . . . I want you to know that it's all okay . . . thank you for everything you've done . . . it's been nothing but wonderful, nothing but wonderful." She was on the threshold between two worlds, where she could see the one before her as clearly as the one she was leaving, and she had gathered the strength to call back to us, reassuring.

She worked hard in her last three days. Her heart was strong, not willing to give up easily. If the life force in her body had been a light, we would have seen it in those days concentrated in a shape like a pear—mouth, throat, heart, lungs, only the parts required to keep her breathing. It would have been a dense light, glowing like a red dwarf star, and falling inward. Her head and belly would have been full of shadows, and her limbs dark—feet abandoned, hands lying flat and limp on the blue cover of the bed. Her eyes filmed over, grew gummy and opaque—she had no use for them any more. Her mouth, half open, was only a hole to pull air through. The light drew in and in until finally, for hours on the last day, it was no more than a faint but stubborn candle flame, and she was a body being breathed, being pumped by whatever force it is in the universe that pumps breath through bodies. The breaths got rougher, halting, more and more shuddering and widely spaced. The last one came in the evening, a little after seven o'clock.

Then we followed the Buddhist way of caring for the dead. We sat with her for forty-five minutes. We washed and prepared her body . . . dressed her in clean sweatpants and a T-shirt, wrapped her in a white sheet, so that only her face showed, with the sheet folded around it like a monk's hood. Under the bed we put branches of bay laurel and sage and pine, and we laid flowers on the bed around her. For three days, the house was open to those who wanted to come. And at the end of three days, on a rainy evening when all the people had gone, we brought in a pine casket that Greg had made and laid her in it. The next day we sat in the chapel adjoining the cemetery's crematorium and waited while the flames in the oven behind the altar burned casket, sheet, flesh, hair, and bone.

I was left with an emptiness where she had been. My mind wrestled with it but made no progress. None of my questions had answers: Where is she? How could she be gone? Is she still here somehow, watching me? Will she come again, in some other form? I can understand the appeal of reincarnation, which holds out the hope that each irreplaceable self will not be obliterated but moved along from one body to another, as if a life history were a long thread winding through the eons, with bodies strung along it like beads, always the same soul housed in one body after another. But I don't see how it can be so neat and linear as that; nothing else is. I imagine instead something more like a vast endlessly fertile jungle, in which everything is always reborn, but no one self ever occurs twice—the way leaves are reborn on a tree every spring, but the exact same leaf that was there last year never appears again. I do not expect to discover, twenty or thirty years from now, a person whose body is the new home for Sylvia's spirit.

I have tried to make death fit into my scheme of life, just as people have tried to do forever, picturing death as a shadowy land on the other side of a river, or a place in the sky full of harp music and white clouds—as if death were another country in life's geography. But I can't make this work. Death is *behind* life, it is the other side of life, not an aspect of life at all, as night is not an aspect of day. In my ordinary mode of operation I am so firmly embedded in life that I can do nothing with death but try to translate it into terms I understand. I look for an answer to it, as though it were a puzzle or a hard mathematical problem, and cling to the belief that if I could find such an answer, I might be comforted.

But there is no comfort, not for the part of me that wants to touch a solid shoulder again and hear the sound of a voice. That self never finds comfort, unless it can believe in a manufactured comfort—that we all go to heaven, that we will be reborn as higher beings, that our loved ones are still themselves only invisible, and will speak to us in their familiar voices if we knock on tables. The one who yearns for that comfort is inconsolable, always. But it has been suggested to me that my small self is held in the arms of another larger kind of being, made of life and death the way time on earth is made of night and day. If my struggling mind were to abandon its efforts, having been confounded at every turn, and collapse its walls so that for a moment it ceased to exist—then I might fall into this greater being and know that death is not something separate that I must try to figure out, but my own self, as impossible to see with my daylight eyes as the back of my head, but just as rightfully a part of me, and just as highly to be valued. Sylvia tried to tell me this, I think, in her last message, and I will take her word for it, though I have not yet died enough to really understand.

·   ·   ·

In the months after Sylvia died, the air turned solid with pain. I could not breathe without taking it in, I couldn't move without feeling it brush against me. It was thickest at home, in the evenings. I sat on the couch with no one opposite me in the striped chair, and looked at the sky through the window above the piano. Twilight was always falling; the sky was always a dead white or a deep hollow gray, and the TV aerials on the rooftops poked up into it desolately, thin and cold. Everything in the house was a word speaking to me about Sylvia. Her handwriting looked up at me from the calendar, where she had marked all the days when the gas man would come to read the meter and I must remember to open the gate. Her clothes hung in her closet, each shirt and shoe speaking of her shape. Her room reeked of the incense we had burned in the last three days, the incense I never wanted to smell again. I put a pan of baking soda in there to absorb it, and then I closed the door.

This is what pain feels like: a fist in the solar plexus. First it hits, and then instead of withdrawing it stays there, pressing and turning. I tried to back away from it, but its arm just became longer and longer, and the fist stayed with me. I could see it coming at the end of the day. It was waiting for me at the table with one placemat, in the hall with the closed door at the end.

Buddhism, says the fourth noble truth, is the path that leads to the extinction of suffering. I wanted to run down that path and get to the place where suffering ceases.

But the path that leads to the extinction of suffering is one of those backward paths like the ones in Alice's looking-glass garden, where the course that seems the most natural and logical is the one that leads you astray. Alice determines to walk to the top of the hill at the end of the garden. She starts up the path with the hill ahead of her, but after a few steps she finds that she is inexplicably walking the other way, with the hill at her back. She takes another path that heads toward the hill, and the same thing happens. All the paths that look as though they'll take her where she wants to go instead perversely shunt her in the opposite direction. Finally she turns and walks away from the hill, and that's when she suddenly finds herself at the top.

It seems to work like this with suffering. You can't walk away from pain in the hope of escaping it; you have to turn around and walk toward it. You have to suffer . . . to end suffering. Zen practice is not a way to slip out from under suffering or to numb yourself to it. Quite the contrary. If your practice isn't hard . . . if it doesn't bring you up against all the things you want least to deal with, if it doesn't require from you great suffering, then you are not really doing spiritual practice. But there is a difference between the suffering that ends suffering and the suffering that perpetuates it. You can learn to distinguish one from the other, and you can, if you are willing to, choose between them.

Night after night in those hard months, I came home hoping I could find a way through the hours of the evening that would take me around the pain instead of through it. But the pain would not be avoided, it was too big. No drink could drown it. No TV show or telephone conversation could silence it. My efforts to stop it had no effect but to darken it with failure.

The more I shrank from pain, the more it crept up behind me like a wave, tugging at my ankles, threatening to pull me off my feet. At last I found that the only way to keep it from swamping me was to do what seemed most perilous—turn to face it. I didn't want to. I would rather have done almost anything else. Nothing else worked.

Writing was my means of confrontation. When all my efforts to fend off the pain had failed and I began to sink, I would force myself to my feet and move across the living room, through fierce currents of resistance, to where the computer stood on its table next to the couch. Heart full of dread, I would flick the switch and plunge in.

The pain streamed through me, out my fingers and onto the screen. Pain was what I wrote about, over and over and over. I looked at it from every angle, described it in all its guises. "It is a dagger," I wrote, "that drives down behind my ribs." "It settles in my solar plexus like a stone and makes my arms limp." "It's as if a hole has been punched out of my middle and the surroundings implode to fill the vacuum, the way air rushes in to fill the vacuum made by a lightning bolt, only in me that result is tears, not thunder." Pain became my familiar—not my friend, but someone whose face I knew. By writing I opened the door to it, I said, "Come in. Run through me." I would write and cry, write and shake, and when I was finished I felt battered but somehow saved.

Months went by, months of this, and although I did not realize for a long time that the pain was ebbing—you can only see that from a great distance, it happens so gradually and with so many backward steps—I *did* notice a change. I began to see that some pain came unavoidably upon me and some I made up myself. The true pain was a sensation, those stabbings and hard blows and aching constrictions. But there was something else as well—a swirling multitude of words that surrounded the pain like a fog. I anguished over what I had done wrong, raged at the past for being how it was instead of how it should have been, recalled words I wished not to have spoken and deeds I wished I had done—as if by denouncing the past, revising it, refusing it, I could repair the unbearable injustice. I knew, in another part of my mind, that this is the way the world is, and worse than this. All I got by fighting it was two pains instead of one: the pain of death and loss and my changed life, and also the pain of my own furious *no!*, my fists balled up, fingernails cutting into my palms. This was extra, added on to the pain. It seemed to happen of itself, and yet I could see, if I looked hard enough, that I didn't *have* to do it.

And here I came upon an unwelcome insight: I was forced to admit that sometimes—often, maybe—I *wanted* to thrash around in my suffering. I didn't want to let the pain go once it had coursed through me, I wanted to hold on to it and recreate it again and again. Something in me was trying to appropriate the pain for its own uses—turn it into a badge I could wear proudly ("Look how I have suffered, much more than you have—I require special treatment"), or maintain me in a broken and helpless condition ("Suffering has ruined my life, not much can be expected from me"). I could feel the terrible seductive sweetness of my pain, the temptation to transform it into something that served my ego and then hang on to it—which is not at all the same as accepting it.

Acceptance is hard. To accept my pain means holding it in my arms, like a package handed to me, my proper burden to be carried. The package may be heavy as lead, or burning hot, or stuck through with razors, but I must concede that it is my package, simply because it has arrived in my life. It is not a mistake. It has not been sent by accident to the wrong person. I may not welcome it, but accepting it means I carry it without protest for as long as necessary—and then I lay it down.

And will it make me happy to follow this hard prescription? I want a guarantee before I start out. But there *is* no guarantee that will satisfy the one who's asking, because it's my ego who wants to know, and my ego is concerned only with my comfort, my pleasures, my success, my importance. Ego rejects all pain, and warns me against it: watch out, this is going to hurt, better protect yourself, better run. Most often I cave in, and my ego smiles and flicks the reins. Every time I am willing to suffer—every time I can say, All right, let it hurt, I accept it—I have flouted ego's authority and loosened a bit the death-grip it has on me.

And this loosening is the path that leads to the extinction of suffering.

There is no end to suffering for my striving, flailing ego-self. It's ego's nature to suffer, and no wisdom is going to improve its nature any more than you can improve an apple so radically that it becomes an orange. It's only outside the ego that there is any end of suffering in sight. Each of the bricks that pave the path must be a pain accepted: a thwarting of the ego.

No one who has ever tried it says this path is easy. It's only preferable to the alternative, which leads down into fear and endless desperate scrambling and the death of the spirit. Nothing guarantees that if I accept my pain I will be a happy person. This path is not concerned with happiness, in the ordinary sense of the word, but with a higher kind of joy, what Buddhists call a "joyful participation in the sorrows of the world." I have seen people who I suspect have come to feel this—Sylvia, at the end of her life, was one. In them the thick wall of the ego has worn papery thin, and they become luminous as lanterns.

SUFFERING AND FAITH

MARTIN LUTHER KING, JR.

In these brief remarks by Martin Luther King, Jr., which appeared in the pages of the periodical Christian Century *in 1960, this prophetic leader reflects on the nature of suffering and redemption in the face of daily trials in the struggle for freedom. "Battered by the storms of persecution" but reluctant "to refer to my personal sacrifices," King meditates on his now-transformed theology: no longer perceiving God as a metaphysical, philosophical abstraction, he now cleaves to a personal, living God.*

... IN RECENT months I have also become more and more convinced of the reality of a personal God. True, I have always believed in the personality of God. But in past years the idea of a personal God was little more than a metaphysical category which I found theologically and philosophically satisfying. Now it is a living reality that has been validated in the experiences of everyday life. Perhaps the suffering, frustration and agonizing moments which I have had to undergo occasionally as a result of my involvement in a difficult struggle have drawn me closer to God. Whatever the cause, God has been profoundly real to me in recent months. In the midst of outer dangers I have felt an inner calm and known resources of strength that only God could give. In many instances I have felt the power of God transforming the fatigue of despair into the buoyancy of hope. I am convinced that the universe is under the control of a loving purpose and

that in the struggle for righteousness man has cosmic companionship. Behind the harsh appearances of the world there is a benign
power. To say God is personal is not to make him an object among
other objects or attribute to him the finiteness and limitations of
human personality; it is to take what is finest and noblest in our consciousness and affirm its perfect existence in him. It is certainly true
that human personality is limited, but personality as such involves no
necessary limitations. It simply means self-consciousness and self-
direction. So in the truest sense of the word, God is a living God. In
him there is feeling and will, responsive to the deepest yearnings of
the human heart: this God both evokes and answers prayers.

The past decade has been a most exciting one. In spite of the tensions and uncertainties of our age something profoundly meaningful
has begun. Old systems of exploitation and oppression are passing
away and new systems of justice and equality are being born. In a real
sense ours is a great time in which to be alive. Therefore I am not yet
discouraged about the future. Granted that the easygoing optimism
of yesterday is impossible. Granted that we face a world crisis which
often leaves us standing amid the surging murmur of life's restless
sea. But every crisis has both its dangers and its opportunities. Each
can spell either salvation or doom. In a dark, confused world the
spirit of God may yet reign supreme.

．　．　．

Some of my personal sufferings over the last few years have also
served to shape my thinking. I always hesitate to mention these experiences for fear of conveying the wrong impression. A person who
constantly calls attention to his trials and sufferings is in danger of
developing a martyr complex and of making others feel that he is
consciously seeking sympathy. It is possible for one to be self-centered
in his self-denial and self-righteous in his self-sacrifice. So I am always
reluctant to refer to my personal sacrifices. But I feel somewhat justified in mentioning them in this article because of the influence they
have had in shaping my thinking.

Due to my involvement in the struggle for the freedom of my
people, I have known very few quiet days in the last few years. I have
been arrested five times and put in Alabama jails. My home has been
bombed twice. A day seldom passes that my family and I are not the
recipients of threats of death. I have been the victim of a near-fatal
stabbing. So in a real sense I have been battered by the storms of per-

secution. I must admit that at times I have felt that I could
bear such a heavy burden, and have been tempted to
a more quiet and serene life. But every time such a temptation
appeared, something came to strengthen and sustain my determination. I have learned now that the Master's burden is light precisely
when we take his yoke upon us.

My personal trials have also taught me the value of unmerited suffering. As my sufferings mounted I soon realized that there were two
ways that I could respond to my situation: either to react with bitterness or seek to transform the suffering into a creative force. I decided
to follow the latter course. Recognizing the necessity for suffering I
have tried to make of it a virtue. If only to save myself from bitterness,
I have attempted to see my personal ordeals as an opportunity to
transform myself and heal the people involved in the tragic situation
which now obtains. I have lived these last few years with the conviction that unearned suffering is redemptive.

There are some who still find the cross a stumbling block, and others consider it foolishness, but I am more convinced than ever before
that it is the power of God unto social and individual salvation. So like
the Apostle Paul I can now humbly yet proudly say, "I bear in my
body the marks of the Lord Jesus." The suffering and agonizing
moments through which I have passed over the last few years have
also drawn me closer to God. More than ever before I am convinced
of the reality of a personal God.

TYLENOL PRAYER BEADS

JARVIS JAY MASTERS

The central concept in Buddhism that all suffering is due to desire and attachment is particularly striking given the circumstances of Jarvis Jay Masters. Born in 1962 and now an inmate on Death Row in San Quentin Prison, Masters received his Buddhist initiation from a Tibetan lama on the other side of a glass partition, over a telephone. In these selections from his book, Finding Freedom: Writings from Death Row, *Masters, alone in his cell, contemplates the karma of his own past actions and, in the midst of the daily violence of prison life, dedicates himself to the Buddhist precepts of purifying body, mind, and speech.*

FOR A LONG time I had been my own stranger, but everything I went through in learning how to accept myself brought me to the doorsteps of dharma, the Buddhist path.

During my death penalty trial, Melody, a private investigator working on my case, sent me books on how to meditate, how to deal with pain and suffering, how to keep my mind at rest. She had broken her ankle and was trying to keep still. She and I were both trying this meditation gig, and like me, she was confronting a lot of things in her past. She was also writing and encouraged me to do so as well.

I began to get up early to try to calm my mind so I wouldn't panic. It was as if my whole life was being displayed on a screen during the death penalty case.

Things I had never realized about myself and my life were introduced to me and the jury at the same time. Questions I'd never asked my mother—like how long she'd been abused, on the street, an addict—were being asked now. Through meditation I learned to slow down and take a few deep breaths, to take everything in, not to run from the pain, but to sit with it, confront it, give it the companion it had never had. I became committed to my meditation practice.

While I was in the holding booth during the jury's deliberation on whether I should get life without parole or the death penalty, I started leafing through a Buddhist journal Melody had left there. In it was an article called "Life in Relation to Death" by a Tibetan Buddhist lama, Chagdud Tulku Rinpoche. I thought, "Wow! This is right up my alley!"

I sent a letter to the address in the journal and got a reply from a woman named Lisa, one of Rinpoche's close students, with a copy of his booklet, Life in Relation to Death. *At the time, I'd gotten into some kind of trouble and was in isolated confinement, stripped down to a pair of shorts and a T-shirt, with only two blankets. In her letter, Lisa asked if I needed help. I always needed help, I still need help, and because of the help she offered, we began corresponding. Then she began to visit me and eventually brought Rinpoche to San Quentin.*

When I first saw Rinpoche through the glass in the small visiting room booth, I thought, "Oh, shit, I'm in trouble now. I'm messing around with a real lama. He's from Tibet. Check him out. I bet everything he's got on is blessed."

I figured there were two ways I could introduce myself. I could greet him in an ordinary way, or I could bow. I bowed. Then he bowed. Why'd I think he wouldn't? He's been bowing all his life.

I thought, "I've been reading about lamas for the last three years and now I have a real one in front of me." I knew that all I could do was tell him exactly what I think. If I lied or shied away from him, he'd know it.

I fell in love with him for the same reasons everybody else does. His life history was my key. He had been a rebellious kid. He wasn't born with a silver spoon. He was a feisty guy who would discipline me when I needed it. He knew what he was talking about, and would say it in a way that I'd get it. He had a certain shrewdness. Compassionate ferociousness. He was a lama who ate beef jerky, got upset, and had jewels of compassion in him. The only thing he didn't do was say all this to me. I just felt it. I thought, "Here's a guy who can take me out of prison even as I remain here. He won't dress me in Buddhist garb, but accept me as I am." I knew he was a tough character.

· · ·

It was past midnight. The prison night watchman was making his routine body count down the tier when I awakened from a late evening snooze with plans to get up and spend the rest of the night doing my meditation practice.

I paced the length of my cell for a while, all eight feet of it, preparing myself with repetitions of the Tara prayer. Suddenly I was struck by an idea for a way to make my own mala, my own prayer beads, which I could use to keep track of the repetitions. I spun around my cell, looking for what I would need.

Since the very first day of learning this prayer, I'd wanted a mala to help me with my practice. My teacher, Rinpoche, and other practitioners who came to San Quentin to visit me had often offered to bring me one, but prison authorities had denied them permission to do so.

I gathered a pair of prison-issue jeans, a *Sports Illustrated,* and a bottle of Tylenol, and sat down at the front of my cell. I picked and pulled at the seams of the jeans until I got hold of a good piece of thread. I unraveled more than I meant to, "Uh-oh!" A gaping hole widened down the leg. "I'll get another pair somehow," I resolved, and put the thread aside.

I opened the *Sports Illustrated* to the middle and took out one of the staples. I straightened it out and sharpened it on the rough concrete floor beside me. I had to be very quiet. If the night watchman heard these strange scratching sounds, the whole cell block might be searched in a panic. Scraping usually meant a weapon was being sharpened.

For almost an hour I ground the staple on the floor, until it was as sharp as a sewing needle.

Now I opened the bottle of Tylenol and began the slow process of poking a tiny hole in the center of each tablet. There were a hundred of them. I had to be as careful as a surgeon. First I poked at the surface of the Tylenol and then with a screwing motion I made a hole all the way through. Taking the thread from my jeans, I passed it through each "bead."

All through the night I sat cross-legged, poking holes in Tylenols and threading them together. It was extremely tedious. My eyes blurred with exhaustion. My fingers began to get sore. I felt foolish. "What in the world am I doing?" I asked myself. But I kept going, determined to finish.

Five and a half hours later I held my first mala, made from trouser thread and Tylenols. I was elated. But when I got up to stretch, my head throbbed, I had an awful headache. I stood silently at the bars of my cell, taking comfort in looking out a window in the opposite wall. A beautiful morning light was peeking in. "I wouldn't mind a Tylenol or two," I thought, "to stop this pounding in my head." I looked down at my hands. "Damn! I don't have any. They're all on this mala."

For a split second I thought the unthinkable, my head was hurting that much. Then I smiled. I realized that after spending all this time making my Tylenol mala, all I needed to do was to sit my butt back down with it and take a few moments—no Tylenols—to do my spiritual practice.

* * *

I was walking out on the exercise yard last week, along the fence, staring up at the beautiful clear sky. It was a gorgeous day. Then something frightening happened: someone got stabbed on the adjacent yard. In the gunmen's tower, prison guards were racking rounds into their rifles. They were shouting at two guys scuffling and fighting and trying to kill each other. I knew immediately that someone was going to die. Either the guards or one of these two prisoners would be responsible for taking a human being's life.

The tower gunmen ordered everyone to lie facedown on the ground as they swung their fully loaded rifles around the three adjacent yards. I didn't know what to think. Since I didn't hear any gunshots, I figured the two guys must have stopped fighting. At least the gunmen had been saved from taking someone's life. But what about the prisoner who had been stabbed? Was he dead? What had I been thinking about before all this happened? Why am I lying here like this? Is this all real? Shit! How long can I go on trying to be a Buddhist in this prison culture that has me lying facedown? Who am I kidding?

Just as I thought my head would explode from so many flashing thoughts, I locked on to a single idea: how some people in this world have only a tragic five seconds to put their entire lives in order before they die—in a car crash or in some other sudden way. I realized that what really matters isn't where we are or what's going on around us, but what's in our hearts while it's happening.

I used to feel I could hide inside my practice, that I could simply sit and contemplate the raging anger of a place like this, seeking inner peace through prayers of compassion. But now I believe love and compassion are things to extend to others. It's a dangerous adventure to share them in a place like S.Q.

Yet I see now that we become better people if we can touch a hardened soul, bring joy into someone's life, or just be an example for others, instead of hiding behind our silence.

The key is in using what we know. This calls for lots of practice. There is this vast space in life to do just that, both as a practitioner and as someone who walks around the same prison yard as everyone else in this place. I've learned how to accept responsibility for the harm I've caused others by never letting myself forget the things I did and by using those experiences to help others understand where they lead.

from *RETURNING: A SPIRITUAL JOURNEY*

DAN WAKEFIELD

Dan Wakefield, a well-known journalist, screenwriter, and novelist approaching middle age, "woke up screaming," wracked with existential pain. An avowed atheist, initially embarrassed to be seen going to his local Unitarian church on Boston's Beacon Hill, Wakefield recounts in Returning *his life-changing move toward God and away from alcohol and drugs, precarious health, and broken relationships.*

ONE BALMY spring morning in Hollywood, a month or so before my forty-eighth birthday, I woke up screaming. I got out of bed, went into the next room, sat down on a couch, and screamed again. This was not, in other words, one of those waking nightmares left over from sleep that is dispelled by the comforting light of day. It was, rather, a response to the reality that another morning had broken in a life I could only deal with sedated by wine, loud noise, moving images, and wired to electronic games that further distracted my fragmented attention from a growing sense of blank, nameless pain in the pit of my very being, my most essential self. It was the beginning of a year in which I would have scored in the upper percentile of these popular magazine tests that list the greatest stresses of life: I left the house I owned, the city I was living in, the work I was doing, the woman I had lived with for seven years and had hoped to remain with the rest of my life, ran out of money, discovered I had endangered my health, and attended the funeral of my father in May and my mother in November.

The day I woke up screaming I grabbed from among my books an old Bible I hadn't opened for nearly a quarter of a century. With a desperate instinct I turned to the Twenty-third Psalm and read it over, several times, the words and the King James cadence bringing a sense of relief and comfort, a kind of emotional balm. In the coming chaotic days and months I sometimes recited that psalm over in my mind, and it always had that calming effect, but it did not give me any sense that I suddenly believed in God again. The psalm simply seemed an isolated source of solace and calm, such as any great poem might be.

In that first acute stage of my crisis I went to doctors for help, physical and mental. I told an internist in Beverly Hills that I had an odd feeling my heart was beating too fast and he confirmed my suspicion. My "resting" pulse rate was 120, and the top of the normal range is 100. An EKG showed there was nothing wrong with my heart, and the doctor asked if I was in the entertainment business. I confessed to television; I had been co-producer of a TV movie I wrote and so earned the title of "writer-producer," giving me the high Hollywood status of a "hyphenate." The doctor nodded and smiled, saying many of his patients in The Industry suffered from stress, as I evidently did now. He prescribed medication that would lower my racing pulse.

The "beta blockers" lowered my pulse but not my anxiety, and I explained to a highly recommended psychiatrist in nearby Westwood (home of UCLA) how I had come out to Los Angeles from Boston nearly three years before to write a TV series called "James at 15" that ran for a season, and then I stayed on doing TV movies and a feature film rewrite I was fired from. I told her how I had grown to feel alien and alienated in Los Angeles; the freeways and frantic pace and the roller coaster of show business were driving me nuts and I couldn't stand the sight of a palm tree. The psychiatrist said I should take a vacation; she suggested Santa Barbara. At that moment the voice of Bob Dylan wailed in my mind the line from "Just Like Tom Thumb Blues"—that my best friend the doctor won't even tell me what I got.

Watching the national weather forecast on "Good Morning, America," I pictured myself on the bottom left-hand corner of the map in the dot of Los Angeles and felt I had slid to the wrong hole on a giant pinball machine, wanting to tilt the whole thing so I could get back to the upper right-hand corner to Boston, where I felt pulled by internal gravity. My Southern California disorientation deepened because I no longer knew when anything happened in the course of a year since all the seasons looked the same to me; when I saw a videotape of Henry James's *The Europeans* the New England autumn leaves and sunlight falling on plain board floors brought tears to my eyes.

I tried to forget about Hollywood by starting a new novel but the room I worked in was next to the swimming pool and the service people who came to test the chlorine were unemployed actors discussing casting calls, making it hard to concentrate; besides, the damp seeped into the pages and stiffened them, giving the manuscript the texture of corpse. I wondered if I might end up as one of those bodies in the movies of Hollywood who float face down in their own swimming pool.

A plumber who came to fix the toilet saw the typewriter and tried to pitch me an idea for a TV pilot about a jewel thief who gains access to rich people's houses by working as a plumber. When he asked if I wanted to get involved I wasn't sure if he meant in a criminal operation or a TV series and each seemed equally unappealing. I longed to leave the land of deals and palm trees and live in a building made of solid brick with a tree outside I could tell the time of year by. Finally, on one of those frantic mornings I stopped in the midst of all I was doing (and failing to do) and called American Airlines, booking a seat on the next flight to Boston.

The city itself was succor, a feast of familiar tradition from the statues of heroes (Alexander Hamilton, William Lloyd Garrison, Samuel Eliot Morison among them) in the wide swath of Commonwealth Avenue to the long wharves on the waterfront reaching out toward Europe. Walking the brick streets of my old neighborhood on Beacon Hill, I felt in balance again with the universe, and a further pull to what seemed the center of it, the source of something I was searching for, something I couldn't name that went far beyond the satisfaction of scenery or local color. I headed like a homing pigeon to the pond in the Public Garden and, without having planned it, sat down on a bench, and at the same time that tears of gratitude came to my eyes the words of the psalm also came to my mind:

". . . he leadeth me beside the still waters. He restoreth my soul."

I recited the psalm from the start and at the end said, "Amen" as if it were a prayer, and it was, of thanks. It would not have occurred to me to go to any church or chapel, but the pond in the Public Garden seemed precisely the place to have offered this.

I thought no further about "religion" on that trip but concerned myself with the more pressing problem of my physical health, which my Boston doctor told me he was frankly worried about. He too found I had a pulse rate of 120, a condition called tachycardia. The EKG showed no heart disease or damage ("yet," he added) but, unlike the internist in L.A., he prescribed not pills but a program of exercise and diet conducted at something called a Stress Lab at Massachusetts General Hospital. I went out of fear, grumbling all the way, wanting a chilled glass of dry white wine instead.

When I came back to Boston a month later, after finishing (or in some cases giving up or fleeing from) my business in Los Angeles, the last thing I wanted to do was return to that damned stress clinic and start their Exercycle program. The principal exercise I had been engaged in the past few years was carrying from the car to the house the case of Almaden chablis half gallons I bought every week as basic sustenance. I was in grief over the breakup of my seven-year relationship that had not survived my move back East from L.A., which was followed a week later by my father's death. The only way I knew how to ease the pain was by drowning it with alcohol, the same "cure" I'd been using for nearly a quarter of a century. I had not done anything for my physical health since I left Boy Scout Camp Chank-tun-un-gi the summer of '48, and only some frayed, shrunken instinct for survival enabled me to make myself go back to see the Exercycle people.

I told Dr. Howard Hartley, the director of the Stress Lab, and the nurse who assisted him, Jane Sherwood, that I was going through a difficult time, I was drinking a lot of wine, and that I did not intend to stop or even cut down. I thought this might provoke them and get me out of the whole thing, but neither of them even blinked. Dr. Hartley was a quiet, thoughtful man about my own age with graying hair and my own sort of Midwestern accent, and Jane was an attractive young blond woman who seemed genuinely concerned about my health. They had disappointed my preconceptions (based on painful experience) about medical people as condescending martinets, and even my aggressive announcement about wine consumption failed to rattle them. Dr. Hartley said all they were asking me to do at that point was work out on the Exercycle a half hour every day, or at least three times a week. I gruffly said if I was going to do it at all I would do the damn thing every day.

I rode for dear life. I rode for my life when I wondered if trying to save it or keep it together was worth the effort. I rode in a fifth-floor walkup apartment I had sublet on Beacon Hill that stifling summer of 1980 in stuffy heat broken by sudden dark thunderstorms that crashed around me like the pieces of my life breaking apart. I rode on a BH Home Bike my old friend Shaun O'Connell helped me buy in some suburban mall sporting goods store and lugged up the stairs for me on a day I was so depressed that after assembling the bike, while I looked on in a sort of paralysis of will, he turned to me before leaving and said in the most optimistic summation of my situation he could muster: "Well, at least you're alive."

I rode watching "All My Children" on a portable black and white television set to see other people's problems in hopes of temporarily forgetting my own; I rode while reading Henri Troyat's biography of Tolstoy and was cheered to learn that the author of *War and Peace* took up bicycle riding for his health at age sixty-seven (he read *Scientific Notes on the Action of the Velocipede as Physical Exercise* by L. K. Popov) and that he and his wife Sonya kept records of their pulse rates in their respective journals, especially noting the elevation after domestic arguments. ("After she left he felt his pulse . . . and noted 'Ninety.'") I rode every day, as ritually as I guzzled my wine every night, and sometimes at lunch to help me make it through to "cocktail time." I rode on days when I didn't even want to get out of bed or get dressed, I rode when I couldn't yet begin the rewrite of the script I had to do to make enough money to pay the rent, I rode when I had a hangover and feared any exertion would make me sick. I rode because some vital if battered part of me wanted to survive, and more than that to live, and when everything else seemed illusory or elusive and out of my control, I knew there was one specific thing I could do to help myself, to keep going, and that was to ride the damned bike. I did it, each day, and nothing I had ever done felt quite so essential as gripping those handlebars and holding on.

There was consolation in being back not only in Boston but in my old neighborhood, the Hill; walking down the main drag of Charles Street, I knew how a soldier felt returning home from war. Old neighbors stopped to shake my hand, and merchants greeted me with welcome and asked what they could do to help me get settled again ("rehabilitated," I thought of it). Ed Jones, a bachelor I thought of as

"King of the Hill," reintroduced me to the regulars at the bar of the Charles Restaurant, and it seemed a haven and shelter, comfortably friendly and dim.

That sodden summer was shot through with shafts of the most intense and unexpected joy, like the moment I came up out of the subway at Harvard Square to the strains of Bach being vigorously played in the foyer of the Coop for coins by street musicians with violins and cellos and it felt like being bathed with love; and the evening Joe Massik took us sailing out of Boston Harbor and we watched the sun go down and the lights come on in the towers downtown like golden signals. Afterward we went to Brandy Pete's for huge platters of chicken and pasta and baskets of fresh bread, and I felt fed as well by friendship and fortune of place.

That fall I found an apartment up on Mt. Vernon Street with big bay windows that looked out on another brick building across the street and a tree, just as I'd dreamed of in Hollywood. I got out the novel whose pages were stiff from the damp of my poolside studio—it felt like something exhumed—and set to work, with the Hill serving not only as home but as inspiration. I could see a slice of the Boston Common from the window I faced when I worked, and as the late autumn sky above it turned the cold royal purple and silver-gray colors I remembered and loved, I told myself I had to finish the book to earn the money—the privilege—of staying on and living here. The Hill was family, too. When my mother died in early November Ed Jones gathered friends from the neighborhood who mourned with me; he made a stew and we drank and dined, and I was comforted. They drove me to the airport and met me when I returned. Home.

Just by moving back to Boston my pulse went down from 120 to 100, and after faithfully riding the Exercycle for three months it was down to the eighties. I was elated by actually making an improvement in my physical condition for the first time in my life, an accomplishment that prompted me to tell Dr. Hartley I'd be willing to try the diet he recommended (a high-complex-carbohydrate regime with no oil, butter, or fat, similar to but not as strict and restrictive as the Pritikin diet). I would try it with the proviso, of course, that I could still drink all the wine I wanted. They told me to do the best I could. In another three months I had lost eighteen pounds and felt almost as miraculously lean as my idol Paul Newman in *The Hustler.*

My faith in Dr. Hartley and Jane Sherwood was now so awesome that they could have asked me to do the impossible, and they did.

They asked me to stop drinking for a month. No alcohol of any kind. No wine. Not a glass, not a sip. Zilch. Cold turkey. Why, I wondered, was such an extreme (inhuman) measure necessary? Dr. Hartley explained that, while they were very pleased with my progress—the weight loss, the increased "work load" as measured on their Exercycle stress test, and my pulse down to the eighties—they felt that, in line with this very improvement, my pulse should really now be in the sixties. They said the only factor they could think of that was keeping it above that was the wine consumption, and they wanted to see for sure if that were true. The only way to find out was for me to stop consuming it for a month.

The longest stretch of time I had done without a drink in twenty years was one week, and the four occasions on which I had performed such a miracle of abstinence had been the most extreme tests of my character, will power, and stamina. In fact, they were torture. I had not had the DTs, but I had suffered such anguish, such torment of desire, such depths of deprivation, that the idea of holding out a day or even an hour longer seemed impossible. Now I was being asked to do it for a month.

I said I would start tomorrow. Declaring it was like diving off the high board; I had to do it right away without thinking or I'd never get up the courage. Dr. Hartley pointed out that this was the end of November, and I'd be having to endure this unaccustomed sobriety during the most difficult time of all, the holiday season. Perhaps I'd prefer to put it off to the first of the year. "No," I said, "I am perverse, and the fact that this is more difficult, that it goes against the grain of society, will somehow make it easier for me." I would start the next day, I pledged, and I meant it.

That night I found one of my drinking pals, a regular from the Charles Restaurant bar, and asked her to join me for a final fling. I was going to load up for the holidays, get loaded in order to endure, as if I could so soak myself in wine that it would somehow sustain me through the dry period. I did my best. I guzzled and gulped, I drank with steady purpose at favorite neighborhood bards, then bought us a half gallon of cheap dry white that I lugged up to my friend's apartment. I poured the stuff down as though I were trying to extinguish a fire (the fear of going without for so long).

I woke not knowing at first who or where I was. Me. Boston. Beacon Hill. My friend's living-room couch. Ouch. I sank back down, dizzy. This was a beaut, this was one of the worst pounding hangovers in my painfully hung-over history. I reeled to the refrigerator for orange juice, gulped, gasped, and flopped back down on the couch. The traumas of the past year began to bloom in my head, and I sought some way of turning them off. It was too early to tune in television in hopes of having my mind blasted empty by the tube, for my faithful drinking companion was still asleep in her bed. Instead, I groped for a magazine or book, some distracting piece of reading matter from the coffee table by the couch where I lay.

I picked up off the top of a pile a book I had never seen before. It turned out to be a journal with sketches that Françoise Sagan had kept while taking the cure in an alcoholic dry-out clinic. It was not the youthfully bittersweet romance of *Bonjour Tristesse*. It was gritty, tough experience, painful and true. Too true. Too close to the mark of the path on which I was painfully about to embark. But so true I couldn't stop reading, either. It was like a personal letter to a fellow boozer on the brink of trying the cure. The last entry, made when the author was sobered and clean and ready to leave, seemed like a message to sustain me in the dry month ahead, a goal to think about during my thirty days in the wilderness of sobriety, a goal that must have seemed as distant and as painful to reach for Mlle. Sagan when she started her cure as it did to me at that moment, but one whose attainment would indeed be worth every deprivation, every exercise of discipline, every resource of nerve and courage it was possible to summon:

"Now I begin to live and write in earnest."

Just before Christmas I was sitting in The Sevens, a neighborhood bar on Charles Street, drinking a mug of coffee while friends sipped their beers. I didn't mind being in bars and around other people who were drinking while I was on the wagon, in fact I preferred it. I was comfortable in the atmosphere, and if I couldn't drink any booze at least I could inhale its nirvanic scents and maybe I even got a kind of "contact high" as musicians were said to do off others smoking grass. A house painter named Tony who was sitting at the table with me and some other neighbors remarked out of the blue that he'd like to go to mass somewhere on Christmas Eve. I didn't say anything, but a thought came into my mind, as swift and unexpected as it was unfamiliar: *I'd like to do that too.*

Since leaving my boyhood Protestant faith as a rebellious Columbia College intellectual more than a quarter century before, I had only once gone to church. Yet I found myself that Christmas Eve in King's

Chapel, which I finally selected from the ads on the Boston *Globe* religion page because it seemed least threatening. It was Unitarian, I knew the minister slightly as a neighbor, and I assumed "Candlelight Service" meant nothing more religiously challenging than carol singing.

As it happened, the Reverend Carl Scovel gave a sermon about "the latecomers" to the Church on a text from an Evelyn Waugh novel called *Helena*. There was a passage in which Helena, the mother of Constantine, addressed the magi, the three wise men who came late to the manger to bring their gifts to the Christ child, and it ended like this:

" 'You are my special patrons,' said Helena, 'and patrons of all latecomers, of all who have had a tedious journey to make to the truth, of all who are confused with knowledge and speculation, of all who through politeness make themselves partners in guilt, of all who stand in danger by reason of their talents. . . .

" 'For His sake who did not reject your curious gifts, pray always for the learned, the oblique, the delicate. Let them not be quite forgotten at the Throne of God when the simple come into their kingdom.' "

I slunk down in my pew, literally beginning to shiver from what I thought was only embarrassment at feeling singled out for personal attention, and discomfort at being in alien surroundings. It turned out that I had a temperature of 102 that kept me in bed for three days with a violent case of the flu and a fearful suspicion that church was a very dangerous place, at least if you weren't used to it.

Maybe my flesh was rebelling against not only the unaccustomed intrusion of spirit but the equally unusual exclusion of alcoholic spirits from my system. For the first time in my adult life I went without wassail through the Yuletide, strictly keeping my pledge of abstinence from alcohol—though the help of a small stash of marijuana from a friend kept it from being a truly cold-turkey Christmas season.

I showed up for my stress test appointment the last day of my most stressful year with my blood completely pure of booze, and Dr. Hartley counted my pulse at an even sixty, exactly as he had predicted it ought to be if I cut out the wine. I was both elated to have reached this healthy rate and disturbed at what it meant. Dr. Hartley's suspicion was correct: the wine was acting as a stimulant to my sympathetic nervous system (the part of the nervous system that controls the heart and blood vessels) and keeping my pulse elevated. Before I could get depressed at the distressing implication—it obviously meant cutting wine drastically down if not altogether out of my daily diet if I wanted to maintain my healthy heartbeat—I took the Exercycle stress test. When I finished pumping and sweating through the last stationary miles, Jane Sherwood announced with elation that I had increased my "work load" by a third, from 120 to 180 watts (units of power generated), since starting the program eight months before.

I was exhilarated by making such dramatic improvement and immediately felt competitive. I wanted to know where I stood now in relation to *other* people, and Jane hurried to her files, coming back smiling and waving a folder. The Stress Lab people kept records of different professional groups they tested, and Jane said proudly I was now "stronger than the average fireman!" I felt like Marvelous Marvin Hagler after winning his first middleweight crown. It was the first time in my life I'd been demonstrably stronger physically than any person or group. The giddy feeling (like a new kind of high) made me think the unthinkable: maybe I could really cut down permanently on my daily wine consumption.

I began to keep a record of my wine intake and how it affected my heart rate. I discovered that if I drank one or two glasses of wine in an evening my pulse was the same the next morning, but if I had more than two glasses my pulse would be higher than it was before drinking the wine the night before. I tried to keep from drinking more than two (well, sometimes three) glasses in an evening, switching to diet tonic before dinner, and coffee after (in the past I rarely drank coffee because it cut the effect of the wine). I began to enjoy the feeling of sobriety, of mornings without hangovers, and a sense of being able to exercise some kind of control over myself. In this new, clearheaded condition, I began to think about other aspects of my life besides the physical that I hadn't considered for a long time. I began to think again about church.

After my Christmas Eve experience at King's Chapel, I was both intrigued and apprehensive about church, and I didn't get up the nerve to go back again until Easter. I did not have any attacks of shivering or chills in the spring sunshine of that service, so it seemed that, even as a "latecomer" and former avowed atheist, I could safely enter a place regarded as a house of God. Still, the prospect was discomforting. My two initial trips of return had been on major holidays, occasions when "regular" people went to church, simply in observance of tradition. To go back again meant crossing the Boston Common on a non-holiday Sunday morning wearing a suit and tie, a giveaway sign of churchgoing. I did it furtively, as if I were engaged in something that would not be approved of by my peers. I hoped they would all be home doing brunch and the Sunday papers, so I would not be "caught in the act." I recalled the remark of William F. Buckley, Jr., in a television interview that if you mention God more than once at New York dinner parties you aren't invited back.

To my surprise, I recognized neighbors and even some people I considered friends at church, on a "regular" Sunday. I had simply assumed I did not know people who went to church, yet here they were, with intellects intact, worshiping God. Once inside the church myself, I understood the appeal. No doubt my friends and neighbors found, as I did, relief and refreshment in connecting with age-old rituals, reciting psalms and singing hymns. There was a calm reassurance in the stately language of litanies and chants in the Book of Common Prayer (King's Chapel is "Unitarian in theology, Anglican in worship, and Congregational in governance," a historical Boston amalgam that became three centuries old in 1986). I was grateful for the sense of shared reverence, of reaching beyond one's flimsy physical presence, while praying with a whole congregation.

The connection of church and neighborhood reinforced one another, gave depth and dimension to the sense of "home" that I had felt so cut off from in Hollywood. Church was not just an abstraction or a separate enclave of my life but a part of the place where I lived, connected with people I knew and encountered in my daily (not just Sunday) life. I think the deep sense of pleasure and solace of *place* I derived from returning to the neighborhood was—along with my physical improvement—part of the process of calming and reassembling myself that nurtured the desire to go to church.

When I lived on the Hill before, I enjoyed it but took it for granted. This time I appreciated it, plugged myself into its rituals. I bought my first pair of ice skates since childhood and on winter afternoons slid precariously but happily over the frozen pond in the Public Garden. I looked up Steve Olesky, my old neighbor from Myrtle Street, a lawyer who served as president of the Beacon Hill Civic Association (he also turned out to be a member of King's Chapel), and volunteered to cook at their annual pancake breakfast in the spring. When I burned my thumb flipping blueberry pancakes at that event, just as I had in years past, I knew I was really back. And I knew by then that I had managed to resuscitate my novel as well as myself.

• • •

How nice it would be if exiles could end their troubles and live happily ever after simply by coming home. But those are the endings of fairy tales. We aren't told what happened to the prodigal son after his father welcomed him back, but the anger of his jealous older brother does not portend a future of sweetness and light. As fulfilling as it was for me to return to Boston and begin a new phase of life in better physical health, it did not make everything smooth. As the usual trials of life continued, I went to King's Chapel not only for inspiration but for solace, a respite from the all too common afflictions of the human condition, from broken furnaces to broken hearts, from bad dreams to flu and taxes.

I began to appreciate what was meant by the Church as "sanctuary." The word itself took on new resonance for me; when I later heard of the "sanctuary" movement of churches offering shelter to Central American political refugees, I thought of the kind of private refuge that fortunate citizens like myself find in church from the daily assaults of pressures and worries, the psychic guerrilla warfare of everyday life.

Caught in an escalation of panic and confusion in my own professional campaigns (more painful because so clearly brought on by my own blundering), I joined the Church in May of 1982, not wanting to wait until the second Christmas Eve anniversary of my entry, as I had planned. I wanted the immediate sense of safety and refuge implied in belonging, being a member—perhaps like getting a passport and fleeing to a powerful embassy in the midst of some chaotic revolution.

Going to church, even belonging to it, did not solve life's problems—if anything, they seemed to escalate again around that time—but it gave me a sense of living in a larger context, of being part of something greater than what I could see through the tunnel vision of my personal concerns. I now looked forward to Sunday because it *meant* going to church; what once was strange now felt not only natural but essential. Even more remarkably, the practice of regular attendance at Sunday services, which such a short time ago seemed religiously "excessive," no longer seemed enough. Whatever it was I was getting from church on Sunday mornings, I wanted—needed, it felt like—*more*.

I experienced what is a common phenomenon for people who in some way or other begin a journey of the kind I so unexpectedly found myself on—a feeling simply and best described as a "thirst" for spiritual understanding and contact; to put it bluntly, I guess, *for God.* I noticed in the church bulletin an announcement of a Bible-study class in the parish house, and I went one stormy autumn evening to find myself with only the church's young seminarian on hand and one other parishioner. Rather than being disappointed by the tiny turnout, as I ordinarily would have been, I thought of the words "Where two or three are gathered together in my name, there am I in the midst of them," and I felt an interior glow that the pouring rain outside and occasional claps of thunder only made seem more vital and precious. I don't remember what text we studied that evening, but I can still smell the rain and the coffee and feel the aura of light and warmth.

Later in the season I attended a Bible-study session the minister led for a gathering of about twenty people on the story of Abraham and Isaac, and I came away with a sense of the awesomeness and power of faith, a quality that loomed above me as tremendous and challenging and tangibly real as mountains. The Bible-study classes, which I later, with other parishioners, learned to lead on occasion myself, became a source of power, like tapping into a rich vein.

Bible study was not like examining history but like holding up a mirror to my own life, a mirror in which I sometimes saw things I was trying to keep hidden, even from myself. The first Scripture passage I was assigned to lead was from Luke, about the man who cleans his house of demons, and seven worse ones come. I did not have any trouble relating this to "contemporary life." It sounded unnervingly like an allegory about a man who had stopped drinking and so was enjoying much better health, but took up smoking marijuana to "relax," all the while feeling good and even self-righteous about giving up the booze. It was my own story. I realized, with a shock, how I'd been deceiving myself, how much more "housecleaning" I had to do.

. . .

I cannot pinpoint any particular time when I suddenly believed in God again. I only know that such belief came to seem as natural as for all but a few stray moments of twenty-five or more years before it had been inconceivable. I realized this while looking at fish.

I had gone with my girl friend to the New England Aquarium, and as we gazed at the astonishingly brilliant colors of some of the small tropical fish—reds and yellows and oranges and blues that seemed to be splashed on by some innovative artistic genius—and watched the amazing lights of the flashlight fish that blinked on like the beacons of some creature of a sci-fi epic, I wondered how anyone could think that all this was the result of some chain of accidental explosions! Yet I realized in frustration that to try to convince me otherwise five years before would have been hopeless. Was this what they called "conversion"?

The term bothered me because it suggested being "born again" and, like many of my contemporaries, I had been put off by the melodramatic nature of that label, as well as the current political beliefs that seemed to go along with it. Besides, I didn't *feel* "reborn." No voice came out of the sky nor did a thunderclap strike me on the path through the Boston Common on the way to King's Chapel. I was relieved when our minister explained that the literal translation of "conversion" in both Hebrew and Greek is not "rebirth" but "turning." That's what my own experience felt like—as if I'd been walking in one direction and then, in response to some inner pull, I turned— not even all the way around, but only at what seemed a slightly different angle.

I hoped the turning would put me on a straight, solid path with blue skies above and a warm, benevolent sun shining down all the time. I certainly enjoyed better health than when I began to "turn" back in 1980, but the new path I found myself on seemed often as dangerous and difficult as the one I'd been following before. Sometimes it didn't even seem like a path at all. Sometimes I felt like a hapless passenger in the sort of small airplane they used to show in black and white movies of the 1930s, caught in a thunderstorm, bobbing through the night sky over jagged mountains without a compass.

·   ·   ·

There was a period around four years after I returned to church that I felt as if finally, with God's help, I was on the right track in my own journey. Then I had an experience that was like running head on into a wall. I turned down a lucrative opportunity to write a movie script because it would have meant making a series of trips back to Los Angeles. I knew I never wanted to live there again, but this would have meant only four or five week-long trips (or so I was assured, though I feared I might be drawn back into the Hollywood orbit by its own powerful suction). I prayed intensely, and felt it was not right to go, but then as soon as I made the decision I fell into panic, fearing I had unnecessarily rejected money I sorely needed. Then I questioned my own prayer, and wondered if in fact I was only reacting to fear, instead of to God's will that I was trying so hard to discern and follow. Or was I simply a fool to try to make business decisions based on prayer?

My agony over what I had done and why I had really done it was made more intense by the question of God in the midst of it all and the fear that I might be misusing Him for my own self-justifications. I felt a sort of psychic pain as unrelenting as a dentist's drill. In the torment I prayed, and there was no relief, and twice I turned back to my old way of dealing with things, by trying to numb the pain with drugs. Throughout all this I never lost faith in God, never imagined He was not there, but only that His presence was obscured. Then the storm broke, like a fever, and I felt in touch again, and in the light. I was grateful, but I also knew that such storms of confusion and inner torment would come again, perhaps even more violently.

I learned that belief in God did not depend on how well things were going, that faith and prayer and good works did not necessarily have any correlation to earthly reward or even tranquillity, no matter how much I wished they would and thought they should. I believed in God because the gift of faith (if not the gift of understanding) was given me, and I went to church and prayed and meditated to try to be closer to His presence and, most difficult of all, to discern His will. I knew, as it said in the Book of Common Prayer, that His "service is perfect freedom," and my greatest frustration was in the constant choices of how best to serve.

· · ·

In times of anguish it was hard to have the faith of an Abraham, and difficult to be reassured by doubts when I seemed to be walking in darkness. Yet there I was, like everyone else, having emerged from all sorts of crises and heartbreak and traumas, events that seemed to have insured my destruction or at least any chance of ever feeling joyous and fulfilled again, and I had gone on, and felt renewed and hopeful all over again, and the very pits of despair most often seemed to have been entries to the next unexpected, unimaginable (while in the pit) emergence and rebirth.

I did not come to thing that "everything works out for the best," certainly not in the earthly, egocentric terms by which we judge the occurrences of our lives, or in the way that the larger events of the tumultuous world of wars and earthquakes, murders and plagues, affect us personally. I was fascinated most by the mystery of it, and of how, to paraphrase William Faulkner, we so often not only endure but prevail.

from *DEBORAH, GOLDA, AND ME: BEING FEMALE AND JEWISH IN AMERICA*

LETTY COTTIN POGREBIN

When her adored mother dies a rapid death from cancer, a fifteen-year-old Letty Cottin Pogrebin experiences not only the pain of this loss but rejection by her father and her religious tradition when she needs them the most. In these selections from Deborah, Golda, and Me, *Pogrebin, a founding editor of* Ms. *magazine and a best-selling author, vividly recalls how, after years as her father's star pupil studying Hebrew, Talmud, and midrash, his refusal to allow her to say* kaddish, *the prayer for the dead, for her mother, alienates her from her family and from Judaism for years to come.*

FEBRUARY 3, 1955. It is an ordinary school night except that my mother is not home; she is in the hospital. After supper, my father takes me into his study, closes the door, and offers me one of his Luckies. He flicks his Zippo lighter for both of us to draw from the flame. I know something terrible is coming. Until now, I had only smoked behind his back. His gesture tells me I am about to be addressed as an adult.

"Your mother has cancer," he says.

There is no preamble. He prides himself on going straight to the point. "The doctors say she has less than six months to live. You'll have to be very helpful and very brave."

That's it. And that matter-of-fact attitude marks his behavior after we bring Mommy home from the hospital to die slowly and painfully in their bedroom. During the whole ordeal, he takes care of things in his no-nonsense, efficient way. There are treatments and medications, doctors to consult, a housekeeper and nurse to hire. No time for reflection. No room for feelings, or ceremony, or despair.

"We all die sometime," he says.

But not my Mommy. Not this wonderful, giving woman who sacrifices for everyone else. Not my mother.

"No use complaining about what we can't help."

But you can help me get through this. Talk to me. Hug me.

"The best thing we can do is to go on with our lives."

And he does.

April 20, 1955. She dies during the night. There are tears in my father's eyes when he awakens me. I won't say he *cries* but they are, to my knowledge, his first tears. He says I can go into their room and kiss my mother goodbye. Then he shifts into his lawyerly mode, making phone calls, giving out assignments, complaining about how much detail work is required by death and dying. Even the modest requirements of a Jewish burial, he says, are too elaborate. "Don't do any of this for me, I just want to be cremated."

(Twenty-seven years later, he is cremated—according to his wishes, and contrary to Jewish law.)

Our week at home sitting *shiva* (the seven days of mourning) is interminable for him. He is impatient with the daytime inactivity, the constant flow of visitors, and the mountains of food accumulating on the kitchen counter. During the evening memorial service, however, he comes into his own. He leads the prayers.

One night, about twenty people are milling about the house, but by Jewish computation, there are only nine Jews in our living room. This is because only nine men have shown up for the memorial service. A minyan, the quorum required for Jewish communal prayer, calls for ten men.

"I know the Hebrew," I say. "You can count *me,* Daddy."

I meant, *I want to count.* I meant, don't count me out just because I am a girl.

"You know it's not allowed," he replies, frowning.

"For my own mother's Kaddish I can be counted in the minyan. For God's sake, it's *your* house! It's *your* minyan, Daddy."

"Not allowed!" says my father.

He calls the synagogue and asks them to send us a tenth man.

May 1955. My father gives away my mother's things. Barely out of childhood, grieving, I do not think to petition for a hope chest of her clothes, or her paintings, or the books, china, or costume jewelry that were precious to her. Unmindful that I might someday have a home of my own and wish to own concrete mementos of my mother's life, my father lets the relatives pick through her closets and drawers like scavengers at a flea market. He lets them load their arms and pack their cars and take away her history.

Summer 1956. I find out that my father has sold our house and most of our furniture. He never asks me how I feel about it. He never gives me the chance to say what objects have special meaning to me. It does not occur to him that I might think of the contents of our house as mine and hers, as well as his.

Everything is sold before I know it. At first, I do not understand. And then I understand. He is getting married. He gets married. His new wife is a Southern belle with an exaggerated drawl, Jewish but unschooled in Judaism and unobservant, fifty-four years old but relentlessly girlish and charming—and self-centered to a fault. She is given to dramatic color-coordinated outfits and dyed black hair styled sleek as patent leather into a chignon at the top of her head. I am in my peasant-blouse-and-black-stockings Bohemian phase. She and I have nothing in common but our mutual distrust. Her Southern baby talk is insufferable. She manipulates my father who dotes on her, serves her, tolerates her domestic ineptitude, seems enchanted by her glamour and helplessness. She is to my mother as polyester is to pure silk. She is a phony. I hate my father's wife. It does not occur to me to hate him for choosing her.

They rent an apartment. The apartment has one bedroom. There is a daybed for me in the foyer. I am a freshman in college. I don't need a whole bedroom just for school vacations, do I? It is clear the new wife doesn't want me around. What my father wants is not at all clear to me anymore.

. . .

November 1958. I needn't dredge up other such recollections. You get the point. That's the Other Father, the one I have to reconcile with the good Daddy before I can fully understand myself and, most particularly, my relationship to Judaism.

In the years after my mother died, incident after incident left me feeling confused and betrayed. At first, I excused my father's behavior, blaming his maleness for his mindless insensitivities, blaming his new wife for everything else. Gradually, it became clear to me that "his behavior" was who he was. I lowered my expectations. It didn't help . . . I withdrew. I closed up. I stopped hoping. This might have been a manageable psychological problem if it had not become an untenable spiritual one.

Somehow, father and faith had gotten all mixed up; I could not separate them. I couldn't mark where one began and the other ended. Both were male-gendered sources of rewarding power. My religion was personified by my Daddy, and I was socially enmeshed in a Jewish world controlled by Jewish men. Whatever honors I had been given or denied were granted or withheld by Jewish men. The creators of historical consciousness and the guardians of privilege were Jewish men like my father, often my father himself. When it suited his needs, Daddy had taken me into his realms; I was *his* little scholar, *his* Bat Mitzvah girl. But when it mattered to *me* to be included, he had exercised his masculine right to shut me out.

In a matter of months, this man who was once my adored mentor had revealed himself to be self-centered, unfeeling—almost a stranger. Because father and faith had been so intertwined, it was only logical that when I broke away from the enchantment of my father, I also cut off my formal affiliation with Judaism. Merge the Jewish patriarch with patriarchal Judaism and when you leave one, you leave them both.

For years, I stayed away from organized Judaism, from the institutionalized Judaism of my father. I married a Jewish man who had never been Bar Mitzvah'd. I raised a Jewish son and two Jewish daughters but did not have a Bar or Bat Mitzvah for any of them. I suppose I did not want those I loved to be covenanted in the faith of the father who betrayed me, the faith that left me out.

Over time, I reconnected to Jewish life. . . . But I have yet to deal with Daddy. The Other Father keeps getting in my way.

.   .   .

"Jew" means man, because males are the only Jews who *count*—literally. I learned this when I was most vulnerable, when I wanted to count—to be counted as a Jew. It didn't matter that I was my father's intellectual heir, my mother's daughter, an educated Jewish student, and a Bat Mitzvah girl. None of it mattered. I may as well have been a Christian, Muslim, or Druze.

A strange man was called in to say Kaddish for my mother, because he was more a "Jew" than I.

In those first weeks after losing my mother I needed to lean on my religion, crawl into its arms, rock myself to Hebrew rhythms as familiar to me as rain. But how could I mourn as a Jew if my Kaddish did not count?

The answer is, I could not.

I refused to be an illegitimate child in my own religion. I could not be a ghost in the minyan. If I did not count, I would not stay.

I mourned as a daughter, and left Judaism behind.

from *REFUGE*

TERRY TEMPEST WILLIAMS

In Refuge: An Unnatural History of Family and Place, *writer and naturalist Terry Tempest Williams juxtaposes the perilous rise of the Great Salt Lake that endangers the wildlife that make it their home with the progression of her beloved mother's breast cancer and eventual death. Williams, who traces her Mormon lineage back to the original mid-nineteenth century Utah pioneers, interweaves meditations on mortality, faith, the sacred, and the interdependence of all life and all worlds—visible and invisible.*

IN MORMON culture, that is one of the things you do know—history and genealogy. I come from a family with deep roots in the American West. When the expense of outfitting several thousand immigrants to Utah was becoming too great for the newly established church, leaders decided to furnish the pioneers with small two-wheeled carts about the size of those used by apple peddlers, which could be pulled by hand from Missouri to the Salt Lake Valley. My ancestors were part of these original "handcart companies" in the 1850s. With faith, they would endure. They came with few provisions over the twelve-hundred-mile trail. It was a small sacrifice in the name of religious freedom. Almost one hundred and fifty years later, we are still here.

I am the oldest child in our family, a daughter with three younger brothers: Steve, Dan, and Hank.

My parents, John Henry Tempest, III, and Diane Dixon Tempest, were married in the Mormon Temple in Salt Lake City on September 18, 1953. My husband, Brooke Williams, and I followed the same tradition and were married on June 2, 1975. I was nineteen years old.

Our extended family includes both maternal and paternal grandparents: Lettie Romney Dixon and Donald "Sanky" Dixon, Kathryn Blackett Tempest and John Henry Tempest, Jr.

Aunts, uncles, and cousins are many, extending familial ties all across the state of Utah. If I ever wonder who I am, I simply attend a Romney family reunion and find myself in the eyes of everyone I meet. It is comforting and disturbing, at once.

I have known five of my great-grandparents intimately. They tutored me in stories with a belief that lineage mattered. Genealogy is in our blood. As a people and as a family, we have a sense of history. And our history is tied to land.

I was raised to believe in a spirit world, that life exists before the earth and will continue to exist afterward, that each human being, bird, and bulrush, along with all other life forms had a spirit life before it came to dwell physically on the earth. Each occupied an assigned sphere of influence, each has a place and a purpose.

It made sense to a child. And if the natural world was assigned spiritual values, then those days spent in wildness were sacred. We learned at an early age that God can be found wherever you are, especially outside. Family worship was not just relegated to Sunday in a chapel.

Our weekends were spent camped alongside a small stream in the Great Basin, in the Stansbury Mountains or Deep Creeks. My father would take the boys rabbit hunting while Mother and I would sit on a log in an aspen grove and talk. She would tell me stories of how when she was a girl she would paint red lips on the trunks of trees to practice kissing. Or how she would lie in her grandmother's lucerne patch and watch clouds.

"I have never known my full capacity for solitude," she would say.

"Solitude?" I asked.

"The gift of being alone. I can never get enough."

The men would return anxious for dinner. Mother would cook over a green Coleman stove as Dad told stories from his childhood—

like the time his father took away his BB gun for a year because he shot off the heads of every red tulip in his mother's garden, row after row after row. He laughed. We laughed. And then it was time to bless the food.

After supper, we would spread out our sleeping bags in a circle, heads pointing to the center like a covey of quail, and watch the Great Basin sky fill with stars. Our attachment to the land was our attachment to each other.

·   ·   ·

WHITE PELICANS

lake level:4209.09'

The Refuge is subdued, unusually quiet. The spring frenzy of court-ship and nesting is absent, because there is little food and habitat available. Although the species count remains about the same, indi-vidual numbers are down. Way down. This afternoon, I watched a white-faced ibis nest float alongside a drowned cottonwood tree. Three eggs had been abandoned. I did not see the adults.

A colony-nesting bird survey has been initiated this spring by the Utah Division of Wildlife Resources to monitor changes in population and habitat use of selected species affected by the rising Great Salt Lake.

The historical nesting grounds on the islands of Great Salt Lake are gone, with the exception of a California gull colony on Antelope Island and the white pelicans on Gunnison. This means colony nesters are now dependent upon the vegetation surrounding the lake for their livelihood.

Great blue herons, snowy egrets, cattle egrets, and double-crested cormorants use trees, tall shrubs, or man-made structures for nesting.

Franklin gulls, black-crowned night herons, and white-faced ibises nest in emergent vegetation such as bulrushes and cattails.

American avocets, black-necked stilts, and other shorebirds are ground nesters who usually scrape together a few sticks around clumps of low-lying vegetation such as salt grass and pickleweed.

Don Paul, waterfowl biologist for the Division of Wildlife Re-sources, anticipates that the white-faced ibis and Franklin gull popu-lations will be the hardest hit by the flood.

"Look around and tell me how many stands of bulrush you see?" He waves his hand over the Refuge. "It's gone, and I suspect, so are they. We should have our data compiled by the end of the summer."

I turn around three hundred and sixty degrees: water as far as I can see. The echo of Lake Bonneville lapping against the mountains returns.

The birds of Bear River have been displaced; so have I.

Nothing is familiar to me any more. I just returned home from the hospital, having had a small cyst removed from my right breast. Second time. It was benign. But I suffered the uncertainty of not knowing for days. My scars portend my lineage. I look at Mother and I see myself. Is cancer my path, too?

As a child, I was aware that my grandmother, Lettie, had only one breast. It was not a shocking sight. It was her body. She loved to soak in steaming, hot baths, and I would sit beside the tub and read her my favorite fairy tales.

"One more," she would say, completely relaxed. "You read so well."

What I remember is my grandmother's beauty—her moist, translucent skin, the way her body responded to the slow squeeze of her sponge, which sent hot water trickling over her shoulders. And I loved how she smelled like lavender.

Seeing Mother's scar did not surprise me either. It was not radical like her mother's. Her skin was stretched smooth and taut across her chest, with the muscles intact.

"It is an inconvenience," Mother said. "That's all."

When I look in the mirror and Brooke stands behind me and kisses my neck, I whisper in his ear, "Hold my breasts."

· · ·

WHISTLING SWAN

lake level: 4208.35'

The snow continues to fall. Red apples cling to bare branches.

I just returned from Tamra Crocker Pulfer's funeral. It was a reunion of childhood friends and family. Our neighborhood sat on wooden benches row after row in the chapel. I sat next to Mother and wondered how much time we had left together.

Walking the wrackline of Great Salt Lake after a storm is quite different from walking along the seashore after high tide. There are no shells, no popping kelp or crabs. What remains is a bleached narrative of feathers, bones, occasional birds encrusted in salt and deep piles of brine among the scattered driftwood. There is little human debris among the remote beaches of Great Salt Lake, except for the shotgun shells that wash up after the duck-hunting season.

Yesterday, I walked along the north shore of Stansbury Island. Great Salt Lake mirrored the plumage of immature gulls as they skimmed its surface. It was cold and windy. Small waves hissed each time they broke on shore. Up ahead, I noticed a large, white mound a few feet from where the lake was breaking.

It was a dead swan. Its body lay contorted on the beach like an abandoned lover. I looked at the bird for a long time. There was no blood on its feathers, no sight of gunshot. Most likely, a late migrant from the north slapped silly by a ravenous Great Salt Lake. The swan may have drowned.

I knelt beside the bird, took off my deerskin gloves, and began smoothing feathers. Its body was still limp—the swan had not been dead long. I lifted both wings out from under its belly and spread them on the sand. Untangling the long neck which was wrapped around itself was more difficult, but finally I was able to straighten it, resting the swan's chin flat against the shore.

The small dark eyes had sunk behind the yellow lores. It was a whistling swan. I looked for two black stones, found them, and placed them over the eyes like coins. They held. And, using my own saliva as my mother and grandmother had done to wash my face, I washed the swan's black bill and feet until they shone like patent leather.

I have no idea of the amount of time that passed in the preparation of the swan. What I remember most is lying next to its body and imagining the great white bird in flight.

I imagined the great heart that propelled the bird forward day after day, night after night. Imagined the deep breaths taken as it lifted from the arctic tundra, the camaraderie within the flock. I imagined the stars seen and recognized on clear autumn nights as they navigated south. Imagined their silhouettes passing in front of the full face of the harvest moon. And I imagined the shimmering Great Salt Lake calling the swans down like a mother, the suddenness of the storm, the anguish of its separation.

And I tried to listen to the stillness of its body.

At dusk, I left the swan like a crucifix on the sand. I did not look back.

.   .   .

There is something unnerving about my solitary travels around the northern stretches of Great Salt Lake. I am never entirely at ease because I am aware of its will. Its mood can change in minutes. The heat alone reflecting off the salt is enough to drive me mad, but it is the glare that immobilizes me. Without sunglasses, I am blinded. My eyes quickly burn on Salt Well Flats. It occurs to me that I will return home with my green irises bleached white. If I return at all.

The understanding that I could die on the salt flats is no great epiphany. I could die anywhere. It's just that in the foresaken corners of Great Salt Lake there is no illusion of being safe. You stand in the throbbing silence of the Great Basin, exposed and alone. On these occasions, I keep tight reins on my imagination. The pearl-handled pistol I carry in my car lends me no protection. Only the land's mercy and a calm mind can save my soul. And it is here I find grace.

It's strange how deserts turn us into believers. I believe in walking in a landscape of mirages, because you learn humility. I believe in living in a land of little water because life is drawn together. And I believe in the gathering of bones as a testament to spirits that have moved on.

If the desert is holy, it is because it is a forgotten place that allows us to remember the sacred. Perhaps that is why every pilgrimage to the desert is a pilgrimage to the self. There is no place to hide, and so we are found.

In the severity of a salt desert, I am brought down to my knees by its beauty. My imagination is fired. My heart opens and my skin burns in the passion of these moments. I will have no other gods before me.

Wilderness courts our souls. When I sat in church throughout my growing years, I listened to teachings about Christ in the wilderness for forty days and forty nights, reclaiming his strength, where he was able to say to Satan, "Get thee hence." When I imagined Joseph Smith kneeling in a grove of trees as he received his vision to create a new religion, I believed their sojourns into nature were sacred. Are ours any less?

There is a Mormon scripture, from the Doctrine and Covenants section 88:44-47, that I carry with me:

The earth rolls upon her wings, and the sun giveth
   his light by day, and the moon giveth her light
   by night, and the stars also give their light, as
   they roll upon their wings in their glory, in the
   midst of the power of God.
 Unto what shall I liken these kingdoms that ye may understand?
 Behold all these are kingdoms and any man who
   hath seen any or the least of these hath seen God
   moving in his majesty and power.

I pray to the birds.

I pray to the birds because I believe they will carry the messages of my heart upward. I pray to them because I believe in their existence, the way their songs begin and end each day—the invocations and benedictions of Earth. I pray to the birds because they remind me of what I love rather than what I fear. And at the end of my prayers, they teach me how to listen.

•   •   •

Dawn to dusk. I have spent the entire day with Mother. Lying next to her. Rubbing her back. Holding her fevered hand close to my face. Stroking her hair. Keeping ice on the back of her neck. She is so uncomfortable. We are trying to work with the pain.

Her jaw tightens. She cramps. And then she breathes.

I am talking her through a visualization, asking her to imagine what the pain looks like, what color it is, to lean into the sensation rather than resisting it. We breathe through the meditation together.

The light begins to deepen. It is sunset. I open the shutters, so Mother can see the clouds. I return to her bedside. She takes my hand and whispers, "Will you give me a blessing?"

In Mormon religion, formal blessings of healing are given by men through the Priesthood of God. Women have no outward authority. But within the secrecy of sisterhood we have always bestowed benisons upon our families.

Mother sits up. I lay my hands upon her head and in the privacy of women, we pray.

•   •   •

BALD EAGLES

lake level: 4211.10'

Rooted. Brooke and I have moved to Emigration Canyon Road, right smack on the trail that Brigham Young and the Latter-day Saints walked down on their way into the Salt Lake Valley.

We planted four Colorado blue spruces today. Housewarming gifts from Mother and Dad. I held the root ball of each tree and blessed them in this supple soil (so unusual for a wintry day), that they might become the guardians of our home.

Dad and Brooke waited impatiently as they leaned on their shovels.

"I'm sorry, Brooke." Dad said. "All this hocus-pocus did not come from me."

I looked at my father as I stood up and clapped the dirt from my hands. "Who are you kidding, Dad? You are the man who taught us as children about divining for water with sticks, taking us out to a job where you had hired a man as a waterwitch to find where a well might be dug."

"Come on, Terry."

"The way I look at it, John," Brooke said. "We're never going to figure it all out, so we might as well acknowledge the intangibles. Who knows, maybe these trees do have souls."

Mormon religion has roots firmly planted in a magical worldview. Divining rods, seer stones, astrology, and visions were all part of the experience of the founding Prophet, Joseph Smith.

Dowsing was viewed negatively by some clergymen, "not because it leads to treasure, but because it leads to information."

Divining rods were understood by many to be instruments of revelation, used not just to locate veins of water or minerals, but to shepherd answers to questions. In folk magic, a nod up meant yes, a lack of movement meant no. Joseph Smith was not only familiar with this tradition, he and his family were practitioners of it—along with use of seer stones, which they used for treasure seeking.

Critics of Mormonism have used this to cast doubt on the origins and faith of this American religion. They dismiss Joseph Smith's discovery of "the golden plates" buried near Palmyra, New York—which contained the holy doctrine translated in the Book of Mormon—as simply an extension of the treasure-hunting days of his youth.

Others claim that Smith's sensitivity to matters of the occult heightened his shamanistic gifts and contributed to his developing spirituality.

For me, it renders my religion human. I love knowing that Joseph Smith was a mystic who ascribed magical properties to animals and married his wives according to the astrological "mansions of the moon."

To acknowledge that which we cannot see, to give definition to that which we do not know, to create divine order out of chaos, is the religious dance.

I have been raised in a culture that believes in personal revelation, that it is not something buried and lost with ancient prophets of the Old Testament. In the early days of the Mormon Church, authority was found within the individual, not outside.

In 1971, when Mother was diagnosed with breast cancer, the doctors said she had less than a 20 percent chance of surviving two years. Mother did not know this. Dad did. I found out only because I overheard the conversation between my father and the doctors.

Months passed. Mother was healing. It was stake conference, a regional gathering of church members that meets four times a year. My father was a member of the stake high council, a group of high priests who direct the membership on both organizational and spiritual matters. President Thomas S. Monson, one of the Twelve Apostles, directly beneath the Prophet, who at that time was Joseph Fielding Smith, was conducting interviews for the position of stake president.

Before conference, President Monson met with my father privately, as he did with all councilmen. He asked him, if called, would he serve as stake president? My father's reply was no. In a religion that believes all leadership positions are decided by God, this was an unorthodox response.

"Brother Tempest, would you like to explain?"

My father simply said it would be inappropriate to spend time away from his wife when she had so little time left.

President Monson stood and said, "You are a man whose priorities are intact."

After conference, my father was returning to his car. He heard his name called, ignored it at first, until he heard it for a second time. He turned to find President Monson, who put his hand on Dad's shoulder.

"Brother Tempest, I feel compelled to tell you your wife will be well for many years to come. I would like to invite you and your family to kneel together in the privacy of your home at noon on Thursday. The Brethren will be meeting in the holy chambers of the Temple, where we will enter your wife's name among those to be healed."

Back home, our family was seated around the dinner table. Dad was late. Mother was furious. I'll never forget the look on his face when he opened the door. He walked over to Mother and held her tightly in his arms. He wept.

"What's happened, John?" Mother asked.

That Thursday, my brothers and I came home from school to pray. We knelt in the living room together as a family. No words were uttered. But in the quiet of that room, I felt the presence of angels.

"What would you have me know?" I asked. "Faith," my great-grandmother Vilate said to me. Mother and my grandmother Lettie and I were helping to pack up her apartment. She was moving herself to a retirement center. "Faith, my child. It is the first and sweetest principle of the gospel."

At the time, I did not appreciate her answer. Faith, to a college coed, was a denouncement of knowledge, a passive act more akin to resignation than resolve.

"Where would faith in the Vietnam War have gotten us? Or faith in the preservation of endangered species without legislation?" I argued.

"My darling, faith without works is dead."

That is all I remember of our discussion. But, today, the idea of faith returns to me. Faith defies logic and propels us beyond hope because it is not attached to our desires. Faith is the centerpiece of a connected life. It allows us to live by the grace of invisible strands. It is a belief in a wisdom superior to our own. Faith becomes a teacher in the absence of fact.

The four trees we planted will grow in the absence of my mother. Faith holds their roots, the roots I can no longer see.

. . .

BIRDS-OF-PARADISE

lake level: 4211.65'

Mother was buried yesterday.

These days at home have been a meditation as I have scoured sinks and tubs, picked up week-worn clothes, and vacuumed.

I have washed and wiped each dish by hand, dusted tables, even under the feet of figurines.

I notice my mother's hairbrush resting on the counter. Pulling out the nest of short, black hairs, I suddenly remember the birds.

I quietly open the glass doors, walk across the snow and spread the mesh of my mother's hair over the tips of young cottonwood trees—

For the birds—

For their nests—

In the spring.

"Wait here, I want to show you something . . ." My friend, who runs a trading post in Salt Lake City, disappeared into the back room and returned with a pair of moccasins.

They took my breath away. The moccasins were ankle-high and fully beaded, including the soles, which were an intricate design of snakes. Cut-glass beads: red, blue, and green, hand-sewn on white deerskin. As I carefully turned them, I wondered how anyone on earth could wear these. To walk in these moccasins would destroy the exquisite handwork.

An Indian woman who had been browsing, smelling the baskets of sweet grass, quietly walked over to the counter.

"Those are burial moccasins," she said. I handed one to her, but she would not touch it. "You won't see many of these."

My friend looked at the woman and then at me. "She's right. A Shoshone woman from Grantsville, ten miles south of Great Salt Lake, brought them in yesterday. They had just buried her grand-mother in Skull Valley with the best they had: a buffalo robe, pendle-ton blankets, jewelry, a beaded dress of buckskin, and the moccasins. The granddaughter made two pairs."

The Indian woman in the trading post identified herself as Chero-kee. She explained how, among her people, they sew only one bead on the soles of their burial moccasins.

I thought of the Mormon rituals that surround our dead: the care Mimi and I took in preparing Mother's body with essential oils and perfumes, the way we dressed her in the burial dress Ann had made of white French cotton; the high collar that disguised her weight loss, the delicate tucks from the neck down, the simple elegance of its lines. I recalled the silk stockings; the satin slippers; and the green satin apron, embroidered with leaves, symbolic of Eve and associated with sacred covenants made in the Mormon temple, that we tied around her waist—how it had been hand-sewn by my great-grandmother's sister at the turn of the century. A gift from Mimi. And then I remembered the white veil which framed Mother's face.

I tried to forget my encounter with the mortician in the hallway of the mortuary prior to the dressing, the way he led me down two flights of stairs, through the maze of coffins, and then abruptly drew the maroon velvet curtains that revealed Mother's body, now a carapace, naked, cold, and stiff, on a stainless-steel table. Her face had been painted orange. I asked him to remove the make-up. He told me it was not possible, that it would bruise the skin tissues. I told him I wanted it off if I had to remove it myself. The mortician left in disgust and returned with a rag drenched in turpentine. He reluctantly handed me the cloth and for one hour, I wiped my mother's face clean.

I remember arriving at the chapel early, so I could check on the flowers and have some meditative time with Mother's body before the funeral. The face paint was back on. I stood at the side of my mother's casket, enraged at our inability to let the dead be dead. And I wept over the hollowness of our rituals.

The same funeral director put his hand on my shoulder. I turned.

"I'm sorry, Mrs. Williams, she did not pass our inspection. We felt she had to have some color."

"Won't you sit down," he said. "Death is most difficult on the living."

"I'll stand, thank you." I said taking my handkerchief to Mother's face once again.

One by one, family members entered the room, walked to the open coffin and paid their respects. This was the first time my grandmother Lettie had seen her daughter since Christmas Eve. Confined to a wheelchair in a nursing home, her only contact had been by phone. My grandfather Sanky stood behind her with his hands on her shoulders. She mourned like no other.

As is customary in Mormon tradition, Steve and I brought the white veil down over Mother's face and tied the bow beneath her chin. I had hidden sprigs of forsythia down by her feet. The casket was closed. Dan and Hank placed the large bouquet of tulips, lilacs, roses, and lilies, across the top. Dad stood back, frozen with protocol.

Friends came to call. The line grew longer and longer. We became public greeters, entertaining their sorrow as we put aside our own.

I cannot escape these flashbacks. Some haunt. Some heal.

Today is Mother's birthday. March 7, 1987. She would be fifty-five. I lay one bird-of-paradise across her grave.

In a dugout canoe, Brooke and I paddle through a narrow channel of mangroves. A four-foot tiger heron peers out with golden eyes, more mysterious, perhaps, than any bird I have ever seen. The canal widens and we find ourselves in a salt water bay reminiscent of home.

We are in Rio Lagartos, Mexico.

Row upon row of flamingos are dancing with the current. It is a ballet. The flamingos closest to shore step confidently, heads down as they filter small molluscs, crustaceans, and algae through their bills before the water is expelled through either side. These are not quiet birds.

Behind the feeders, a corp de ballet tiptoes in line, flowing in the opposite direction like a feathered river. They too are nodding their heads, twittering, gliding with the black portion of their bills pointing upward. They move with remarkable syncopation.

American flamingos. Gray. White. Fuchsia and pink. They span the red spectrum. Feathers float in the water. Delicately. Brooke leans over the gunnels of the canoe and retrieves one. It contracts out of water. He blows it dry.

The birds are a pink brushstroke against the dark green mangroves. A flock flies over us, their necks extended with their long legs trailing behind them. Pure exotica. In the afternoon light, they become flames against a cloudless blue sky. Early taxonomists must have had the same impression: the Latin family name assigned to flamingos is *Phoenicopteridae,* derived from the phoenix, which rose from its ashes to live again.

There is a holy place in the salt desert, where egrets hover like angels. It is a cave near the lake where water bubbles up from inside the earth. I am hidden and saved from the outside world. Leaning against the back wall of the cave, the curve of the rock supports the curve of my spine. I listen:

Drip. Drip-drip. Drip. Drip. Drip-drip.

My skin draws moisture from the rocks as my eyes adjust to the darkness.

Ancient murals of ceremonial art bleed from the cavern walls. Pictographs of waterbirds decorate the interior of the cave. Herons, egrets, and cranes. Tadpoles and serpents stain the walls red. Human figures dance wildly, backs arched, hips thrust forward. A spear-thrower lunges toward fish. Beyond him stands a water-jug maiden faintly painted above ferns. So lucent are these forms on the weeping rocks, they could be smeared without thought.

I kneel at the spring and drink.

This is the secret den of my healing, where I come to whittle down my losses. I carve chevrons, the simple image of birds, on rabbit bones cleaned by eagles. And I sing without the embarrassment of being heard.

The men in my family have migrated south for one year to lay pipe in southern Utah.

My keening is for my family, fractured and displaced.

PINTAILS, MALLARDS, AND TEALS

lake level: 4211:85'

April 1, 1987. Great Salt Lake has peaked for the second time at 4211.85'.

The birds have abandoned the lake. Borders are fluid, not fixed. There is no point even driving out to the Refuge. For now it is ocean. I hardly know where I am.

Since Mother's death, I have been liberated from my optimism. I have nothing to hope for because what I hoped for is gone.

There are no mirages.

A Sunday morning in April. It is General Conference. A gathering of Saints. Mormons from all over the world convene on Temple Square to sit on the wooden pews of the tabernacle (pews stained to look like oak, even though they are pine) to hear the latest counsel and doctrine from the Brethren.

I drive by the cast-iron gates, heading west with the gulls. Red light on North Temple. I stop. With my windows rolled down, I can hear the Tabernacle Choir singing "Abide With Me, 'Tis Eventide," as it is being broadcast throughout the grounds.

Abide: to wait for; to endure without yielding; to bear patiently; to accept without objection; to remain in a stable or fixed state; to continue in a place. "Abide with me," I have sung this song all my life.

Once out at the lake, I am free. Native. Wind and waves are like African drums driving the rhythm home. I am spun, supported, and possessed by the spirit who dwells here. Great Salt Lake is a spiritual magnet that will not let me go. Dogma doesn't hold me. Wildness does. A spiral of emotion. It is ecstasy without adrenaline. My hair is tossed, curls are blown across my face and eyes, much like the whitecaps cresting over waves.

Wind and waves. Wind and waves. The smell of brine is burning in my lungs. I can taste it on my lips. I want more brine, more salt. Wet hands. I lick my fingers, until I am sucking them dry. I close my eyes. The smell and taste combined reminds me of making love in the Basin; flesh slippery with sweat in the heat of the desert. Wind and waves. A sigh and a surge.

I pull away from the lake, pause, and rest easily in the sanctuary of sage.

Ten miles east, General Conference is adjourned.

In Mormon theology, the Holy Trinity is comprised of God the Father, Jesus Christ the Son, and the Holy Ghost. We call this the Godhead.

Where is the Motherbody?

We are far too conciliatory. If we as Mormon women believe in God the Father and in his son, Jesus Christ, it is only logical that a Mother-in-Heaven balances the sacred triangle. I believe the Holy Ghost is female, although she has remained hidden, invisible, deprived of a body, she is the spirit that seeps into our hearts and directs us to the well. The "still, small voice" I was taught to listen to as a child was "the gift of the Holy Ghost." Today I choose to recognize this presence as holy intuition, the gift of the Mother. My prayers no longer bear the "proper" masculine salutation. I include both Father and Mother in Heaven. If we could introduce the Motherbody as a spiritual counterpoint to the Godhead, perhaps our inspiration and devotion would no longer be directed to the stars, but our worship could return to the Earth.

My physical mother is gone. My spiritual mother remains. I am a woman rewriting my genealogy.

EXPLORATION

and

ENCOUNTER

from *SALVATION ON SAND MOUNTAIN*

DENNIS COVINGTON

Southern-born journalist Dennis Covington travels to poor, white Appalachia to cover the murder trial of a Holiness snake-handling preacher, and finds himself inextricably drawn to their particular mix of religious dogma and ecstasy. In this excerpt from Salvation on Sand Mountain, *his vivid and often disturbing chronicle of his experiences with the handlers, Covington at last comes face to face with his own attraction to danger and surrender in the biggest rattlesnake he's ever seen.*

MY JOURNEY had come back around to the congregation on Sand Mountain, the remnant of Glenn Summerford's flock that had left the converted service station on Wood's Cove Road in Scottsboro and then met under a brush arbor in back of J.L. Dyal's house until the weather got too cold. After worshiping for a while in the basement of an old motel, they finally found a church for sale on the mountain. It was miles from nowhere, in the middle of a hay field south of Section, Alabama, home of Tammy Little, Miss Alabama 1984. The nearest dot on the map, though, was Macedonia, a crossroads consisting of a filling station, a country store, and a junk emporium. It was not the kind of place you'd visit of your own accord. You'd have to be led there. In fact, Macedonia had gotten its name from the place in the Bible that Paul had been called to go to in a dream. Paul's first European converts to Christianity had been in Macedonia. But that was, you know, a long time ago and in another place.

.   .   .

The church happened to be sited in the very center of a grove of old oak trees. Fields of hay surrounded the grove and stretched to the horizon. As you approached the church along a dirt road during summer heat, the oak grove looked like a dark island in the middle of a shimmering sea of gold and green.

That's the way it looked to me, anyway, on a bright Sunday morning in late June . . . when Jim and I drove up from Birmingham for their first annual homecoming. Brother Carl had invited us by phone and given us directions. He was scheduled to preach at the homecoming. Other handlers were coming from all over—from East Tennessee and South Georgia, from the mountains of Kentucky and the scrublands of the Florida panhandle. If we hadn't had Carl's directions, we'd never have found the place. The right turn off the paved road from Macedonia was unmarked. It was one of several gravel roads that angled off into the distance. Where it crossed another paved road, there finally was a sign, made of cardboard and mounted at waist level on a wooden stake. After that, the gravel turned to dirt. Dust coated the jimsonweed. The passionflowers were in bloom, and the blackberries had begun to ripen in the heat. There were no houses on this road, and no sound except for cicadas, a steady din, like the sound of approaching rain.

For once, Jim and I were early. We stepped up on a cement block to get through the back doorway of the church. The door itself was off its hinges, and none of the windows in the church had screens. There were no cushions on the pews and no ornaments of any kind, except a portrait of Jesus etched into a mirror behind the pulpit and a vase of plastic flowers on the edge of the piano bench, where a boy with a withered hand sat staring at the keys. We took our places on a back pew and watched the handlers arrive. They greeted each other with the holy kiss, women with women, men with men, as prescribed by Paul in Romans 16. Among them was the legendary Punkin Brown, the evangelist who I'd been told would wipe the sweat off his brow with rattlesnakes. Jamie Coots from Kentucky and Allen Williams from Tennessee were also there. They sat beside Punkin on the deacons' bench. All three were young and heavyset, the sons of preachers, and childhood friends. Punkin and Jamie both wore scowls, as though they were waiting for somebody to cross their paths in an unhappy way. Allen Williams, though, looked serene. Allen's father had died drinking strychnine in 1973, and his brother had died of snakebite in 1991. Maybe he thought he didn't have anything more to lose. Or maybe he was just reconciled to losing everything he had. Within six months of sitting together on the deacons' bench at the Old Rock House Church, Jamie, Allen, and Punkin would all be bit.

The church continued to fill with familiar faces, many from what used to be The Church of Jesus with Signs Following in Scottsboro, and the music began without an introduction of any kind. . . .

·   ·   ·

Brother Carl himself walked in with a serpent box containing the biggest rattlesnake I'd ever seen. Carl smelled of Old Spice and rattlesnake and something else underneath: a pleasant smell, like warm bread and apples. I associated it with the Holy Ghost. The handlers had told me that the Holy Ghost had a smell, a "sweet savor," and I had begun to think I could detect it on people and in churches, even in staid, respectable churches like the one I went to in Birmingham. Anyway, that was what I smelled on Brother Carl that day as he talked about the snake in the box. "I just got him today," he said. "He's never been in church before." Carl looked over his glasses at me and smiled. He held the serpent box up to my face and tapped the screen until the snake started rattling good.

"Got your name on him," he said to me.

A shiver went up my spine, but I just shook my head and grinned.

"Come on up to the front," he said. I followed him and sat on the first pew next to J.L. Dyal, but I made a mental note to avoid Carl's eyes during the service and to stay away from that snake of his.

Billy Summerford's wife, Joyce, led the singing. She was a big woman with a voice that wouldn't quit. *"Remember how it felt, when you walked out of the wilderness, walked out of the wilderness, walked out of the wilderness. Remember how it felt, when you walked out of the wilderness. . ."* It was one of my favorite songs because it had a double meaning now. There was the actual wilderness in the Old Testament that the Israelites were led out of, and the spiritual wilderness that was its referent, the condition of being lost. But there was also the wilderness that the New World became for my father's people. I don't mean the mountains. I mean the America that grew up around them, that tangled thicket of the heart.

"Remember how it felt, when you walked out of the wilderness. . ." My throat tightened as I sang. I remembered how it had felt when I'd sobered up in 1983. It's not often you get a second chance at life like that. And I remembered the births of my girls, the children Vicki and I had thought we'd never be able to have. Looking around at the familiar faces in the congregation, I figured they were thinking about their own wildernesses and how they'd been delivered out of them. I was still coming out of mine. It was a measure of how far I'd come, that I'd be moved nearly to tears in a rundown Holiness church on Sand Mountain. But my restless and stubborn intellect was still intact. It didn't like what it saw, a crowd of men dancing up to the serpent boxes, unclasping the lids, and taking out the poisonous snakes. Reason told me it was too early in the service. The snakes hadn't been prayed over enough. There hadn't even been any preaching yet, just Billy Summerford screaming into a microphone while the music swirled around us like a fog. But the boys from Tennessee and Kentucky had been hungry to get into the boxes. Soon, Punkin Brown was shouting at his snake, a big black-phase timber rattler that he had draped around his neck. Allen Williams was offering his copperhead up like a sacrifice, hands outstretched. But Brother Carl had the prize, and everyone seemed to know it. It was a yellow-phase timber, thick and melancholy, as big as timber rattlers come. Carl glanced at me, but I wouldn't make eye contact with him. I turned away. I walked to the back of the church and took a long drink of water from the bright yellow cooler propped up against a portrait of Jesus with his head on fire.

"Who knows what this snake is thinking?" Carl shouted. "God knows! God understands the mind of this snake!" And when I turned back around, Carl had laid the snake down and was treading barefoot on it from tail to head, as though he were walking a tightrope. Still, the snake didn't bite. I had heard about this, but never seen it before. The passage was from Luke: *Behold, I give unto you power to tread on serpents and scorpions, and over all the power of the enemy: and nothing shall by any means hurt you.* Then Carl picked the snake back up and draped it around his neck. The snake seemed to be looking for a way out of its predicament. Carl let it nuzzle into his shirt. Then the snake pulled back and cocked its head, as if in preparation to strike Carl's chest. Its head was as big as a child's hand.

Help him, Jesus! someone yelled above the din. Instead of striking, the snake started to climb Carl's sternum toward his collarbone. It went up the side of his neck and then lost interest and fell back against his chest.

The congregation was divided into two camps now, the men to the left, with the snakes, the women to the right, with each other. In front of Carl, one of the men suddenly began jumping straight up and down, as though he were on a pogo stick. Down the aisle he went and around the sanctuary. When he returned, he collapsed at Carl's feet. One of the Summerford brothers attended to him there by soaking his handkerchief with olive oil and dabbing it against the man's forehead until he sat up and yelled, "Thank God!"

In the meantime, in the corner where the women had gathered, Joyce Summerford's sister, Donna, an attractive young woman in a lime green dress, was laboring in the spirit with a cataleptic friend. She circled the friend, eyeing her contortions carefully, and then, as if fitting her into an imaginary dress, she clothed her in the spirit with her hands, an invisible tuck here, an invisible pin there, making sure the spirit draped well over the flailing arms. It took her a while. Both of the women were drenched in sweat and stuttering in tongues by the time they finished.

"They say we've gone crazy!" Brother Carl shouted above the chaos. He was pacing in front of the pulpit, the enormous rattlesnake balanced now across his shoulder. "Well, they're right!" he cried. "I've gone crazy! I've gone Bible crazy! I've got the papers here to prove it!" And he waved his worn Bible in the air. "Some people say we're just a bunch of fanatics!"

Amen. Thank God.

"Well, we are! *Hai-i-salemos-ah-cahn-ne-hi-yee!* Whew! That last one nearly took me out of here!"

It's not true that you become used to the noise and confusion of a snake-handling Holiness service. On the contrary, you become enmeshed in it. It is theater at its most intricate—improvisational, spiritual jazz. The more you experience it, the more attentive you are to the shifts in the surface and the dark shoals underneath. For every outward sign, there is a spiritual equivalent. When somebody falls to his knees, a specific problem presents itself, and the others know exactly what to do, whether it's oil for a healing, or a prayer cloth thrown over the shoulders, or a devil that needs to be cast out. The best, of course, the simplest and cleanest, is when someone gets the

Holy Ghost for the first time. The younger the worshiper, the easier it seems to be for the Holy Ghost to descend and speak—lips loosened, tongue flapping, eyes rolling backward in the head. It transcends the erotic when a thirteen-year-old girl gets the Holy Ghost. The older ones often take time. I once saw an old man whose wife had gotten the Holy Ghost at a previous service. He wanted it bad for himself, he said. Brother Charles McGlockin started praying with him before the service even started, and all through it, the man was in one attitude or another at the front of the church—now lying spread-eagled on the floor, while a half dozen men prayed over him and laid on hands, now up and running from one end of the sanctuary to the other, now twirling, now swooning, now collapsing once again on the floor, his eyes like the eyes of a horse that smells smoke, the unknown tongue spewing from his mouth. He got the Holy Ghost at last! He got the Holy Ghost! you think, until you see him after the service eating a pimiento cheese sandwich downstairs. His legs are crossed. He's brushing the crumbs from his lap. He agrees it was a good service all right, but it sure would have been better if he'd only gotten the Holy Ghost. You can never get enough of the Holy Ghost. Maybe that's what he means. You can never exhaust the power when the Spirit comes down, not even when you take up a snake, not even when you take up a dozen of them. The more faith you expend, the more power is released. It's an inexhaustible, eternally renewable resource. It's the only power some of these people have.

So the longer you witness it, unless you just don't get into the spontaneous and unexpected, the more you become a part of it. *I* did, and the handlers could tell. They knew before I did what was going to happen. They saw me angling in. They were already making room for me in front of the deacons' bench. As I said, I'd always been drawn to danger. Alcohol. Psychedelics. War. If it made me feel good, I'd do it. I was always up for a little trip. I figured if I could trust my guide, I'd be all right. I'd come back to earth in one piece. I wouldn't really lose my mind. That's what I thought, anyway. I couldn't be an astronaut, but there were other things I could do and be. So I got up there in the middle of the handlers. J.L. Dyal, dark and wiry, was standing on my right; a cleancut boy named Steve Frazier on my left. Who was it going to be? Carl's eyes were saying, you. And yes, it was the big rattler, the one with my name on it, acrid-smelling, carnal, alive. And the look in Carl's eyes seemed to change as he approached me. He was embarrassed. The snake was all he had, his eyes seemed to say. But as low as it was, as repulsive, if I took it, I'd be possessing the sacred. Nothing was required except obedience. Nothing had to be given up except my own will. This was the moment. I didn't stop to think about it. I just gave in. I stepped forward and took the snake with both hands. Carl released it to me. I turned to face the congregation and lifted the rattlesnake up toward the light. It was moving like it wanted to get up even higher, to climb out of that church and into the air. And it was exactly as the handlers had told me. I felt no fear. The snake seemed to be an extension of myself. And suddenly there seemed to be nothing in the room but me and the snake. Everything else had disappeared. Carl, the congregation, Jim—all gone, all faded to white. And I could not hear the earsplitting music. The air was silent and still and filled with that strong, even light. And I realized that I, too, was fading into the white. I was losing myself by degrees, like the incredible shrinking man. The snake would be the last to go, and all I could see was the way its scales shimmered one last time in the light, and the way its head moved from side to side, searching for a way out. I knew then why the handlers took up serpents. There is power in the act of disappearing; there is victory in the loss of self. It must be close to our conception of paradise, what it's like before you're born or after you die.

I came back in stages, first with the recognition that the shouting I had begun to hear was coming from my own mouth. Then I realized I was holding a rattlesnake, and the church rushed back with all its clamor, heat, and smell. I remembered Carl and turned toward where I thought he might be. I lowered the snake to waist level. It was an enormous animal, heavy and firm. The scales on its side were as rough as calluses. I could feel its muscles rippling beneath the skin. I was aware it was not a part of me now and that I couldn't predict what it might do. I extended it toward Carl. He took it from me, stepped to the side, and gave it in turn to J.L.

"Jesus," J.L. said. "Oh, Jesus." His knees bent, his head went back. I knew it was happening to him too.

Then I looked around and saw that I was in a semicircle of handlers by the deacons' bench. Most had returned their snakes to the boxes, but Billy Summerford, Glenn's buck-toothed cousin, still had one, and he offered it to me, a medium-sized canebrake that was rattling violently. I took the snake in one hand without thinking. It was smaller than the first, but angrier, and I realized circumstances were different now. I couldn't seem to steer it away from my belt line. Fear had started to come back to me. I remembered with sudden clarity what Brother Charles had said about being careful who you took a snake from. I studied the canebrake as if I were seeing it for the first time and then gave it back to Billy Summerford. He passed to to Steve Frazier, the young man on my left. I watched Steve cradle it, curled and rattling furiously in his hands, and then I walked out the side door of the church and onto the steps, where Bobbie Sue Thompson was clutching her throat and leaning against the green shingles of the church.

"Jesus," she said. "Jesus, Jesus."

It was a sunny, fragrant day, with high-blown clouds. I looked into Bobbie Sue's face. Her eyes were wide and her mouth hooked at the corner. "Jesus," she said.

I thought at first she was in terrible pain, but then I realized she wasn't. "Yes. I know. Jesus," I said.

.   .   .

At the conclusion of the service, Brother Carl reminded everyone there would be dinner on the grounds. Most of the women had already slipped out, to arrange their casseroles and platters of ham on the butcher paper that covered the tables the men had set up under the trees. . . .

.   .   .

I found Brother Carl by his pickup truck. He was talking to J.L. Dyal. They'd just loaded the big yellow-phase rattler into the bed of the truck, and they were giving him one last look.

Carl hugged me when I walked up. "I sure am proud of you," he said.

I asked if he was leaving for Georgia already.

"I've got to get back to God's country," he said.

While Carl went to say goodbye to some of the others, J.L. and I stared at the snake in the back of the truck. I told J.L. I just couldn't believe that we'd taken it up.

"It's something, all right," he said.

I asked what it had been like for him.

"It's love, that's all it is," he said. "You love the Lord, you love the Word, you love your brother and sister. You're in one mind, one accord, you're all combined together. The Bible says we're each a part of the body, and when it all comes together. . . Hey!" He whistled through his teeth. "What was it like for you?" he asked.

I didn't know what to say.

It's hard for me to talk about myself. As a journalist, I've always tried to keep out of the story. But look what had happened to me. I loved Brother Carl, but sometimes I suspected he was crazy. Sometimes I thought he was intent on getting himself, and maybe the rest of us, killed. Half the time I walked around saying to myself, "This thing is real! This thing is real!" The other half of the time, I walked around thinking that nothing was real, and that if there really was a God, we must have been part of a dream he was having, and when he woke up. . . *poof!* Either way, I worried I'd gone off the edge, and nobody would be able to pull me back. One of my uncles by marriage was a Baptist minister, one of the kindest men I've ever known. I was fifteen, though, when he killed himself, and I didn't know the whole story. I just knew that he sent his family and friends a long, poignant, and some have said beautiful letter about how he was ready to go meet Abraham, Isaac, and Jacob. I believe he ran a high-voltage line from his basement to a ground-floor bedroom. He put "How Great Thou Art" on the record player. Then he lay down on the bed, reached up, and grabbed the live wire. He left a widow and two sons. My uncle's death confirmed a suspicion of mine that madness and religion were a hair's breadth away. My beliefs about the nature of God and man have changed over the years, but that one never has. Feeling after God is dangerous business. And Christianity without passion, danger, and mystery may not really be Christianity at all.

from *THE SEARCH FOR GOD*
AT HARVARD

A R I L . G O L D M A N

As the religion correspondent for The New York Times, *Ari L. Goldman,
an Orthodox Jew, was the detached journalist, protected by his reporter's
notebook. But when Goldman, now a professor of journalism at Columbia
University, enrolled in the Harvard Divinity School to study comparative
religion, he had to put aside his shield against authentic encounter with
the feared "Other" and face the challenge of the non-Jewish world.*

FOUR WENT down to the orchard. One fell gravely ill and
died, one became a heretic, one went mad and one, Rabbi Akiba,
emerged whole. I thought of this story from the pages of the Talmud
often when, at the age of thirty-five, I moved to Massachusetts with
my wife and our infant son to enroll as a graduate student at Harvard
Divinity School.

The Talmudic story of the rabbis and the orchard had thrilled me
ever since I first heard it as a youngster. These were clearly no ordinary rabbis. The ones I usually learned about in Jewish day school
were the type who stayed in the study hall morning to night, learning
the holy books and answering the queries of the faithful. Rabbis were
not the type who took chances. But this tale provided another model,
four adventurers going off like so many early-day versions of Indiana
Jones, their black fedoras cocked at rakish angles, heading for the
orchard . . . and trouble. But where were they going? This obviously

was no simple orchard of dates and apples. What trouble were the rabbis courting? And why the ominous three-to-one odds? One survivor. One heretic. One madman. One dead.

There are several interpretations of this Talmudic tale, which dates to the first century. The explanation that has always made the most sense to me is that the adventurers were embarking on a perilous interfaith journey. Rome beckoned, with its philosophy, art, science and letters. So did Christianity, with its message of love in an era when rabbinic Judaism was being set into law with the Mishna, the legal code that often appeared to emphasize Judaism's rules over its compassion. Alternatives to Judaism were there, gleaming and shining and easily within reach, like fruits on a tree in an orchard. As God had once told Adam and Eve, the Talmudic story had an implicit warning about these tempting fruits: "Don't touch."

I was born nearly two thousand years later and two continents away, in 1949 in Hartford, Connecticut. Still, the story of the rabbis and the orchard resonated. Well into my adulthood, the threat of the pagan and Christian worlds loomed large for me. The "Don't touch" signs still hung beside the trees.

Now, in 1985, as an adult, I was enrolling as a student at Harvard Divinity School, the result of an unusual leave of absence from my job as a reporter for *The New York Times*. I was going to Harvard for a year to study comparative religion—and all I could see were forbidden fruits. What could I expect from my encounter with Harvard Divinity School? Would I emerge whole, like Rabbi Akiba, or suffer the fate of Elisha Ben Avuya, the brilliant young Jewish scholar who emerged the heretic? Or worse, would I go mad or simply expire?

These might seem like strange and powerful fears for someone who had been exposed to just about every human and municipal failure as a reporter working for ten years in New York City. Before going to Harvard, I had written about—and rubbed shoulders with—corruption, murder, drug addiction, disease, crime, the subways, City Hall and the Statehouse. The study of the development of religious thought would seem tame, almost pure, to most people. But my apprehensions, complete with the Talmudic parables dancing in my head, were far more emotional—and even mystical—than they were rational.

Maybe it was the words of my great-aunt Minnie, a regal women in her nineties who blended religious piety with a strong streak of superstition. It was Aunt Minnie who had helped raise me after my parents were divorced when I was six years old. Now, three decades later, Aunt Minnie was very much opposed to my going to study religion at Harvard. "You have one of the best schools for religious studies right here in New York—Yeshiva University," she told me. But when she realized that I was going to Cambridge despite her entreaties, she gave me her blessing. "Remember," she whispered in my ear at a family gathering shortly before I left for Cambridge. "You can study all the religions, but Judaism is the best."

In my family, Judaism meant only one thing: Orthodoxy. I come from an unusual American Orthodox family. The most unusual thing about it is that it is still Orthodox. There is an ugly adage about American Jewry that I was brought up on, although not until years later did I realize it was not only ugly but false. The adage goes like this: The first generation is Orthodox, the second is Conservative, the third is Reform and the fourth is Christian. I am a third-generation American-born Orthodox Jew. All four of my grandparents were born in the United States, all of them, in fact, on the Lower East Side of Manhattan, the sons and daughters of the migration in the late 1800s of Russian and Polish Jews. For over a century, we kept "authentic Judaism," as we saw it, and that burden of family history weighed heavily on my shoulders.

Enrolling at Harvard University was yet another step in the sometimes reluctant worldly education of an Orthodox yeshiva boy who was not always sure it was worthwhile to be worldly. I was brought up in a warm cocoon of Orthodox observance, and when I cautiously ventured forth, propelled by a curiosity and a hunger to experience the world, I often felt it was a mistake. Maybe I should have stayed home.

The story of my religious exploration is different from that of some of my friends who were brought up in assimilated Jewish homes and then spent their adulthoods looking for their Jewish roots and the meaning of religion in their lives. . . .

.   .   .

I never had to search. My parents gave me the Hebrew name Ari, which means "lion," then backed it up with the somewhat redundant middle name Lionel, just in case I needed or chose to avail myself of a Christian name. (As it has turned out, I've never used Lionel.) If anything, over the generations, my family—which found refuge in America from the persecutions and economic hardships of Eastern Europe—was becoming more and more confident of its religious place in the world.

. . .

For me, the challenge was not Judaism, but the non-Jewish world. First, as a reporter for *The New York Times* on a variety of subjects, I encountered the secular world, taking in its pleasures with mixed emotions. Later, as a religion writer for *The Times*, I was plunged into New York's diversity of churches, synagogues, mosques, temples and other, more private, forms of religious expression. Through it all, I remained the outsider, knowledgeable enough about my subject to write about it, but detached enough not to feel it. Not feeling it, in fact, is supposed to make you a better reporter, truer to the journalistic god of objectivity. If for the sports reporter there is no cheering in the press box, then for the religion writer there are no "Amens" after the sermon and no humming along with the church choir.

After a year of writing about religion with the detachment that had always served me well as a reporter, I approached my editors with a request for a one-year leave of absence. The idea was that I would go to Harvard—the most prestigious of American divinity schools—for a dispassionate encounter with Christianity and the religions of the East, then return to *The Times* to write about religion with greater knowledge and authority.

. . .

At Harvard Divinity, I learned that there is little dispassionate about the study of religion. From my first day at the Div School, as it was known on campus, I was emotionally engaged and spiritually challenged.

At first I tried to resist. In those opening days of school, I carried a small reporter's notebook wherever I went, ostensibly as a way to record the experience. It was one of those lean spiral books that fit neatly in one hand, just right for jotting down the sounds and sights of a train wreck. The notebook has also served another purpose; it has long been my shield against getting involved. In church, it assured me I was not a Christian; in the hospital, it said I wasn't sick; in the police station, it said I wasn't in trouble; at the gay rights parade, it said I was straight.

My shield seemed to work fine for the reporter on the street, but it was wrong for the student of religion. I had to come to terms with the fact that the incessant scribbling was a way of hearing but not feeling. After several days at school, I put the notebook down and allowed myself to enter the worlds I had so feared. Cautiously, I let myself experience Buddhist meditation, Christian hymns, Muslim poetry.

No, I did not convert. My deeply nurtured Jewish identity never seriously came under siege. But what did happen was an extraordinary dialogue, one between the religious ideas that I encountered and the Jewish ideas within myself. The dialogue continued every day in the classroom, in the words of the New Testament, the Koran, the Upanishads and in fellowship at my own Sabbath table, around which I assembled people of various faiths. As a result of these encounters, I learned how others experience their faith. But more important, I developed a richer and fuller understanding of myself and my own Judaism.

In many ways, the year at Harvard helped knit together the many diverse facets of my life, my stormy childhood, my disordered education, my passion for journalism and the powerful, mystical pull faith continues to have on me.

.   .   .

Every pollster will tell you that there is a renewed interest in religion today among Americans of all faiths. The problem is that the interest of most people ends at the doors of their own churches or synagogues or mosques. By and large, Christians are interested in Christianity, Muslims care about Islam and Jews want to know about Judaism. It is a phenomenon that goes back to the first century, when the Talmud fretted over the four searchers who went down to the orchard.

This is . . . what happened to me when I went down to the twentieth-century version of the Talmudic orchard. To say that it changed me forever is only the beginning of my story.

.   .   .

It began with a funeral. I bounded up the gray stone steps leading to the cathedral-like Divinity School building in the northern reaches of the Harvard campus with excitement and an extra measure of the normal fears that accompany any new enterprise. It was a sunny and crisp fall day, the kind that New England is famous for. The leaves on the tall patrician trees on Francis Avenue had already put on their autumnal colors and made a blazing canopy for my arrival. I reached the great oak doors of Divinity Hall, put my hand on the heavy brass door latch and then I spotted the sign: "Due to the Funeral Mass of

George MacRae, HDS Orientation Has Been Canceled for the Morning."

Five days before orientation was to begin, the Reverend George W. MacRae, the acting dean of Harvard Divinity School, collapsed and died while leading a spiritual retreat at a Catholic seminary in nearby Brighton. He was fifty-seven years old. MacRae was a Jesuit, a member of that intellectual and progressive order of Catholic clergy that spawned the peace activist Daniel Berrigan and Father Robert Drinan, the liberal member of Congress who gave up his congressional seat at the insistence of the Vatican. MacRae, a New Testament scholar and member of a committee preparing a new Protestant translation of the Bible, seemed like an appropriate person to be the first Catholic to head Harvard's very Protestant divinity school. He had received the appointment less than two months before his death.

Disoriented by the death of a man I never knew, I followed a solemn line of students and faculty across Harvard Yard and into St. Paul's Roman Catholic Church for the funeral mass. I took my seat among the mourners as the organ played sad and robust melodies. A procession of white-robed priests, led by Bernard Cardinal Law of Boston, entered, followed by deacons and an assortment of altar boys. An all-boys choir sang.

I shifted uncomfortably in my seat. No matter how many times I have been in church—and, as a reporter, I often find myself in one— I never feel right. One of the Orthodox rabbis of my youth, a Rabbi Siegel, always seems to catch up with me there, waving his finger in my face even before he starts talking. "A church? What are you doing in a church? Didn't you study Jewish history? Don't you know what they did to our people in the name of that cross? Didn't I tell you that it is forbidden to step into a church? No. No excuses. I don't care who died. I don't care if there is a storm outside. I don't care if the whole world is on fire and this is the only escape. Out of the church. Out. Out. Out."

I took my spiral reporter's notebook out of my pocket and impulsively began jotting down words from the eulogies. Most of them, including Cardinal Law's, were pretty prosaic. ("His ministry continues in the lives of us all.") But I was struck by the words of MacRae's nephew, Gordon MacRae, like his uncle a Roman Catholic priest. "The most profound search of my uncle's life was not for wisdom or knowledge, but for peace." the young MacRae said. What a fine tribute to a man who, after all, was a scholar. The nephew looked out into the church, which was crowded with MacRae's colleagues and students, and said, "My family shared George's blood, but you have shared his soul." A cut above, I thought. I was able to see the profound influence George MacRae had had on this young priest and understood why he had chosen to follow in his uncle's footsteps; maybe he was the son that MacRae could never have as a celibate Catholic priest. For a moment, I mourned George MacRae, or maybe I mourned that I would never be touched by him.

Cardinal Law, a strappingly handsome Harvard graduate with a full head of white hair, celebrated the funeral mass.

.   .   .

Law stood at the altar surrounded by a dozen priests, who looked at him in what seemed like genuine awe as he lifted the communion wafer above his head and recounted the words of Jesus, words that in the Catholic belief would transform the wafer into the body of their Lord. "He broke the bread, gave it to his disciples and said: 'Take this, all of you, and eat it. This is my body, which will be given up for you.'" I noticed the assembled priests silently mouth the words of Jesus along with the cardinal.

Law put down the broken wafer and lifted the cup. "When supper was ended, he took the cup. Again he gave you thanks and praise, gave the cup to his disciples, and said: 'Take this, all of you, and drink from it.'" Again I saw the lips of the assisting priests move in unison. "'This is the cup of my blood, the blood of the new and everlasting covenant. It will be shed for you and for all, so that sins may be forgiven. Do this in memory of me.'"

I've always admired the Catholic Mass as it moves from this moment of consecration to the sharing of communion with all members of the church. It is so much more dignified than the Jewish *kiddush*, the collation of sweet red wine and sponge cake that follows the Sabbath service. After the synagogue prayers on Saturday morning, the crowd descends to the social hall and stands chattering around the tables of food while waiting for the rabbi to say the *b'racha*, the blessing, on the wine so that everyone can begin. I grew up with these b'rachas, an essential part of the everyday life of an Orthodox youngster. *"Baruch atah Adonai Eloheynu Melech Ha'olam hamotzi lechem min ha'aretz,"* one says before eating bread. "Blessed are you, God, King of the Universe, who brings forth bread from the ground." There is another b'racha for vegetables (". . . who brings forth the produce of the ground") and another for pastries (". . . who created different kinds of cakes"). And then there is a whole different category— b'rachas that you say when you see lightning or a rainbow, b'rachas after recovering from an illness and, most routinely, a long laundry list of b'rachas in the daily prayers—giving thanks for waking up, for freedom, for new clothes, for the ability to study Torah—there is even one, recited by boys and men, thanking God for not making us women, and another, recited by males and females, praising God for not making us Gentiles. Upon leaving the bathroom, we make a b'racha thanking God for our internal plumbing system. In yeshiva, our rebbe taught us that "a good Jew" has to say one hundred b'rachas a day.

My mother spent my childhood years on b'racha patrol, making sure that nothing would pass my lips without thanks to the Almighty properly expressed. After she gave me a cookie, she would watch closely for the mumble. Saying b'rachas is a habit that never left me, and it still sometimes looks like I am talking to my food before I pop it in my mouth. It is an involuntary act and, on those rare occasions when I think about what it is that I'm doing, I kind of like it. In the great scheme of things, it seems only right to give thanks.

Still, with all this reflexive Jewish background and a thousand b'rachas on my tongue, I feel irresistibly drawn to Communion, the high point of the Catholic Mass. Unlike the kiddush after the synagogue service, at Communion there is no need to reach across the table and secure a piece of sponge cake and a shot glass of wine. For the Catholic, it is total submission. Open your mouth and the wafer is placed there. Open your mouth and the cup is placed on your lips, "so that sins may be forgiven." There is no work involved. Just give yourself over to Jesus and you will be saved. It is entirely different from the Jewish approach; the Jew must work for his redemption, whether at the kiddush table, in the study hall or in the marketplace.

I am sitting in church at George MacRae's funeral and imagine myself lifted from my pew. In my daydream, I join the line of Catholics—good, confessed and fasting Catholics—leading up to the cardinal, who stands at the altar in his white robe and embroidered stole. A gold cross dangles from a chain around his neck. Some open their mouths reverently and the cardinal places the wafer on their tongues; others, in accord with the reforms of Vatican II, hold out their hands, accept the wafer and put it in their mouths themselves. I am now standing face to face with the cardinal, and I hear him whisper the words "Body of Christ" as he directs the wafer to my mouth. I say my b'racha, thanking the Almighty for the bread of the earth. I open my mouth and I eat His flesh.

PAPA OGOU, DO YOU TAKE THIS WOMAN?

KAREN MCCARTHY BROWN

The academic world has long prided itself on "objective" scholarship, but Karen McCarthy Brown, Professor of the Sociology and Anthropology of Religion at the Graduate and Theological Schools of Drew University, has extended the boundaries of her discipline with her multi-textured narrative, Mama Lola: A Vodou Priestess in Brooklyn. *Brown, who spent a dozen years immersing herself in the daily life, culture, and religious practices of Alourdes, known as Mama Lola, moves from observer to participant, "marrying" Papa Ogou, one of the Vodou spirits, in an elaborate ritual, foreshadowing her own formal initiation into this mysterious, and much maligned, religion.*

EARLY IN the summer of 1980, Alourdes read the cards for me, as she does from time to time. That day we were considering whether or not I should undergo the Vodou marriage to Papa Ogou. My first trip to Haiti had been in the summer of 1973. Starting with that trip, every priest or priestess who chose to make a diagnosis told me that Papa Ogou was my *mèt tèt*.* In 1977 a *manbò* I had never met before made her way across a crowded temple dance floor just to tell me that she could see Papa Ogou "around my head."

A person's *mèt tèt* can be identified in several ways, most often

*Principle protective spirit.

through divination or consultation with the spirits during possession. *Manbo* or *oungan** with the intuitive powers called "the gift of eyes" are said to see protective spirits directly. Diagnosing someone's *mèt tèt* is more than a surface labeling of personality types. It often works at a deeper level, where it zeros in on significant latent characteristics. Even though the diagnosis of Ogou[†] as my *mèt tèt* did not fit easily with my own self-image, I could see the wisdom of it.

Although I had witnessed many Vodou marriages and been fascinated by them, I originally had no intention of going through the ritual myself. Then, one day in 1980 when I was alone in my apartment and full of rage (I had some things to be angry about in that period of my life), I found myself muttering, "Stop trying to make the anger go away. It only makes it worse. It's yours. Marry it!" I picked up the phone and called Alourdes.

This spontaneous decision marked a new stage in my relation to Haitian Vodou. It also brought new and deeper understandings of how Vodou actually works in the lives of individuals. The contents of Vodou rituals—from private healing consultations to public dances and possession-performances—are composed from the lives of the particular people performing them. When I began to bring my own life to the system for healing, I began to understand more of what it meant for Haitians to do that. But there were also new risks. In a way, I was setting out to do fieldwork on my own psyche. I remain convinced that this was the best and perhaps the only way for me to move my understanding of Vodou beyond external description into the deep places where it takes up the dreams and fears, hope and pain of an actual life. I try to exercise caution in not claiming more authority for my experience than it can bear. What I have gained from participating in Vodou is a kind of knowledge that exists in the seam between two cultures, where the various strands of the fabric can never be disentangled.

As Alourdes laid out the cards for my reading, we talked. She said to me, "Karen, you very intelligent person. Only thing about you, you don't push yourself. You just stay right where you are." In two quick gestures, her hands framed a small, tight box. "You could push faster. . . yes." In Vodou, there is a pervasive contrast between being immobile and blocked and having a life of energy and flow. The goal

---

*Vodou priestess/vodou priest.
[†]Vodou warrior spirit.

of all Vodou ritualizing is to *echofe* (heat things up) so that people and situations shift and move, and healing transformations can occur. Heating things up brings down the barriers, clears the impediments in the path, and allows life to move as it should. When Ogou discussed Maggie's initiation with her, he used another metaphor for energy and movement, telling her that if she would make the commitment to take the *ason**, then *"dlo klè va koule devan ou* [clear water will flow in front of you]."

The opposite of this openness, heat, and flow is the state of being arrested or stopped *(rete)* or, worse, of being bound *(mare)*. Charms and amulets made by every Vodou healer, which are designed to control the behavior of others in limited ways, are *mare,* bound or tied, round and round with thread, wire, or rope. Slave chains are even kept in some temples, where they are part of the iconography of "left-hand work," a type of Vodou ritualizing directed at much more extreme forms of control. When Alourdes said, "You just stay right where you are," she was not suggesting that I was the victim of left-hand work; instead, she was suggesting that my own behavior boxed me in.

After Alourdes delivered this verdict, the room was quiet save for the tapping noise her middle finger made as it descended two or three times in quick succession on a card here and there in the four neat rows of eight cards in front of her. "Karen, you got to fight. You got to be a fighter," she said. More silence and tapping followed. "Look, if you decide you going marry Papa Ogou, you got to do it for yourself. Don't do nothing for me. Do it for yourself." More silence. More tapping. "Karen, you think too much!" "What?" I asked. "Drink too much?" Alourdes laughed. She told me to come back the next Wednesday and she would call Papa Ogou for me.

It was eight-thirty on a hot summer evening when I returned. Maggie was in the living room. All the lights were off except a tiny one on the portable sewing machine where she was working. The door between the living room and Alourdes's bedroom was open. Alourdes lay on her stomach on the bed. I sat on the edge of the bed, and we talked. The conversation moved in fits and starts, focusing mainly on a familiar topic, money problems. Alourdes yawned repeatedly. So did I. After almost two hours of labored talk and long silences, I began to think that Alourdes had forgotten her promise to call Ogou. Or perhaps she had concluded that it was too hot to work.

---

*Sacred rattle of priests and priestesses.

I decided not to press the issue, to wait for another occasion when she was more in the mood. But I was annoyed. I had traveled from Manhattan at the end of a busy day and in weather that sapped my energy and fogged my mind. Ending an especially long silence between us, I stood up and said I thought it was time to be on my way.

Alourdes rolled over slowly onto her back, a questioning look on her face. "You don't want to talk with Papa Ogou?" she asked. This is often how it works: Alourdes pulls through just when I am thoroughly frustrated and ready to give up. Our attitudes toward time are very different. I hoard it and spend it like a miser; she rides the rhythms of the day like a surfer. She lets things happen when the time is right for them to happen. Alourdes recognizes the right moment only when it is upon her.

Together, we went to the basement. Alourdes knocked three times on the door to the altar room, and we went in. She struck a match and pushed the wick of a candle stub into the flame. She anchored the small white candle on the edge of her work table and settled herself on a low stool next to the table. I was asked to reach into Ogou's altar cabinet for a bottle of rum. She poured a dollop or two of the amber liquid onto a red metal plate and then dropped matches on the thin film of rum until it ignited. Alourdes sat staring into the fire while tipping the plate from side to side to keep the blue flames dancing across its surface. Her free hand was held to her forehead like a sunshade, which paradoxically kept the light in rather than shutting it out. Narrowing her eyes, Alourdes sought the focused state of mind that creates a portal through which ordinary consciousness slips away.

For a *manbo* as accomplished as Alourdes, the struggle that marks the onset of trance is usually pro forma. During community rituals, when energetic singing and hand-clapping bring on possession, the struggle between her *gwo bònanj** and the spirit who seeks to possess her is over in minutes. First, her eyes narrow. Then her head bends forward as if she had a weight on the back of her neck (the spirits are said to ride on the back of the neck), and her facial features go slack. She often loses her balance and requires support from bystanders. Assistants remove her shoes and take the *ason* from her hand. Soon, the personality of the *lwa†* is in full control of her body and voice.

*Big guardian angel, consciousness or personality.
†Vodou spirit.

When Alourdes does not have the energy and support of a crowd to push her along, this process can be slower, as it was on this night.

As she concentrated on the slippery blue flame, a light tremor passed through her body from time to time, and she squeezed her eyes shut. Once, she jerked her left hand away from her forehead and shook it vigorously as if it had gone numb. But, like a restless sleeper, Alourdes seemed to wake with a start each time she dipped below the surface of the waters of consciousness. At one point, her body shook so much I was sure the spirit had come. But the crisis passed.

Alourdes sighed and reached for the rum bottle to refuel her small fire. Again, there was intense concentration, and this time it worked. Barely perceptible tremors became intense shaking, and then the energy shot out her arms and legs, making them do a stiff staccato dance in the air. When the shaking stopped, Alourdes's body was drawn up straight, and keen black eyes were staring at me with interest. Papa Ogou had arrived.

"*Bonjou, bèl ti fi* [Hello, pretty little girl]," Papa Ogou said in the nasal speech of the spirits. "*Ba'm nouvèl ou. Sa ou genyen? Kouman ou ye, pitit?* [Give me news of yourself. What's going on with you? How are you, little one?]" Ogou asked with paternal concern. Then, without waiting for answers, he requested his red scarf and his *shouga,* spirit talk for *siga* (cigar). He tied the scarf tightly around his head and lit the cigar. Then he leaned back and eyed me from head to toe.

When I asked if he thought I should marry him, Ogou continued staring and did not respond. I put the question in another form, and Ogou still said nothing. I began to tell him about the things that made me angry—my marriage breaking up, packing, moving, too much work, tension on the job. Ogou nodded sympathetically but without comment. Things went on like this for a long time. I felt like a chicken senselessly flapping its wings, unable to take off. The room was full of my clucking. He was as unmoveable and silent as a mountain.

When I was close to the end of my patience, Ogou spoke. He asked quietly: "What can I do for you?" "Tell me what to do," I sputtered. "Should I do the marriage or not?" Ogou's body snapped forward, and a thick cloud of cigar smoke shot into my face along with his forceful reply: "*Pran tèt ou* [Get ahold of your head]! Do what you want! Do you want to marry me?" I had tried to get Ogou to tell me what to do, and he had been waiting for me to say what I wanted. In the end, I said I wanted to have the ceremony. I had made the decision, and I intended to carry it through.

"*Bon!*" Ogou said and sat back, puffing contentedly on his cigar. "You have the spirit all around you," he observed. "Did you know the Ginen spirit can love a white person? You don't know that? I think you have a *rasin* Ginen [an African root] in you. . . an Indian root. . . Jewish, too! You are a very intelligent woman. You could be a doctor, a lawyer. But no, you choose this. You don't have to come here. But you are searching. . . searching. You are digging. Why did you choose this? Because you have an African root in you! Do you understand what I am saying to you?"

The marriage took place the next month at Ogou's regularly scheduled July birthday party. Around two o'clock in the morning, when the songs summoning Ogou began, I excused myself from the twenty-five or so people gathered around Alourdes's sumptuous altar tables. I went upstairs to change into my wedding clothes—a bright red sundress purchased especially for the occasion and, on my head, a red satin scarf. When I came down the stairs half an hour later, everyone oohed and aahed over my fine attire. Everyone, that is, except Papa Ogou.

He had mounted Alourdes in my absence, and I found him decked out in his own finery, his red velvet military jacket with the gold epaulets. But Ogou ignored me. I stood by patiently while he talked to one person after another without even acknowledging my presence. No matter how I maneuvered, he always managed to keep his back to me.

Everyone was getting nervous. One woman said, "Papa Ogou, your beautiful bride is here, behind you. Don't you want to talk to her?" Ogou ignored the question. Then a man whispered in my ear, "Go on!" and gave me a shove in front of Ogou. The spirit looked me over with a cold eye. "What do you want?" he asked. I found my voice: "I am here to marry you. You promised me you would marry me. You have made me wait a long time. I am ready." Papa Ogou threw back his head and laughed. It was a deep, rich laugh. "Begin the ceremony!" he shouted, and, taking my arm, he propelled me toward the largest of the altar tables. Once again, Ogou had taught me the warrior's lesson: know what you want and fight for it.

Two chairs were placed in front of the table. Papa Ogou and I sat, and the four people who were "godparents" for the wedding gathered behind us. Willy, functioning as *prètsavann**, stood in front of us. *"Liberté, égalité, fraternité,"* he began, reading from a paper bearing the official stamp of the Republic of Haiti. (Blank forms are available near the big Iron Market in Port-au-Prince for four cents apiece; my Acte de Mariage had been written out in ballpoint pen on the first page of the folio sheet.) "In the year one thousand nine hundred and eighty in the state of New York. . . ." Willy continued in French.

"Make it fast!" Ogou snapped. Willy laughed, put the paper down, and began to ad lib in Creole. "Do you, Ogou Badagri, take this woman, Karine. . . uh. . . uh. . . Brown, as your wife? And do you promise to give her protection?" "Yes!" answered Ogou, thumping his sword on the floor for emphasis. "Do you take Monsieur Ogou Badagri as husband?" Willy asked me. "To be faithful. . . to give him one night each week?" "Yes!" I said.

From the altar Ogou took a saucer holding the ring with a small red stone that I had purchased earlier in the week. He doused the ring in Florida Water and rum and set it on fire. While the ring was still warm, he slid it over the middle finger of my left hand. He held my hand up to each of the four directions. Four times he blew a fine mist of rum over my hand and the ring. Then Papa Ogou plucked a red carnation from a bouquet on the table and doused it in the mixture of rum, perfume, and cool blue fire. He handed me the flaming flower, as Willy intoned the final words in French: "Maître Ogou Badagri and Mademoiselle Karine are united by marriage!"

People cheered. A champagne cork popped. Ogou refused champagne, preferring a long swig from his rum bottle. He also refused to eat any of the wedding cake, but he did cut it. With his sword, he removed a circular piece from the center of the cake and instructed me to take it home to feed friends, family, and spirits. Everyone present signed the marriage document, including Ogou Badagri, who scratched a big "O.B." with a red felt-tip pen.

---

*Vodou functionary who plays the role of a Catholic priest in certain types of ritualizing.

SATAN; SAVED

MALCOLM X

In these excerpts from his highly influential autobiography, El-Hajj Malik El-Shabazz, known as Malcolm X—born Malcolm Little in 1925 and slain in 1965—recollects his prison years when he referred to himself as "Satan," always ready to denounce God. Malcolm's hostility to religion is challenged by his brothers who have joined the Nation of Islam, "the natural religion for the black man." Encountering Islam, Malcolm X grapples with the transformation required to become a Muslim—one who literally surrenders to God.

I SERVED A TOTAL of seven years in prison. Now, when I try to separate that first year-plus that I spent at Charlestown, it runs all together in a memory of nutmeg and the other semi-drugs, of cursing guards, throwing things out of my cell, balking in the lines, dropping my tray in the dining hall, refusing to answer my number—claiming I forgot it—and things like that.

I preferred the solitary that this behavior brought me. I would pace for hours like a caged leopard, viciously cursing aloud to myself. And my favorite targets were the Bible and God. But there was a legal limit to how much time one could be kept in solitary. Eventually, the men in the cellblock had a name for me: "Satan." Because of my antireligious attitude.

The first man I met in prison who made any positive impression on me whatever was a fellow inmate, "Bimbi." I met him in 1947, at Charlestown. He was a light, kind of red-complexioned Negro, as I was; about my height, and he had freckles. Bimbi, an old-time burglar, had been in many prisons. In the license plate shop where our gang worked, he operated the machine that stamped out the numbers. I was along the conveyor belt where the numbers were painted.

Bimbi was the first Negro convict I'd known who didn't respond to "What'cha know, Daddy?" Often, after we had done our day's license plate quota, we would sit around, perhaps fifteen of us, and listen to Bimbi. Normally, white prisoners wouldn't think of listening to Negro prisoners' opinions on anything, but guards, even, would wander over close to hear Bimbi on any subject.

He would have a cluster of people riveted, often on odd subjects you never would think of. He would prove to us, dipping into the science of human behavior, that the only difference between us and outside people was that we had been caught. He liked to talk about historical events and figures. When he talked about the history of Concord, where I was to be transferred later, you would have thought he was hired by the Chamber of Commerce, and I wasn't the first inmate who had never heard of Thoreau until Bimbi expounded upon him. Bimbi was known as the library's best customer. What fascinated me with him most of all was that he was the first man I had ever seen command total respect . . . with his words.

Bimbi seldom said much to me; he was gruff to individuals, but I sensed he liked me. What made me seek his friendship was when I heard him discuss religion. I considered myself beyond atheism—I was Satan. But Bimbi put the atheist philosophy in a framework, so to speak. That ended my vicious cursing attacks. My approach sounded so weak alongside his, and he never used a foul word.

.   .   .

One day in 1948, after I had been transferred to Concord Prison, my brother Philbert, who was forever joining something, wrote me this time that he had discovered the "natural religion for the black man." He belonged now, he said, to something called "the Nation of Islam." He said I should "pray to Allah for deliverance." I wrote Philbert a letter which, although in improved English, was worse than my earlier reply to his news that I was being prayed for by his "holiness" church.

When a letter from Reginald arrived, I never dreamed of associating the two letters, although I knew that Reginald had been spending a lot of time with Wilfred, Hilda, and Philbert in Detroit. Reginald's letter was newsy, and also it contained this instruction: "Malcolm, don't eat any more pork, and don't smoke any more cigarettes. I'll show you how to get out of prison."

My automatic response was to think he had come upon some way I could work a hype on the penal authorities. I went to sleep—and woke up—trying to figure what kind of a hype it could be. Something psychological, such as my act with the New York draft board? Could I, after going without pork and smoking no cigarettes for a while, claim some physical trouble that could bring about my release?

"Get out of prison." The words hung in the air around me, I wanted out so badly.

I wanted, in the worst way, to consult with Bimbi about it. But something big, instinct said, you spilled to nobody.

Quitting cigarettes wasn't going to be too difficult. I had been conditioned by days in solitary without cigarettes. Whatever this chance was, I wasn't going to fluff it. After I read that letter, I finished the pack I then had open. I haven't smoked another cigarette to this day, since 1948.

It was about three or four days later when pork was served for the noon meal.

I wasn't even thinking about pork when I took my seat at the long table. Sit-grab-gobble-stand-file out; that was the Emily Post in prison eating. When the meat platter was passed to me, I didn't even known what the meat was; usually, you couldn't tell, anyway—but it was suddenly as though *don't eat any more pork* flashed on a screen before me.

I hesitated, with the platter in mid-air; then I passed it along to the inmate waiting next to me. He began serving himself; abruptly, he stopped. I remember him turning, looking surprised at me.

I said to him, "I don't eat pork."

The platter then kept on down the table.

It was the funniest thing, the reaction, and the way that it spread. In prison, where so little breaks the monotonous routine, the smallest thing causes a commotion of talk. It was being mentioned all over the cell block by night that Satan didn't eat pork.

It made me very proud, in some odd way. One of the universal images of the Negro, in prison and out, was that he couldn't do without pork. It made me feel good to see that my not eating it had especially startled the white convicts.

Later I would learn, when I had read and studied Islam a good deal, that, unconsciously, my first pre-Islamic submission had been manifested. I had experienced, for the first time, the Muslim teaching, "If you will take one step toward Allah—Allah will take two steps toward you."

My brothers and sisters in Detroit and Chicago had all become converted to what they were being taught was the "natural religion for the black man" of which Philbert had written to me. They all prayed for me to become converted while I was in prison. But after Philbert reported my vicious reply, they discussed what was the best thing to do. They had decided that Reginald, the latest convert, the one to whom I felt closest, would best know how to approach me, since he knew me so well in the street life.

.   .   .

I hadn't heard from Reginald in a good while after I got to Norfolk Prison Colony. But I had come in there not smoking cigarettes, or eating pork when it was served. That caused a bit of eyebrow-raising. Then a letter from Reginald telling me when he was coming to see me. By the time he came, I was really keyed up to hear the hype he was going to explain.

Reginald knew how my street-hustler mind operated. That's why his approach was so effective.

He had always dressed well, and now, when he came to visit, was carefully groomed. I was aching with wanting the "no pork and cigarettes" riddle answered. But he talked about the family, what was happening in Detroit, Harlem the last time he was there. I have never pushed anyone to tell me anything before he is ready. The offhand way Reginald talked and acted made me know that something big was coming.

He said, finally, as though it had just happened to come into his mind, "Malcolm, if a man knew every imaginable thing that there is to know, who would he be?"

Back in Harlem, he had often liked to get at something through this kind of indirection. It had often irritated me, because my way had always been direct. I looked at him. "Well, he would have to be some kind of a god—"

Reginald said, "There's a *man* who knows everything."

I asked, "Who is that?"

"God is a man," Reginald said. "His real name is Allah."

Allah. That word came back to me from Philbert's letter; it was my first hint of any connection. But Reginald went on. He said that God had 360 degrees of knowledge. He said that 360 degrees represented "the sum total of knowledge."

To say I was confused is an understatement. I don't have to remind you of the background against which I sat hearing my brother Reginald talk like this. I just listened, knowing he was taking his time in putting me onto something. And if somebody is trying to put you onto something, you need to listen.

. . .

The hardest test I ever faced in my life was praying. You understand. My comprehending, my believing the teachings of Mr. [Elijah] Muhammad had only required my mind's saying to me, "That's right!" or "I never thought of that."

But bending my knees to pray—that *act*—well, that took me a week.

You know what my life had been. Picking a lock to rob someone's house was the only way my knees had ever been bent before.

I had to force myself to bend my knees. And waves of shame and embarrassment would force me back up.

For evil to bend its knees, admitting its guilt, to implore the forgiveness of God, is the hardest thing in the world. It's easy for me to see and to say that now. But then, when I was the personification of evil, I was going through it. Again, again, I would force myself back down into the praying-to-Allah posture. When finally I was able to make myself stay down—I didn't know what to say to Allah.

For the next years, I was the nearest thing to a hermit in the Norfolk Prison Colony. I never have been more busy in my life. I still marvel at how swiftly my previous life's thinking pattern slid away from me, like snow off a roof. It is as though someone else I knew of had lived by hustling and crime. I would be startled to catch myself thinking in a remote way of my earlier self as another person.

from *THE EXPERIENCE OF NO-SELF*

BERNADETTE ROBERTS

---

*To lose oneself in contemplation of God was no mere metaphor for
Bernadette Roberts, a former Catholic nun, who has written about her
remarkable inner spiritual encounter in* The Experience of No-Self.
*In this opening section to her book, Roberts recounts turning her attention
within and finding only the unending silence of God.*

THROUGH PAST experience I had become familiar with
many different types and levels of silence. There is a silence within; a
silence that descends from without; a silence that stills existence; and
a silence that engulfs the entire universe. There is a silence of the self
and its faculties of will, thought, memory, and emotions. There is a
silence in which there is nothing, a silence in which there is something; and finally, there is the silence of no-self and the silence of God.
If there was any path on which I could chart my contemplative experiences, it would be this ever-expanding and deepening path of
silence.

On one occasion, however, this path seemed to come to an end,
when I entered a silence from which I would never totally emerge.
But I must preface this account by saying that on previous occasions,
I had come upon a pervasive silence of the faculties so total as to give
rise to subtle apprehensions of fear. It was a fear of being engulfed
forever, of being lost, annihilated, or blacking out and, possibly, never

returning. In such moments, to ward off the fear, I would make some movement of abandoning my fate to God—a gesture of the will, a thought, some type of projection. And every time I did this, the silence would be broken and I would gradually return to my usual self—and security. Then, one day, this was not to be the case.

Down the road from where I lived there was a monastery by the sea, and on afternoons when I could get away, I liked to spend some time alone in the silence of its chapel. This particular afternoon was no different from others. Once again there was a pervasive silence and once again I waited for the onset of fear to break it up. But this time the fear never came. Whether by habit of expectation or the reality of a fear held in abeyance, I felt some moments of suspense or tension—as if waiting for fear to touch me. During these moments of waiting, I felt as if I were poised on a precipice or balanced on a thin tightrope, with the known (myself) on one side and the unknown (God) on the other. A movement of fear would have been a movement toward the self and the known. Would I pass over this time, or would I fall back into my self—as usual? Since there was no power of my own to move or choose, I knew the decision was not mine; within, all was still, silent and motionless. In the stillness, I was not aware of the moment when the fear and tension of waiting had left. Still, I continued to wait for a movement not of myself and when no movement came, I simply remained in a great stillness.

Sister was rattling the keys of the chapel door. It was time to lock up, and time to go home and prepare dinner for my children. Always in the past, having to abruptly pull out of a deep silence was difficult, for my energies were then at a low ebb, and the effort of moving was like lifting a dead weight. This time, however, it suddenly occurred to me not to think about getting up, but to just *do* it. I think I learned a valuable lesson here, because I left the chapel as a feather floats in the wind. Once outside, I fully expected to return to my ordinary energies and thinking mind, but this day I had a difficult time because I was continually falling back into the great silence. The drive home was a constant battle against complete unconsciousness, and trying to get dinner was like trying to move a mountain.

For three exhausting days, it was a battle to stay awake and ward off the silence that every second threatened to overpower me. The only way I could accomplish the minimum of chores was by persistently reminding myself of what I was doing: now I'm peeling the carrots, now I'm cutting them, now I'm getting out a pan, now I'm putting water in the pan and on and on until, finally, I was so exhausted I would have to run for the couch. The moment I lay down I immediately blacked out. Sometimes it seemed I was out for hours, when it was only five minutes; at other times, it seemed like five minutes when it was hours. In this blackout there were no dreams, no awareness of my surroundings, no thoughts, no experiences—absolutely nothing.

On the fourth day, I noticed the silence easing up so I could stay awake with less effort and, therefore, I trusted myself to go shopping for groceries. I do not know what happened, but suddenly a lady was shaking me and asking, "Are you asleep?" I smiled at her while trying to get my bearings because, for the moment, I had not the slightest idea how I got in the store or what I should be doing. So I had to start all over again: now I am pushing the basket, now I must get some oranges, and so on. The morning of the fifth day, I could not find my slippers anywhere, but when getting breakfast for the children, I opened the refrigerator and what I found there was unbelievable, positively ludicrous.

By the ninth day, the silence had so eased up I felt assured that a little while longer and all would be normal again. But as the days went by, and I was once more able to function as usual, I noticed something was missing and I couldn't put my finger on it. Something, or some part of me had not returned. Some part of me was still in silence. It was as if some part of my mind had closed down. I blamed it on the memory because it was the last to return, and when it finally did, I noticed how flat and lifeless it was—like colorless slides on an antique film. It was dead. Not only was the distant past empty, but also the past of the previous minutes.

Now when something is dead you soon lose the habit of trying to resurrect it; thus, when the memory is lifeless, you learn to live as one who has no past—you learn to live in the present moment. That this could now be done effortlessly—and out of sheer necessity—was one good outcome of an otherwise exhausting experience. And even when I regained my practical memory, the effortless living in the present never left. But with the return of a practical memory, I discounted my earlier notion of what was missing and decided that the silent aspect of my mind was actually a kind of "absorption," an absorption in the unknown, which for me, of course, was God. It was like a continuous gaze at the great, silent Unknowable which no activity could interrupt. This was another welcomed outcome of the initial experience.

This interpretation of the silent aspect of my mind (absorption) seemed sufficiently explanatory for about a month, when I again changed my mind and decided that this absorption was actually an awareness, a special kind of "seeing" so that what had really happened was not a close-down of any kind, but actually an opening-up—nothing was missing, "something" had been added. After awhile, however, this notion also did not seem to fit; it was somehow dissatisfying; something else had happened, so I decided to go to the library to see if I could solve this mystery through someone else's experience.

What I found out is that, if it cannot be found in the works of John of the Cross, it will probably not be found at all. While the writings of the Saint were well known to me, I could not find there an explanation of my specific experience; nor was I able to find it anywhere in the library. But it was coming home that day, walking downhill with a panorama of valley and hills before me, that I turned my gaze inward, and what I saw, stopped me in my tracks. Instead of the usual unlocalized center of myself, there was nothing there; it was empty; and at the moment of seeing this there was a flood of quiet joy and I knew, finally I knew what was missing—it was my "self."

Physically, I felt as if a great burden had been lifted from me; I felt so light I looked down at my feet to be sure they were on the ground. Later I thought of St. Paul's experience, "Now, not I, but Christ lives in me," and realized that despite my emptiness, no one else had moved in to take my place; so I decided that Christ WAS the joy, the emptiness itself; He was all that was left of this human experience. For days I walked with this joy that, at times, was so great, I marveled at the flood gates and wondered how long they would hold.

For me, this experience was the height of my contemplative vocation. It was the ending of a question that had plagued me for years: where do "I" leave off and God begin? Over the years, the line that separated us had grown so thin and faded that most of the time I couldn't see it anymore, but always my mind had wanted desperately to know: what was His and what was mine? Now my quandary was over. There was no "mine" anymore, there was only His. I could have lived in this joyous state the rest of my life, but such was not in the Great Plan. It was just a matter of days, a week perhaps, when my entire spiritual life—the work, the suffering, the experiences, and the goals of a lifetime—suddenly exploded into a million irretrievable pieces and there was nothing, absolutely nothing left.

from *AMBIVALENT ZEN*

LAWRENCE SHAINBERG

Lawrence Shainberg's wealthy, philosophically inclined father, preoccupied with existential worries and the lamentable human condition, introduced his young son to everything from psychoanalysis to the wisdom of the East. Shainberg, now a Manhattan-based writer and a seeker himself, wrestles with enlightenment, personal sacrifice, and the enigmatic and often comical teachings of his Zen master.

SOON AFTER Kyudo Roshi and I go up to Yankee Stadium, I have what I take to be an enlightenment experience. His remarks about sacrifice have been almost constantly in my mind, but suddenly, while sitting in meditation, it seems to me that I am living them out instead of merely understanding them. My mind is unmarked space. Memories, fears, expectations—everything falls away. There is no self. I've sacrificed everything. For the next half-hour I live in a blissful state of immediacy, each instant a self-contained unit, untainted by past or future. So great is my exhilaration that when I stand up from my cushion I phone Roshi at once. I have never done this sort of thing before, but then again, I have never *felt* this sort of thing before. Isn't it his job to confirm, as masters have since Zen began, the enlightenment of his student? He listens patiently while I describe my experience, and then, as I ought to have known he would, takes it all away from me. "Larry-san, listen to me, OK? In the word, 'Buddha,' even the letter *B* is nothing but dust."

Dust is his word for all that's ephemeral, all that, if one becomes attached to it, gets one into trouble. In other words, all that, at Yankee Stadium, he admonished me to sacrifice, everything the Buddha relinquished when he sat beneath the Mucalinda tree. The logic is always the same: the source of fear is attachment to the impermanent. Conversely, if you befriend impermanence instead of denying it, you won't be afraid of anything. What complicates the issue is that ideas like this are dust as well. Since Buddhists become attached to Buddhist theory more than anything else, there is no greater source of dust, as he's just pointed out to me, than Buddhism itself. Once I asked him if monks "improved" as a result of their training, which is to say the training he had himself received, and he said: "No. Usually become more worse. Develop fixed ideas. Develop pride." It isn't Zen practice or meditation he questions. It is Zen concepts, Zen excitement. Zen ego. He views the mind in general as a dust factory and meditation as a means of wiping dust away. He likens our formal meditation—zazen—to taking a shower, advises us to think of our breath as a windshield wiper which, sweeping back and forth with inhalations and exhalations, cleans dust from the mind as wipers clean a windshield.

Between internal and external dust he makes no distinction whatever. To wash this dish perfectly or clean this mirror till it shines or handle a vacuum cleaner with authority is no different from sitting with one-pointed concentration—washing away your mental dust with the vacuum cleaner of awareness—on your cushion. Ask him about his plans for the weekend, and without a trace of irony, he'll answer, "Clean zendo," or "I washing my undershirts." Such chores, far from being onerous, are in his view therapeutic, purifying. A student who complains of depression is advised to clean his toilet, a woman contemplating suicide to wash her car. He cleans the zendo three or four times a week and resists all offers of help. It is not just that he believes we don't know how to clean properly but that, as he admits, he is selfish and doesn't want to share his pleasure. There is no cleaning chore—dish-washing, window-cleaning, snow-shoveling, etc.—about which he is unkowledgeable or unenthusiastic. He mops with his hands, at high speed, bending from the waist and sweeping a rag across the floor, cleans the brush attachment of the vacuum cleaner with a pair of tweezers. If he catches you vacuuming perpendicular to the seams of the floor so that you are not picking up the dust that collects between the boards, he concludes that you are a child and, even though he knows he is supposed to teach rather than penalize, will do his best to see that you are not assigned this job again.

An immaculate shoe rack, cleaned every day, stands just inside the door of the loft that contains our zendo. A rag, freshly dampened twice a day, is placed at the door of the zendo itself so that we can clean our feet of this, if not the deeper, dust we bring from the outside world. You don't step inside the loft and then remove your shoes. You wipe them on the doormat—also cleaned every day, of course—and remove them before you enter. In the dressing room, you hang your clothes on one hanger, preferably the one from which you've just removed your robe. He does not like to be explicit about it, but he views the use of more than one hanger as taking up more space than you need. In other words, an egoism, an act of selfishness, inattention. The way in which you wear your robe is crucial. More than once, he has told us that he can look at a Zen student, especially a monk, and discern from his robe how long he's been practicing. All of this seems compulsive until it strikes you, as it does with greater and greater frequency the more you hang around him, that your wrinkled robe or your sloppy habits with the vacuum cleaner are symptoms of inattention and distraction, the mindless fog in which most of your life is spent. During retreats, when you go to the kitchen for food and bring it back to your cushion, you walk behind rather than in front of others because if you don't, "dust come out" in the direction of their food. The vacuum cleaner is stored with the hose folded on top just so on this particular shelf with the orange extension cord wound like a rope with its plugs connected to each other. For loan when the weather surprises us, six umbrellas on which he's painted SOHO ZENDO hang from the shoe rack. We have two floor brushes for the vacuum cleaner, one labeled ZENDO, which is not to be used anywhere else in the loft. In the bathroom, hand towels hang from labels he's cut in half so that they fit neatly around the hook. Replacement facial and toilet tissue are as carefully centered on the toilet tank as the Buddha, the water bowl and the incense burner are centered on the altar. On a recent Saturday, he tells me, he went out early in the morning and did not return until late at night. In his mail, he found a telephone bill. He climbed to the zendo on the fourth floor, removed his shoes, went to his desk, wrote out a check, placed it in an envelope, put on his shoes again, went downstairs and walked to the corner mailbox in order to send it on its way. It was mid-December, very cold, almost midnight, and he was fifty-five years old. "Why the hurry?" I asked. "Why not wait until you went out again?" "No!" he cried. "I want to clean it up!"

On the other hand, one of his favorite expressions is "Fish not grow in pure water." Though he is orthodox and reverent and attentive to the precepts, nothing arouses his revulsion like piety. "You in jungle, tiger attacking you, you raise your rifle and think, 'Oh, no, cannot shoot! I Buddhist!' Such a one not Buddhist! Such a one attachment to Buddhism! Not understand at all!" He proudly describes how he killed cockroaches while living in the monastery. "I help cockroach! Cockroach help me!" If Buddhist excitement is dust, Buddhist orthodoxy is mud. Any suggestion that he is "religious" strikes him as insulting. Most spiritual seekers are "like drunk." Though his reverence is obvious when he speaks of the Buddha, he never tires of reminding us that, just before his death, after teaching for sixty years, Shakyamuni said, "I have taught nothing at all!"

· · ·

Confused about a decision I must make, I go to Roshi for advice. My girlfriend and I are having problems, and I know it's because we've both got one foot out the door: should we break it off or take the leap into commitment? Never mind that this is a man who went to all-male schools before he entered the monastery, who's never had the sort of relationship I'm talking about and, by his own testimony, never had sex in his life. On the day he graduated high school, sitting around with a group of classmates, he suddenly announced, "I never marry!" When I ask him why he made this decision, he says, "I don't know. Just come out!" But a moment later he makes a stab at it. "You know, Larry-san, marriage very beautiful. Two people live together, do each other laundry, cook each other. Slowly two people become one. But me—I one already!" It is seventeen years since he left the monastery, and he still finds it difficult to look at a woman. Only recently, he tells me, has he overcome the impulse to turn his head away when he sees a man and woman kissing on television. Now fifty-six, he likes to brag about his diminishing potency. "Until I fifty, my sausage much stand up! Now, almost never! Very good for practice! All my energy for zazen!"

We're having tea at the zendo before evening zazen begins. While he stands at the sink preparing the Japanese brew he serves (along with a bowl of Pepperidge Farm cookies), the telephone rings, and we hear a voice on the answering machine. It's a prospective student, seeking our zendo schedule, leaving his name and address so that we can send him information. "Larry-san," Roshi begins, pointing to the notepad next to the phone, "please you take down name." But then he pauses for a moment, listening hard to the man who's speaking. "No, don't bother—insincere voice."

Not too long ago, another man found our number in the phone book, and this time Roshi answered.

"Are you a Zen master?"

"Yes, I am."

"I need to talk to you. I want to commit suicide."

"Good idea!" Roshi said. "Right away! Don't hesitate!"

In contrast to our usual, informal meetings, when we discuss business matters (taxes, membership dues, etc.) relevant to my role of vice president or make small talk, Roshi has donned his robes and assumed a serious demeanor, as if to remind us both that my request for advice this afternoon requires him to be my teacher rather than my friend. We sit at the table in his kitchen which serves as his living and dining room. The only social area in this loft, it is adjacent to his tiny, windowless bedroom, the interior of which is hidden behind a sliding glass door and a set of venetian blinds. The zendo is down the hall, a large, sunlit room with an immaculate altar, tropical plants, scrolls on the walls and of course the cushions on which we sit in meditation. Looming above us, covered with a yellow brocade altar cloth embroidered with Japanese calligraphy, is his favorite possession, the television set and VCR the membership gave him for his birthday last year. His favorite show is professional wrestling—especially when Hulk Hogan fights—he he also fancies reruns of "Kojak" and "Dallas" and beauty contests like those to select Miss Universe and Miss America.

When I've finished describing my quandary, he remains silent for several minutes. Erect in his chair, eyes half closed, it's as if he's doing zazen in order to give me full attention. Finally, he says, "Larry-san, must make great decision." He makes a fist and extends it slowly, like a piston, into the air between us. "Even if terrorist gun to your head, you not change your mind!"

"Well, sure, Roshi, I know that. But it's not so easy. Something tells me we won't be able to make it, but I can't bear the thought of hurting her."

"Always, you too kind! Want to please everybody! Irresponsible, Larry-san! In the end, cause more pain."

"But isn't Dharma about compassion? Aren't we supposed to think of others before we think of ourselves?"

"The Dharma," he says, "is only going in one direction. You make great decision, you make great Dharma. You wandering, you wasting your life. Forty-seven years old, Larry-san! You wandering now, you wandering under cemetery."

This is not, of course, the first time I've heard such advice from him. Such is his belief in willpower and self-motivation that no aspect of behavior seems beyond their influence. Even one's own neuro-chemistry can be mastered with the proper mix of faith and courage. Depressed? "I give you advice," he said to one woman, "must cheerful!" And to another, despondent about the failure of her marriage, "You make decision, Sarah-san: forget it!"

What else should one expect from a man who believes that any problem can be dissolved by keeping one's back straight and watching the mind in which confusion percolates? He likes to quote the Buddha's famous parable about the wounded warrior on the battle-field. Though dying from an arrow in his back, he resists when some-one offers to remove it, insisting that he must first know who shot it, what direction it came from, what mistake he made that caused him to be hit, etc. The belief that growth proceeds from understanding and description, unraveling the chain of cause and effect, is a recipe for paralysis. The first arrow is the analytic mind. How can you hope to heal your wound with more analysis?

There are days when I am amenable to this point of view, but today, as it happens, is not one of them. I feel as if he's dismissing my pain, offering bromides. What's the good of advising a man who can't sleep and has no appetite and, most important, is suffering from a paralyz-ing case of indecision, to "make a great decision"? It's as if I've got a broken leg and he's telling me to run the marathon.

"Listen, Roshi, I've come to you with a problem. I don't know what to do, OK? In America we call this 'indecision.' Are you familiar with the word?"

"'Indecision?'" He pronounces it "indeeseeshun" with accent on the last syllable. "Yes, I understood, Larry-san. Cannot decide. Wandering mind. Indeeseeshun. Very good word!"

"And yet you're telling me that the cure for it is to make a decision?"

"Yes, yes. Great decision! Never shaking! Never turn back!"

"But Roshi . . . I've just been telling you. A decision is just what I can't make. Have you never had that problem?"

He puts out his cigarette and reaches for another. Again and again, like other students here, I've complained about his smoking, arguing that he owes it to us, if not himself, to care for his body so that he can remain healthy and be our teacher as long as possible. "Why I want that?" he says. "I live too long, everybody die, then I lonely!"

"Of course I have that problem," he says. "Twice."

"Twice!"

"Yes, after high school, when I cannot decide what to do. And again before I go to monastery."

"Before the monastery! That was thirty years ago! C'mon, Roshi, admit it. You don't know anything about indecision! I'm a fool to ask you for advice. It's like I'm crawling up a mountain and you fly past me in a helicopter."

"Hellicopper?" He squints at me, puzzled. "What you mean 'hellicopper'?"

Thinking he's trying to evade the issue, I snap, "It's a kind of airplane."

He hands me a piece of paper. "You write for me, OK?"

I print out "helicopter" while he fetches his dictionary from the bedroom. Still annoyed, I watch his lips shape the word while he searches out the definition. At last, pronouncing the Japanese word, he cries: "Yes! Yes! Hellicopper! I hellicopper! You crawling on mounting! I flying! You crawling! Ha! Ha! Ha!" He takes a long drag on his cigarette, stubs it out in the ashtray, then suddenly turns serious again. "Listen, Larry-san. I fly over you, I see what you not see."

"What's that?"

He presses his thumb against his forefinger and holds them poised together above his teacup. "You and mounting-top—only this far apart."

AROUND THE KA'BA AND OVER
THE CRICK

MOHJA KAHF

Now a professor of English at the University of Arkansas, Mohja Kahf, a Muslim of Syrian origin, was raised in a small Indiana farming town in a world in which her religion and family customs were decidedly "other." While growing up, Kahf learned to deflect daily taunts and threats and took refuge in the safety and love of her isolated and insular Muslim community. But when her family relocates to a religiously and ethnically diverse area in the Northeast, the cultural landscape shifts and Kahf finds herself ill-prepared and reluctant to now encounter "the Other" in her midst.

OVER BY the "crick" out back, scuffing the chain-link fence, and dashing through a couple of neighbors' backyards, was the shortcut to the bus stop when I was in the sixth grade at Van Buren Elementary School in the small farming town of Plainfield, Indiana. The "crick" was tiny but beautiful to us; blue-green dragonflies zigzagged over it and creepy "crawdads" crawled in the muddy bank. But as a Muslim in Plainfield, the chasm I traveled each day between school and home was wider than the little creek my brother and I hopped on the way to school.

Once, in sixth grade, I even had to leap over hellfire, singeing my toes. I was in music class, and the words "dear Lord Jesus" came up suddenly in the song I was singing, full-throttle, with the rest of the class. What else could I do? All that my parents taught me, my religion, my catechism, my *tawhid*—Islamic monotheism—forbade these words. What was very important in my Muslim tradition seemed to be invisible here. Years later, I would read these words by Adrienne Rich—*"When someone with the authority of a teacher, say, describes the world and you are not in it, there is a moment of psychic dis-equilibrium, as if you looked into a mirror and saw nothing"*—and I would recognize my own experience, day after day, in Plainfield.

My equilibrium teetered on those choir bleachers, where nothing I knew from home had a foothold. Pressing around me were the imperatives of the moment, the bodies of my classmates, and the presence of the music teacher. He was oblivious to the theological battle furiously being waged inside my head as I stood in the third row with my eternal fate in my hands. I sang the words in a dread-filled mumble, and of course I never told my parents. I added it to the load I carried over the crick every day between my two worlds.

Dogging the early years of our life in Plainfield, Indiana, was a lawsuit filed by the "Concerned Citizens of Hendricks County." Though most Plainfielders were decent folks who went about their own business, this ad hoc group was formed specifically to oust from its site the Islamic Society of North America (ISNA), the organization for which my father worked and for which we had moved to Plainfield. Neighboring towns in our concerned citizens' county, such as Danville and Morrisville, were reputed to be Ku Klux Klan enclaves. We were reminded of this by the graffiti that regularly defaced ISNA property. Daughters of those pursuing the lawsuit would goad me in the girl's room about the progress of the case, and Klansmen's boys would boast to me about their vandalism.

My parents did their best to deal with the situation after their own fashion. They held an open house after we moved into the neighborhood; they drove us to Muslim friends in Indianapolis, and took us to Islamic gatherings all over the States. Their knowledge of their children's experience was limited, however, their reserves of understanding based on their own childhoods in another country. And let's be clear: My parents and the other Muslims who made up our little immigrant-dominated community in those early days in Plainfield were truly modern-day Puritans, as earnest and righteous in their outlook as any who set foot on Plymouth Rock in 1620. They saw themselves as an island of faith, an outpost of God in the moral wilderness, and it was their mission to see that we did not risk drowning in the waters of American society. We would venture out as a family only far enough so the local natives might have a chance at salvation too. How a part of my immigrant community ever expected to settle in America and have their children emerge not one whit differently than if they had grown up in a conservative Muslim environment back home remains beyond my comprehension. It is a little comic to me, in retrospect, why fate chose to juxtapose those particular immigrant Muslims with these kind of Americans. . . . Of all the ornery people God could find to throw together!

When I was in junior high, one of those "Americans" who would brag about spray-painting "KKK" on the Islamic Society's placard was a gorgeous football player, and it gave me goose-bumps to be faced with him. In that heartbeat that lasts an eternity for a teenage girl, I would be entranced by his halo of blond hair and chiseled features. Then he'd open his mouth and say crude, hateful things right at me, and I realized that I wasn't even a girl to him, just an undifferentiated enemy. My religious community, for its part, expected me to see his being a non-Muslim male as the sole significant factor defining my interaction with him and preferred that I had no interaction with him at all. And I complied, except for brief moments when some other possibility seemed imaginable. Yet, these were the encounters that characterized this period of my life: Beauty overtaken by ugliness too quickly for it to operate as beauty should. My two worlds refused to meet.

It was natural, with the sense that we had of being besieged by bigotry, that the farm where ISNA was located felt like a haven. My brother and I loved to accompany our father to his office on the ISNA property. We climbed its apple trees, collected international stamps from indulgent staff members who handled the mail, and skipped through the dusty book warehouse in the old red barn. At least in those golden cornfields we could traipse without fear of being chased out by a rifle-toting local. I remember some moonlit evenings when our little group of Plainfield Muslim families, which included Pakistanis, African-Americans, Euro-Americans, and Arabs, gathered in the mosque room of the wood frame farmhouse for some event, followed by night prayers. I took a big gulp of safety and love, knowing it would have to last me through the school week. It would have to carry me through the name-calling in the hallway: Ayatollah, camel jockey, King Tut—I collected the tags like war medals. And then through the hoots in the cafeteria while I stood balancing my tray of

Salisbury steak and apple crisp and searching, Forrest Gump-like, for a place to sit, for a friend. It would have to take me past the corridor lined with older boys where I walked a gauntlet of verbal threats on each of the four hundred and forty-four mornings of the Iranian hostage crisis.

The derision was especially sharp when it came to the way I dressed. After making *hajj*, the pilgrimage to Mecca to the Ka'ba, the holiest place on earth for Muslims, with my family during the seventh grade, I had decided to wear the head scarf associated with conventional Islamic notions of womanly propriety. Contemporary Muslim discourse calls this dress *hijab*. Choosing hijab helped junior-high-school-me marshal the resources of my family and faith community. In fact, my parents were so proud of me that I am still running into relatives in the Arab world who heard about my *hijab*. Aunt Wadia, a vivacious African-American Hoosier who worked at ISNA and who, with her little son Malcolm, had adopted our family, took me to a fabric store to choose material. I still have a scarf she edged for me, clusters of pale mauve flowers on an off-white background.

"You're in America now," the be-jeaned girls and boys would jeer, flipping their Farrah Fawcett and Fonzie hair. "Whyn't you dress like everybody else?" "It's a free country!" I'd retort. With *hijab* as an alternative, I could reject their Barbie-and-Ken teenage conformity. The headcloth reminded me that even if no one in Plainfield connected with me, there were whole worlds of people, thousands of whom had thronged around me at the Ka'ba, with whom I did have a connection, with whom I was real and legitimate and belonged. The *hajj*, the pilgrimage, re-oriented me to an internationalist Islamic identity so that I did not have to feel second-class at home because I lacked the typical national identity of whoever surrounded me, be they Arab or American. *Hijab* seemed like a way to hold on to that awareness once I was back in Plainfield. With *hijab*, then, I shored up my identity—far too entirely. With supreme naiveté, I believed I could pin my self-formation upon this already overloaded bit of fabric. I suppose, given the circumstances, it worked: the scarf did its job; it helped me navigate through a sea wherein I could have broken down psychologically and capsized.

Years later, I met a beautiful person who, just by being who she is, has taught me volumes about being a human being, a friend, and a Muslim. An Arab-American like me—although from a very different type of family—she had grown up only a few dozen miles away from

Plainfield. "Surely you visited the ISNA farm," I asked, delighted at the common ground we'd tread, unbeknownst to each other.

"I went to look at books a few times," she said. "I always slunk out quickly, feeling uncomfortable."

"Why ever so?" I asked, completely surprised.

"I don't think they approved of the way I dressed or looked. They seemed to disapprove of the kind of Muslim I was," she explained.

Maybe it was because she did not wear the head scarf that the folks at the ISNA did not feel she was quite kosher—so to speak. Whatever was the cause, I began to see that every closed place has its shadows. My one-time haven could be, in its turn, a cold and intolerant place for certain others who were outside a carefully drawn circle. And it is easiest, I learned, to remain silent about the dark spots in one's own community—and one's self.

Since the 1970s, Plainfield and INSA have both changed; eventually, these two communities adjusted to each other—somehow. Though nothing in the Muslim community ever compared to the viciousness of the Klan, yet for both my Muslim community and the Plainfield citizenry at that moment in history, the religion and ethnicity of an individual or a group created a near-impenetrable boundary that negated the potential of any possible spiritual, or just-plain-human encounter. And in those days, I was a Muslim with a capital "M." As a young woman, I was far from questioning the structure of an us-versus-them opposition, even as I fought for an end to the harassment. Some ways of battling discrimination and bigotry can also stunt your own spiritual growth, block the imagination, and keep you at the level of parrying blows and living angry, exhausted, and defensive.

My family moved to New Jersey when I began the tenth grade. After physically leaving Plainfield, Indiana, I slowly began to leave it in other ways: emotional, intellectual, and spiritual. At Passaic Valley High, in a student body almost entirely made up of second-generation Polish- or Italian-Americans, there was yet another lesson in store for me. I learned that being different was not so different after all. It turned out that my Plainfield experience, although revelatory, was neither representative of, nor unique to, Muslims. From a metropolitan, East Coast, perspective, America looked less homogenous, and thus it became easier for me to find my niche. I found out within my first few weeks at PV High that some of the "regular American" kids in my classes even had Arab parentage! They were from an earlier generation of immigrants who had settled down and became a part of

America and owned gas stations or delis or worked in "The City" (New York—is there any other?).

"Hey, so do you also eat, like, *yabra'* n' shit?" Marlene says to me, snapping her gum as we change into gym sneakers. I start with delighted recognition when I hear her use the word for stuffed grape leaves, Syrian-style. I am also shocked at the casual cussing, and from a girl with Arab ancestry! "Americans," I always thought, were the ones who used profanity, not "us." Here in this New Jersey high school, I had my first encounter with Arab Christians, with children of interfaith marriages, and with new mixtures of identity that had not occurred to me. I would now have to rearrange all my mental charts and binary oppositions.

"*Yabra'* 'n shit." How cool, how tough, how exquisitely an expression of both Arabness *and* Americanness, how totally Jersey. I could do this!—maybe. In reality, I was ill-prepared to explore friendships across cultural or religious boundaries, first dipping in a toe, then bounding back from the shoreline. Now that my social scene permitted new kinds of opportunities for friendships, it turned out that I had a poverty of personal resources for engaging "the Other," those outside the particular conservative Muslim identity which I then embraced. It was the nourishing "spring rain" of such friendships that would finally enable my stunted little soul to grow beyond the rigid dichotomies to which I held fast.

When I could allow myself to love, it would be friendship that would reveal human beauty—beauty that surely must be a reflection of the Divine. Maybe that is why, in the poetry of Islamic mysticism, one of the poet's code words for God is "The Friend." "Fundamentally, all loves relate and refer to the True Beloved," writes Muzzaffer Ozak in *The Unveiling of Love.* "However, he continues, "the manifestations appear variously. . . ."

Intellectually, I began to learn how to connect the jagged halves of my two worlds when I entered college. I went to a school with a long-standing commitment to the development of womens' potential—Douglass College, a part of Rutgers, the State University of New Jersey, and continued at Rutgers for a doctorate in comparative literature. There, in the form of feminist theory and civil-rights movement history, I learned that the individual is embedded in ideological structures, and the knowledge which comes from personal experience is not just an irrelevant, slightly shameful burden to be shed at the threshold of real, objective knowledge. In particular, leftist thought spoke to me because it validated experience as a source of theory and seemed to empower those who stand outside of what is dominant and mainstream. In graduate school, I came back down from the deterministic extremes of this idea that the individual is defined solely by larger structures toward a more pragmatic medium ground.

I was not sure how to reconcile all this progressive thought, particularly the feminist part, with Islam as I knew it, but I decided to hang on to both sides, including the *hijab,* and let things work themselves out gradually. Insight would come, I felt, through intuition and experience, not through more theory. Or, to quote Ghazali, the twelfth-century Muslim who details his journey from traditional belief through the stages of skepticism, theology, philosophy, and finally veering toward mysticism, "It became clear to me that the last stage could not be reached by mere instruction, but only by transport, ecstasy, and the transformation of the moral being."

This kind of engaged self-transformation, I am embarrassed to admit, was a new frontier for me. You mean being "religious" is not merely a matter of conforming to massive rule books handed down by generations of legalistic scholars? I actually have to think about things like "manifesting the beauty Divine" in the here and now, not just follow a crime-and-punishment logic to please a Grand Inquisitor God? Years of imbibing a rather confident missionary stance made me wary of more easy talk of God. The beauty part I could understand, however: poetry, song, music, glorious Form. Yes, these are paths to another dimension; yes, I want to go to that planet.

Spiritually, what I have been experiencing since leaving Plainfield, and leaving and leaving, is a slow draining of silt, layer after layer of the sediment of racism, sexism, and prejudice—my own. Every time I think I have finished with the last layer I find another. I have glimmers that in doing so I am making room for some beautiful dimension of reality that has escaped me, even though the emptying out can be wrenching, especially on my relationships.

I wonder what it might be like to become a muslim with a small "m," turning toward the etymological root of the word: the giving over of one's self, surrendering to the Divine—as opposed to the social-religious community that currently owns the label of Muslim with a capital "M" and carries with it all the accumulated historical doctrines and assumptions about what being a Muslim should entail. The contemporary liberationist Farid Esack explores this question in his book, *Qur'an, Liberation, and Pluralism,* showing how the Qur'an uses the terms "islam" and "muslim" in far more dynamic ways than traditional Muslim thinking allows. After all, there are no capital letters in Arabic, the language of the Qur'an. To seek the living manifestation of spiritual and ethical values themselves, regardless of the label they come under, is to discover unexpected kinship with persons from utterly different social and religious backgrounds. In this view, faith is no longer a matter of allegiance to a specific community or identity, but a ceaseless search for the beautiful ways to realize the human potential in every given age and place. "Every new encounter with ourselves and others, every deed that we do or refuse to do, is a step in our perpetual transformation," Esack says. There's that word again—transformation.

The spiritual path before me is still dim. All I know for certain is that it lies in the direction of love. Somewhere, a dragonfly, blue or green—both or neither—moults through metamorphosis after metamorphosis, preparing to swoop over a zigzaggy creek and into the whitehot flame of an unimaginable beauty.

from *PLAIN AND SIMPLE: A WOMAN'S JOURNEY TO THE AMISH*

S U E   B E N D E R

Sue Bender, a Berkeley-based wife, mother, artist, and family therapist, lived a frenetic life, surrounded by lists and things to do. In 1967, when she was in her early thirties, she came upon Amish quilts, and later, their "faceless" dolls, whose austerity and simplicity beckoned her. In Plain and Simple, *she describes being inspired by these everyday objects to seek out an Amish family in order to discover an antidote for her compulsive busyness in the world.*

I HAD AN obsession with the Amish. Plain and simple. Objectively it made no sense. I, who worked hard at being special, fell in love with a people who valued being ordinary.

When I told people I wanted to live with an Amish family everybody laughed. "Impossible," they said. "No Amish family will take you in."

I didn't know when I first look at an Amish quilt and felt my heart pounding that my soul was starving, that an inner voice was trying to make sense of my life.

I didn't know that I was beginning a journey of the spirit, what Carlos Castaneda calls following "a path that has heart."

I thought I was going to learn more about their quilts, but the quilts were only guides, leading me to what I really needed to learn, to answer a question I hadn't formed yet:

"Is there another way to lead a good life?"

I went searching in a foreign land and found my way home.

. . .

Can an object go straight to your heart?

Twenty years ago I walked into Latham's Men's Store in Sag Harbor, New York, and saw old quilts used as a background for men's tweeds. I had never seen quilts like that. Odd color combinations. Deep saturated solid colors: purple, mauve, green, brown, magenta, electric blue, red. Simple geometric forms: squares, diamonds, rectangles. A patina of use emanated from them. They spoke directly to me. They knew something. They went straight to my heart.

That was the beginning. Innocent enough.

"Who made these quilts?" I demanded.

"The Amish."

I went back to Latham's every day that summer, as if in a trance, not noticing it at first, just something I did in the midst of all the other things I was doing. Visiting the quilts became a practice, something like a spiritual practice, the one constant in days that were otherwise filled with the activities of summer.

I stared at the quilts. They seemed so silent: a "silence like thunder." It was 1967, and I was thirty-three years old.

. . .

The quilts spoke to such a deep place inside me that I felt them reaching out, trying to tell me something, but my mind was thoroughly confused. How could pared-down and daring go together? How could a quilt be calm and intense at the same time? Can an object do that? Can an object know something?

. . .

How opposite my life was from an Amish quilt.

My life was like a CRAZY QUILT, a pattern I hated. Hundreds of
scattered, unrelated, stimulating fragments, each going off in its own
direction, creating a lot of frantic energy. There was no overall structure to hold the pieces together. The Crazy Quilt was a perfect
metaphor for my life.

A tug-of-war raging inside me.

In contrast to the muted colors of the Amish, I saw myself in
extremes: a black-and-white person who made black-and-white
ceramics and organized her life around a series of black-and-white
judgments.

I divided my world into two lists. All the "creative" things—the things
I valued, being an artist, thinking of myself as undisciplined and
imaginative—were on one side, and the boring, everyday things—
those deadly, ordinary chores that everybody has to do, the things I
thought distracted me from living an artistic life—were on the other
side.

I was an ex-New Yorker living most of the time in Berkeley, California; a wife and mother of two sons; an artist and a therapist with
two graduate degrees, one from Harvard, one from Berkeley. That
was my resume.

I valued accomplishments.

I valued being special.

I valued results.

The driven part didn't question or examine these values. It took
them as real, and believed it was following the carrot "success" whole-
heartedly. Didn't everyone believe in success? I never asked, "Success
at what cost?"

A part of me is quiet. It knows about simplicity, about commitment, and the joy of doing what I do well. That part is the artist, the child— it is receptive and has infinite courage. But time and my busyness drowned the quiet voice.

In the world in which I grew up, more choices meant a better life.

It was true for both my parents and my grandparents. I was brought up to believe that the more choices I had, the better.

Never having enough time, I wanted it all, a glutton for new experience. Excited, attracted, distracted, tempted in all directions, I thought I was lucky to have so many choices and I naively believed I could live them all.

A tyranny of lists engulfed me. The lists created the illusion that my life was full.

· · ·

I never thought to stop and ask myself, "What really matters?" Instead, I gave everything equal weight. I had no way to select what was important and what was not. Things that were important didn't get done, and others, quite unimportant, were completed and crossed off the list.

Accumulating choices was a way of not having to make a choice, but I didn't know that at the time. To eliminate anything was a foreign concept. I felt deprived if I let go of any choices.

· · ·

I never questioned my frantic behavior. When I looked around, most of my friends were like me, scurrying around and complaining that they never had the time to do all the things they really wanted to do.

Only now, looking back, can I hear a child's voice inside me calling "*STOP,* I want to get off. The merry-go-round is spinning faster and faster. Please make it stop."

At the time I thought I was extremely lucky. But something was missing, and though I could not have said what that "something" was, I was always searching, believing there was *something out there*—and if only I could find it. That "if only" kept me trying to change. I took classes—trying to improve, hoping I'd be a better person. A friend laughed, "I'll know you've changed when you stop trying to change."

I didn't know that my addiction to unrelenting activity produced a quiet desperation that permeated every cell of my being. In the world of "if only," nothing I was doing would ever be enough.

Spinning frantically, I left myself out.

·   ·   ·

I had become an artist by chance.

In 1960, three months before the birth of my first child, I stopped teaching history at New Rochelle High School in New York and joined a clay class. The timing was perfect: I had planned to miss only three months of teaching before school began again in September. I never returned. In those few months, I fell in love with clay. Clay was soft and responsive. It had its own rhythm, its own heartbeat, a timing sensitive to moods and the atmosphere, just like a person. It didn't make demands, but it did ask me to pay attention and to listen. I thought being receptive meant being "out of control," so I had a lot of difficulty with that part of the relationship. On damp days, the clay took longer to harden. Impatient, I put the pieces in my kitchen oven, willing them to dry faster.

For all the abuse I gave the clay, I also had a natural connection with the material. Clay became part of me, not just something I did. But I never saw myself as just a potter. Refusing to make regular or practical forms, I felt I was something more, an *artist*. To me "regular" meant ordinary. I was determined to stand out.

Growing up in New York, my parents' message had been *"Be a Star,"* though these words were never said out loud. The first things I made were beautiful, shining ceramic stars, with real gold luster. I loved making them. The child in me was still dreaming of becoming a star.

I spent many years in school. Achieve, achieve, I heard, and along with the words came a clear picture of the right way to be. Even the air I breathed seemed to agree. Clay was different. It was flexible, encouraging me to take a chance.

I tried to learn the potter's wheel but I resisted its discipline and was singularly unsuccessful at using it. To explain my ineptness, I told myself I was afraid I would get hooked on the technology of the wheel, and end up making perfectly thrown, characterless pots. I never understood that while the clay was whirling around on the wheel, centering a pot meant centering myself. At that time I was too scattered to find that calm inner focus.

In the summer of 1967, I had my first show.

The pieces were impractical, fanciful objects and whimsical creatures from my imagination. *"More, more!"* my demons demanded, for in their world "more" meant better. It was a year of hell. Instead of enjoying the work, I pushed myself, trying to make each piece more original than the previous one. The more I willfully tried to force something fresh, the more I failed. Never pausing to take a breath, I raced around on full power until, exhausted, I finally caved in. Only then, when my frantic pace was temporarily halted, could I make pieces I felt good about.

At the opening of my show people came up to greet me.

"You must be such a happy person. Your work is so filled with fun," said one guest.

"If I made ceramics that looked the way I felt this year, the work would be gnarled and hideous," I replied.

. . .

Each time I went back to look at them that summer, those stoic Amish quilts with their spartan shapes, sent shock waves through me—a grown woman mesmerized. These are dramatic words, but that's what it felt like. The connection was immediate and electric.

My busyness stopped. The fragments of my life became still. I was coming home, connecting to a part of me that I had ignored, even depreciated. I felt calm.

.   .   .

Though I never thought of buying an Amish quilt, I spent the next years searching for them. Quilt dealers who knew of my growing interest called when they returned from buying trips. Each time I made a pilgrimage to see them, I returned home calm. My head was filled with questions. What was the intention of the woman as she began making a quilt for her daughter? Was her life embodied in her quilt? Was she telling me something of her hopes and dreams?

Many years after I had seen my first Amish quilt, in the fall of 1981, I walked into Ed Brown's Folk Art Gallery in San Francisco and saw three strange-looking dolls that had no features drawn on them—the eyes, noses, mouths, fingers, and toes were missing. One was stuffed with straw, another with quilt batting, and the third with rags. Their bodies were covered with hardy unbleached muslin. Dressed in tattered, dark, old-fashioned clothing and bonnets, they were quite unlike the pink doll babies I had known as a child. Like voodoo dolls, they cast their spell.

Astounded, I asked Ed Brown, "Where do these odd dolls come from?"

"The Amish."

"Why are their faces blank?" I asked.

"The rule comes from their religion," he said. "The Bible says, 'Thou shalt not make any graven image, or any likeness of anything that is in heaven above, or that is in the earth beneath.'"

For generations Amish mothers have made their dolls for their daughters. Always the same, no need to change or embellish or improve them. They just need to be durable enough to withstand lots of use.

I stood looking at these three old tattered dolls, and each week I went back to stare at them. On the surface they looked the same, but when I looked closer, each one had a distinct personality, the unique mark of the mother who made the doll for her child. Finally, just looking at the dolls wasn't enough. Thinking about the dolls, daydreaming about the quilts, I realized I had to know more. Back in New York that summer my husband and I, tourists like everyone else, drove off to Lancaster County, Pennsylvania, to visit the Amish.

What we saw wasn't quaint, make-believe Williamsburg, nor a reenactment of country living in the nineteenth century. These people weren't acting. They were quietly minding their own business as they drove their neatly painted black horse-drawn buggies down the narrow country lanes. The Amish call those people who aren't Amish the "English" (the "other sort of people"). We "English" were creating a traffic hazard, stopping to take their pictures.

If the Amish were bothered by the intrusion of these gaping English outsiders, they didn't show it. Although they were a major attraction for masses of aggressive, curious tourists, they moved around unhurried, as if in a contemplative world of their own. Their somber expression, staring straight ahead, their faces encased in large black bonnets—all this created an atmosphere that made me uncomfortable.

Surrounded by grossly commercial motels, neon signs flashing "Plain and Fancy," the Amish had created a world in sharp contrast. The fields looked like their quilts—rich, lush, orderly, and serene.

This was their world, and we were voyeurs, looking at them with the same curiosity we might look at someone in a freak show. I hated it—and had to leave. "Are there any Amish communities where the people don't live in a fish bowl?" I asked the surprised woman at the tourist bureau. She suggested a somewhat remote county several hours away, in Ohio.

We left small country roads for even smaller lanes, meandering with no plan, leaving behind the world of road markers. That was unusual for us, getting unhooked from the world of road maps and certainty.

I was looking for an excuse to begin a conversation, so when we arrived I began asking Amish women if they could tell me where the nearest Amish dry goods store was, saying I wanted to buy a faceless doll and some solid colored cotton material.

The stores were hard to find, tucked away on back-country roads, looking like every other Amish house, a white wooden building with black trim, no sign outside. After a while I could spot them by the hitching posts and buggies standing outside. I learned to recognize Amish homes by the absence of electrical wires leading to the house. Several homes used windmills, but the easiest clue was the clothesline, full of trousers and blouses in dark, vibrant Amish colors, hung neatly on the line in order of size.

"Do you sell faceless dolls?" I would ask.

"No, we don't sell them," I was told everywhere. "Every mother makes her own doll."

"Do you know anyone who might be willing to make a doll for me?"

Finally, lost on a small country lane, we met an old woman who sold a few basic sewing supplies from a room in the back of her house. "You can try down the road. The two sisters who live there are midwives and I think they make dolls for the new babies."

We found the house. "Hello? hello?" I called, knowing there would be no doorbell. After a long wait, a young freckle-faced woman came out of the house and walked toward us with a definite, unhurried step. Barefoot, wearing a long black dress almost to the ground, and a kelly-green blouse that complemented her red hair, she looked determined.

"Why are you here?" she asked, brusquely, I thought. The quizzical look on her face seemed to say, "What could these people possibly want?" The look of guarded suspicion remained as I asked her if she would make me a faceless doll.

"Why would you want one?" she asked. "They're so ordinary."

I told her the truth, knowing how odd that explanation must have sounded. "I thought they might teach me something."

"Why do you call them faceless?" she wanted to know.

"All the dolls I'd seen before had their eyes, noses, and mouths drawn in. I call them faceless because the contrast is so startling."

She seemed alternately suspicious and curious, unable to make up her mind. Finally after several minutes, she opened the door and invited us in. Her name was Sarah. Once inside, she was pleased to show us around. To the left was a large kitchen with a black, immaculately polished woodburning stove and a kitchen table with ten chairs around it. To the right was a living room with an old floppy sofa, two straight-back chairs, a small table, bare walls except for a few paper calendars, and a lot of empty space.

Everything in the rooms was sparkling clean.

This was her sister Becky's house, Sarah explained. Becky had nine children, and Sarah, who was not married, lived with her, doing chiropractic work and helping Becky with the children and the garden. "I help Becky catching babies."

"What's that?"

"We're midwives," she said, and went on to explain "We fixed up the two rooms next to the living room with hospital beds so the mothers would be comfortable."

Bursting with curiosity, I blurted out questions. "How do you know when a mother's about to have a baby?" I asked, seeing that as a real problem in a community without telephones.

"They just show up when they're ready. Some come from quite a distance, but we're always around."

"Doesn't a buggy take too long?"

"Oh, some of the women hire drivers to bring them here," Sarah explained matter-of-factly.

After visiting for half an hour I began to feel uneasy taking up Sarah's time. "Will you make a doll for me?" I asked, hoping to have an excuse to stay in contact with her.

"Yes, but I can't tell you exactly when I can send it. I'll have to wait till I have a bit of free time. Is that all right?" She finally agreed to make two dolls for me as long as I understood—I almost had to promise that I understood—they were nothing special.

Then we argued about the price. She said, "Five dollars for each doll."

I said, "You're charging too little." We finally agreed. I would pay fifteen dollars for the two dolls.

Several months later the dolls arrived in a recycled shoe box with a note on lined white paper. I opened the box and saw two serious Amish dolls looking up at me.

The note read, "I hope they are all right. Let me know if you are dissatisfied."

A week later another note arrived, this time from a woman named Ruth, who identified herself as Sarah's cousin. "I hear you like Amish dolls. Would you like me to make you one?" I wrote back, pleased to have an excuse to write to another Amish woman and receive more direct statements on lined white paper.

Over the next six months, I received twelve dolls from seven Amish women.

The dolls surrounded me, silent and serene. I was overcome by the collective energy radiating from them.

Everywhere I looked there was a faceless doll. Some watched while I worked in the studio, a few kept me company upstairs in the room where I saw my clients, two sat on the living room sofa, and several were housed in an old Shaker basket on the dining room table.

Their spirit permeated the house.

They were made by seven ordinary women who spoke no "shoulds."

There was no pecking order there. None was better, none was worse than the others. They didn't have to perform or prove anything. No voice said, "Be happy, cute, or pretty." No voice said, "Be a Star."

In my world everyone has a face, and many of us try to stand out. In their simplicity, these faceless dolls said more with less. They left more to the imagination. Maybe accepting who they are, they don't waste their strength trying to change or compete.

Looking at the dolls, I imagined them worthy companions, friends, allies, and guides for young girls. But were they allowed to cry or be angry, were they itching to be wild and free? Was I talking about myself?

"Tell the truth," they seemed to say. "Don't be afraid. We'll help. Go on! Go on!"

"Where?" I asked. "You'll know! You'll know! Risk. Your heart's desire."

It was hard to admit to myself what I wanted: "To go and live with an Amish family."

Impossible, I told myself. Everyone agreed: no Amish family would take me in. They were religious, hard-working farmers. They didn't reach out to strangers, and they didn't try to proselytize. They chose to live apart from the world and its temptations.

The dolls stood silently by, cheering me on.

from *ENCOUNTERING GOD: A SPIRITUAL JOURNEY FROM BOZEMAN TO BANARAS*

DIANA ECK

The cremation pyres on the banks of the Ganges were a far distance from the banks of the Gallatin River in Montana where Diana Eck grew up riding horses and spending summers in the Methodist Youth Fellowship. Now an esteemed professor of comparative religion and Indian studies at Harvard, Eck writes in Encountering God *that she had never experienced a challenge to her faith until, as a college sophomore in 1965, she journeyed to Banaras, India's holiest city, and met Hindus as devout as the Christians she knew back home.*

I GREW UP in Bozeman, Montana, in the Gallatin Valley, one of the most beautiful mountain valleys in the Rockies. The Gallatin River cuts through a spectacular canyon to the south, then flows like a stream of crystal through the fertile farmlands of the valley. I had three horses stabled on our land by the Gallatin and spent hours every week riding along the river. By the time I was twenty, I had made my way "back East," as we called it, to Smith College, and then much further east to India, to the Hindu sacred city of Banaras, set on the banks of another river, the Ganges. Banaras was the first real city I ever lived in. It was a city in the time of the Buddha, twenty-six hundred years ago, and the guidebooks called it "older than history." Bozeman had been settled for scarcely one hundred years.

As a twenty-year old, I found Banaras to be about as far from Bozeman as any place on earth. The smoke of the cremation pyres rose
night and day from the "burning ghats" along the river. The Ganges
is a much bigger river than the Gallatin; it is a powerful river that
seemed to flow with authority and peace as it slid along the ghats, the
great stone steps of the city, where Hindus bathed by the thousands at
dawn. Today these two places, Bozeman and Banaras, both convey
the spiritual meaning of the word *home* to me. And these two rivers,
the Gallatin and the Ganges, both flow with living waters I would call
holy. Worlds apart, they carry currents of life and meaning whose
confluence is in me, deep in my own spiritual life. All of us have such
rivers deep within us, bearing the waters of joining streams.

. . .

The church I grew up in, the First Methodist Church on South Will-
son, was the oldest Methodist church building in the state. The foundation stone had been laid in 1873 by the first minister, the Reverend
T.C. Iliff, in the days when Bozeman was still a frontier town with dirt
streets and Saturday night shootouts.

. . .

Our Methodist church camps were summer meeting places where I
got my first taste of a wide and vibrant sense of the church. Various
churches built their own cabins in Luccock Park, the camp in the hills
above the Paradise Valley near Livingston. Those log cabins, named
for our towns "Bozeman," "Livingston," "Billings," and "Big Timber," nestled like miniatures below the towering mountains we called
Faith, Hope, and Charity. There in our summer camps we teenagers
in the Methodist Youth Fellowship, the M.Y.F., enacted the rites of
bonding and commitment that are so formative in the adolescent
experience of religion: confessing our secrets and dreams, singing
round the campfire at night, sitting in silence and prayer as the fire
began to die down, holding crossed hands in a circle of commitment
around the glowing embers. When I became the state M.Y.F. president, I also went to the Flathead Lake camp, nearly four hundred
miles away in the northwest part of the state. There the cabins were
called "Kalispell," "Missoula," and "Great Falls," and there we sat on
logs in the outdoor chapel at Inspiration Point for what we called
"morning watch," looking out at daybreak past the wooden cross,
over Flathead Lake toward the Mission Range.

I did a lot of building as a teenager in the Montana M.Y.F.—roofing, mixing cement, pounding and pulling nails. There were work camps every summer. We built a dining hall at Luccock Park under the supervision of my father, an architect and builder. We built a church at a little settlement called Babb on the Blackfoot Reservation in the grassy, windy prairie land east of Glacier National Park. We lived for a month in two spacious tepees, talking late into the night, sleeping in sleeping bags around the fire, and rising early for morning watch on the hilltop just above our campsite. We took an old schoolbus to Mexico, again with my father and mother, and built a silo on a rural-development farm near Patzcuaro. Our workdays included drilling holes for dynamite, blasting, and mixing cement for the master masons from the little village of Huecorio to use in raising the stone walls of what had to be the most elegant and durable silo in all of Mexico. There our days began with morning watch on the rooftop terrace, where the twenty of us studied the Bible and sang hymns looking out over the farmlands towards Lake Patzcuaro with its island village of Janitzio.

The most durable product of these teenage summers, at least for me, was a sturdy faith in God, a very portable sense of what constitutes the church, and a commitment to the work of the church in the world. I arrived at Smith College in the fall of 1963 straight from the March on Washington, where I had been with the national M.Y.F. delegation. I joined these friends again during the spring vacation of my freshman year to lobby in Washington, D.C., for the Civil Rights Bill. Civil rights and the Vietnam War, racism and militarism, were the issues that shaped the whole context of college in the sixties, during the years I was at Smith. They came together in complex ways. One of my first summer jobs was a short stint working for the Montana Board of Health on the Northern Cheyenne Reservation out of Lame Deer in southeastern Montana. I saw at first-hand the racism of my own state, where I had rarely met an African American, but had also rarely seen the real conditions in which most of the Native American peoples lived. After two weeks in Lame Deer, I was invited to an all-night prayer meeting of the Native American church. As we settled into a circle around the fire in the tepee, my host told me that the service was to pray for the Cheyenne boys who were serving in Vietnam. There were six from the tiny town of Lame Deer alone. The night was unforgettable: rounds of peyote, chanting, prayer, drumming. It was a form of worship I had never seen, among people who were virtual neighbors and yet virtual strangers to me in Montana, people whose sons and brothers were disproportionately drafted for service in Vietnam.

It was in this context of the Vietnam War that I first went to India. The move had only an indirect logic to it, a logic animated by the concern and yet the inadequacy so many American college students felt about the U.S. war in Asia. As a sophomore in college, I was aimed toward the study of Latin America. But when I saw the announcement of the University of Wisconsin's College Year in India program posted on the bulletin board in Wright Hall during midyear exams, I was immediately drawn to the possibility. Nothing and no one in my past had prepared me for an encounter with that part of the world. I knew nothing of Asia. In fact, the Vietnam War seemed a tragic testimony to how little most of us in America knew about Asia. The boys from Lame Deer were there. A few friends from my high school were there. My friends from Amherst thought of nothing but how to avoid going there. So I applied to go to India. It was Asia. Close enough. Maybe I would learn something. I took a spring term course taught by a visiting professor from Poona on the thought of two of India's most important twentieth-century thinkers, Gandhi and Aurobindo. That summer—which was for some a Mississippi summer, for some a Vietnam summer—I spent in the language labs at the University of Wisconsin learning Hindi.

In September of 1965, with a new group of friends from the summer of language study in Madison, I arrived in India. There was not much in Bozeman or Northampton, or even in Patzcuaro, that could have prepared me for Banaras, a vibrant, congested city sitting high on the banks of the River Ganges. Its intensity was overwhelming. I had been in Banaras only a few days when I wrote home, "Wandering half-scared through the side-walk narrow streets near the Chowk market today was an exhausting experience, exhausting because it was as if I had walked through all of India, seen, felt, tasted, smelled it all in three hours. There were too many people, too many faces, too many cows, too many catacomb streets and dead ends, too little air. The utter concentration of life, work, misery, odor, and filth in this area of the city was staggering."

Despite my feelings of claustrophobia and bewilderment, I was immediately impressed by the religiousness of Banaras. There religion was surely *the* most important observable fact of daily life. The whole city seemed to revolve on a ritual axis. There were temples everywhere, large and small, inhabited by images of gods and goddesses whose names I did not know, whose multiarmed forms I could not even distinguish one from the other, and whose significance was totally beyond my grasp. The bathing ghats along the Ganges were the scene of morning rituals for pilgrims. We had not been there more than a day or two when we rose before dawn and took rickshaws to the riverfront to see the sights for which Banaras is so famous. Thousands of Hindus were there at Dasashwamedh Ghat, bobbing in the water, standing waist deep their hands folded in prayer, chanting to a crescendo of bells as the sun rose over the river. Perhaps the one piece of my Montana past that I brought with me to the comprehension of that first dawn on the Ganges was "morning watch." For two miles along the ghats, Hindus bathed in the Ganges and worshiped as the sun broke the horizon. The city pulsed with the life of faith as vibrant as any I had known, and as different.

That year I came to know, for the first time, people of faith from a tradition not my own. I did not know any Jews, let alone Hindus or Muslims, when I set off from Montana for Smith College. I knew little of the faith of others, but at that point in life I was quite clear about the center of my own Christian faith: love, justice, human dignity, and the steady sense of being linked in kinship to Christ and to the Christian community. It was a faith nourished, as all faith finally is, by people—energetic, loving, committed, visionary people. The only people of that sort I knew—and I had the good fortune of knowing quite a few of them as a teenager—were Christians.

It was in Banaras that I experienced the first real challenge to my faith. Not surprisingly, it did not come in the form of ideas, even though I was enrolled in a course in Advaita Vedanta philosophy at the Banaras Hindu University. It came in the form of people— Hindus whose lives were a powerful witness to their faith. I had conceived a completely naive fieldwork project on "Hinduism and the Indian Intellectual." Knowing little about Hinduism myself, I concocted a set of questions about the gods, the meaning of *karma*, the meaning of reincarnation, and so forth, and set out on my bicycle to meet scholars, poets, and professionals in Banaras and to ask what they believed. It was not a very good project, but I couldn't have found a more interesting introduction to India.

One of those I met was Achyut Patwardhan, a former freedom fighter who had spent his share of years in prison in the service of the nonviolent movement for India's independence. He was a man of simple, self-giving love. Like the civil rights leaders I had admired at home, he had put his life on the line in the service of justice. "You see suffering," he said to me, "and you don't debate about it or make yourself act. Those who love simply act, respond naturally with the spontaneous good that is human. Perhaps all you can do is take another person's hand. This, then, is sufficient." Patwardhan was, to me as a twenty-year-old, a man of God and a great spiritual friend at a time of my life when questions were tumbling through my mind. He was a man whose life was a witness to love and justice. He was very much like the people I had most loved and admired as a teenager. But he was not a Christian. He did not find an example and a companion in Christ, as I did. To my surprise, it did not seem to me that he somehow ought to be a Christian. What did this mean about some of the biblical claims of my own tradition?

In November I met J. Krishnamurti, a man who did not fit any category at all. He was giving a series of daily talks at Rajghat in Banaras. Not only was he not a Christian, he was not a Hindu, not a Buddhist. That was just his point. "Truth is a pathless land," he said. "You cannot approach it by any path whatsoever, by any religion, by any sect." He did not say, Follow me. On the contrary, he said, "I desire those who seek to understand me to be free, not to follow me, not to make out of me a cage which will become a religion, a sect." He did not care for the labels of any religion. Indeed, he observed the way in which we fearfully, anxiously, shape our whole lives by religious, political, cultural, and personal labels and names—all of which function as a buffer zone of security between ourselves and the experience of life.

Krishnamurti posed my first real encounter with the "otherness" of a worldview. No one in my world had ever asked about the value of labeling, judging, discriminating, and categorizing experience or suggested that by doing so we distance ourselves from experience. We call it a beautiful sunrise on the Ganges and don't ever really see it because we have dispensed with it by giving it a name and label. Perhaps we write a poem about it to capture it in words or take a photograph of it and feel satisfied that we "got it." We name so-and-so as a friend or an enemy. The next time we encounter that person, the pigeonhole is ready. Are not our minds perpetually busy in these maneuvers? I must admit, at twenty it had never occurred to me to ask such questions. And what about religion? Is it really just a name? I had to ask myself about being a Christian. Did the name matter? Did the label provide me with a shelter or barrier to shield me from real encounter or questioning? What did I have invested in this name? Everywhere I turned I saw question marks.

.   .   .

During the years in Banaras I worked and studied with two teachers, both men in their eighties, whose equanimity and patience, love of learning, love of God, and love of the Ganga, the River Ganges, were luminous. They became family to me, and I to them. In my study of the Hindu tradition, I asked many questions of them. But I was not the only one with questions. They had questions, too. "Why do you pour yogurt on the gods?" I would ask, astonished. "Is it true that Christians in the West wear their shoes right into churches?" they would ask, equally astonished. When I asked about the worship of Shiva and Krishna, I was also asked about Christ.

I could hear them sizing me up, interpreting me in their own world of meaning. Who was this woman who had come from so far away, who asked so many questions about temples and gods, who studied Sanskrit and made so many mistakes? My friends in Bozeman may have wondered, as I have myself, how it was that a young woman who grew up in the high valleys and fresh air of the Rocky Mountains was so drawn to the city of Banaras, studying temples in its crowded alleyways and breathing the air of the cremation grounds. But this posed no problem to my teachers and friends in Banaras. "You must have been a Hindu in your last lifetime," said one. "You lived here in Banaras in a former life, which is why you have such a feeling for this city," said another. "You were part of our family, which is why you have come to be among us now," said another. One of my teachers, Kuber Nath Sukul, insisted, "You are my granddaughter, because your mother was born just about the time my only daughter died. Welcome home."

In our relationship, I surely was a witness to my own faith as a Christian. They knew I was a Christian, that I was a Protestant, and that even so I went to the little Catholic church that met in an apartment building called Vishnu Bhavan at the end of Lanka Street. But I was not the only one to bear witness to my faith. So did my teacher Ambika Datta Upadhyaya, whom I addressed with the reverential and affectionate title Pandit-ji, when he spoke with quiet confidence about the meaning of death, even his own death. So did his wife, whom I called Mata-ji, in her observances of fasting and prayer.

. . .

One day in Banaras Pandit-ji's cousin came to visit. He was introduced to me as "Uncle." Like Pandit-ji, he was in his eighties, but unlike Pandit-ji he had rarely met a Westerner. Uncle was fascinated to discover I was a Christian; I may have been the first he had ever met. He asked me to tell him about my *ishtadevata,* my "chosen god," Jesus Christ. I must admit I was not quite sure what to say. I had not practiced this Hindi vocabulary, and for a fleeting second I found myself wishing I had done a Hindi study course at Landour, the old mission station in the hills north of Dehra Dun where the lessons were geared to the explication of terms like "Son of God" and "the Word made flesh." I told him that Christ was fully God and fully man. I used the words *Parameshvara,* "supreme God," and *manushya,* "man," as they would be used in the Hindi translation of the Bible. The word *incarnation* does not appear in the New Testament, but I decided to try to convey that sense of divine embodiment. Jesus Christ was the incarnate presence of the supreme God, right here on earth. I used the term *avatara,* which is only approximately accurate, and means, literally, a "divine descent" of God into the world of name and form.

The *avatara* notion is a powerful one in the Hindu tradition. According to the Bhagavad Gita, when righteousness has declined and injustice prospers, God comes into being, in age after age, to reestablish order. The stories of the "divine descents," *avataras,* of the supreme Lord Vishnu are stories of rescuing the righteous and protecting the faithful. In the sequence of *avataras,* God weaves his saving power through all the realms of creation. As a fish he guides Manu, India's Noah, through the great flood. As a boar he dives deep to rescue the sunken earth from the bottom of the sea. As a man-lion he kills an arrogant demon and rescues the young boy Prahlada, his most ardent devotee. As a dwarf he humbly asks for three paces of land from a world-conquering demon and then expands to stride through all the earth, the heavens, and the beyond with his three steps. As the fully human Rama, he nobly embodies righteousness, renouncing his kingdom on a matter of principle and protecting humanity by slaying the demons of the forest during his fourteen years of exile. As Krishna he ecstatically lifts the heart to love.

I do not for a moment doubt the transforming and sustaining power of these stories for Uncle. Indeed, they are moving stories for me. There is much that I find captivating, but, to be honest, much that I don't find captivating: the endless battles; the *avatara* Parashu-rama, who killed his mother and then slew all the world's warriors seven times over. There is much that I find appealing theologically: the fact that the forms of God's embodiment move through the strata of life with a kind of theological Darwinism—a sea-going fish, a land-to sea-going tortoise, a mammal, a half-man/half-lion, a dwarf, a human, a superhuman. Among them all, it is especially Krishna who moves my heart religiously and expands my mind theologically.

"Is it true," Uncle asked as if verifying an outlandish rumor, "that Christians believe Jesus was the *only* avatara?" I recalled in my mind all the language about the decisiveness, uniqueness, and finality of Christ—language I was uncomfortable with, but which I knew was still the common Christian understanding. "Yes, most Christians do," I responded. "Christians say he was unique, the only one." "But how is it possible," he asked, "to believe that God showed himself only once, to one people, in one part of the world, and so long ago?" The implications were clear in the expression of Uncle's face: What kind of stingy God would that be? What kind of small-minded, self-centered people would believe in such a God? To him it was clear that the full, embodied disclosure of God to men and women was not only multi-ple in time and place, but potentially infinite. Uncle went on to ask about the story and attributes of Jesus. Did he have a goddess or con-sort? Did he have a vehicle or animal mount? Did he have special powers? I did my best, but between my inadequate Hindi and my inadequate theology, I am afraid Uncle was disappointed in Jesus.

WHEN A CHRISTIAN CHANTS
THE QUR'AN

GEORGE DARDESS

Wanting to know more about Islam beyond the sensationalist stereotypes offered by the media, George Dardess, a devout Roman Catholic, visited his local Islamic Center in Rochester, New York, first to study Arabic, and then to learn to chant the Qur'an. Dardess, an English teacher, explores in this reflection his deep attraction to this monotheistic tradition and realizes the surprising paradox of interreligious encounter: his own Christian faith is strengthened the more his love of Islam grows.

WHEN DR. MUHAMMAD SHAFIQ, imam of Rochester's Islamic Center, entered the center's main prayer area (the *masjid* or mosque), I was chanting the Qur'an with my teacher Siddiq Abdul Hakkim. The two of us were sitting on the carpet near the back wall. Dr. Shafiq came over and said something that startled, even alarmed me. He invited me to join the prayer line with the other men at *salat*, the prayer performed daily at five prescribed times.

Why was I startled? Because as a Roman Catholic Christian, I had somehow assumed that my taking part in *salat* was off limits to me in the same way as Communion in my church would be off limits to Dr. Shafiq. Didn't every religion have its boundaries beyond which outsiders might not pass? Yet here was the leader of a Muslim congregation inviting me, a Catholic, over that boundary, and doing so in the gentlest way possible, as if the invitation, from his point of view,

447

involved no boundary violation whatsoever. Where I saw a wall, Dr. Shafiq saw an open path leading directly in front of the *masjid*.

Later on I asked Dr. Shafiq what he'd had in mind when he made the invitation. His answer—which I'll give in due course—didn't surprise me. From the start, I understood him better than I understood myself. I knew right away, for example, that my alarm had nothing to do with an effort on Dr. Shafiq's part to convert me to Islam. I had known him for almost two years, ever since my first coming to the center to take his course in Arabic. I'd been moved to do so by my dismay at my ignorance of Islam, an ignorance which had forced me to rely on the mass media's distorted accounts during events like the Salman Rushdie controversy and the Persian Gulf War. After the course, I asked Dr. Shafiq if I might study the Qur'an. For it was now clear to me, as I had often been told, that without such study I wouldn't have a way of knowing Islam with any degree of intimacy. At this point Dr. Shafiq arranged for me to take lessons from Siddiq. Meanwhile, our relationship grew closer. Dr. Shafiq gave me good counsel during an illness in my family. I brought my high school English classes to visit the *masjid* during Friday prayers. A year ago, Dr. Shafiq invited me to speak at the center to Muslim teenagers about the meaning of Christmas from a Christian perspective. He has asked me on occasion to edit his writings on Islam. In short, it is a relationship based on mutual trust and personal liking. He has been happy to see my degree of commitment or dissuade me from it. I don't say he wouldn't be happier still to see me become a Muslim, but, as the Qur'an says, "let there be no compulsion in religion"—a verse Dr. Shafiq quoted for me early in our friendship. One's way of worshiping God must be freely chosen or else it is no meaningful choice at all.

So if I ask again why I was so alarmed at his invitation, I'm forced to look inside myself for an answer. Some of this answer lies, as I have said, in my uncertainty about what is allowable to outsiders, and specifically to Christians, in the practice of Islam. But most of the answer lies at a deeper level, and so is harder to get at: in my own attraction to Islam. What began for me out of a sense of civic and intellectual responsibility—as a desire to cut through my ignorance of a religion practiced by a good proportion of the earth's population, a religion often misrepresented in the Western press—had become a passion. For how else than as the result of a passion could I account for the fact that I was returning to the *masjid* week after week to study the Qur'an with Siddiq and with my other brother in Islam, Navid Aslam? Why was I including within my daily Christian prayers others I'd learned at the *masjid*—for example, the *Fatiha*, the opening chapter of the Qur'an, which stands in approximately the same relation to Muslims as the Lord's Prayer does to Christians? And didn't my alarm at Dr. Shafiq's invitation indicate that my attachment to my study had become stronger than I was aware of? Didn't my alarm really signify my sudden awareness, not of a boundary in front of me, but of one behind me, one I had crossed already without knowing it?

But what was this boundary? And where exactly was I now? And in general, how far can I or any Christian go in following an attraction to Islam?

First things first! I cannot answer these more general questions without returning to my own uncertain position at the moment of Dr. Shafiq's invitation. In moving along the path toward—into?—Islam, I knew I was following a strong attraction. But precisely to what?

To people, primarily—to Dr. Shafiq and Siddiq and everyone else I had met at the center. I would not have proceeded down the path opened for me there unless I had felt welcomed at every step.

Yet surmounting these strong attractions to people—surmounting but supported by them, and unimaginable to me without them—is my attraction to the Qur'an, and particularly to its voice. I was slow to hear that voice because of the inevitable difficulties any Westerner has with Arabic's alphabet, grammar, and, above all, with its vocalization. Arabic's various throat, velar (middle of the palate), and nasal intonations are ones we don't make unless we are choking or clearing our throat and sinuses. Gradually, however, my body and my understanding accommodated themselves to the language's demands. And then, last summer, came an event I count as a special blessing. I was able to take lessons in Qur'anic *tajwid* or chanting with Qari Muhammad Khursheed Ali. Qari Muhammad (*qari* means "reciter") is the *mu'adhan* or *muezzin*, the one who calls the faithful to prayer, at the Faisal Masjid in Islamabad, Pakistan. His chanting of the Qur'an verses is treasured throughout Pakistan. Very fortunately for me and others at the center, Qari Muhammad was able to come to Rochester for a few weeks to teach *tajwid* to American Muslims. Such instruction is not an "extra." The Qur'an—which means "recitation"—is meant to be heard aloud. The Prophet Muhammad (peace and blessing be upon him) delivered the verses orally as he heard them from the angel Jibreel (Gabriel), who was himself reciting the very words of Allah. Many *hadith* (traditional stories about the Prophet's sayings and actions) establish the spirit in which one is to vocalize the Qur'an's verses: other traditions not only set down technical rules for pronunciation and rhythm but also indicate where and how far one may extemporize, especially in the changing of pitch and the free shaping of lengthened vowels. A *qari* like Muhammad Khursheed Ali studies and follows such prescriptions carefully, finding in them the source of a centuries-old discipline and of a constantly renewed freshness. The result is that when one hears the Qur'an chanted by a good *qari*, one is hearing it reembodied, as if the Prophet's voice were revived in the voice of the chanter.

To hear this voice—and not only to hear it but to learn to embody it in oneself through *tajwid*—is to experience a beauty that stretches the heart. It is an invigoration of the mind and body, as if one stood, at each moment of vocalization, at the edge of all time and space, themselves merely the Creator's doorstep. No matter that after attempting to follow Qari Muhammad through a verse phrase by phrase, my sinuses ached, my nose became runny, my breath became short. These are happy birth pangs as a new creature enters what the Qur'an calls, in one of its most memorable verses, the "light of lights."

But how new is this "new creature," as I call myself? What exactly is different about the relationship I hope I have with God as a result of this transformation by the Qur'an's voice?

For me this is the key question, one whose answer I must approach delicately.

I spoke earlier of a tradition of recitation. Each chanter chants the same text chanted by every other chanter through the ages, but the chant takes form in each throat differently. The laws of *tajwid* allow, as I have said, for certain freedoms of expression. Such freedoms are themselves rooted in each chanter's individual gifts, musical and spiritual, as they manifest themselves at the moment of utterance. In this sense, recitation of the Qur'an is a continuous prayer, an audible sign of the inner disposition or Islam, submission, of the chanter. (The word Muslim means, "one who submits.") It is not a mere musical performance that Qari Muhammad gives, or that his student gives in imitation of him, but the evidence of a sincere longing for what the voice promises, again and again, in verse after verse: reward. Reward is the Garden, the land of delight and fulfillment after death where the only conversation is the word *salam*, peace, the fruit and climax of all voices raised in Qur'anic prayer.

But a strong taste of that peace is realized here on earth when one finds echoing in one's own body and soul, despite their imperfections, the Qur'an's true and original voice, God's own. This voice, mediated from a great distance above and behind one, through lines of transmission from Allah to Jibreel to the Prophet (peace and blessing be upon him) to *qaris* throughout the ages, is nevertheless disconcertingly or perhaps reassuringly near—"closer than their jugular vein," as one Qur'anic verse puts it. It is the voice, the message, the tone conveyed by the Hebrew prophets—overwhelming, magisterial, commanding, glorious, and so on and on, in adjectives derived from our experience of anyone who has ever spoken to us with true authority. And because it speaks with authority, it is not a bullying voice. Its power is not flaunted. It simply soars out high above us without interruption from the beginning of the Qur'an to the end, effortless and unhurried, even in modulations of tone from the joyful to the grim to the ironic to the reassuring. Yet without sacrificing its grandeur it seems to swoop low as well, to listen closely to our own inner voices, including the secret conniving voice in which we resist to try to ignore this penetration. The Qur'anic voice speaks often of our not listening to it, and records with short, devastating strokes the consequences of this indifference: the turbulence of heart, the violence of behavior, and the terrible end in the fire of final judgment. The effect, however, is not to frighten but to warn. We are not helpless in meeting the voice's challenge. We possess the strength to listen, and God—"*ar-Rahman ar-Rahim*" (the beneficent, the merciful)—never tires of trying to catch our ear and enter it.

My understanding is that being Muslim means just this, allowing the voice of the Qur'an, God's voice, to penetrate one's heart, with the result that one's behavior radically changes. The Qur'an's ethical dimension is rooted in this joyful submission. One simply cannot afterward, for example—in keeping with behavior the Qur'an most frequently condemns—neglect the poor, play the hypocrite, or set oneself (or anyone or anything else) up as an idol. Such behavior is not simply proscribed; it is impossible in the creature one is invited to become.

But what of myself as a Catholic Christian, coming to the Qur'an not from discontent or atheism but from a kindred belief in God's might and from a kindred ethical orientation? Could my experience of the Qur'an be said to have changed me in any way? If so, am I less of a Christian than I once was, as I become more of a Muslim? Or could the opposite be true, that I am more of a Christian as a result? What would "more of a Christian" in this sense mean?

Whatever the ambiguities of my position in the *masjid*, whatever my doubts about the degree to which I may take part in the practice of this religion to which I have been drawn, I do find myself "more of a Christian" as a result of my experience—meaning that I am more joyfully and wonderingly a Christian than before.

This is so because the Qur'an has enlarged my sense of the Word of God.

How? To start with John's Gospel, Jesus is the "Word made flesh." He is the creative power of the Father come down from heaven to share fully in our humanity and to sacrifice himself for that humanity on the cross. That sacrifice, for a Christian, is not a bitter but a joyous event since it leads to resurrection. Our fallen humanity is transformed by Christ's saving action, a transformation that begins here on earth in our celebrations of Communion and which is perfected after death in heaven, when our union with Christ becomes complete.

The Word of God in the Qur'an is not transformative in the same way or to the same degree. Islam vigorously denies that human nature has fallen so low as to require God's salvific action. But in its power to enter the heart through the body and to lift both heart and body toward the light of God's mercy the Qur'anic Word is fruitfully close to the "Word made flesh." What the Qur'an "adds" for me—though, for God, there can be no question of a deficiency, of an adding or a subtracting—is a reinvigorated emphasis on the voice as the agent of embodiment. At Catholic Mass, the Word of God is made flesh both in the scriptural Word which our mouths proclaim and in the Eucharist which we consume. But though the Second Vatican Council declared the indivisibility of the Liturgy of the Word and of the Eucharist, we Catholics tend to tip this balance forward, emphasizing the Eucharist at the expense of the Word. The Eucharist then becomes the climax of a liturgical drama to which the Word is mere prelude. A prayerful recitation of the Qur'an, which requires that key ingredient of Muslim worship, *taqwa,* or absolute attentiveness to God's "signs," primarily to those given in the Qur'an itself, has led me to a more prayerful attention to the Christian Word at Mass and in private Bible reading. Word presence is real presence. The force of this truth, acknowledged by me before, but often lukewarmly, has been quickened by my Qur'anic chanting.

But can the Qur'an's voice lead me farther? Has it had only an oblique usefulness, in invigorating a somewhat dulled consciousness of the power of the spoken Word in my own religion? What of the message of that voice? How much of it can I absorb as my own without peril to my love of the risen Christ? I speak here of the level of importance the Qur'an assigns to Jesus. For while, as Geoffrey Parrinder convincingly demonstrates in his *Jesus in the Qur'an* (Oxford University Press, 1977), the Qur'an speaks of Jesus in terms surprisingly close to those used in the Gospels, he is mentioned in only 93 of the Qur'an's 6,226 verses. "He receives many honorable names but he is placed in the succession of the prophets, and teaching about the prophets is only one element in the Qur'an." Given the Qur'an's apparent minimizing of Jesus' role in God's plan for humankind, how far can I, or any Christian, go in my reverence for the Qur'an as God's Word? As attractive as the Qur'an may be, for all the reasons I have stated, doesn't its seeming indifference or blindness to Jesus' centrality divide it from me, force me always to hear it with a certain detachment? The Vatican II document *Lumen gentium* (16) may say that "the plan of salvation also includes those who acknowledge the Creator. In the first place among those are the Moslems . . . ," but nothing whatever is said or implied about the value or indeed the legitimacy of a Christian's worshiping with them. If, as almost all Christians, including myself, believe, there can be no salvation except through Christ, how can I chant the Qur'an sincerely without assuming—against all evidence—that the Qur'an is also, at some level, the language of the Gospels?

But for me—I cannot speak for all Christians—my love of Christ is not reducible to a series of dogmatic declarations. This love is a presence that accompanies me at every moment of my life, in moments of folly, weakness, and misery as well as in happier states. It is the atmosphere in which I "live and move and have my being." Put another way: the risen Christ is present to me, not only at Mass, but at every beat of my heart, in every circumstance. There is no limit to this penetration. Similarly with everyone else, including those who do not know him as risen Lord, or who do not know him at all. Yet my belief in his universality does not entitle me to make claims of superior knowledge. I could never confront Dr. Shafiq with the statement that, whatever he may think to the contrary, Jesus is with him. Not good manners but humility prohibits my doing so. What Saint Paul calls "the language of the cross" is not like the language we use with each other, where we deal with equals. This language bridges heaven and earth. We humans did not invent it. God purified and transformed an instrument of torture, the cross, as his vehicle for communicating with his creatures. In his unfathomable wisdom he performed a not dissimilar miracle with the language of an obscure Semitic people, the Arabs, purifying and transforming that language into a vehicle of his almost direct utterance. As I stand before the cross chanting the Qur'an, I do not find myself, God's creature, moved to argue about discrepancies, even ones as significant as those involving Jesus' true nature or importance. My conviction that the language of the Qur'an is also God's language overrides what would otherwise bring me to disagree with it as a mere human utterance. In such moments of enthusiasm—and they come often—I find nothing to hinder me from making the Muslim *shahada,* the credal statement of faith in one God and in Muhammad as his prophet.

For Dr. Shafiq too, God's *Tawhid* or Oneness resolves all tensions in belief. I mentioned earlier that I finally asked him, once I had gotten over my surprise, what he'd had in mind when he invited me to pray with the others at *salat.* His answer was, simply, that he already saw me as a Muslim in the truest sense, in that I believed in the one God. I myself might think I'm also something else, but in his view, Allah had brought me to Rochester's Islamic Center to become a part of the community of the monotheistic religions. "Islam and Christianity and Judaism are different only on cultural, not on spiritual levels. People don't see this larger picture because of a lack of knowledge," he said. As for my taking part in *salat,* Allah is the judge of my intentions, not people. But Dr. Shafiq thought *salat* would be good for me since it is a humbler form of prayer than the prayer of chanting the Qur'an. I did not press him on this point, but reflecting on it now, I think he meant to say that *salat*—whose formulas are largely composed of Qur'anic verses, especially those in the *fatiha*—enforces the Qur'an's egalitarianism. Qur'anic chant by itself might foster a certain intellectual and spiritual arrogance. *Salat* brings the believer side by side with every other person smitten by the voice of the Qur'an, not just with those adept at *tajwid.*

Smitten as I continue to be, however, I have not—yet—answered the *adhan,* or call to prayer. While I trust Dr. Shafiq and agree with his vision of the oneness of religion under one God, I nevertheless feel a restraint about taking a step which to me, rightly or wrongly, expresses a form of trespass. It isn't simply a fear of what my fellow Catholics would say of my doing so, let alone of what Muslims less enlightened than Dr. Shafiq might think to find me, a Christian, at their side during *salat.* It's that the communal action of prayer, as opposed to the more private version of it represented by chanting the Qur'an, assumes a full commitment to those with whom one prays. By "full commitment," I don't mean tithing only, or serving on committees, or regular participation at liturgies, though of course these things are part of what a full commitment means, and of what they mean to me in my service to my local parish and diocese. It means primarily a desire to make one's religion one's home. In marital terms, it means monogamy. Was it chance or God's will that I married the woman who is still and I hope will always be my wife? Given different circumstances, I might have married someone else—or no one. But the marriage I made, though a limitation in one sense, has also enabled me to be open to people in ways I doubt I could have managed otherwise. Similarly with my Catholicism. I was baptized as a Catholic Christian thirteen years ago. Given different circumstances, I might have become a Protestant or a Muslim—or remained agnostic. Yet my baptism and confirmation, from one point of view a deliberate narrowing of my options, gave me the security I hadn't possessed earlier, to open myself to God everywhere, since that is where my church told me to look for him. Without the security thus granted me, would I have approached the Islamic Center at all? And if I had managed to get so far, would I have been able to look at the Qur'an as anything but an important cultural text, the way the Bible itself is viewed in secular society?

Yet all such analogies, persuasive and binding on my behavior in the *masjid* as they seem, could evaporate instantaneously under the "light of lights." While I was flustered by Dr. Shafiq's invitation, I wasn't left speechless. What I said to him at the time in answer still makes sense to me—at least I have not been able to improve upon it, in all my replayings of the scene. I described my reluctance to take part in *salat* as a form of fasting, comparing it to my fast when, as a catechumen, I awaited baptism and confirmation as a Catholic Christian. As I watched at Mass the congregation file up to the altar to receive Communion, I felt keenly a hunger for the Eucharist. But I also felt joy for the hunger itself, as if it were important in God's plan that I experience fully the hunger before I knew its satisfaction. So in my reply to Dr. Shafiq, I spoke in similar terms of performing *salat*—that, in holding myself from performing it at present, I was putting myself in the position of knowing fully the extent and meaning of my desire.

Unlike my fast from the Eucharist, however, I undertake my fast from *salat* without the certainty that the fast will end. Yet it well might. I doubt I would find such suspense tolerable if I weren't sure in my heart that my love for God in Jesus Christ has brought me to it. When I mentioned earlier feeling "more wonderingly" a Christian than before coming to the Islamic Center, I was referring to my amazement (not untinged by humor) at the predicaments into which a commitment to Christ can lead one—even to the threshold of a different religion! When I mentioned feeling "more joyfully" so as well, I was referring to the new way given me, in the Qur'an, to embody the Word of God. During this growth, some categories have been broken. An old wineskin has begun to split. So be it. May all Christians know the complex delight granted me to know our God at the boundary of our practice and understanding.

ENCOUNTERING A JEWISH JESUS

JAMES (K) KARPEN

James Karpen—known as K—now just past forty, came of age on Long Island, wanting to be a rabbi—except he wasn't Jewish. Now a Manhattan-based Methodist minister currently completing a joint doctorate from Union Theological Seminary, a Protestant graduate school, and the Jewish Theological Seminary across the street, Karpen revisits his many encounters with Judaism—through Hebrew songs and prayers, the study of Talmud and midrash, sharing his church with a synagogue, but also through his love of Jesus, the Jew. In this highly personal, sermonic-style essay, Karpen lays bare the tender places where these two monotheistic traditions meet and part—on the pages of scripture, in the land of Israel, and in his life.

WHEN I WAS growing up, I wanted to be a rabbi. My brother, blessed with a beautiful voice, wanted to be a cantor. I came closer than he did. He's a systems programmer. I'm a Methodist minister.

It's not that we grew up Jewish. We grew up Methodist. My mother, also with a beautiful voice, worked as a soloist at St. Mark's Methodist Church in Rockville Centre, Long Island, an imposing stone structure a half hour's drive from our home in Massapequa. Every Sunday we spent five hours at that church. There were choir rehearsals, Sunday school classes, worship, coffee hour (always with plain brown doughnuts) and meetings. Our job was to run around, jump the stairs, and not get caught. We got used to it.

On Fridays, my mother had a different job. She sang at Central Synagogue, a Reform temple down the street from St. Mark's. My sister, who was six, was in love with the cantor. My brother wanted to *be* the cantor. I was not exactly sure what a rabbi was or what one did. But I wanted to be one.

I understood one thing about rabbis from the beginning. A rabbi was someone who was close to God. A rabbi was someone who knew something about God. A rabbi could teach about God and talk to God. I knew one other thing about rabbis from reading my Bible. Jesus was a rabbi. And I knew I loved Jesus.

My mother loved to sing to us. That's not exactly correct. My mother sang to herself whenever the three of us began to make noise. My mother sang so she could hear herself think. She usually just sang whatever she was working on at the time. On Fridays, we always got Hebrew prayers.

It worked. We usually stopped and listened. There is something compelling about the sung word. So it happened that before we learned the Lord's Prayer, we knew the Hebrew blessing over the wine: *Baruch ata adonai, eloheinu, melech ha-olam; boray p'ri ha-gafen.* Somehow with the words we absorbed a love for Judaism.

I never became a rabbi. But I came close.

My mother's first professional singing job had come her way back when I was four years old. She was hired to sing for the High Holy Day services at Congregation B'nai Jeshurun, a small, struggling synagogue on the Upper West Side of Manhattan.

Years later, when I began working as a United Methodist pastor at the Church of St. Paul and St. Andrew on 86th Street and West End Avenue, I met the rabbis from B'nai Jeshurun: Marshall Meyer (of blessed memory) and Rolando Matalon. Roly Matalon and I walked home one day from a clergy meeting at another church, and he offered to show me the B'nai Jeshurun sanctuary. It was gorgeous. Mysteriously gorgeous. He and Marshall invited me to join them for worship some *shabbat,* and I did. Together with my colleague at St. Paul and St. Andrew, the Reverend Ed Horne, we began working together on plans for our congregations to get together.

A near-tragic accident at the synagogue hastened those plans. Late on a Friday night in May of 1991, the ceiling of the B'nai Jeshurun sanctuary collapsed. No one was hurt, but when Saturday morning dawned, the congregation was left without a place to worship. When Ed and I called to offer our sympathy and support, we left a message for the rabbis, "Whatever we can do, just let us know." Marshall and Roly called back and said, "There may be something. . . ." The next thing we knew, we were making arrangements for our church building to be shared with B'nai Jeshurun.

The first B'nai Jeshurun event in our church was *Selichot,* the midnight prayer service the week before *Rosh Hashanah.* Ours is a large but plain sanctuary without a lot of Christian symbolism. Large angelic figures perch in each of the four corners of the ceiling. A banner, built by choir members from both congregations, had just been installed over the one visible cross, proclaiming the words from the 133rd Psalm, "How good it is when brothers and sisters dwell together in harmony." When the first songs went up in Hebrew, my wife Charlene leaned over to me and said, "I think the angels are smiling."

On *Rosh Hashanah* our ninety-five-year-old sanctuary was filled with more than a thousand worshipping Jews, and a handful of curious Christians as well. At one point in the service it was time to recite the *Sh'ma:* "Hear, O Israel, the Lord your God, the Lord is One." At that point those words seemed to be profoundly true. Ed and I were invited up to welcome the B'nai Jeshurun congregation to their new home. We spoke of our delight at this new and evolving partnership, and I recited Psalm 133 in halting Hebrew. The sanctuary erupted into applause. They knew they were home. Oddly, that night I also felt like I had come home.

The next morning a man came up and introduced himself. His name was Isaac, and as a young boy he had been imprisoned in the Nazi death camps. "I never thought I would ever be inside a Christian church," he said.

The following Sunday morning, I noticed that the sanctuary felt different to me. It was as though the Hebrew prayers and songs had left a holy residue. The place felt more sacred.

One day soon after, when I was attending a *shabbat* service, Marshall introduced me as the pastor of B'nai Jeshurun. It was a joke. But I was profoundly honored. It was the next best thing to being a rabbi.

From the beginning, I was a child of the church. I loved hymns and Gospel music. I loved the stories of Jesus. When I was nine, we left St.

Mark's for a church nearer home. Some of my deepest long-term friendships were formed there.

As a teenager, church provided a refuge from the negative culture of high school. I'm the only person I know who cut classes to go to church. Not because there was anything happening there in the middle of the day. Just because it was quiet. It was safe. I went to talk to the church secretary. I went to talk to the nursery school director. I went to have long theological discussions with the minister.

I love Christianity, but much of Christian doctrine mystifies me. It always seems that people are trying so hard to prove what cannot be proven. To prove what can only be felt. I didn't believe in God because anyone could prove God to me. I knew God as a reality in my life.

When I was 16, my Sunday School teacher, a remarkable and dedicated man named Cliff Knowles, announced that people had created God. He wasn't trying to startle us, he was just stating the facts the way he saw them. God is a creation of the human mind.

I found the whole idea so odd, I went to see my pastor, Duncan MacKenzie. He talked to me for a while and then suggested a book called *The Question of God* by Heinz Zahrnt. I still have it. Ten years of graduate theological training, and I still can't figure out what it's about. But it didn't really matter. I knew he had suggested the book because he respected my struggle, and took me seriously.

Reading through centuries of theological works, the ones I have found compelling are the ones which deal with God as a reality to be experienced and sometimes understood, rather than a supposition to be defended. While studying at Union Theological Seminary, I was assigned a book on the prophets by Rabbi Abraham Joshua Heschel. Here was someone who knew about the reality of God. "In the beginning was the relation," Heschel said. Not the proposition. Not the supposition. The relation. We know God because we are known by God.

Heschel wrote that when the prophets of Israel received the word of God, they heard it one syllable at a time. There are times in my life when I yearn for even that much from God. Just one syllable, God. That will last me a long, long while. And there are other times when God's voice finds me when I am not expecting it.

I first heard the voice of God in an empty high school gym locker room. By ninth grade I was very much a lost soul. I had drifted into a pattern of activities which were destructive and illegal. My friendships and my identity were bound up in these activities, and I was stuck. Late for gym class, I walked through the empty locker room, trying to remember which locker was mine, and I heard the words, "K, you don't have to do what you're doing."

Two things struck me about this *bat kol,* this message from God. First, God knows me by name. Second, God is not interested in condemning me. God was giving me permission to take my life in a different direction. God was making contact, and letting me know I wasn't alone. In the beginning was the relation. At the time it did not seem at all odd that God had chosen a rancid-smelling locker room for this moment of revelation.

Since then, I have heard God's voice at several other times. Usually in response to a desperate prayer. Always just a syllable or so at a time.

Strangely, Heschel helped me to understand what I love about Jesus. He opened me up to a world of Jewish writings I had known nothing about. I had viewed Jewish tradition the way most Christians probably do: as a baffling tangle of rules and requirements. Heschel taught me that the most important thing in Judaism is not getting the rules right. The most important thing is the *kavanah,* the intention, with which a Jew approaches God and the faith. The laws, the commandments, the *mitzvot,* are not stumbling blocks to trip over, but opportunities for blessing God and blessing other people. To me, Heschel sounded like the Jesus of the synoptic Gospels.

Soon I was studying Talmud and midrash at the Jewish Theological Seminary. I began to see Jesus more clearly. I began to understand Jesus within his Jewish context. Understanding Jesus in this way made me see what it is that I love about him.

In 1995 I decided to go to Israel for the first, and so far only, time. Roly Matalon was leading a B'nai Jeshurun tour, and I got a letter inviting me to go. I thought the letter was sent to me by mistake, but when I called Roly to check, he said, "Sure! You should definitely come."

Seeing Jerusalem, the Judean wilderness, and the Galilee in the company of seventy Jews was an amazing experience. To be in the desert. To climb Masada before sunrise. To sing the *Shehechyanu* before entering Jerusalem. To pray at the Western Wall. To see *eretz* Israel, the land of Israel, through Jewish eyes.

There were times when it was just hard, though. The day our bus drove through Nazareth, and then across the Jordan River, without slowing down, I felt like I had made a mistake. Maybe it is not possible to cultivate a Jewish love of *eretz* Israel without ignoring the significance of this land to Christianity. But I found my love for both Judaism and Jesus growing the longer I spent in Israel.

I had to sneak off to see the Christian sites that were important to me. The Mount of Olives and Gethsemane in East Jerusalem. Bethlehem. When an opportunity came to travel to Capernaum, though, three friends from the synagogue joined me. Together we tried to picture the everyday life of Jesus. Hanging out at Peter's mother-in-law's. Looking out across the lake. Walking to the synagogue.

Marshall Meyer used to say that if Jesus came to New York he'd come to our church on Friday night or Saturday morning for B'nai Jeshurun's synagogue services and feel right at home. It would never occur to him to come back for Sunday—the Lord's Day—*his* day.

In the Galilee, we stayed at a *kibbutz* on the north shore of the Sea of Galilee. To the west we could see Magdala and Tiberius. To the east was Capernaum. As I sat there on the grass near the shore one day I got this powerful conviction that Jesus had walked by the spot I was sitting many times. I felt an overwhelming connection with the historical Jesus.

That night I was asked to speak to the group about what it was like for me as a Christian to be in Israel. I was flattered and a little confused. Still, I shared my thoughts, followed by what felt like hundreds of questions. Finally, someone in the group asked me, "You obviously have a love for Judaism. Why aren't you Jewish?" The answer came to me. "Jesus." My love of Jesus has led me to Judaism. But my love of Judaism has led me to a more profound love and appreciation of Jesus.

It seems sad to me that the figure who links Judaism and Christianity together is also the one who has driven them apart. As Christianity moved further away from Judaism it sought to portray Jesus as less Jewish, less particularistic, more universal, more "Christian." As Judaism distanced itself from Christianity, it too began to portray Jesus as less Jewish.

Dorothee Sölle describes the Christian religion as "the attempt, which has failed and been betrayed a thousand times, and which still cannot be abandoned . . . to remain true to the God of Israel, who was also the God of Jesus." Christianity's Jewishness is not an interesting sidelight or an embarrassing secret, it is central to the health of the faith. The more I study, the more I realize that what attracts me to Christianity is the religion of Jesus. And that religion is Judaism.

The decision several years ago by the Southern Baptist Convention to begin a formal effort at converting Jews reminded me of my own early efforts at evangelism. At the age of seven or eight I had learned enough in Sunday School to realize that Christianity and Judaism were two separate faiths, and that Jews did not believe in Jesus. This was presented to us as a problem—even a challenge. Jews needed to know about Jesus to have a shot at salvation.

My best friend William was Jewish. I decided he would be a good place to start. "William," I asked him one day after school. "Do you know who Jesus is?" "Yeah, he's the son of God," said William, "Why?" But he had taken my line. I had nothing else to say.

My more recent experience with Jews and Christians has taught me that we have a lot to learn from each other. My study of Judaism, my time with the Talmud, my worship of the one God of Israel in settings Jewish and Christian and my encounters with the living faith of Jews and Christians have enriched my life and my faith.

Will I ever convert from Christianity to Judaism? I doubt it. Not without a clear message from God. But I think Christianity may need to do a little converting—of itself.

A DARK WEBBING OF SPIRIT

JAMES OAKLEY

*James Oakley, now in his mid-twenties, looks back at his teen years sub-
merged in Christian fundamentalism when he was saved and born again,
and what followed: a wayward life on the road, getting high and running
away. In college now, steeped in writing and film-making, philosophy
and poetry, Oakley recounts in vivid, sometimes startling language and
imagery, his search for God in the midst of both ecstasy and anguish.*

MEMORY SEEMS to cloud here on these nights in this
northern town; not much comes out of hiding. A ghost of an idea or
some sweep of longing mixes with the sweat on my chest and I howl
out. The only things I remember are the yearning for some connection or the way the sky felt during a certain season. On summer afternoons where I grew up in the south it would always rain at about four
o'clock, leaving the streets shiny. Then the sun would come back and
cars would slide all over the roads on their way home from work. This
is where God would hide during those long burning days; he'd creep
up alongside a quick shower so we all could enjoy the wet pavement.

Memories will sift through the brain like a sandstorm, stinging and
blinding. Sometimes you welcome the pain, but mostly it leaves a big
purple bruise on your day. On some evenings God finds us unaware.
His joy moves all over tonight and I am struck with it, coming subtler

than a kiss and then damaging, like a storm. It comes and goes. The wretchedness is the absence. The sweetness is the longing.

I was fourteen when I first noticed it. I was sent out to the Midwest to some Christian camp where I found Jesus. They said Jesus loved us more than anyone else and that we were to give our lives to him. I was shown photos and films of sin, taught about what happened if I sought pleasure in the world. I remember so many of the other boys were so cavalier about all of this. They snuck into the woods to smoke cigarettes and look at porno mags during break times. They talked of boners and of sex. I was appalled. How, when they knew Jesus was watching, could they be so careless? They did not have the fear of the Lord that my counselor told me would have made them hunger for righteousness. I hungered to be righteous. I seemed to buy what the camp leaders said cuz I never was one not to believe.

The first few days of camp I was inconsolable without my mother around. I cried morning to night. The other campers stared at me with these looks of wonder, like where did this sissy come from? This stung being that I did not have much skin to protect me because it had all been burnt off at school. Burning everyday as I tried to fit in with all the other malleable objects of middle school. Burning off when I faced the rejections of youth. Never did fit in with any potato-chip brand of fellow, always the freaks. When you are a misfit your tongue becomes your fist then your pain becomes your security. My need, my banner, my loss.

The camp was the strictest fundamental Bible haven. They dissected the Book of Revelations with joy to tell us that the end-time was near. We were taught to pray before all activities, to never think about sex, to live the "I'm Third Life"—God first, others second, and I'm third. Our role models were all the men and women who were the counselors. They were the pictures of purity. Never a cuss word nor any negative talk. Positive positive positive was the way there. Good clean living and wholesome people all about. The message was so attractive that I immediately began praying to this Jesus character they spoke of.

One night during the evening worship they called for people who had recently accepted Jesus into their hearts to come up and testify. I stood and got up on stage to the sound of uproarious applause. I witnessed that I had indeed met the Lord and would live the rest of my days as his servant. Little did I know that these actions would change

my brain for many years to come. Little did I know that Jesus would
become my banner like one wears a shield or a mask. I wore that
identity for all to see. So proud to have found the answer. So proud to
be saved.

Tonight here in this northern town a hurricane is just down the coast,
the winds blow through the buildings, boys and girls are all out. I
know that I am the refugee. Somehow saved from that prison from
whence those dealers in salvation shoved me. Some sort of grace must
have whipped through my room one night as I knelt and begged for
God to make me whole. Now, I am not a big proponent of the idea of
grace. It seems to point to a God who gives gifts to some and lets others be maimed and starve, yet I am without answer as to how I made
it to this pen and paper, to you. The years after that summer evening
when I stood and spoke aloud my new salvation were ones of fright
and yelling. I think I musta yelled for ten years. Yelled at someone or
at god or some asshole. My skin was quite uncomfortable to live in.
Problem children don't know what else to do but run. I ran and ran
from Louisville to Austin to San Fran, all over this damn place. Didn't
know what else to do but drive and smoke cigarettes. I never could
escape my thoughts of the Maker, though. Never could see beyond
that hunger. I do know that on that summer evening I met some sort
of spirit, maybe Jesus himself. It is not important now. Some lost
ghost was sucked down through my bones as the smoke from my
prayers burnt up the night leaving me seared and marked.

First Avenue is dead around my house. I take Avenue A when I walk
home. Tonight the moon is bright and September has begun. There
is a constant journey going on beneath my skin, running on in mythic
scenes. Running on black nights and angst days, cheap words and
hiding from the looks of strangers. Hunting and diving down to pick
up anything, looking for God. We all take such long journeys. Come
to the surface, go to the dry cleaners or the deli, and then back down
swimming looking for Him. I'd failed outta my second high school
when I started looking elsewhere for some guidance. Maimed by the
family of God I went searchin' into other realms. I struggled and
eventually the drugs won out. No amount of Bible reading could take
the place of getting high. School went from bad to worse and I
couldn't have cared less. It held no interest for me; travel and drugs
were all I wanted. The prison of Christianity or conservative America

gets really old. I'da shot myself if I hadn't found some other pathway to new languages. Drugs brought a whole nother thing into my life. Took me to another country but don't believe I was free of the old. Voices in my head as I hit the pipe, sin far from god not holy no good help.

It all made me some part fractured. Air filled the space between my thoughts and words came out a lot slower, and as I called everyone brother and sister I bought a new identity again. I could never deal well with the normal racket of eating and doing work or just interacting with a traffic cop, these were never my strong suits. When acid made me more air-filled I had a hard time navigating any patterns. I did believe that I was close to God when I was high. I probably should have been a teenager in the sixties and not the late eighties; these things were a little out of vogue. I wrote to communes to see if I could join; I changed my name to Star, because I felt I was a star out in the universe. I dated a girl named Rainbow Fire. Identity to identity, some call it searching. It is not without humor that I tell these stories. This was probably the most fun time I had. Went to Colorado and swallowed a puddle of liquid acid and saw myself become the snow. Gave my soul to Jerry Garcia in a ceremony out in the forest, tried to take up witchcraft, and thought being bisexual was the only way. This is when it was all still safe and new, before the demons came to rest in my bones.

The road between Flagstaff and Oklahoma City is bright in the gaze of my mind. I am sittin' here in this tenement, but only my body—I am really driving down a dark freeway. A long road back to that bird in flight, to loose those feathers, to shake the tether, to rid myself of language. Words are such fuck-ups, centuries of hatred upon their backs. Never doing justice to any tear or pain. We talk and talk about us selling our wares to any pedestrian rambling by on the avenue. I am struck deaf and dumb everyday with the lack of words to describe the light or the way I love my best friend. Without a language to reach anyone else, without the ability to touch inside another body. Then they will talk of spirit like the movie on the late show. They will say God this or I am this, claiming grace while burning up the planet. My friend David just hung himself, a knife into my grace. I do not really ever understand anything. Mercy, calling mercy for me, too. I am at a loss as to how we ever make it through these pains. Stumbling in turmoil, calling crying flying falling.

I once had a friend named Molly. She was dead late one July

evening. She would always laugh and laugh at me for being so God-swayed. We would drive around smoking pot and listening to Joni, lookin at the rich people's houses. One November we went to a church retreat where they taught us of *caritas*—a free gift—it seemed so nice. I ate up the idea of some god giving us gifts, she just laughed. She was too smart for their wiles; she wouldn't buy any of their speeches or words. I always idolized her; she was so light and sure. Never one to buy bullshit of talkers and sellers. She did too much that July and didn't make it back. I know she was too pure for this place. Angels wear all sorts of masks, and Molly taught me the most. I'll never walk anywhere without her again. Some nights when God is around I will call out to her crying Molly Molly Molly. I became a little less the night she died, lost a foot or something. After she was gone my own demise started courtin' me with the coke I was shovin' up my head. I ran.

Spending years God-fucked makes one have many lines in their head. Division of OK and not OK. Horizon lines inside where one could just trail off at any given party and fall into some closet. The demise of my fancy free powder up nose bad movie of the week life came with the insanity of birthdays passing, slowly. I was wearing thin and the Wal-Mart would not even give me a job, shopping in any bookstore for a new plan. I called and kept callin out to the sky. Spent my days trying to buy my redemption. Wanting to be good and pure and true. Driving here again, moving there, shoved into some rehabs around Tucson, sleeping with any offerer. Texas, Denver, southern New Mexico, wild out like a wolf and lost with other runners. Drove all night to get to the water, California the end of it. Wanting to not be so crazy, God mixin with heroin mixin with dicks. Sucking and fixing up the house clean the yard want to smell the roses. Barstow to L.A., broke down snortin drugs and selling my body for no good reason at all. Cocaine all over the floor of the Bell-Age Hotel on Sunset—here is my potential. I slept so many days, the spirit musta took a vacation in Malibu while I ran down ole Hollywood Boulevard. Dark webbing of spirit causing the earthquakes and firestorms. Dark spirit that stood as I lost my mind, that crawled with me on the floor, this is no redemption song no claim of goodness only a scar of some past after-noons.

Once I had a girlfriend who prayed with her legs open. She longed for the ultimate lover, this was really the only place we could relate. Months and months of horror passed, turning into years and me face down on the floor. Walked away from trying to be good. Fast and far. Alone now with my glasses and plates and anger, today the fall is hitting us. Maybe that is what grace is, when fall brings its first cool day and that nightmare of August runs towards China.

Years away from drugs. Years away from being a born again. Roads slick with many stop lights and a slow car. God hungry, people hungry. All I know about God is that it is the broken heart of all of us. Too many sentiments from all around proclaiming too much. Sun in my window this morning, light crashing through tall buildings, lonely at the cafe, my best friend can't ever get out of bed. I take a shower, read the daily horror paper and try to find some distraction. Woke to the sound of the hum of my fan then the pit again then the empty bed swallowing me. Mutter a prayer, mercy for us in the mornings. The night brings a color that takes everything in, day is so bright, thousands of beams of bricks and mortar. School is open and Jesus loves everyone. I am only talking about these things. A tear for the loss, for the growth endured. Demons and rebels are my lot now, grace has given me misfits to know and afternoons in the sun with no safety net. I claim my Grace cause I was saved from those things taught by the servants of God. I run to that hilltop and take Jesus down from the cross. We take a car to the coast, lovers free on the highway.

Permissions Acknowledgments

Grateful acknowledgment is made to the following for permission to print or to reprint the following material:

Adler, Margot. Edited excerpts from *Heretic's Heart* by Margot Adler. Copyright © 1997 by Margot Adler. Reprinted by permission of Beacon Press, Boston.

Augustine. Edited excerpts from *The Confessions* by Saint Augustine, translated by Henry Chadwick. Copyright © 1991 by Henry Chadwick, reprinted by permission of Oxford University Press.

Balmer, Randall. "The Generation of Faith," by Randall Balmer. Copyright © 1999 by Randall Balmer. Printed by permission of the author. All rights reserved.

Barnes, Kim. From *In The Wilderness* by Kim Barnes. Copyright © 1996 by Kim Barnes. Reprinted by permission of the author. All rights reserved.

Belton, Don. "My Father's House" by Don Belton from *Wrestling With the Angel*, edited by Brian Bouldrey. Copyright © 1995 by Brian Bouldrey. Reprinted by permission of Riverhead Books, a division of The Putnam Publishing Group.

Bender, Sue. Edited excerpts from the Prologue and Chapter One from *Plain and Simple: A Woman's Journey to the Amish* by Sue Bender. Copyright © 1991 by Sue Bender. Reprinted by permission of HarperCollins Publishers, Inc.

Brown, Karen McCarthy. From *Mama Lola: A Voodou Priestess in Brooklyn.* Copyright © 1991, The Regents of the University of Califor-

Gandhi, Mohandas. Excerpts from *The Story of My Experiments with Truth* by M. K. Gandhi. Copyright © 1927, 1929, 1940, 1957 by M. K. Gandhi. Reprinted by permission of the Navajivan Trust, India.

Gilman, Richard. Edited excerpts from *Faith, Sex, Mystery* by Richard Gilman. Copyright © 1986 by Richard Gilman. Reprinted with the permission of Simon & Schuster.

Goldman, Ari L. Edited excerpts from *The Search for God at Harvard* by Ari L. Goldman. Copyright © 1991 by Ari L. Goldman. Reprinted by permission of Times Books, a division of Random House.

Gordon, Mary. Edited excerpts from *The Shadow Man* by Mary Gordon. Copyright © 1996 by Mary Gordon. Reprinted by permission of Random House, Inc.

Harrison, Barbara Grizzuti. Excerpts from *Visions of Glory: A History and Memoir of Jehovah's Witnesses* by Barbara Grizzuti Harrison. Copyright © 1978 by Barbara Grizzuti Harrison. Reprinted by permission of Georges Borchardt, Inc. for the author.

Harrison, Kathryn. "Catherine Means Pure" / "Saint Catherine of Siena" by Kathryn Harrison from *A Tremor of Bliss: Contemporary Writers on the Saints* by Paul Elie. Copyright © 1994 by Kathryn Harrison. Reprinted by permission of Harcourt Brace & Company.

hooks, bell. Both selections in this anthology from *Bone Black* by bell hooks. Copyright © 1996 by Gloria Watkins. Reprinted by permission of Henry Holt and Company, Inc. and by David Higham Associates, London.

Jung, Carl. From *Memories, Dreams, and Reflections* by C. G. Jung, translated by Richard and Clara Winston. Translation copyright © 1961, 1962, 1963, and renewed 1989, 1990, 1991 by Random House, Inc. Reprinted by permission of Pantheon Books, a division of Random House, Inc. and by HarperCollins Publishers, London.

Kahf, Mohja. "Around the Ka'ba and Over the Crick." Copyright © 1998, 1999 by Mohja Kahf. Printed by permission of the author. All rights reserved. Portions of this essay appeared in *Religion and Education,* Vol. 25, Nos. 1 & 2, Winter 1998, under the same title.

Karpen, James (K). "Encountering a Jewish Jesus." Copyright © 1999 by James F. Karpen. Printed by permission of the author. All rights reserved.

Kehoe, Louise. Edited excerpts from *In This Dark House* by Louise Kehoe. Copyright © 1995 by Louise Kehoe. Reprinted by permission of Pantheon Books, a division of Random House.

ABOUT THE EDITOR

Katherine Kurs has a Manhattan-based private practice as a spiritual/pastoral counselor and teaches religious studies at Lang College of the New School for Social Research and at Empire State College of the State University of New York. She holds a Master of Divinity degree from Harvard Divinity School and a Ph.D. from the Royal College of Art, London. She can be contacted at soulbio @aol.com and you can visit her website at http://www .searchsoul.com